# Assault
# Against
# Children

# Assault
# Against
# Children

## Why It Happens
## How To Stop It

*Edited by*

**John H. Meier, PhD**
*Director, Research Division*
*CHILDHELP U.S.A./International*

COLLEGE-HILL PRESS, San Diego, California

**COLLEGE-HILL PRESS, INC.**
4284 41st Street
San Diego, California 92105

**Library of Congress Cataloging in Publication Data**
Main entry under title:

Assault against children.

    Bibliography: p.
    Includes indexes.
    1. Child abuse—Addresses, essays, lectures.
  2. Child abuse—Treatment—Addresses, essays, lectures.
  3. Child abuse—Prevention—Addresses, essays, lectures.
  I. Meier, John H., 1935–
  HB713.A87  1984     362.7'044     84-28563
  ISBN 0–88744–120–3 (soft)

47,380

**Printed in the United States of America**

# DEDICATION

To Sara and Yvonne, who, rather than cursing the darkness, have lighted up countless young lives for the past 25 years and graciously enabled me, with the help of God, to participate in this magnificent humanitarian effort; to Henry (1923–1984), who not only alerted and enlightened the world and me about battered children but also enlarged my perspective and commitment to make positive differences in their lives, families, and environments.

JHM

# CONTENTS

# CONTRIBUTORS

**Joan Carney, LLD**
Commissioner and Judge (pro tem), Los
   Angeles Juvenile Court
Los Angeles, CA

**Perry Cook, MS**
Certified Marriage and Family Counselor,
   (MFCC)
Oxnard, CA

**Diane Gallinger, MS**
Certified Marriage and Family Counselor
   (MFCC)
Riverside, CA

**Marshall Jung, DSW**
Director, Riverside Family Services
   Association
Riverside, CA

**C. Henry Kempe, MD**
Late Professor and Chairman
   Pediatrics and Microbiology Departments,
University of Colorado School of Medicine
Denver, CO

**John H. Meier, PhD**
Director, Research Division, CHILDHELP,
   U.S.A./INTERNATIONAL;
Adjunct Clinical Professor, Medical
   Psychology/Neuropsychiatric Institute
University of California, Los Angeles, and
Lecturer, Departments of Psychology and
   Education,
University of California,
Riverside, CA

**Morris Paulson, PhD**
Professor, Department of Psychiatry
   Neuropsychiatric Institute
University of California at Los Angeles, CA

**Roland Summit, MD**
Associate Professor of Psychiatry
School of Medicine
University of California, Los Angeles, and
Community Consultant re: Child Abuse
Harbor General Hospital
Torrance, CA

**Richard D. Willey, MA**
Lieutenant and Commander of the Child
   Abuse Detail
Los Angeles County Sheriff's Department
Los Angeles, CA

# PREFACE

The topic of assault against children is inherently repugnant and generally avoided for leisure reading or in polite social conversation. It is not uncommon in prisons for even the most hardened of criminals to be so offended by the presence of another inmate who has assaulted a child, that they viciously assault their fellow prisoner or actively exclude any child molester from their group of more respectable criminals. It is difficult for many professional persons, even those well trained to understand and cope with this cruel human behavior, to work objectively and dispassionately toward the reunification of assaultive adults with their assaulted children. Indeed, it is often nearly impossible for the perpetrators and victims themselves to address openly these unspeakable and inhumane experiences. Ironically, the lay public has steadfastly resisted exposure to the gruesome details of domestic violence between parents and their children, while simultaneously feeding the fires of adult interpersonal violence, which is clearly related to assault against children (Gelles, 1972), by supporting dramatizations of such violence in the popular literature and media.

A review of the annals of mankind's existence reveals that child assault and its precipitating causes have always been present, and remain largely unresponsive to the intervention and prevention efforts thus far attempted throughout the world. It is paradoxical to be living in an age where many enlightened and civilized persons are concerned about increasingly impersonal computerized lifestyles, yet are seemingly unconcerned about the startling statistics reporting the prevalence of the primitive killing and brutalizing of hundreds of thousands of fragile and helpless children (a conservatively estimated one million child victims annually for the past several years in the United States alone, according to the American Humane Association, 1984; for example, 1.4 million verified cases were cited for 1982 by the National Center on Child Abuse and Neglect).

Nevertheless, motivated by a genuine determination to improve the human condition, several concerned professionals and organizations have begun to reveal the details of child assault and have developed and implemented numerous noteworthy systematic efforts to treat and ultimately to prevent this travesty and tragedy in the human community. It is now acceptable, and perhaps even somewhat faddish, to study and write about various kinds of assaults against children. The current news media have been paying unprecedented attention to numerous cases of out-of-home assaults against children, most noteworthy of which is the recently alleged (Stewart, 1984) series of episodes of child sexual molestation and exploitation, evidently occurring over more than a decade, at the now infamous preschool in Manhattan Beach in Southern California. Because of the large numbers of helpless young children and outraged parents involved in this and other similarly implicated child care programs throughout the United States, public awareness and desire to do something about stopping such assaults has never been more extensive or intensive.

The term *assault* smacks of the harsh legal reality that most reportable incidents of child abuse would be legally considered as assault and battery among adults and prosecuted accordingly; the term falls somewhere in the middle of the same constellation of cruelty suggested by slaughtered, battered, maltreated, abused, or neglected as gut-level descriptors. A number of serious and systematic efforts to understand the causes and consequences of this complex phenomenon have been under way for the past two decades and are beginning to yield insights and trends that warrant being mined, refined, and deposited in the bank of scientific and clinical information.

This book is another deposit in the data bank, to be drawn on for more clearly defining the problem, identifying some additional efficacious procedures for treating individual cases, and generalizing some principles for enabling the human society at large to reduce more effectively the incidence and prevalence of assault against children throughout the world. Since no individual or discipline has a monopoly on the accumulating wisdom, this book contains contributions from several well-informed and experienced individuals, representing a wide diversity of disciplines and a profound depth of backgrounds and resources. It seems prudent to invest in a diversified portfolio of expertise to ensure maximum interest and dividends for the broadest possible spectrum of beneficiaries. The multidisciplinary contributors of various chapters in the book are identified in the List of Contributors, are briefly introduced in the Acknowledgments, and eloquently speak for themselves in their respective contributions. This book is intended to document the most interesting current and promising insights and practices regarding the burgeoning field of child assault, organizing and updating these to be shared with colleagues working in a variety of professional and paraprofessiona! circumstances where they are confronted with these incredibly complex human problems.

Of course, interested and informed laypersons are also encouraged to read this book, since volunteers and other concerned citizens have been behind some of the most successful campaigns to correct physical and social ills in this country. If it were not for the volunteer March of Dimes to fight poliomyelitis—which, incidentally never claimed as many lives or crippled as many children as assault does—the vaccine against poliomyelitis might not yet be available. Everyone is motivated to work toward the elimination of life-threatening disease, such as cancer, since it might strike them, too. Just as cancer is referred to in many medical settings, assault (or child abuse) may also be abbreviated CA. A major difference is that assault against children is a symptom of a pernicious cancer of the soul (Krugman, 1983), a cancer which is spreading (metastasizing) throughout the human race. If left unchecked, this malady will victimize more and more children and families, creating colonies of "Swiss cheese" children whose very spiritual and emotional constitution is riddled with holes, scars, and festering wounds, even though they may appear physically intact after plastic surgery and other superficial repairs have been performed. The volunteer armies of energetic, talented, and dedicated citizens, recruited and marshalled by CHILDHELP, U.S.A., and by other private organizations such as the National Committee for the Prevention of Child Abuse, represent the core of a private sector volunteer movement that promises to reach critical mass in the near future and gradually eradicate assault against children—first in the United States, then elsewhere in the world.

Although a major part of the material deals with successful practices and revealing research findings, some attention is given to theory and model building in order to bind together logically these apparently disparate procedures and discoveries. Hall and Lindzey (1957) state that there is nothing more practical than a good theory, since it is from such rationale that innovative practices spring. Moreover, it is from a unifying theoretical perspective that practical considerations are put into meaningful context (Meier, 1976a; Newberger, Newberger, and Hampton, 1983). On the other hand, the text avoids sheer speculation, except in those rare instances in which an untested hypothesis or heuristic insight seems to have great promise of leading to some enlightening empirical confirmation from future research. Hence, there is a continuous effort to strike a balance between theory and practice to avoid either a paralysis of analysis or the heresy of action, neither of which would be optimally efficacious in treating and ultimately preventing this human disease.

Following the Acknowledgments and Introduction, Chapter 1 defines the topic of assault against children and thereby establishes the scope of the entire book. A multifactorial model of the dynamics of child assault elucidates the many facets of this very complex subject. Recent estimates of incidence and prevalence of child assault locally, statewide, nationally, and internationally are included. After Chapter 1 defines the subject matter and describes its magnitude, subsequent chapters address some of the more widely accepted and empirical explanations for why child assault occurs and what its short- and long-term consequences are, primarily with regard to the child victims. Since there are many causal explanations offered and multiple consequences suggested, only a few of the representative ones have been selected for inclusion, especially if they seem to shed new theoretical or empirical light on previous statements available elsewhere. The state of the art and science is documented by a thorough review of the pertinent literature, which is woven into the entire text for further reference for those who wish to pursue any particular issue in greater breadth and depth.

Some of the more recent concerns, such as sexual assault, are given greater emphasis. The interactions among the child victims, the adult perpetrators, and the stressful environments underscore a human problem that is related to various handicapping conditions, genetic predispositions, cultural traditions, and bureaucratic machinations. The consequences clearly cut across the entire developmental spectrum of the child's physical, social, emotional, intellectual, and spiritual growth and development, as well as having negative impact upon the perpetrator and the society at large, since often the victims subsequently perpetuate the transgenerational vicious cycle of interpersonal violence by becoming delinquent, criminal, and, all too frequently, perpetrators of one or more forms of assault against their own or others' offspring.

A wide variety of modalities and methodologies for treating assaulted children and their assaultive families are offered, as are descriptions of some of the more promising preventive programs and approaches that are available. Various case studies of assault against children are presented (and profiled using the model) and must be dealt with by law enforcement authorities, the juvenile sociolegal system, the child protective system, and the out-of-home care system as these systems typically function (and dysfunction) throughout the United States. Special consideration is given to several new therapy modalities and techniques, such as art or pet therapy, treatment of sexually abused children and their families, self-help groups, some family systems approaches, and some major interdisciplinary community-based approaches.

Included is a description of an exemplary comprehensive treatment and prevention program, which incorporates and orchestrates the best that is currently known for total intervention in serious child assault situations requiring the removal of the children from their life-endangering or severely debilitating home environments. The agonizing dilemmas posed by removal of children from their natural parents and planning for their more permanent disposition in the future are discussed. The various alternatives of foster care, adoption, and reunification are presented and discussed, with some attention given to techniques and instruments that are useful in evaluating whether or not an intervention or prevention effort is working satisfactorily.

This book is written by practitioners for practical application—with a selective sprinkling of theoretical insights to stimulate interest and make various intervention and prevention methods more understandable and easier to apply. A wide variety of interdisciplinary expertise is herein assembled so that the practitioner, regardless of his or her individual disciplinary background, can benefit from a broad perspective, complete with many of the subtle nuances each discipline has to contribute toward understanding, evaluating, treating, and preventing assaults against children. It samples the best of what is known and practiced in light of the current state of the art and science. It serves as a handy reference for those who are already totally immersed in one or more aspects of the multifaceted work with assaults against children. It also provides information and, it is hoped, inspiration to students and lay persons who wish to become actively involved in identifying, reporting, and perhaps helping to treat assaulted children and the assaulting parents or caregivers—and ideally to prevent it from happening whenever possible.

Furthermore, this book serves as a textbook or supplementary reading for graduate and undergraduate courses on child abuse, family violence or dysfunction, human developmental disabilities, and other related topics. It is a ready reference for child caregivers, foster parents, adoptive parents, parent educators, pediatricians, psychologists, psychiatrists, marriage and family counselors, social workers, judges and attorneys, other child and adult therapists, law enforcement personnel, educators, nurses, and concerned humanitarians the world over. The book was written in response to multiple requests received from throughout the world for updated statements about what is now known and being successfully practiced in the struggle to alleviate and eliminate assaults against children.

As the Acknowledgments testify, this book is actually the latest in a series of essays toward better understanding and coping with the challenges presented by assaults against children in the world society. This editor–writer has had the privilege and pleasure of associating with the giants in the field and, having learned from them, has put into practice many of their findings and recommendations in a unique laboratory for the study of the causes and consequences of child assault. The many requests from scholars and other interested persons throughout the world, as well as the obvious progress made by individual assaulted children and their troubled families, have served as rationale for writing this book and as encouragement to see it through to press when the competing demands of everyday lives in trauma preempt most of the physical and psychic energy of the contributors. Obviously, no one has all the answers; it is hoped, however, that the collective wisdom assembled here will engender more informed questions and enable more efficacious intervention and even prevention approaches to be found for this cancer of the human soul and the society of mankind.

# ACKNOWLEDGMENTS

It is instructive occasionally to reflect upon one's career and to identify the major influences which have had a profound impact upon its evolution. A critical path analysis reveals that numerous persons, various events (usually planned but occasionally serendipitous), and personal predilections contributed to my being and becoming. Expressing some of this personal evolution through a book in itself signifies another milestone in the process. Given that one's history is prologue, this Acknowledgments section is deliberately autobiographical and suggests that, God willing and with the help of others, there is much yet for us to do on behalf of those less fortunate human beings in this world. In this widely heralded and somewhat ominous year of 1984, it seems propitious to contemplate the past and present in order to distill the spirit of future intoxicating challenges. Although Orwell's *1984* (1949) has not yet become a total reality, and we are not yet drowning in Toffler's predicted *Third Wave* (1981), there is the continual danger of reverting to less civilized behaviors toward one another, as in *Lord of the Flies* (Golding, 1978).

Although I accept full responsibility for everything I have written here, when I began to reflect upon the many persons and various experiences which informed and influenced me to engage in human service, the list grew very long. Reducing it to a bare minimum of the highlights was difficult, leaving a rich residue of memories of unmentioned giants on whose shoulders I have stood, and through whose eyes my own tunnel-visioned perspective has been immeasurably broadened. My present work with victims of nonaccidental assault is by no means accidental, since for some 25 years now I have been intentionally involved in working with various handicapped populations, whether their handicaps were due to acts of God or rites of families (Meier and Sloan, 1983).

In the late 1950s and early 1960s, while working as a preschool and elementary school teacher, researcher, psychotherapist, academician, and administrator, in both rural and urban settings, with impoverished and affluent children and their families, I encountered numerous children who had suffered from various forms of assault. However, this was before the knowledge of assault against children was in the forefront as it is now on the professional's and lay person's consciousness. I have on various occasions reconstructed the many poignant and pernicious details of each of those assaulted children's lives and consequently have become doubly committed to work toward better treatment for those who now suffer the unspeakable crimes of assault against children and, insofar as it is possible, to prevent such traumatic experiences from taking place in the lives of coming generations.

Consequently, I would first acknowledge the reality-based and unforgettable education I received from clients and victims of child assault, who have suffered from family dysfunction, environmental deprivation, and even the well-intentioned but inadvertently harmful intervention of some "do-gooders" driven by their peculiar rescue fantasies. One of the indelible lessons is the practical application of the physician's Hypocratic Oath, requiring that one should always be careful to at least do no additional harm to a patient or victim. This is especially germane to out-of-home care and to reducing or eliminating the systemic assault many child assault victims suffer after they have been "rescued" from a life-endangering and developmentally harmful situation—only to be cast into a limbo of interminable indecision, chaos, multiple placements, and other iatrogenic causes of further physical and psychic pain.

At the same time that I was totally immersed in providing and administering services, conducting research, and providing training for students and colleagues, I had the good fortune of interacting with a number of experts regarding child development and child assault. Although it would be impossible to adequately acknowledge the subtle contributions of all of these luminaries toward enlightening my understanding, I would like to herein extend a special thanks to several of the persons who made most important contributions to my entrance into and enduring dedication within this universe of endeavor.

I am deeply grateful to Sara O'Meara and Yvonne Fedderson, co-founders of IOI (now CHILDHELP, U.S.A./INTERNATIONAL), who had the foresight to incorporate research into CHILDHELP's developing programs (see Chapter 8) at its inception and thus made possible this work—including this book. Moreover, thanks are due for the wisdom, generosity, and the continued support of their beloved husbands, Don Fedderson and the late (1981) Robert O'Meara, plus the many other devoted friends of CHILDHELP, who have given these leading women and the CHILDHELP organization the courage and conviction to make many an impossible dream come true, despite the numerous nightmares that are inevitable in any effort of such momentous magnitude.

Just prior to uprooting our fourth-generation Colorado family to move to California and undertake this challenging opportunity, I had spent nearly a decade as an Associate Professor in the Department of Pediatrics under the inspiring leadership of the recently deceased (March, 1984) C. Henry Kempe, M.D., widely known as the principal scientist behind identifying "the battered child" syndrome (Kempe et al., 1962) and as the crusading pioneer relentlessly seeking to end such assaults against children.

Dr. Kempe and other authorities in the field of child assault repeatedly observe that the state of the art and science is still quite imperfect. Aristotle wrote many centuries ago that it is a terrible error to make a science more exacting than its subject matter allows. Unfortunately, research studies too often focus on the significance of statistical differences between experimental and control subjects while at the same time they ignore the fact that the differences are not really significant or that other matters are far more significant insofar as the people's real lives are concerned. This book focuses on what really matters in helping these people get their lives back together. Dr. Henry Kempe, whom I consider to have been one of my most profound mentors, makes these points poignantly clear in his Foreword to this book, wherein he cautions the professional or other worker in the field of child abuse that there are no simple cause-effect relationships or ready-made answers to the enormously complex questions raised by each case.

Although most of the problems are not new ones, and many of the intervention-prevention solutions are not altogether innovative, it is important to assemble and disseminate the best that is now known to prevent busy practitioners from wasting their precious time and talent reinventing the wheel. Historical accounts of childrearing practices down through the recorded history of mankind's existence cite concern for the abandoned or maltreated youngster, while at the same time recording practices of infanticide and sacrificial rites whereby either the handsomest or the most grotesque male or female offspring were offered up to various gods to seek their more favorable disposition. From the slaughter of the innocents in King Herod's time to the concern with pedophiles in ancient Greece and Rome, to the custom of practically abandoning babies in the French tradition of mothering (Badinter, 1981), to the current concern for children's welfare expressed by an International Year of the Child sponsored by the United Nations in 1979, the history of treatment of children is discouraging or encouraging, depending on whether an optimistic or pessimistic point of view is taken toward the status of children in today's society. Regardless of any individual's disposition, enough children have been sacrificed on sacrilegious altars of twisted tradition and bizarre family rites.

The cliché that prophets are neither popular nor believable in their own country is based in part on the fact that their critics, who are the pessimists in the equation, can informedly cite all of the reasons why a given plan will fail and even set about to ensure its failure. On the other hand, one of the reasons why some prophesies seem to be self-fulfilling is that the prophets themselves are of such an optimistic turn of mind that they are not persuaded by the reasons advanced why something cannot be done but are indefatigably driven by the reasons for which something *must* be done—and do it. Sara, Yvonne, Henry, and a few other seemingly superhuman crusaders energize and inspire the rest of us to keep struggling in the face of seemingly insurmountable odds and take courage in seeing just noticeable differences for the better. Therefore, this book is dedicated to them in particular.

When I first became Director of the John F. Kennedy Child Development Center at the University of Colorado Health Sciences Center, I was somewhat mystified to learn that several of the offices were occupied by members of the Department of Pediatrics who served on what was called the "Child Battering Team." It was in this capacity that I first met Dr. Ray Helfer, who was then in transition to Michigan State University. Dr. Harold Martin, who subsequently became Associate Director with me at the JFK Center, also served on this team to investigate and to help treat assaulted children, along with attorney Brian Fraser who went on to Chicago to help establish the National Committee for the Prevention of Child Abuse. These three continue to influence me and the field itself through their administrative, clinical, and scholarly work, including the numerous excellent articles and books they have written about assault against children. I had the honor and pleasure of writing a preface (Meier, 1976b) to the book, *Child Abuse and Neglect: The Family and the Community* (edited by Helfer and Kempe, 1976), and am doubly delighted to have Dr. Kempe's reciprocal Introduction here in this volume.

Through the seven year involvement of my wife, Ann, as one of the first lay therapists (family home visitor/parent aide) at the C. Henry Kempe National Center for the Study and Prevention of Child Abuse in Denver, I also became acquainted with the insightful and compassionate clinical work and magnificent personalities of psychiatrists Drs. Ruth Kempe and Brandt Steele and super social worker Helen Alexander as they formulated and refined the pilot efforts of the Kempe Center, recently named after its inspiring founder. It is truly gratifying that CHILDHELP's consummate success has enabled it to underwrite a family evaluation component at the Kempe Center.

Weekly seminars and grand rounds with Drs. John Conger, René Spitz, David Metcalf, Bob Emde, Joe Campos, Charles Kaufman, and Lulu Lubchenko, to name a few, continued to stimulate my interest in the multiple factors that interact in producing various developmental aberrations in children and families. This certainly enlivened my related interest in the relationships between developmental and learning disabilities (Meier, 1976a). It has since become even more clear how child assault contributes to both learning and developmental disabilities, as this present volume attests.

Several of the regional and national research and training efforts in which I have been involved have sharpened my sensitivity to the overriding needs of assaulted children. Prior to locating at the University of Colorado Health Science Center in Denver, I enjoyed working at the University of Northern Colorado and the Rocky Mountain Educational Laboratory, where I learned a good deal from Glen Nimnicht, with whom I helped to develop several compensatory programs for environmentally disadvantaged children, who are now defined as neglected children—a sort of passive assault. We established a prototype program and laboratory, called the New Nursery School, for demonstrating effective intervention with children from the poverty cultures (Meier, 1970). We helped to lead the way to Project Head Start, which over a decade later I had the responsibility of protecting and enlarging through Congressional testimony at the Federal level (Meier, 1977a). In my opinion, Head Start remains this nation's and the world's finest and largest example of early childhood enrichment, compensation for neglect, and protection from assault; it is also a vehicle for the early detection of developmental problems, regardless of whether their cause is an act of God or rite of mankind, at a time when the problems are more amenable to effective intervention and prevention.

During my tenure at the University of Colorado, I had the honor of being appointed to serve in the dual roles of Director of the U.S. Office of Child Development (now renamed the Administration for Children, Youth and Families [Meier, 1978]; this office is responsible for Head Start, and similar programs) and Chief of the United States Children's Bureau (responsible for all of the nation's child welfare programs, including the newly authorized National Center on Child Abuse and Neglect [Public Law 93-247]). From this vantage point I had the opportunity to become acquainted with many of the key professionals and major programs devoted to handicapped and assaulted children throughout the United States. My colleague, attorney Doug Besharov, who was then the first Director of the Federal Government's National Center on Child Abuse and Neglect, and I were able to influence the direction of federal legislation, funding, research, and training in child assault programs for several years. Some of the initial programs described in this text are only now demonstrating their value, underscoring the fact that some worthwhile efforts require considerable time before they can deliver any discernible payoff.

This federal position also afforded a view of the international scene.

On several occasions—such as one in Paris in 1976, while planning for the 1979 International Year of the Child—my perspective on the plight of the child in the world was abruptly broadened. Several developing countries protested loudly that they were not particularly concerned about physical or psychological assault against their children, since they were having difficulty keeping their children alive. As reported at the Fourth International Congress on Child Abuse, held in Paris in 1982, even worse conditions existed in the Third World, owing to increased population and worsened worldwide economic difficulties.

In addition to all of the aforementioned background influences, I am most grateful to each of my colleagues within the CHILDHELP organization who have collaborated with me on this book; their cooperation and competence are deeply appreciated. Since books are seldom merely written, but are rewritten over and over, the patient and competent retyping of the manuscript by Patti Hosburg and the general help of Tricia Albers, Sandra Davis, Nancy Valdivia, and other Research Division staff are all readily and happily noted. Thanks, too, are in order to our "landlord" Bob Lippert, the conscientious Administrator of The Village of CHILDHELP and to his capable staff, including especially psychologists Drs. Bill Nelson, Jim Scholz, and Michael Sloan, plus others too numerous to mention, all of whom helped to gather data and to interpret findings from the numerous studies done in our large natural laboratory, The Village of CHILDHELP. With the growth of its continuum of services, CHILDHELP has recently added the talents of Brian Cahill as Executive Director, and I deeply appreciate his ability to understand and support the interdisciplinary challenges of increasing the coherence and efficacy of an extraordinarily complex and unique organization.

Although each of the contributing authors is identified in the List of Contributors and they speak eloquently for themselves through their individual contributions, it would be a grievous omission not to gratefully acknowledge their individual and collective cooperation and competence as reflected in their works contained herein. Joan Carney has reportedly heard more child assault cases in her capacity as a long-term Judge in the Los Angeles Juvenile Court System than any other judge in the world; her diminutive size and humorous humility are exceeded only by her knowledgeable and compassionate decisions in the best interests of literally thousands of children and families. Perry Cook and Marshall Jung worked successfully together at the nearby Family Services Association, helping to rehabilitate seriously dysfunctional families, including reuniting assaulted children with their previously assaultive parents. In his leadership role, Marshall also stimulates considerable excitement about new ideas and practices in family therapy as he extends his training with S. Minuchin and colleagues. Diane Gallinger worked at The Village of CHILDHELP for several years in a variety of capacities while completing her training in marriage and family counseling. Starting as a child caregiver living with many assaulted children in our residential program, Diane's quiet competence enabled her to take on many increasing responsibilities, including giving substantial assistance to the research division and the production of this manuscript. I trust that the above comments about and dedication of this book to Henry Kempe do some justice to his influence on me, my colleagues, and the thousands of needy children and families throughout the world; his untimely death is grieved by us all who are beneficiaries of his unparalleled legacy. Morris Paulson is a rare combination of a deep thinker who refuses to allow the ivory tower of academia to separate him from the real world agonies and ecstasies of helping severely disturbed persons get their lives back together and training other clinicians to do the same. Roland Summit has demonstrated such excellence in academic and clinical circles that the demands for his wisdom and skills are practically overwhelming; his seasoned brilliance, applied to such cases as those in the Manhattan Beach preschool, has already advanced the state of the art and science another great stride. Dick Willey has also been working in the proverbial trenches for a number of years in the very county that can make the questionable claim to fame for more cases of reportable child assault, not to mention general family violence, than any other county in the world; he is a first-rate practitioner who is simultaneously having an immense impact on those who make, enforce, or break the law. These consummate professionals and busy practitioners not only gave freely of their time and expertise but also generously agreed to waive royalties in order to keep the cost of this book as low as possible to enable its wider dissemination. Moreover, any net profits are returned to CHILDHELP to further its pioneering work against child assault.

Last but not least, as I review the experiences of assaulted children and their assaultive families throughout the world, I am repeatedly moved to thank God, not only for the healthy and happy family my parents provided me but also for my own family of Ann, my loving wife and an excellent mother, and our wonderful three daughters, Rebecca, Rita, and Rhonda (our "3R's"), all now pursuing greater wisdom and fulfillment in various universities of California. They have enabled me to experience and enjoy the lighter and brighter side of life as a part of a joyful family, which all too often I neglected in order to pay greater attention to the plight of other less fortunate children and families.

As indicated in Henry Kempe's Introduction, we have come a long way toward addressing and eliminating assault against children around the world; however, whenever tempted to relax and admire our collective accomplishments, I am reminded of the lines Poet Laureate Robert Frost recited in his sonorous voice and inimitable style to us as undergraduates at Dartmouth College many cold winters ago (1954):

> The woods are lovely, dark and deep,
> But I have promises to keep,
> And miles to go before I sleep,
> And miles to go before I sleep.

(Robert Frost, *On Stopping by the Woods on a Snowy Evening*, 1923)

John H. Meier
July, 1984

# Introduction: International Perspective and Prospects Regarding Assault Against Children

## C. Henry Kempe

All of us concerned with the welfare of children the world over must remember that to this very day vast numbers of children, and particularly those living in portions of the Third World, still face malnutrition and infectious diseases as the two major problems of survival. Nations concerned with malnutrition and the prevention of infectious diseases must first address these primary needs, but it is interesting that even in countries struggling with these basic concerns, the problem of assault against children is now being considered. In Europe and North America we see that, as birth rates drop, each child is expected to survive. Without concerns about malnutrition or infectious diseases as likely causes of death, many additional threats to the child's life and health are increasingly considered, among them child assault. In a sense, therefore, the very consideration of assault against children as a problem worthy of the public's concern means that children have reached a certain plateau of basic care.

The International Year of the Child (1979), by order of all 149 member states of the United Nations, was a worldwide effort to better the lot of children. Broadly based national committees all over the world planned what each country wanted most urgently to do for her children. Many of the national committees considered plans for improved childhood nutrition, immunization, and education. There was a consensus among national committees working in each member country that the rights of children should be prominently considered, and assault against children was named as a topic by a number of them. The International Year of the Child saw broadly ordered programs throughout the world dedicated to emphasizing the unique needs of the child, and for the first time, on an international basis, addressed the rights of all children. The United Nations is on record as saying that it is not enough for a child not to be abused, not to be neglected, not to be starved, and not to be sexually assaulted. On the contrary, the Children's Charter states that all children have the right to be in a setting that will attempt to develop each child to his or her greatest potential. To do so children need to be born well, to be valued, to enjoy optimal growth and development, to be in a nurturing family environment, to learn the skills necessary for success, to receive health assessment and health maintenance, anticipatory guidance, health education for self-care, easy access to competent medical and dental treatment, and to share in the advances made possible by biomedical and biosocial research.

In Geneva (the First International Congress on Child Abuse) many diverse professionals were brought together who could freely exchange experiences and views. This led to collaboration and striking cross-fertilization of ideas.

Six selected areas in which significant progress has occurred are considered:

1. Change from a closed system of child protection to a more open system involving many professions and the public at large. Perhaps the greatest progress has been in the general recognition that social workers have carried the entire burden of protective services alone for too long a time, and that they have lacked the needed support of physicians, nurses, police, the judiciary, and, finally, the population they serve. Wherever the system has remained so rigidly isolated as to preclude an interdisciplinary approach, progress has been slow. Pressure from the outside, primarily from enlightened and sometimes enraged citizens, has been required to bring about needed change. But in many thousands of communities throughout the world, broad interest shown by the public and all helping professionals has brought about reorientation toward joint concerns by involving the community as a whole with all its professional and lay talents. This has greatly improved the lot of needy families as well as the lot of primary workers in the child protection field. It is now well understood that, because of the enormous emotional stress produced in coping with child abuse, the fatigue and burnout of workers in the field is great. Primary care child protection workers have been the only public servants willing to constantly stretch their case load to meet any demands. They do so because they are not a militant profession with defined duties. In the process, however, they do an injustice to their clients and to themselves. The answer lies in the increasing use of lay family aides as social work extenders.

We now understand that the phenomenon of worker fatigue and burnout can be prevented by enlisting professional and community support. The complex problems of assault against children, with the long treatment required for families, the difficult-to-treat parents and very needy children, are in themselves such a challenge to the social care system that there is a chance that, once progress has been made, it might later be lost in an exhaustion phenomenon of the system itself. It is not possible to say that it is too expensive or too time-consuming to try to treat treatable families by pronouncing them all to be untreatable. Having once committed ourselves to helping families to prevent and treat child assault, we must not once again leave it to the constituted authorities to slide back to the isolationist days so recently overcome.

It is not surprising that every country I have analyzed goes through a specific sequence of developmental stages in addressing the problem of assault against children.

Stage One is denial that either physical or sexual assault exists to a significant extent. Serious assault that surfaces is ascribed to a psychotic, drunken, or drugged parent or to foreign guest workers with different styles of child raising—"nothing to do with us."

Stage Two is paying attention to the more evident assault against children—the battered child—and beginning to cope in more effective ways with physical assault, including early intervention when it is perhaps not so severe.

Stage Three comes when physical assault is better handled and attention is now beginning to be paid to the infant who fails to thrive, an example of passive assault, and to the general area of significant physical neglect.

Stage Four comes in recognition of emotional assault and neglect. Its more severe form is seen in the child who is rejected, scapegoated, unloved, and so emotionally deprived that it significantly interferes with normal physical, intellectual, and emotional growth and development.

Stage Five is paying attention to the serious plight of the sexually assaulted child, including the youngster involved in incest.

I am certain that these sequences of events occur in every country, and, provided that your country has already passed through all these phases, you might ask yourself when you might come to face Stage Six, that of guaranteeing each child that he or she is truly wanted, and is provided with loving care, decent shelter and food, and first class preventive and curative health care.

If any country has solved the problem of assault against children, I have not discovered it. Some nations have moved forward in this field through stages One through Five; they do possess the understanding and technical know-how to provide proper services. But even in these so-called advanced countries there are as yet only islands of excellence in a sea of ineptitude and insufficient political and financial commitment. There may yet come a time when children are seen as such a precious national resource and so deserving of total civil rights that society at vill take a benevolent interest in their welfare from the time of conception through prenatal care, and from birth into infancy, early childhood, and through the school years. One of the paradoxes of our century is that society has, indeed, involved itself materially in the child's life at school age, but in many nations there remains an enormous hiatus in the protection afforded the child from conception until age six.

The question of the rights of parents to be left alone must be weighed against the rights of the child to be protected from parents unable to cope at a level assumed to be reasonable by the society in which they reside.

2. Early treatment of the assaulted child and his or her siblings. Another relatively recent development has been the acceptance of the concept that we cannot wait to begin the emotional reconstitution of the physically or sexually assaulted child, regardless of age. Treatment of the child is a relatively new concept for protective service workers who have hitherto, of necessity, had to focus on the mother while the father was largely unavailable. This was known as the "trickle down" theory by which giving nurturing help to the mother was thought to improve her total life and marriage and would then permit her to be a more competent mother and wife. It was the credo of protective service work for 100 years, and it turned out to be woefully lacking. It should come as no surprise to anyone that it took parents 25 years to become what they have become; as a result, it is difficult to change their child-raising practices and, even in a modest way, their character in a period of a year or two. On the other hand, it has been very encouraging to us to see how relatively quickly their children can be reconstituted emotionally, provided only that they receive skilled, reliable emotional support at once. Individual and group treatment must be tailor-made to each child's needs. To fail to address the emotional needs of the assaulted child effectively—and from the very first—should nowadays be regarded as malpractice.

3. The growing recognition that sexual assault is as prevalent and, in many ways, as serious as physical assault in considering the long-term welfare of children. More and more is being done to prevent child assault and to intervene successfully as early as possible, before it is a major threat to the child's life or growth and development. This has not yet been possible in a major way in the field of sexual assault, although even there we see inroads being made by early inclusion of family life education in schools, and by providing effective rescue once sexual assault comes to light. Let me add here that those who believe that incest had best be left a "family affair"—that it is not of serious emotional import as judged by the fact that many victims have gone on to lead apparently

normal lives—fail to take into account the enormous emotional costs paid by many of these children and the scars they bear for a lifetime. Recent studies show that a disproportionate number of prostitutes have been involved in incest in early years, and that most children involved in incest do not grow up to have happy lives. The frequency of incest is very large, and the reported number of cases is now fully equal to that of physical assault in our Center.

Early treatment of these children, regardless of age, appears to be important in order to be successful in many cases, with some spectacular failure in others. But remember that incest is as yet hardly talked about in many countries; it is, indeed, the "last taboo." Discussing incest even at a professional level often leads to hostile responses similar to those we heard 20 years ago when discussing the battered child.

4. The institutional assault against children, which occurs when society's intervention is more harmful than if intervention had not occurred. Our concept of prevention and, when that fails, of early intervention does assume that intervention is better than doing nothing. But there are times when we clearly intervene badly and do unintended harm. An intelligent treatment plan must be made that does full justice to the rights of the child without subjecting him or her to the alternative, institutional assault of unduly prolonged and frequently changing foster care or institutional placements. Many a child, having been robbed of his or her family for his own good, is subsequently robbed of each new family substitute in turn, a truly devastating blow to any attempt at bonding for the child. The incredible inertia of child protection and judicial systems the world over requires public attention and action to ameliorate this kind of institutional assault against children.

Consider the plight of children who have committed no crime but are placed in temporary shelters which are in fact juvenile correction institutions, training schools, and security detention facilities—all alternatives used by society to cope with children who simply have no place to go because they are assaulted at home. In many instances the money spent by the public on institutional care of such children could be better spent in treatment of the family, with the child given additional safeguards because of the increased development of helping services. But above all, the child who is in limbo is really suffering the most. When families cannot be reconstituted, making prompt adoption available would certainly be preferable to shuttling the child from pillar to post over a period of many years.

Since our last meeting there has been lively debate about the relative importance of societal assault of the parents by suggesting that assault against children is essentially a product of young families caught up in the stresses of poverty, racism, unemployment, and poor housing; these crises trigger the attack on the child and are the primary cause of physical assault against children. This concept does not, of course, take care of the failure-to-thrive syndrome or sexual assault, but it does take the therapist somewhat off the hook by blaming society's shortcomings for the parents' assaultive behavior. Without underestimating the importance of external crises as a trigger phenomenon, let me just point out that we are very struck with the high incidence and serious nature of child assault among a group of individuals who do have jobs, housing, cheap food, free comprehensive health care, are married, and live surrounded by potentially helpful people. I am talking here about a group of military families who enjoy all these societal advantages and still have a very significant problem of child assault, with five child deaths occurring in a single military camp in my state in the past 12 months. Clearly internal and external stresses combine to trigger attacks.

5. The two legal concepts of the law guardian and the legal requirements of involuntary termination of parental rights and the freeing of the assaulted child for adoption. Two legal advances, which are rapidly coming to the foreground, have been the concept of a guardian *ad litem*, an adult who may not necessarily have legal training, who is assigned by the court to be the advocate of the child in all situations in which the child is deemed to be in need of protection by the court. All of our states have the possibility of providing guardians ad litem to assaulted children, but an increasing number of states now mandate it.

Similarly, a number of states have now more clearly defined the situations under which involuntary termination of parental rights can be accomplished. This usually entails either a particularly brutal or sadistic form of assault against children by imprisonment or starvation or abandonment for a period of six months or more. Also considered are serious and incurable psychopathology on the part of the parent which places the child in immediate danger and is not amenable to treatment, and finally those situations in which a serious effort at treatment has failed and it is believed by the court that a child cannot successfully be raised in his or her family. Such termination of parental rights is never undertaken lightly, but if information is well documented by a social worker, a pediatrician, and a psychiatrist (psychologist), we have yet to see it overturned on appeal. Early termination of parental rights to make the child available for adoption will, in years to come, be seen as a key element in the chain of progress for assaulted children.

6. Prevention of assault against children. Since our last meeting there

has also been debate about the ethics of identifying, or some people say labeling, of some families as "in need of extra services" or "at risk." Pediatricians have always preferred prevention to treatment. We have felt that it was far better to develop the poliomyelitis vaccine to prevent polio than to try to improve the iron lung respirator used by the victims of the disease. There are now a number of well-controlled studies that show that it is possible to identify families who might be expected to have problems in bonding and to assist many of them by an extra effort of kindness and care. It is particularly important to those of us who work in the fields of obstetrics, midwifery, pediatrics, and nursing that every effort be made by paying careful attention to families' attitudes toward their babies before, during, and after their births, and to find those to whom we will need to reach out in order to provide extra help if parenting should fail partially or completely, and before disasters occur. There are those who believe that even looking at a mother and a child after delivery is unethical and an invasion of their privacy. Not so! We health professionals are employed by our families to help bring into the world a healthy child with the least trauma both physically and emotionally to the baby and its parents. As part of comprehensive health care by obstetrics and pediatrics, we must pay attention to early bonding and adjustment needs of families. Failure to provide this comprehensive health care is medical and nursing malpractice.

It should not be surprising to anyone that, even when we do a better job of providing early help to families in need of extra services and of educating families to seek such help when they encounter crises, we will be left with the residue of impossible-to-treat, assaultive parents who will appear to us to be more and more sick. Unless we license parenthood, this will be our lot in years to come, if we are successful in preventing the majority of instances of serious assault against children.

# CONCLUSION

The second International Congress represented a truly unique opportunity to listen and to learn: to have a totally open mind, to be humble and not dogmatic, and to assume that we all know very little.

To those who for professional satisfaction insist on a high percentage of "cures," the field of child assault has little to offer. But to those who find an immense satisfaction in bringing happiness, even for a time, to children and to their parents, to see them all grow and develop, and to go from constant misery to at least intermittent times of joy and satisfaction, it is indeed a most satisfying field. It is hard to measure the ultimate effect of our care. One simply has to see hundreds and hundreds of such families to be persuaded that humane and skilled efforts in their behalf have brought about changes for the better, and this is particularly so for the children who have been neglected so long in our early rush to help their parents.

Although international meetings serve a splendid purpose of acquainting us with the contributions made by many diverse groups in many countries, I should warn you that it is not always possible to transfer a program from one country to the next, even when they are neighboring countries. Differences in professional attitudes, laws, and society's readiness for change all govern and all are important. On the other hand, it would be quite wrong to assume that just because a piece of work was done here it cannot be useful somewhere else. Science would not have progressed if people had persisted in having to reinvent the wheel.

In closing let me quote the preamble to the Declaration of the Rights of the Child adopted by the United Nations in 1959:

"Mankind owes the child the best it has to give."

Doctor Kempe (deceased March, 1984) was Professor of Pediatrics (Chairman) and Microbiology and Director of the C. Henry Kempe National Center for the Prevention and Treatment of Child Abuse and Neglect, University of Colorado Health Services Center, Denver, Colorado. This Introduction is essentially an address entitled "Recent Developments in the Field of Child Abuse" presented by Dr. Kempe at the Second International Congress on Child Abuse convened in London, England, in 1977; it was published in *Child Abuse and Neglect* (2:261–267, 1978) and is included here by gracious permission of the writer. Its timeless observations still establish a current and appropriate point of departure for this book. The terms abuse and neglect have been changed to assault for reasons given in the Preface, and a few other slight editorial changes have been made for continuity with the following chapters.

*Chapter 1*

# Definition, Dynamics, and Prevalence of Assault Against Children: A Multifactorial Model

### *John H. Meier*

## DEFINITION

The multiple dynamic factors that contribute to child assault are kaleidoscopic, subtle, and complex. This means that any definition or model of the dynamics of child assault must be multifaceted. Even the definition of child assault itself is highly variegated, contributing to confusing incidence explanations and prevalence statistics, contradictory estimates of the efficacy of various treatment and prevention programs, and inconclusive research findings in general (Besharov, 1981; Giovannoni and Becerra, 1979; Zigler, 1979). For purposes of this chapter, child assault is broadly defined as "the physical or mental injury, sexual abuse or exploitation, negligent treatment, or maltreatment of a child under the age of eighteen by a person who is responsible for the child's welfare under circumstances which indicate that the child's health or welfare is harmed or threatened thereby" (U.S. Department H.E.W., 1975, p. 3).

After several months of intensive and extensive debate, the above definition is being amended to include "the withholding of medically indicated treatment from disabled infants with life-threatening conditions" (Holden, 1984). This controversial addition, popularly referred to as the Baby Doe Compromise, leaves decisions to treat an infant up to a physician's reasonable medical judgment and would generally exclude treatment when the infant is irreversibly comatose or the intervention would be judged to be futile, inhumane, or merely a prolonging of the death process. Since this most recent addition has just been approved, it is too early to comment further on its contribution toward reducing assault against children.

Gelles (1973) calls child assault a political term which, as such, "defies logical and precise scientific definition." He goes on to say, "Malnourishment, sexual abuse, failure to feed and clothe a child, allowing a child to live in a deprived or depraved environment, and helping a child stay out of school have all been defined at various times and in various laws as 'child abuse.' The definition of child assault varies over time, across cultures, and between different social and cultural groups" (Gelles, 1973, p. 612). Regardless of the lack of definitional precision, rigor, or simplicity, assault against innocent children is occurring and increasing throughout the world. It is crucial to understand the dynamics underlying child assault, however defined, in order to identify, treat, and prevent it. As mentioned in the Preface, the term *assault* is used throughout this text since it repeatedly reminds the reader of the criminal or legal implications which are more or less strongly suggested in the past and present literature by such terms as slaughter, batter, maltreat, abuse, or neglect.

## DYNAMICS OF CHILD ASSAULT: A MULTIFACTORIAL MODEL

The reasons for a given child's being assaulted arise from factors which are divided into three major categories: (1) Parental Factors; (2) Child Factors; and (3) Ecological Factors. In each of these categories are many possible factors, which may occur in a wide variety of combinations and permutations to cause or contribute to any actual episodes or patterns of assault against children. Since the possible interactions among these multiple factors are so numerous, there is no single set of characteristics that might be assembled into a singular profile of the assaultive parent–perpetrator, the assaulted child–victim, or the assault-conducive ecology or environment. In fact, the inherent complexity of contributing factors in each idiosyncratic case of child assault is a significant challenge to authorities when they attempt to ferret out the peculiar constellation of factors causing or contributing to a given episode of child assault or a chronic series of such episodes.

Nevertheless, it is hoped that, as the state of the art and science advances, identification of certain prevalent profiles, patterns, syndromes, typologies, and characteristic causes of child assault will become more clear (Sloan and Meier, 1983c). This would in turn make it more feasible for planning for primary prevention—that is, prevention of child assault before it occurs even once in a child's life. Although the complexity is presently perplexing, because the contributing factors cut across the fabric of the entire human condition, there are some common threads that can be teased out and rewoven into a multifactorial model for better understanding the sometimes crazy-quilt dynamics in a given case of child assault. This understanding is important, not only for the planning and implementation of long-range primary prevention programs, but also for the more informed treatment of current child assault cases. In this regard, the model serves to indicate or at least implicate some salient causative factors and thus proves most helpful in planning long-term secondary prevention—that is, prevention of any recurrence or recidivism in a given child–victim's life.

A multifactorial model of child assault dynamics is presented in Figure 1–1 to serve as a gestalt with its many component parts being described briefly in this chapter. Each of the major factors mentioned herein is addressed in greater detail in other chapters of this book and in various CHILDHELP Research Division publications, wherein additional differentiation clarifies the many more subtle nuances and interrelationships among the factors. The model, then, serves both as a conceptual skeleton to be fleshed out later and as an operational definition of child assault, without which incidence and prevalence statements and intervention or prevention efforts cannot be meaningfully addressed and researched because they have no commonly understood context. In this regard, a theoretical model becomes quite practical, as observed by Hall and Lindzey (1957) and Newberger, Newberger, and Hampton (1983). This more comprehensive perspective in itself should help to dispel any simplistic notions about the perpetrators, the victims, or the circumstances of child assault and might in itself eliminate some of the more superficial "Band-Aid" or unidimensional approaches to treating, preventing, or even discussing assault against children.

The actual entries included in Figure 1–1 are intended to be representative and suggestive but are by no means an exhaustive list of the many factors mentioned in a more detailed treatise regarding the dynamics of child assault. The model was developed by Meier (1978) and has been further informed by the following sources: Achenbach (1978); American Humane Association National Survey (1977); American Psychiatric Association, Diagnostic, and Statistical Manual (DSM III) (1980); Gaines, Sandgrund, Green and Power (1978); Garbarino and Crouter (1977); Gelles (1977); Helfer and Kempe (1976); Holmes and Rahe (1967); Meier (1984a); Parke and Collmer (1975); and Wodarski (1981).

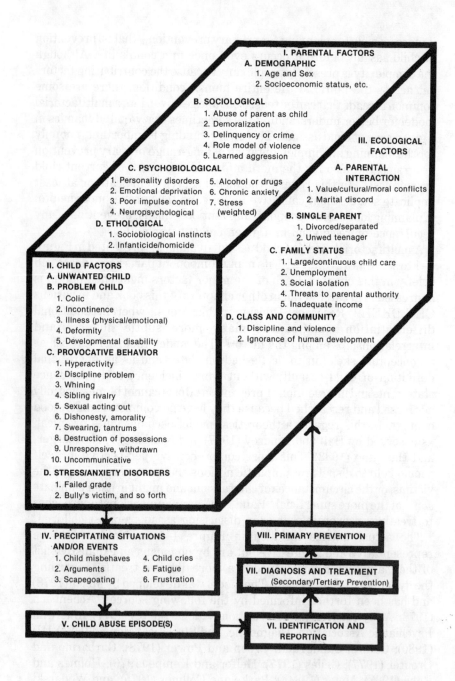

**Figure 1–1.** Model of child abuse dynamics. Developed by John H. Meier.

The three-dimensional portrayal is designed to illustrate the simultaneous mutual interaction among the factors contributing to an episode of child assault. Understanding the causes and consequences of assault against children is a far more demanding challenge than solving the popular Rubik's Cube; this model is intended to be a rudimentary "Rubrics Cube" for illustrating and explaining the complex dynamics and rubrics of various forms of child assault.

## Parental Factors

Since over three fourths of reported child assault cases, which are later verified to be legitimate cases, can be attributed to one or both natural parents of the child, it is necessary to review the variety of contributory factors that must be considered with regard to the biological or surrogate parents of the child. As indicated by the data from the American Humane Association National Surveys (1977, 1979, 1983) and The Village's residential population (Meier, 1984, and Chapter 8), over 70 per cent of the perpetrators of child assault were biological mothers; this is explained primarily by the fact that the mother spends the most time with the child and has the greatest responsibility for caring for the child. Other perpetrators include fathers, boyfriends, relatives, neighbors, babysitters, and others, in descending order of frequency.

### *Parental Status*

**Age of Parent–Perpetrator.** The age of the perpetrator is related to the probability that child assault will occur and is somewhat predictive of the kind of assault. On the lower end of the childbearing age continuum there is presently in the United States a virtual epidemic of unwed teenage pregnancies which are being carried through to birth more frequently than in previous generations. Moreover, most of the young mothers are choosing to keep their offspring rather than relinquishing them for adoption, as was more customary in the past. These young mothers, who themselves are still adolescents frequently in need of considerably more mothering, ordinarily do not have sufficient fiscal, physical, psychic, or parenting resources for providing all that a newborn child requires (Calderone and Johnson, 1981). The many reasons given by these young women for bearing their own babies at such a youthful age include, to name a few: (1) a desire to finally have someone to love them (and perhaps to even act as mother to them—a type of role reversal);

(2) to prove their arrival as fully functioning females (the counterpart of the male "macho" phenomenon); (3) as a source of income through Aid to Families with Dependent Children (AFDC) and other welfare programs (not to mention the business of bearing babies to sell them in several illegal markets); (4) as an achievement to which their culture attributes great meaning and admiration; (5) the naive notion that babies are cute little playthings to keep them company and occupy their spare time; or (6) perhaps as the result of sheer ignorance about contraception, accidental conception, and a subsequent unwillingness to undergo an abortion, whether for fear of pain or for cultural, religious, personal, or moral reasons.

At the other end of the childbearing age continuum are those middle-aged persons, 35 years of age and older, who had not planned to have any children at all or at least did not wish to bear and rear any more children. For one of several reasons they have a surprise pregnancy and choose to go through with it, often to realize that their physical resources or emotional reserves have become depleted during the past several years and they are no longer an adequate match for the unrelenting demands of a dependent newborn child. Moreover, even though these people may be at the prime of their earning capacity, when they realize that it will require about $100,000 over the coming 18 years to provide for this new human being, the frightening financial prospects may become overwhelming.

Several studies have implicated unplanned or unwanted births as major contributors to some cases of child assault (Gelles, 1973; Oates and Hufton, 1977; Parke and Collmer, 1975). For example, Gelles (1973) suggests that the unplanned child is beaten not because of a projection or "transference psychosis" but because the child is seen as a source of stress and an additional unbearable burden. A possible additional complication is that mothers (and probably fathers) at either end of the childbearing age continuum have a higher risk of producing a neurologically defective child who is likely to be even more demanding, frustrating, and expensive to raise than a normally developing child (Meier and Sloan, 1983).

**Sex of Parent–Perpetrator.** As alluded to in the above section, the sex of the parent–perpetrator may be a contributing factor. The father or male adult may believe that sons are made tough or are prevented from becoming sissies by learning to endure being knocked around, perhaps as he was when of a similar age. Or the mother may have some hangup about cleanliness for little girls and severely reprimand or corporally punish a daughter for making a normal child's mess of something. Alternatively, the parent(s) may simply be disappointed that their daughter is not a boy, or vice versa, since they had great fantasies for a child of the opposite sex. For example, one mother, who expected a son, had picked out blue baby clothes and planned to breast feed her baby; when a girl was born, she refused to even hold her newborn daughter and had her placed on bottle feeding immediately, neither of which augurs well for the maternal bonding and infant attachment behavior deemed so important by Ainsworth (1980), Bowlby (1969), Klaus and Kennell (1976), and others.

Socioeconomic Status. Socioeconomic status (SES) is a two-factor index, proposed by Hollingshead (1957), reflecting income and occupation, which are highly related to level of education. The relationship between child assault and SES is well expressed by the title "The Myth of Classlessness in Child Abuse" (Pelton, 1978, 1981). Although it is true that child assault is found in families ranging from the bottom to the top of the SES continuum, the highest documented prevalence is definitely within lower SES families (American Humane Association, 1977, 1983; Gelles, 1973; Gil, 1970a).

Smith and Bohnstedt (1981) report data on approximately 1,000 child assault cases; they found no significant differences between assault, neglect, and molestation in terms of SES. All three groups were composed of members of predominantly lower SES as indicated by their receiving financial aid. Regardless of the type of child assault, significantly more victims' families receive financial aid than families without child assault. In cases of neglect there is a preponderance of lower incomes and menial occupations (or unemployment, as discussed later and as documented by Krugman, 1984), which prevent the family from providing adequate food, shelter, and clothing as well as intellectual, emotional, and cultural enrichment, all of which are more available in middle and upper class homes parented by better educated adults. It has been argued that reported neglect is also higher among low SES families because they must use various public welfare programs, such as Aid for Dependent Children, maternal and infant clinics, medicare services, food stamps, and other societal welfare benefits for low SES persons. They are thus more likely to be brought to the attention of government or other authorities when there is any suspicion of a child's being neglected. Nevertheless, Smith and Bohnstedt (1981) found this relationship of financial aid and victimization not likely to be either (1) an artifact resulting from the detection of need for financial aid; or (2) an artifact of an eligibility worker's rendering financial aid and incidentally detecting victimization by the close relationship with the families receiving aid.

It is argued that although neglect is less likely to occur for reasons of monetary or educational inadequacies in middle and upper SES homes, when it does occur, it is less likely to be reported to the authorities and to become a documented statistic. In a similar manner, in cases of physical or sexual assault, such child maltreatment is less likely to be suspected, let alone reported, in middle and upper class families who have private physicians and an abundance of other resources. Until mandatory reporting laws were enacted in all 50 states during the past decade (Van de Kamp, 1983; see also Chapter 3), professionals avoided reporting such cases for fear of reprisal, court complications, or withdrawal from their patient population. They were more inclined to give their personal patients and friends the benefit of the doubt and even the benefit of various cover-up procedures, such as making more benign diagnoses for nonaccidental injuries to children by simply calling them accidental or using some exotic explanation, such as *osteogenesis imperfecta* (an extremely rare condition of very brittle bones) and not probing further. Legislation requiring reporting of assaults now makes failure to report suspected child assault a felony punishable by a fine, jail sentence, and, more devastatingly, loss of professional licensing and credibility. Such legal sanctions have reduced this cover-up behavior and probably have contributed substantially to the noteworthy increase in reported and substantiated child assault cases throughout the United States (see Chapter 3).

## Psychosocial Factors

**Abuse of Parent as a Child.** A frequently cited cliché in the field of child assault is that in most child assault cases there are two victims, the adult perpetrator and the child, implying that the adult is not only a desperate and needy person at the time when she or he assaults a child, but that there is a high probability that she or he was assaulted as a child only one short generation earlier. Adams (1976), Jenkins (1970), Solomon (1973), and Steele and Pollock (1968) report that most assaultive parents had been assaulted as children. Similarly, Green, Gaines and Sandgrund (1974) and Main and Goldwyn (1984) report childhood rejection, criticism, and severe punishment as having been experienced by assaulting mothers. Oliver and Taylor (1971) describe an account of five generations of ill-treated children in the analysis of one family's pedigree. This transgenerational tradition of child assault within families is documented to be true in only about 50 per cent of the reported cases in the National American Humane Survey (1983), but was found to be much higher (80 per cent) among parents of seriously assaulted children

(Meier, 1980c, 1984a). This discrepancy may be explained by the fact that the American Humane Survey is a relatively superficial questionnaire of all reported assaultive persons, whereas the CHILDHELP parent population (and other clinical populations) are verified assaulters whose own detailed biographies are exposed gradually through prolonged involvement in multiple therapy and parenting education sessions. One of the more intriguing research questions is the following: on the one hand, why do a large number of children who are assaulted in their childhood grow up to be exemplary parents, practically bending over backwards to assure that their children do not suffer the same plight? On the other hand, why do those children who grow up in relatively humane and gentle circumstances subsequently become assaultive as parents? The many developmental factors contributing to differential parenting skills and intuitive childrearing myths are addressed in other chapters of this book and other CHILDHELP literature.

**Demoralization.** Demoralization is a term proposed some time ago (Frank, 1961) and recently reiterated by Frank (1981) as a general description of what has happened to many adults before they seek or need psychotherapy. It is characterized by one or more of the following symptoms in various combinations: a sense of general incompetence, loss of control over one's life, overall distress and depression, anxiety, loneliness, occasional thought disorders, and inability to cope with everyday, not to mention extraordinary, demands. Frank postulates that as much as 25 per cent of the adult population suffers mild forms of this demoralization syndrome, 10 per cent of cases being severe enough to warrant psychotherapeutic help for the patient (this was corroborated by a massive NIMH national survey reported in 1984). Those who have found a network of socioemotional supports and spiritual guidance from other persons or groups reported a noteworthy decline in anxiety, depression, and general emotional problems. Such values clarification or inculcation evidently constitutes a kind of remoralization for persons who have experienced demoralization. The apparent absence or inadequacy of moral development in assaultive adults (and assaulted children, for that matter) has prompted the CHILDHELP Research Division to sponsor an extensive collaborative research network at several major universities throughout the United States to investigate such relationships (see Chapter 8; Jensen and Meier, 1983).

**Delinquency and Crime—History of Antisocial Behavior.** Individuals with the so-called psychopathic personality often commit crimes against property and other human beings; such personality types may be more common than statistics suggest, since it is a difficult

...ation to diagnose adequately. Baldwin and Oliver (1975) report a significant association between child assault and criminality. Similarly, Smith and Bohnstedt (1981) have identified criminal histories as quite prevalent among child assaulters. Alfaro (1978), Garbarino and Plantz (1984), Hunner and Walker (1981), Meier (1979b), and the Senate of Canada (1977–1979) have marshaled considerable evidence for a high correlation between child assault and juvenile delinquency, which is frequently a stepping stone to adult crime.

The psychopath has traditionally been defined as a predominantly amoral or antisocial person characterized by impulsive, irresponsible actions satisfying only immediate and narcissistic interests without concern for obvious and implicit consequences, accompanied by minimal outward evidence of anxiety or guilt. The Diagnostic and Statistical Manual of Mental Disorders (American Psychiatric Association, 1980) redistributes some of these characteristics and places several of them, including child assault itself, under "Conditions not Attributable to a Mental Disorder." This suggests that child assaultive behavior results  from a moral or ethical disorder—a disorder or deficiency of character, the sort of deterioration or lack of sociopsychological maturation and prosocial behavior suggested by demoralization as conceptualized by Frank (1961) and already discussed.

The stages of moral development proposed by Kohlberg (1976) would place many parent–perpetrators of child assault at a relatively primitive level exemplified by an eye-for-an-eye and a tooth-for-a-tooth belief system of retaliative justice (Jensen and Meier, 1983). Thus, if a child bites an adult, the adult literally bites back to let the child know how it feels. The resort to inflicting corporal pain and suffering is also commonplace, whether by commission of real physical beatings or omission of food (causing hunger and other distress) or the withdrawal of affection, without the critical parental sensitivity to or empathy for the child's feelings (Feshbach and Howes, 1983). It is noteworthy that on the part of a representative sample of assaulted children at The Village there is a relatively reduced sense of pain or at least fewer somatic complaints (see Chapter 8) which in turn may be due to having experienced so much pain—a kind of psychic anesthesia. This may lead to these children's not being aware of how much others hurt when similar pain is inflicted upon them, contributing to an inability to empathize with others who are suffering from psychic or physical pain; on the other hand, it is conceivable that those who have suffered child assault will become exquisitely sensitive to the suffering of others, thus being more empathic, altruistic, and even therapeutic toward others.

**Role Model of Violence.** Children tend to identify with the psychological parent(s) in their lives, and if that parent is one who prescribes and practices violent solutions for life's inevitable problems ("never force anything, just get a bigger hammer"), it is likely that the child will identify with this aggressor. Whether a person subscribes to the Freudian notions of identification and introjection or the Piagetian ideas of assimilation and accommodation, this learned violent attitude seems to be passed on to the next generation (Galdston, 1971; Gelles, 1979, 1984).

Hence, such a violent attitude is thought amenable to intervention through systematic substitution and learning of more gentle and humane ways of shaping one's own and other's behavior. Some reeducation is often necessary to enlighten violent persons about alternatives to expressing violence, whether they direct it inwardly (intropunitive) or outwardly (extrapunitive). Rosenzweig (1944) has researched this bipolar approach to frustration resolution and sheds additional light on this aspect of child assault dynamics.

**Learned Aggression.** Instead of presenting his or her self as an aggressive role model, sometimes a very passive and withdrawn, yet significant, parent figure will systematically teach a child to become aggressive, to be tough, and to act in an aggressive manner, which the adult was never able to do but enjoys doing vicariously through his or her offspring. This may be exemplified in a socially acceptable form in various children's sports in which the parents seem to be the real protagonists, albeit on the sidelines. In the extreme, this can lead into the role reversal phenomenon, in which the child is expected to become the champion for the adult's needs and even serve as the adult's spokesperson and procure those things that the adult alone is unable to obtain. Some parents may even teach the child to commit crimes or sexual acts which the adult does not have enough courage to attempt. Such behaviors, which have been systematically reinforced, have to be unlearned and replaced with more socially acceptable behaviors. Chapter 5 addresses specific theoretical and practical aspects of such antisocial and maladjusted behavior along with methods of treatment and prevention.

## Psychological Factors

**Personality Disorders and Mental Illness.** Although fewer than 10 per cent of the adult or parent perpetrators of child assault can be technically classed as schizophrenic or psychotic (Steele, 1975), those who are so diagnosed have a particularly guarded prognosis (some designated as "untreatable" by Jones, 1984) since, for the most part, such severe underlying psychopathology does not respond to psychotherapy rapidly enough, if at all, for the parents to catch up with the child's developmental needs and meet their own peculiar needs simultaneously. Hyman and Parr (1978) found a higher degree of moderate chronic psychiatric disorder in mothers of assaulted children; Heinicke (1984) cites early family dysfunction due to parental personality characteristics as a major responsible factor. Griswold and Billingsley (1969) found that female assaulters obtained high scores on the subscales of the Minnesota Multiphasic Personality Inventory (MMPI) (Hathaway and McKinley, 1967), indicative of psychotic inclinations. In another study, Hyman and Parr (1978) compared 37 assaulting and 37 matched control parents on the Sixteen Personality Factors Test (Cattell, 1965); the assaulting parents had significantly lower ego control and ego integration and higher suspiciousness. Call (1984) proposes a cogent case for the psychiatric syndrome, reactive attachment disorder of infancy, being operative as a source of early hostility between new parents and their newborns. Paulson, Afifi, Chaleff, and Thomason (1975) analyzed the MMPI profiles of assaultive parents. Assaultive mothers were excessively aggressive; male assaulter profiles had significantly more psychotic overtones. Such disturbed parents have often created such bizarre home environments and early learning experiences for the child(ren) that considerable unlearning of inappropriate behaviors and attitudes must precede any constructive rehabilitation. These abnormal early experiences may be so wanting or distorted as to contribute to the development of so-called "Swiss cheese" children (Meier, 1976a), who have not received appropriate or adequate cognitive and affective input during various critical developmental stages and remain somewhat incomplete as to feeling good about themselves. When these persons become parents they are dealing from an incomplete or damaged deck of cards in their behavioral and underlying cognitive and affective repertoires.

**Emotional Deprivation.** It is noteworthy that many assaulting adults are described not only in terms noted previously but also frequently manifest an overall lack of emotional expression, sometimes called a flatness of affect. They seem not to have had sufficient emotional input as youngsters and thus have depleted reservoirs of feelings to draw upon for expressing love, hate, fear, and so forth. This lack of emotional input, from not being cuddled as infants to not being loved as adults, makes it unlikely that they will have much, if any, deep emotional input to pass on to their offspring. Simplistic bumper stickers asking, indeed recommending, "Have you hugged your child today?" represent the notion that every human appreciates and even needs such basic physical expressions of emotional caring. One author addressing emotional developmental somewhat whimsically prescribed four hugs a day for survival, eight for maintenance, and twelve for optimum emotional growth (Simon, 1976); it seems analogous to the folk wisdom in the advice, "a pinch to grow an inch but a smile to grow a mile."

**Poor Impulse Control.** The aphorism "There but for the grace of God, go I" is one frequently iterated in discussions about who are the perpetrators of child assault. This suggests that without some mystical insight and control anyone might assault his or her child(ren). Although it is true that parents do have the physical, psychological, and economic power to inflict assault on their children, most do not. Each person seems to have a threshold of tolerance for frustration and there seem to be different thresholds among people and even within the same person at different times. Spinetta and Rigler (1972) describe child assaulters as having a general defect in character (demoralization?) that allows aggressive impulses to be expressed freely. To put this in perspective, it is interesting to note that the DSM III (American Psychiatric Association, 1980) classifies behaviors such as pathological gambling, kleptomania, and pyromania in the same category with intermittent or isolated explosive disorders. People have varying levels of fascination or irresistible attraction to gambling, stealing and arson, and perhaps there are related drives toward violence. For example, some people are known to have a "short fuse" and to easily "fly off the handle," whereas others are known as "slow burners" who have a great deal of tolerance and patience, and the ability to count to ten before or instead of resorting to violent expressions of anger. Furthermore, the same person, during different stages of life (Levinson, 1978) or even during different periods of the day (due to such things as hunger, fatigue, and so forth) may have an undulating and unpredictable variation in threshold of frustration tolerance. Other people remain calm and easygoing under the most adverse of circumstances.

These individual differences are important with respect to the prognosis for family reunification and estimates about potential further child assault episodes (recidivism). Such behaviors are very difficult to test systematically and objectively since it is difficult to simulate the kinds of stresses which might precipitate a loss of control. Moreover, ethical and professional considerations preclude deliberately inducing such frustration to prompt episodes of child assault or adult breakdowns.

Another interpretation of a lack of tolerance refers to the inability of a parent or child caregiver to tolerate child behavior that may be quite normal for a given child. Due to unrealistic expectations imposed upon the child, he or she is almost certain to fail in the eyes of the adult, who may then resort to unwarranted and assaultive corrective procedures. Such parental lack of understanding and tolerance for normal child growth, development, and behavior was evident in over one half of The Village cases of severe child assault, underscoring the crying need for parenting education.

**Neuropsychological Disorders.** This is a controversial factor referring to the effects of brain damage or neurological dysfunction on the adult's impulse control system. It implies that the perpetrator is not totally in control of his or her emotions because of minimal brain dysfunction or damage (MBD). This MBD may have been caused by traumatic insults to the neuropsychological system, such as head injuries, perhaps sustained from assault as a child. Hanley's description of a post-concussive syndrome (1984) further implicates previously undiagnosed brain insult in both child and adult violent behaviors. Alternatively, the dysfunction may be due to a genetic predisposition and consequent endocrinological imbalances; for example, having an XYY sex chromosome constitution, instead of the standard XY sex chromosome complement, has been suggested as predisposing a male to more active and violent behavior (Mednick, 1977).

One of the functions of the ascending reticular activating system in the human central nervous system is to filter out stimuli that are irrelevant from those on which the organism must focus either for survival or for optimum functioning. Malfunction of this system is frequently manifested in behavior characterized as distractible and even hyperkinetic. However, most of the behavioral manifestations attributable to such dysfunction are of a sensorimotor nature and use observations of bodily activity levels to determine normal or abnormal functioning. A person experiencing difficulties in this neuropsychological realm has difficulty in learning information and skill that require concentration. It is believed that many learning disorders, with their attendant behavioural aberrations and emotional distress, are attributable to MBD, and vice versa (Brown and Rosenbaum, 1983).

In addition to the elevated incidence of MBD and learning disabilities found among assaulted children and their parents, demonstrated on psychometric tests of intelligence and achievement (Meier, 1983c; see also Chapter 8) and inferred through clinical and anecdotal observations and histories, there is a remarkable increase in the amount of psychopathology and sociopathology. Recent neuropsychological theory indicates that one of the principal functions of the frontal lobes is analogous to the ascending reticular activating system but responsible for filtering cognitive and affective input and giving feedback to the rest of the brain and entire organism regarding appropriateness of behavior. Frontal lobe impairment or immaturity is implicated in a lack of flexibility or ability to correct behavior even when an error is perceived, a lack of ego strength and personality integration, a lack of verbal regulation of behavior, and a general lack of abstraction and problem-solving abilities, to name several prominent and relevant deficiencies (Walsh, 1978). Since the specific functions of the frontal lobe remain somewhat unclear and since they are the last sections of the brain to become fully myelinated and hence the last to reach developmental maturity (sometime during adolescence), it has been suggested that the frontal lobes may be the seat of many complex sociobehavioral mediators as yet not well understood or documented. The brain–behavioral relationships and the stages of moral development that occur with other types of maturation intimate a relationship between moral development and behavior and frontal lobe maturation and function. In addition to the many other functions attributed to the frontal lobes, the experience with assaulted children and assaultive parents suggests that because of the extraordinarily inconsistent and chaotic social milieu in which they are immersed, they are probably unable to make sense of the confusing and contradictory inputs and are neuropsychologically or experientially rendered unable to distinguish appropriate from inappropriate behaviors in various interpersonal social settings. This may, in a vicious cycle, lead to additional assault.

**Alcohol or Drug Dependence.** Alcohol and drug abuse among parent-perpetrators of child assault and neglect is found in at least a fifth of the verified cases. The interaction of several phenomena is usually found, such as the fact that the substance abuser is often seeking an escape from many real or perceived stresses in his or her life. As the alcohol or drug dulls the person's normal inhibitory system, more primitive and violent behavior is permitted and expressed. Although it is true that these substances typically increase sexual desire but reduce ability to perform, they do not reduce the relatively overwhelming strength and power an adult has compared with a small child. The adult's sense of propriety (morality) may be so dulled that not only are sexual liberties taken with the child but physical damage is inflicted; subsequently memory may be so impaired that there is no remorse—an apparently psychopathic, demoralized reaction.

**Chronic Anxiety.** Some people are referred to as being "high strung" or nervous types who are often overly active or distractible and seem to have a high level of energy or free-floating anxiety, which can readily be elicited by any number of seemingly minor events. It is conceivable that some of these persons are adult versions of hyperkinetic children and, possibly for neurological reasons, are unable to relax mentally or even to sit still. Others are so fear-ridden or guilt-ridden that the anxiety from their state of mind can take a reverse form and render them paralyzed, gradually sinking into withdrawal and even deep depression, which occasionally leads to suicidal (intropunitive) attempts. The apparent prevalence of debilitating depression among assaulted children is noted and discussed later (see Chapter 5). Such anxiety or agitated depression may be a part of a larger state of demoralization discussed earlier (Frank, 1961).

**Stress.** Holmes and Rahe (1967) have devised a Social Readjustment Rating Scale of normal life events and assigned to each event a weighted numerical value equivalent to the event's contribution to a person's stress. These events range from the death of a spouse (100 points) to being put in jail or other institution (63), being fired (47), or even such a seemingly benign event as a vacation (13). Each event is placed in an hierarchy ranging from one to 100 points. The stressful events occurring in a given person's life during the past year are assigned points which are added. If the cumulative score is 300 or more, for example, there is an 80 per cent risk that the person will suffer some sort of major health breakdown in response to the overload of stress in his or her life. Another promising procedure for tapping numerous lesser daily hassles and uplifts (Kanner, Coyne, Schaefer, and Lazarus, 1981) helps to identify the proverbial "straw that broke the camel's back." It is remarkable how many of these events are present in the case histories of assaulting parents. In a noteworthy related study, Egeland, Breitenbucher, and Rosenburg (1980) administered a modified version of Cochrane and Robertson's Life Events Inventory to a sample of 267 primiparous women at risk for assaulting their children. The inventory, administered 12 months after the birth of the infant, differentiated between a subsample of 32 mothers who mistreated their children and a subsample of 33 mothers who provided adequate care. Since the majority of stressed mothers did not assault their children, it remains to be answered why some stressed mothers assault their children whereas others, experiencing similar amounts of stress, do not. Justice and Duncan (1976) found that assaultive parents showed much higher levels of stress and change in their lives than nonassaultive parents with problem children. The intriguing interaction among stress, empathy, and moral development provided a heuristic lead presently being studied to help answer this question (Meier, 1984).

This entire series of factors is reminiscent of the book by Alvarez (1956) in which he made the generalization that transmission of psychophysical vulnerability, developmental deviations, and behavioral anomalies all seem interrelated and seem to repeatedly manifest themselves from generation to generation within certain families, suggesting various expressions of an underlying genetic predisposition to malfunction. However, they may take a different form, depending upon the vulnerable organs or psychic systems (some people develop ulcers whereas others develop hypertension or colitis), and some individuals resort to adult criminal behavior, whereas others may become child assaulters. Some become homicidal and others suicidal depending on whether they have learned to turn their violent feelings outward (extrapunitive) or inward (intropunitive).

## *Ethological or Sociobiological Factors*

**Sociobiological Instincts.** Although customarily it is unthinkable or at least very controversial, considerable evidence from research findings regarding instincts and patterns of survival in nonhuman animals suggests that similar primitive drives remain subtly active in mankind as well (Leak and Christopher, 1982; Van den Berghe, 1979). Prominent ethologists and comparative sociobiologists have advanced many other analogues of child assault and neglect which seem to be manifested in primates and other animal species. For example, the anxious attachment (Ainsworth, 1980) of assaulted children with the assaultive mothers was also found in infant monkeys who were assaulted by their mothers (Harlow, 1958). The aggression displayed by primates and children as a result of repeated frustration both suggest the possibility of similar dynamics occurring naturally and instinctively in nonhumans and humans alike. Empirical studies reveal that stepparents are more likely to assault stepchildren (Meier and Sloan, 1984; Russell, 1984), an ominous finding in light of the growing rate of family dissolutions and remarriages. This has been tentatively explained by the notion of "inclusive fitness," whereby a male adult seeks to establish his dominance by killing the offspring fathered by other competitive males and then impregnating the available female(s) to ensure his impression on the tribe or family; a primitive proclivity to destroy or disown nonbiological children may be operative on at least an unconscious level.

**Infanticidal or Homicidal Tendencies.** One example has to do with the Darwinian notion of survival of the fittest. Carried to one extreme, this drive is expressed by some bird species, which will restrict egg production lest they have more hungry offspring than the estimated available food supply and their anticipated energy resources can satisfy. Examples of nonhumans exposing their weaker offspring to certain death by abandoning them to other predators is regarded as natural. Obviously, this becomes quite a different issue when it involves infanticide or homicide in the human race, since this directly violates the principle of a society's quality being judged by how well it cares for its weakest members. The infanticidal or homicidal practices of such groups as the Spartans in ancient history and the Nazis in contemporary history sends shivers of fear up the spines of most civilized people. To further complicate matters, the bioethical discussion about deliberate abortion and euthanasia, in view of the rapidly rising cost of raising a normally developing child, not to mention a handicapped one, simply adds to the flames of heated discussion. Some posit that an argument against evolution is the contrast between instinctual drives in lower animals toward protecting the fittest and eliminating the weakest versus the very reverse inclination of civilized humans toward protecting the weakest through the concerted efforts of the more fit. Others of a eugenics persuasion argue that mankind should use scientific knowledge and skills to ensure that only the fittest children be born and raised. Defining fitness, however, becomes a seemingly unending philosophical debate, prolonging resolution of these sociomoral dilemmas well into the future.

# Child Factors

**Unwanted Child.** The Judeo-Christian ethic prevails in Western culture and mandates that all children are sacred human beings. Influential groups place nearly irresistible pressure upon adolescents to have and to keep children, whether they want them or not. The technological advances in contraceptive devices and procedures have reduced the numbers of unwanted children and contributed to the phenomenon of zero population growth within the United States and in many other developed countries. Now more and more couples are saying that they intend to have only one or perhaps two children when they are ready. China has instituted negative sanctions against couples who have more than one child. Nevertheless, many unwanted children are conceived and carried to full term, born into circumstances where many mixed emotions flow (such as the joy of the parent's coming of age, the resentment towards having an unwanted child, the guilt about those feelings, and an unwillingness to relinquish the loved child), all coupled with the frustrated desire to be footloose and fancy free. Such conflicted feelings would certainly compromise the optimum parent-child attachment sought in more ideal relationships.

Gelles (1973) suggests that the unwanted–unplanned child is beaten not because of a projection or transference psychosis, but because the child is concretely seen as a source of unbearable responsibility, stress, and trouble. Oates and Hufton (1977) found that 92 per cent of the 24 failure-to-thrive children in their sample resulted from unplanned pregnancies. Seventy-five per cent of these children were the youngest in their families and were born within 18 (mean) months of the next sibling.

## Problem Child

**Colic.** Ounsted, Oppenheimer, and Lindsay (1974) report the frequency of colic, irritability, and crying among battered children. A child with colic can be exasperating to parents who are mature and competent but even more so to parents who have many other problems in their lives. If a colicky child cannot be soothed and cries all day and night, the parent often interprets this as rejection or failure as a parent because of his or her inability to quiet this persistently noisy and inconsolable human being, often referred to as a "little monster" as patience wanes. Such feelings of failure may only precipitate further resentment and prevent a satisfactory caring relationship from developing. Some children's cries have especially irritating sound qualities for adults, adding fuel to an already enraged disposition.

**Incontinence.** Children develop their ability to control bladder and bowel movements at varying ages and some have more difficulty and delay in achieving control than do others. If parents have a preconceived notion as to when children should stop wetting or dirtying their diapers and their child fails to comply, they may become quite frustrated and attempt to force the child to learn proper elimination habits before the child is ready. In some cases the child trains the parent, who jumps to all sorts of cues which the child emits, in order to rush the child to the toilet, often too late and amid such a flurry that the child is further flustered and unable to perform.

Other factors compound this, such as an insufficient income to supply plenty of disposable diapers or to keep the washing machine in good repair. It is not difficult to identify with the tired, unemployed adult's frustration and consequent anger when a child gets diarrhea in the middle of the night and, just as the last clean diaper is in place, proceeds to fill it again with foul-smelling, messy excrement, possibly due to inappropriate diet or sickness. A vicious downward cycle of interaction might ensue, with the enraged parent inflicting punishment upon the bottom or the genitalia, which only further complicates the episode. There are examples of hips being displaced by an angry parent's jerking the legs of the child apart when the child seems not to be cooperating in the diapering process. Persons visiting China and witnessing childrearing techniques there are quite impressed with the apparent absence of tension and crying and the ease with which toilet training is achieved, typically cued by a whistle; of course, societal pressures and sanctions in China encourage each family to have only one child, and there have been reports that many aborted fetuses are found by authorities, with a worrisome preponderance of females, since males are more highly regarded as the family's only allowed child.

**Illness—Mental or Physical.** If an infant or toddler is not feeling well and yet cannot talk and explain the nature of his or her discomfort, it can be quite difficult for the parent to interact effectively with the child. Chronic illnesses, which require additional care and supervision, in some cases only speed up the potential process of progressive disenchantment, which occurs when the parent–caregiver has the responsibility for continuous child care with no outside help or support system to make this task bearable. Sherrod, O'Connor, Vietze, and Altemeier (1984) found that having an ill child is another source of stress which may even trigger assault. On the other hand, there are occasional martyr-like parents who seem to thrive on illnesses in their children, perhaps because it gives them an increased sense of importance, and they may unconsciously contribute to the prolongation of the illness, a kind of iatrogenic exacerbation of the debilitating relationships and ecology. This sometimes results in infantalizing or smother loving of older children whose parents will not let them mature and become independent.

**Deformity.** Most parents have in their minds and may even express in their conversation a conceptualized ideal child who will grow up to become some idealized adult. The reality of caring for a helpless, demanding, dependent, self-centered infant is a difficult enough challenge, but when the children are deformed in visible ways that make them look different from the beautiful pictures on babyfood containers, the parents may become quite disappointed and distraught. Gil (1970b), Meier and Sloan (1983), and Ounsted and colleagues (1974) discuss the role of physical handicaps in the assaultive process. In a hospital survey of maltreated children, Birrell and Birrell (1968) found a direct relationship between physical deformities, prematurity, and child management problems. These factors therefore place the child at higher risk for one or more kinds of child assault. It is noteworthy that geneticists estimate that approximately one third of the offspring from an incestuous relationship will have one or more mental and physical abnormalities.

In such instances, it may be necessary for the parents to go through a process similar to the imagined death of the idealized child, who is never to be theirs. They must come to the realization that this real, physically deformed infant is theirs and must be substituted for the nonexistent ideal child. This may require going through several stages of reconciliation, including the denial that the handicapped child is theirs, the grief that in fact this is their child and, ultimately, the philosophical acceptance of such acts of God. They may have to deal with any guilt they may feel for somehow causing or contributing to these deformities and eventually develop a realistic adjustment and determination to now care for this new, nonideal individual, whom they can and usually do learn to love very much but not always very well.

**Developmental Disability.** There is at present a good deal of discussion and investigation into the relationship between various handicapping conditions and child assault. Various patterns of the dynamics among a vulnerable child, assaulting parents, and high risk environment are a challenge to unravel and understand both theoretically and practically (Solnit, 1984). In some cases it is difficult to ascertain whether a child's handicap contributed to his or her assault or the assault was the cause of the handicap, as suggested by Meier and Sloan (1983). In the more dramatic cases of fragile infants who, for example, are vigorously shaken and sustain subdural hematomas (Carter and McCormick, 1983), it is clear that the assault is the cause of the brain damage and handicapped condition of the child; however, in some instances, it is not clear whether the reason the child was vigorously shaken was due to some other provocative behavior or possibly some gross mismatch between child and parent (Chess and Thomas, 1980; Green et al., 1974). For example, some children are much more active than others; when a very active mother gives birth to a lethargic child, or a lethargic mother has a very active child, this mismatch in activity level or temperament alone (Johnson, Floyd, and Isleib, 1983) may lead to a child assault incident that may subsequently result in developmental delay or disability. Moreover, different patterns of child assault have different developmental consequences, as cogently presented by Egeland, Sroufe, and Erickson (1983).

There is a wide range of severity for damage inflicted on an infant. Some early insults may not manifest themselves until later stages of growth and development (Kempe and Helfer, 1973; Martin, 1976). For example, a child who does not seem to be developing language adequately may be shown on audiometric testing to have some loss in the ability to hear certain sounds in the spoken language and therefore not be able to imitate these sounds in his or her own speech. A significant number of the Village children who have endured physical assault are found to be afflicted with what are known as "soft" neurological signs, such as mild hearing loss (Billingslea, 1979), probably caused by slapping or other trauma to the head. Such head trauma may cause not only damage to the delicate ear organ itself but also possibly result in minimal cerebral dysfunction, which does not show up until later, more advanced stages of development and cognitive functioning are reached (Hanley, 1984).

In the Village population the distribution of tested mental functioning is skewed toward the lower end of the intelligence range, with significantly lower scores on verbal subtests than on performance subtests (see Chapters 5 and 8; Meier, 1984). This intelligence deficit may be due to damaged or deficient cortical tissue in the brain which enables more abstract thinking processes to occur or to underdeveloped brain capacity owing to a lack of experience in problem-solving and information learning opportunities (Diamond, 1984). Elmer (1967) presents an excellent discussion of the developmental characteristics of assaulted children, which suggests that the developmental delays are due to multiple physical, interactional, and ecological deficits.

Hyman and Parr (1978) report a developmental lag in assaulted children as measured by Bayley Tests; the mean motor and mental scale quotients were 89 and 94.6, respectively (compared with average of 100). They also suggest that these developmental deficits are presumed to arise from the inhibiting assaultive home environment. Additionally, Oates and Hufton (1977) found that one third of the assaulted children in their three year follow-up study were developmentally delayed. Parke and Collmer (1975) also identify cognitive damage in assaulted children, including mental retardation and developmental lags. Finally, Elmer and Gregg (1967) and Gaines and colleagues (1978) report a higher incidence of mental retardation among physically assaulted children. It should be noted, however, that Starr and Dietrich (1984) have marshaled and reported evidence that mild assault is no more prevalent

and aftermath of what may escalate into fierce fighting. Inconsistent and inequitable treatment of different children in the same family also contributes to some of the rivalry problems. Arguments and fights may be precipitated if a child perceives himself or herself as always coming out second in whatever transaction occurs among siblings, whether it be in terms of affection, clothes, food, toys, or whatever. The child may be desperately struggling for an equal share of attention (love) from the parents—and even negative attention is better than none at all. Of course not all sibling relationships are filled with rivalry and strife; moreover, siblings may be quite protective of one another when threatened by outside agents (this factor directly led to the CHILDHELP Brothers and Sisters Emergency Care Program, designed to keep siblings together when they are removed from their life-endangering homes and parents—see Chapter 8).

**Sexual Acting Out.** In spite of the alleged enlightenment of this culture regarding human sexuality, sex remains a generally delicate if not taboo topic. When young and innocent children demonstrate a natural curiosity about sexual matters, they often elicit all sorts of negative or anxious feelings from their adult caregivers, who themselves may have severe conflicts in this aspect of human behavior. Sexual activities are considered by some to be the result of evil forces or the devil. This may provoke adults to somehow try to drive out or exorcise these evil inclinations from a toddler or a young child, who does not even begin to comprehend the adult's interpretation of his or her behavior. Sexual behavior among children may elicit the guilt of parents, who are inappropriately interacting with their children in sexually provocative ways. Some multiply molested children begin to model adult sexual behavior, which appears to be precocious and seductive but in fact may be a counterphobic reaction on the part of the terrified child (de Young, 1984). It is a behavioral way for the child to tell on the adult, whose need to deny this might be expressed in vigorous corporal punishment, verbal belittling, or "loving secret incest," the most insidious of all (Justice and Justice, 1976).

**Dishonesty, Amorality.** Various transparently dishonest child behaviors can elicit from an adult a response designed to teach the child a lesson, often in such a painful manner as to far exceed the seriousness of lying, cheating, or stealing. Some diabolical adults even set the children up to commit an infraction and then descend on him or her with a vicious vengeance. Dishonesty frequently is learned, either as a means of avoiding punishment for forbidden behavior or in an effort to obtain something that does not rightly belong to the person. A child may attempt to compensate for an adult's not being satisfactorily gratifying in other realms by stealthily taking something as a token of love from that adult. It is also likely that, at earlier stages of development, a child is simply not yet able to distinguish ownership of material possessions, since in very young children's typical egocentric universes everything and everyone revolves around them and thus belongs to them as desired. Some considerable although still inconclusive research has been done on the moral development of children (Hoffman, 1970; Kohlberg, 1976; Lickona, 1976). New thrusts to study moral development (and its counterpart, demoralization, discussed previously) in assaulted children and assaultive adults are now being sponsored by CHILDHELP, U.S.A. in its National Collaborative University Network (Mayeda and Meier, 1983; Meier, 1982). At this writing it appears that assaulted children manifest a lower level of sociomoral reasoning and prosocial behavior than do their nonassaulted controls; assaultive parents and other adults likewise display reduced empathy, less parental awareness of morality, and relatively immature sociomoral reasoning (Jensen and Meier, 1983; see also Chapter 8).

**Swearing, Tantrums.** One of the most dramatic ways of getting an adult's attention is to use that adult's choice swear words with adult intensity and voice inflection. Sometimes this verbal behavior is accompanied by violent physical behavior such as "throwing a tantrum." Johnson and Morse (1968) noted that physically assaulted children are prone to severe tantrum behavior. Ironically, if this behavior elicits shocked or other obviously inept responses on the part of the adult, the child may in fact be encouraged or reinforced to become even better at it. Of course, when a child learns to swear and throw a tantrum in a public place, such as a supermarket, the response of the adult caregiver may be even more dramatic and thus satisfying to the child. The adult's inability to control the child's behavior often embarrasses the adult, forcing the adult to even more drastic kinds of corrective disciplinary tactics, such as clobbering the child, in an effort to give the child something real to cry about. The apparent escalation of severity in both the child's behavior and the adult's response is a phenomenon familiar to authorities dealing with child assault; however, the escalation phenomenon is not well studied or understood, thus warranting further research.

**Destruction of Possessions.** Very young children have a natural inquisitiveness about the world around them and frequently will attempt to take something apart or break it apart to see what is inside or what makes it operate. If this becomes a means of gaining additional attention from parents–caregivers, such destructive behavior may become more persistent within the home. If this is the most effective way for the child to gain adult attention, much like temper tantrums, the breaking of items throughout the home may become the child's means of communicating a desire for attention or showing anger at an item's owner. Frequently parents will point to those very items they wish to protect and instruct the child not to touch them, which simply cues the child in to those very things that will be most effective in getting a rise out of the parents. Moreover, the child may have observed the parents' becoming frustrated and hitting the source of their frustration, including the child, and may imitate this behavior with toys that frustrate him or her; similarly when the child is frustrated by adults, he or she may destroy those objects that are known to be highly valued by the adults (Schaefer, 1978).

**Unresponsive, Withdrawn Behavior.** Although very aggressive, acting out, and boisterous behavior can be quite obnoxious, the very passive and withdrawn child can be equally if not more exasperating to parents–caregivers who are attempting to elicit specific desired behaviors from the child. Such a lack of responsiveness to verbal interaction could conceivably be due to a hearing loss and this certainly should be ruled out first.

More frequently, however, withdrawn and unresponsive behavior is a way for the child to express deeply festering anger, fear, or depression by simply turning inward and refusing to communicate. This may be a form of passive aggression to express internal rage. Taken to its extreme, such apparent flatness of affect may be one of several symptoms found in childhood autism, in which case children so completely turn inward that they seem to be out of contact with the outside world and other people. This becomes very frustrating to any caregiving adult, who expects interaction with or at least some response from the child.

In a study of ten assaulted toddlers and ten matched controls, George and Main (1979) found that assaulted children were much less likely to approach caregivers in a daycare setting in response to friendly overtures and also exhibited approach-avoidance behavior in response to friendly peer and caregiver overtures. In another study designed to assess responsiveness, Hyman and Parr (1978) made controlled video observations of five to six year old assaulted children; assaulted children tended to avoid interaction of either a positive or negative kind with their mothers. On the other hand, observations of assaulted young children and primates show that they cling to the assaulting parent (Harlow, 1958) and indiscriminately approach and hang on to strangers in what Ainsworth and colleagues (1978) describe as "anxious attachment." This rapid and often inappropriate familiarity is frequently misinterpreted by some adults, who want to believe that they are some kind of magical Pied Pipers instead of the unwitting foils of anxious children seeking security and even coming to them with insincere expressions of affection in exchange for unwarranted favors or goods. Normal human development becomes distorted by child assault, which further alters the discontinuities described by Harmon, Morgan, and Glicken (1984) and is partially explained by the notion of social referencing advanced by Campos (1984).

**Uncommunicative or Other Provocative Behaviors.** Just as with unresponsive or withdrawn children, the uncommunicative child can be very provocative and frustrating to parents or caregivers, who would like to know what the child is thinking or feeling. Nonetheless, the child refuses to communicate even with body language, let alone with spoken language. This behavior represents a refusal to give anything, even a nod, back to a parent–caregiver, who may become increasingly desperate to interact. In Hyman and Parr's study (1978), assaulted children also had significantly lower levels of vocalization with their mothers compared with normally developing children.

Other provocative behaviors include a wide range of behaviors, which are too numerous to enumerate, let alone discuss. Many noteworthy ones are listed on such instruments as the Child Behavioral Profiles (Achenbach, 1978) under categories such as somatic complaints, schizoid behaviors, obsessive-compulsive behavior, depression, social withdrawal, hyperactive, delinquent, aggressive, and other behaviors, all of which are broken down into over 100 distinctly observable and quantifiable behaviors. These in turn are clustered under two large headings, internalizing and externalizing, according to whether a child acts out or turns inward as a characteristic response to stress, anxiety, frustration, or child assault.

**Stress.** Just as a series of weighted stressors (Holmes and Rahe, 1967) and numerous less stressful uplifts and hassles have been identified for adults (Kanner, Coyne, Schaefer, and Lazarus, 1981), there is a similar litany of events for children's lives that cause either chronic or transient stress. For example, besides experiencing a great deal of stress over common human crises like the death of a parent, sibling, or other loved one or experiencing a move to an unfamiliar location from a familiar one, where friends and associations were comfortable, children may also experience considerable stress over more child-specific traumatic episodes such as being held back a grade in school, failing an important test, not being chosen for a particular team, or being teased by fellow students or other children in the neighborhood. A child who is experiencing stress may not understand its source and become generally anxious, causing difficulty in concentration. A child may do poorly at certain demanding, cognitive tasks and may become even more active or "hyper" owing to an inabilility to focus on specific learning or problem-solving tasks. This is not to say that all stress is to be avoided; in fact, some stress, called *eustress* (Selye, 1956), is described as positive and may increase an individual's ability to cope with change and survive life's inevitable crises.

## Ecological Factors

Child assault ordinarily does not occur in an environmental vacuum. Various situational or contextual factors outside the adult or child influence their behavior and interaction. Some of the more salient ecological or environmental factors are presented and briefly discussed below.

## *Parental Interaction*

**Value–Cultural–Moral Conflicts.** Several cultural anthropologists have reviewed the kinds of traditions that may contribute to child assault. Korbin (1980) presents a cross-cultural perspective on child assault and gives examples of various tribal traditions that would be considered child assault by American cultural standards. Such practices as molding the shape of the head, lips, or feet by various appliances, or the sacrificing of one's prized firstborn son to the gods, seem inhumane to our "more enlightened" civilization. Accepted American practices such as circumcision, cosmetic orthodontia, and cosmetic plastic surgery, however, demonstrate the cultural relativity of such judgments.

Traditional convictions such as "spare the rod and spoil the child," a widely cited childrearing maxim paraphrased from the Bible (Proverbs 13:24), may guide childrearing practices and may encourage assault against children in order to beat the devil or the hell out of them (and goodness into them?). An alternative interpretation to the ambiguous word rod is that of a measure of land (16.5 feet) or a symbol of authority ("Thy rod and thy staff comfort me," Psalm 23, Verse 4), and would refer to the importance of giving children limits or standards and consistently enforcing them lest one spoil the children by not establishing meaningful expectations for their acceptable behavior. By the same token, parents of different cultural backgrounds may observe different standards of childrearing. Such differences may give rise to child assault for the child who is caught in the middle of conflicting value systems and becomes the battleground for their resolution.

In the United States, child assaulters generally have espoused values that include acceptance of the use of force on children by assaultive adult caregivers (Gil, 1970a). Justice and Justice (1976) described parents as having inappropriate values about the legitimacy of their needs gratification as compared to their child's; Radbill (1974) documented the multiple persuasions in the American society that justify violence; Gelles (1973) discussed the values and norms of violence in assaulting families; and Geis and Monohan (1976), Gil (1970b), Palmer (1972), and Pickney (1972) have all argued that the frequency and intensity of assault against children in Western society is partially due to a cultural approval and even encouragement of physically violent acts. Often, when parents differ in beliefs about the use of physical punishment, the more violent parent is the more assertive and wins the arguments.

**Marital Discord.** High on the list of family factors present in child assault cases is either a broken family (42 per cent) resulting in single parent situations (25 per cent) or pervasive marital discord (38 per cent) (American Humane Association, 1977). The interpersonal strife between warring parents can and often does reach levels of such intensity that intervening in domestic violence is considered to be the most hazardous duty of law enforcement agencies. A child who is conceived in an act of love and caring passion is often regarded as the embodiment of a caring relationship between a man and a woman. Conversely, when the relationship turns sour, that same love child may represent the embodiment of the deterioration and painful situation and may in fact become the personification of the dysfunctional relationship and become the target for the exasperation with each other. Parke and Collmer (1975) discuss in greater detail the major role marital discord seems to play in assault against children.

It is occasionally reported, and it is true of some cases at The Village, that a woman will live with a violent man and be somewhat relieved when his violence is directed at their children instead of at her. Moreover, she may have gotten into the relationship because she was accustomed to being the victim of such violence as a child and may have the unspoken conviction that this is in part what childhood is supposed to be like. This seems especially true in role reversal circumstances wherein the children assume an adult capacity for meeting one or both of the parents' childish needs and are expected to bear, instead of their parents, the brunt of the cruelties of the adult world (Justice and Duncan,

1976; Justice and Justice, 1976; Morris and Gould, 1967; Steele, 1970).

There are developmental studies (Martin, 1976) suggesting that a meaningful relationship exists between the stage of a given child's development and the concomitant stages of the adult's development when she or he was assaulted in the preceding generation. It may be far more difficult for a parent to cope with a child's going through the genital stage of development (from a Freudian psychoanalytical frame of reference) when the parent had difficulty mastering the same developmental tasks and may still have some hangups about them. The child's behavior may unconsciously, if not openly, remind the parent about these unresolved conflicts and revive much of the anxiety and stress the parent had experienced in the past. Adding to this complexity is the symbiotic nature of many marital relationships (Bergler, 1946) wherein one parent chose his or her spouse in an effort to fulfill vicariously certain developmental needs through the other so that the couple present several unfulfilled stages of development. Thus, one parent may be sparked to assault the offspring at one stage and the other parent may be irresistibly provoked to child assault at a later stage of the child's development.

## Single Parent

**Divorced or Separated.** With over one third of marriages in the United States now ending in divorce and many others being in stressful stages of progressive disenchantment toward dissolution, there are many single parents, usually mothers, who are attempting to meet the unrelenting needs of their offspring singlehandedly. In spite of the wishful thinking on the part of many single parents, the evidence is mounting that children raised in such circumstances generally do less well than children in intact families in terms of subsequent academic and personal lives (Jacobson and Margolin, 1979; Jellinek and Slovik, 1981; Kelly and Wallerstein, 1976). In some instances, the elimination of the interpersonal stress between father and mother through physical separation has salutary effects on the home atmosphere and may make life more tolerable for all involved, despite the concomitant disadvantages.

**Unwed Teenager.** Compounding the problems inherent in being a single parent are other factors, such as the financial, physiological, and emotional problems characteristic of most teenage parents. The fact that there is an epidemic of teenage mothers who are reluctant to interrupt their pregnancies, who choose to bring their pregnancies to term, and who then choose to rear their babies does not augur well for the future of many of these children (Furstenberg, 1976; Miller, 1983; Ooms, 1979). Society is faced with a difficult dilemma in these cases, since condemning them makes the plight of the mother and child even worse, whereas condoning unwed pregnancies by giving them special attention and services may be an encouragement to have more jeopardized children. An additional insidious incentive for some youngsters to produce babies is to sell them eventually to some questionable or illegal adoption agencies.

## Family Characteristics

**Large Family–Continuous Child Care.** Parents who have too many children, now popularly defined as more than two, may find the responsibility and constant demands on their time and energy to be simply too much for them to cope with satisfactorily. The physically and psychically draining nature of childrearing can eventually exhaust even the most committed parents, but it is especially a problem when there are unwanted or difficult children and there is no way to obtain even temporary physical or psychic distance from them (Bishop, 1971; Gelles, 1973; Light, 1973). Baldwin and Oliver (1975) report that 75 per cent of the 34 families of several assaulted children had four to nine children. The phenomenon of burnout in trained child care workers and others in the helping professions eloquently testifies to the potential hazards of childrearing, even for persons who are trained and who willingly entered such a field of endeavor (Freudenberger, 1974). Unless there are other supportive resources to refill an individual's physical and psychic reservoirs of coping energy, the person caring for one or more children may in fact run dry and be at his or her wit's end (threshold of violence) until some precipitating event provokes an episode of exasperated or revengeful child assault.

**Unemployment.** If both parents are unemployed and the family income can only meet the bare necessities, resources may not be adequate for getting even occasional relief from childrearing, including babysitters, vacations, and day care. Garbarino and Crouter (1977), Justice and Duncan (1976), Kempe and colleagues (1962), Oates and Hufton (1977), and Pelton (1978) clearly document the relationship between unemployment and child assault. Unemployment is particularly a problem for the unwed teenager who has no marketable skills and may even be too young to compete successfully for sufficiently gainful employment. Moreover, as the economy recedes, these inexperienced employees are ordinarily the first to be laid off or terminated and the last to be rehired, thus further adding to the depth of the economic disaster and loss of self-esteem.

**Social Isolation.** In earlier times, part of the system for helping parents cope with childrearing responsibilities was the extended family, which provided a bottomless resource of folk wisdom and experience-based advice, as well as a willing and supportive network when the parent(s) became desperate for assistance or respite. Because of the high mobility in the United States today, most extended families have been disintegrated and new parents typically find themselves quite isolated from their next of kin.

In many cases, this isolation from what used to be an extended family is a deliberate move away from in-laws, who may have been assaultive parents themselves. Elmer (1967) found that assaultive parents fail to use social support systems that are made readily available and are also high on anomie, distrust, and retreat from society. Similarly, Lenoski (1973) reports that 81 per cent of the assaultive families in his sample preferred to "resolve crises alone" and that 89 per cent of the assaultive families with telephones had unlisted numbers; in contrast, only 12 per cent of nonassaultive families had unlisted numbers. Young (1964) noted that 95 per cent of several assaultive families had no continuing relationships with others outside the nuclear family; 94 per cent of these families did not belong to or participate in any organized groups. On the other hand, Norton and Huttonlocher (1983) observed and recorded on videotape numerous families at high risk for assault who lived in urban ghetto settings in which a wide variety of children and adults drifted in and out of their living quarters before suspected assault was ever reported and verified.

**Threats to Parental Authority.** New parents, who are already feeling somewhat insecure about assuming a role for which they have had precious little formal or even informal preparation, may react to such a challenge by becoming quite authoritarian. They do not want to be confused by the facts when their minds are already made up about appropriate childrearing practices. This unyielding certainty, which may be a facade to mask a panic of uncertainty, often results in a very uptight approach to childrearing and an unwillingness to learn more about or make allowances for the wide variations in normal child growth and development. Instead, there is a relentless enforcement of their own narrow views and values upon the growing and developing child. Data from both the American Humane Association (1984) and CHILDHELP (Meier, 1980c; see also Chapter 8) reveal that many assaulting parents simply lack an understanding or cannot tolerate some of the behaviors of normally developing children, let alone accept the abnormal and often more disturbing behavior of developmentally disabled children.

Some of the unrelenting pressure on the child to conform to very restrictive and unrealistic expectations may arise in part from a need for the parents to bolster their own sense of self-worth; the child is at least one person whom they can manipulate and control. And, as pointed out earlier, if these childrearing beliefs and the means of instilling them differ radically between the two parents, additional stress and friction surrounds the child. Of course it is preferable when parents (and other caregivers) are consistent in disciplining their children by catching them when they were behaving well (instead of misbehaving) and rewarding that desirable behavior, a practice leading to optimum child growth and development (Gordon, 1970).

**Inadequate Income.** Frequently coupled with the many aforementioned ecological factors is the inability of the parent(s) to provide an adequate home environment for a growing and developing child. When it is understood that an approximately $125,000 (1985 estimate) will be needed to raise a child to the age of majority (18 years old), not including college, most parents must be prepared to make many sacrifices and have a fairly constant income in order to provide the basic necessities of food, clothing, shelter, and education for each of their children. Although it is quite difficult to prove conclusively that a given home's condition is sufficiently inadequate to constitute legal neglect and fall within the definition of assault against children, there is growing evidence that homes defined to be inadequate in accordance with widely accepted standards, which are presently being refined and promulgated, do contribute to child maldevelopment. Caldwell (1979) demonstrated that the level of stimulation found in a home was the single most predictive index to the child's subsequent overall performance in elementary school and on individual or group tests of intelligence. Garbarino and Crouter (1977) found that low economic status accounted for the largest portion of variance as a contributor to child assault.

**Discipline and Violence.** Whenever there is a power struggle between an adult and a child, the bigger and stronger adult typically wins. If childrearing is regarded as a process of breaking a child's will and rendering the child malleable, subservient, and dispirited (demoralized), this can be done through various violent intrusions on his or her physical body and psychic space. Too often the term discipline gets translated into corporal punishment and child assault, when in fact the term should reflect its common origins with the word disciple, which means a devoted student or learner who does not have to be taught to the tune of a hickory stick (Meier, 1982, 1983b). People in poverty live in an environment where violence is often the standard means for solving interpersonal problems. This attitude permeates the childrearing process as well (Gelles, 1973). Disborn, Doerr, and Caufield (1977) found that physical punishment by assaultive parents is the preferred disciplinary tactic. Furthermore, parents who assaulted their children opted for corporal punishment more frequently and used nonpunitive tactics less often than did nonassaulters. In another study, Reid, Taplin, and Loeber (1982) found that assaultive mothers displayed more verbal and physical aggression toward their children than did nonassaulting mothers and distressed nonassaulting groups. The tradition of domestic violence is not only self-perpetuating but self-escalating in severity, requiring heavier doses to get the same results, as the victims become increasingly tough, anesthetized, or resilient.

**Ignorance Regarding Human Development.** This section is clearly related to the previous discussion about parental authority. The folklore of childrearing passed down through the generations suggests that in addition to the maxim that grandmother knows best, "grandmother handed down a lot more than her china" (National Committee for Prevention of Child Abuse, 1981). The family tradition of beating or inflicting emotional stress or sexual assault upon helpless children is a transgenerational passing on of brutal rites, which ignore the human rights of children to pass happily and gently through normal stages of growth and development. However, it has been clearly demonstrated that the majority of persons who are parents for the first time have had neither experience nor formal or even informal training to acquaint them with the normal milestones of human growth and development. Often they engage in a kind of competitive game to see if they can train their children to cry less, smile more, be toilet trained earlier, and speak earlier and better than the neighbor's or relative's children. It is ironic that the society establishes multiple competencies and qualifications for a person to be licensed to drive an automobile, operate a restaurant, perform surgery, and so forth—all presumably to protect the lives of the citizenry—whereas there are no formal requirements for the bearing and rearing of children.

Tracey and Clark (1974) report that child assaulters lack knowledge of child development and proper child care. Similarly, McClelland (1973) proposes that assault perpetrated by otherwise "normal" individuals stems in part from lack of parenting skills and general knowledge about child development. Parke and Collmer (1975) also relate child assault to parental lack of knowledge and unrealistic expectations about children. Moreover, such unrealistic expectations may be applied to a child who has developmental delays in which cases the developmental discrepancies become even more visible and frustrating to the parents.

## Precipitating Situations or Events

Situations and events leading to child assault may take many forms and are typically not anticipated. The following are some common conditions implicated in child assault cases.

**Misbehavior of Child.** If a child accidentally or intentionally fails to behave as parents expect, possibly causing some embarrassment or frustration for the parent, the parent may strike out at the child in order to stop the misbehavior or aggravation. The misbehavior may be something as inconsequential as spilling a glass of milk or failing to pick up his or her clothes; or it may be as serious as destroying a prized family heirloom or setting fire to the draperies. If the parents are already operating under considerable stress and possibly disagreeing about how to manage misbehavior, it is a ripe situation for one or both of the parents to step in and "teach the child a lesson" through psychological, verbal, or physical assault of one kind or another.

**Argument.** In arguments between parents or between parent and child an attempt may be made to resolve the difference with some physical confrontation or verbal putdown with which the parties cannot deal effectively, and thus they resort to violence to show who is boss, regardless of right or wrong, since "might makes right."

**Scapegoating.** In many instances, when adults reach the limit of their tolerance for stress from all sources and a child happens to misbehave in their presence, that child may be the "last straw" and become the scapegoat to suffer for all of the accumulated pain and anger the parent is feeling about innumerable other hassles and stressful life situations.

**Child Crying.** One of the most frequently mentioned precipitating events is a child's crying for a prolonged period of time for reasons not understood by the adult. A child who is inconsolable can make a parent feel quite helpless and exasperated. It may cause the adult to resort to the statement, "I'll give you something to cry about," followed by visible physical damage to replace whatever invisible reasons the child had been crying about earlier.

**Fatigue.** Persons who are not getting sufficient rest or sleep to renew their physical and psychological resources are particularly prone to "flying off the handle." Aircraft manufacturers and others are aware of the danger that metal, under constant stress, becomes fatigued before it breaks down totally. Unfortunately, we do not have equally refined testing devices for assessing the state of fatigue in the human being nor predicting the probability of a breakdown as a result of having been under constant stress for a prolonged period of time. The identification and weighting of stress factors mentioned earlier is a step in the desired direction. With appropriate refinement, such criteria will become increasingly useful and sensitive for assessing human mental fatigue and predicting physical or psychological breakdowns or burnout due to accumulating wear and tear, even taking into consideration that people have varying levels of coping ability and stress tolerance.

**Frustration.** A sense of frustration is experienced when an individual is confronted with a perplexing situation and when every effort to resolve a given problem seems to fail. For example, attempting to obtain employment and being told that there is nothing available for inexperienced persons, for those who have no opportunity for gaining experience, can be most exasperating. Such frustration typically engenders anger at the perceived source of the frustration. If the anger is turned inward, the person may feel worthless and have a low sense of self-worth; if turned outward, some other target may be identified, such as one's child(ren), who may be perceived as having prevented the individual from obtaining the necessary experience and training when it was available. A mild form of misbehavior by a child in such an explosive situation can release a disproportionate reaction, which may astound everyone involved, including the perpetrator who later protests, "I don't know why I got so carried away and violent."

## CHILD ASSAULT–NEGLECT EPISODE(S) AND PREVALENCE DATA

Any one or combination of previously cited or similar situations and events may lead to an episode of child assault. The legal and other technical identification criteria for reportable child assault are dealt with in other CHILDHELP publications and have been carefully dissected by several authorities (Besharov, 1981; Giovannoni and Becerra, 1979). The official definition promulgated by the National Center for Child Abuse and Neglect is mentioned at the outset of this chapter (U.S. Department of H.E.W., 1975). Local resources, such as the offices of state Attorney Generals, often offer definitions and interpretations compatible with that state's other laws. The California Attorney General's Office produced an exemplary publication that contains the following brief definition of child assault, which is described in detail on the next 15 pages of the publication:

To many, assault against children is narrowly defined as having only physical implications. In reality, child assault is any act of omission or commission that endangers or impairs a child's physical or emotional health and development. This includes:

- Physical assault and corporal punishment
- Emotional assault or deprivation
- Physical neglect or inadequate supervision
- Sexual assault and exploitation

The infliction of injury and the resulting damage, rather than the degree, is the determinant for intervention. A parent or caregiver may begin inflicting minor injuries and go on to cause more serious harm over a period of time. Therefore, detecting initially inflicted small injuries and intervening with preventive action may save a child from future permanent injury or death. Of course, inflicted physical injuries, physical neglect, and malnutrition are more readily detectable than the subtle, intangible injuries that result from emotional maltreatment or deprivation (Van de Kamp, 1983).

To give the reader some appreciation of the actual numbers of cases of prevalence of child assault reported internationally, in the United States, within local counties, and within The Village of CHILDHELP, the following summaries are included.

**International.** More children under five years of age are reported to die each year as a result of deliberately inflicted injury in developed countries than in underdeveloped countries. In developed countries reporting the number of childhood deaths that result from homicide or an injury inflicted by another person, the United States is second only to Northern Ireland in number of children per thousand who are deliberately killed (Christoffel and Liu, 1983). Of the 52 countries reporting the number of intentional childhood killings, the United States ranks ninth behind El Salvador, Nicaragua, Mexico, Thailand, Puerto Rico, Columbia, Paraguay, and Northern Ireland. With regard to the intentional killing of children under the age of five years, the United States ranks seventh behind Hungary, Cuba, Japan, Austria, Uruguay, and Czechoslovakia. These rankings are not to be taken very seriously since so many nations failed to report such data at all and others openly admit that they really do not know how accurate their reports are. On official (U.S. State Department sponsored) visits to Russia and China, for example, this writer and colleagues inquired about the incidence and prevalence of child assault and were told that it was not permitted.

**National–United States.** During the past decade the number of reports of child assault in the United States has been steadily increasing each year, both in absolute numbers of verified cases and in relative severity (the data are from the 1980 National Census, which is conducted every ten years). Child assault is reported most often by nonprofessionals, who include friends, neighbors, victims, responsible caregivers, perpetrators (self-report), other family members, and so forth. Of professionals, social service personnel do the most reporting of suspected child assault, followed by school, law enforcement, and medical personnel, in that order. Neglect is the most common form of child assault reported nationwide. Over three quarters of a million reports of child assault were documented in the nation during 1980. This includes only verified child cases of child assault, not simply suspected cases. Table 1-1 (from Besharov, 1981) lists differences in child assault prevalence data, which reflect the wide variations in definitions and reporting of child assault.

According to extrapolations from repeated surveys (American Humane Association, 1983) and one large incidence study underwritten by the National Center on Child Abuse and Neglect (Burgdorf, 1980), over one million children are victims of active or passive assault each year in the United States. Over 500,000 children in the United States are known to have been deprived of the basic necessities in 1980, and at least another 50,000 were sexually assaulted—and this estimate is considered by Finkelhor and Hotaling (1984) to represent only the proverbial tip of the iceberg; well over 200,000 children are physically assaulted and probably over 2,000 children die each year as a result of assault by their adult caregivers. Gelles (1984) and Straus, Gelles, and Steinmetz (1980) would argue for considerably higher figures based on their extensive research on domestic violence.

Although in a little over half of the homes in which child assault is detected, there is only one male or one female caregiver, nearly 40 per cent of the nation's homes are occupied and managed by female adults alone. Children are almost always (76 per cent of cases) assaulted by their own parents.

Nearly 75 per cent of assaultive families characteristically have family interactional problems, such as spousal assault, family violence, inability to cope with parenting, marital problems, new babies, and associated stressful situations. Approximately one half of all assaultive families are plagued by economic problems (including unemployment—see earlier discussion), and about 40 per cent experience health problems. About 17 per cent of families that have assaulted children are characterized by alcohol dependence.

**Table 1-1. Selected Incidence Studies**

| Investigator | Definition of Countable Situation* | Finding |
|---|---|---|
| *Abuse:* | | |
| Gil (1970a) | Abuse that resulted in some degree of injury | 2.4–4.1 million |
| Helfer and Kempe (1976) | Officially reported abuse | 60 thousand |
| Light (1973) | Reanalysis of Gil's data | 200–500 thousand |
| Nagi (1977) | Officially reported abuse | 167 thousand |
| Nagi (1977) | Unreported abuse | 91 thousand |
| Gelles (1977) | Parent-to-child violence | 1.4–1.9 million |
| American Humane Association (1978) | Abuse officially reported to social services agencies | 111 thousand |
| *Neglect:* | | |
| Light (1973) | Neglect and other forms of maltreatment, excluding abuse | 465 thousand |
| Nagi (1977) | Officially reported neglect | 432 thousand |
| Nagi (1977) | Unreported neglect | 234 thousand |
| American Humane Association (1978) | Neglect officially reported to social services agencies | 202 thousand |

*Refer to Besharov (1981) for the definition used.

Perpetrators of child assault are most often between the ages of 20 and 35 years, with the number of cases decreasing with the age of perpetrator. Nearly one third of assaulted children are under the age of four years, and nearly 50 per cent are under the age of seven. A gradual shift toward older child and adolescent victims has occurred as sexual assault detection and reporting increases. Sexual assault occurs more often with male perpetrators and female victims, whereas female perpetrators more frequently are cited for deprivation of necessities. Sexual assault is much more commonly reported with female than male children, regardless of age; however, Finkelhor's retrospective survey of college students revealed that 28 per cent of the girls and 23 per cent of the boys surveyed had had inappropriate sexual experiences with relatives or family friends (1979a). Chapter 8 also contains comparative statistics between national and Village populations.

**California.** Much of the statistical data of California parallel that of the United States as a whole–that is, percentage of neglect versus physical versus sexual assault cases, the persons who tend to report such cases, family stresses, and the dynamics depicted and discussed in the model presented earlier (Fig. 1–1). However, there were by far more cases of child assault reported in California in 1980 (U.S. Census) than in any other state; in fact, California alone accounted for 12 per cent of all reported cases in the United States (this means that more than 200 California children die annually as a result of child assault). In California in 1980 over 50,000 children were reported to be neglected, over 20,000 reportedly were assaulted physically, and another 6,500 reportedly were assaulted sexually (Van de Kamp, 1983). With the exception of California, the West Coast states report many fewer cases of child assault per capita than do the East Coast states.

The number of referrals accepted (i.e., considered worthy of follow-up) in the state of California is greater than the total number of reports (accepted or not) in any other single state. The State of California received 97,329 reports of maltreatment in 1980; Florida received the second highest number, with 67,627; New York was third, with 55,937; and Texas received 45,030. If only the number of reports that were accepted and verified by investigation were considered, California claimed 69,624, which is still higher than any other state's total number of reports. At an approximately 30 per cent rate of attrition, the number of reports accepted would be reduced as in the following table:

| State | Total Number of Reports | Reports Accepted |
|-------|------------------------|------------------|
| California | 97,329 (0.004)* | 69,624 (0.003)* |
| Florida | 67,627 (0.006)* | 47,399 (0.005)* |
| New York | 55,937 (0.003)* | 39,156 (0.002)* |
| Texas | 45,030 (0.003)* | 31,521 (0.002)* |

* Percentage of total population

**Counties.** Los Angeles County alone reported nearly one third of the child assault cases in California in 1980. Second in number of cases reported was San Diego County, with not quite one tenth of the cases. Over 18,000 children reportedly were neglected in Los Angeles County in 1980 and another 6,000 were reported to be assaulted physically. Nearly two thirds of the reportedly assaultive families in Los Angeles County receive public assistance.

Of 3,693 cases of child assault referrals accepted in Riverside County in 1980, 1,688 were labeled neglected, 952 physically assaulted, 272 sexually assaulted, 383 intentionally deprived, and 398 for other reasons. In Riverside County, which is the third largest geographic county in the United States and the host county for the Village of CHILDHELP, referrals for child protective services have risen from 1,973 cases in 1976 to 4,244 cases in 1982.

In nearly all reported cases in California, the most common reasons for closing a case was that the family had "stabilized." In Los Angeles County almost half of the cases closed were for this reason and in Riverside and San Diego Counties this was true for more than half of the cases closed. Further complicating and confounding the aforementioned observations is the reported practice by responsible agencies to use what has been called an "inverted triage" procedure, whereby only the most severe cases, which have the most guarded prognoses, are investigated. When there is no evidence of severe and life-endangering high-risk circumstances, cases are placed on the "back burner" only to be tragically reintroduced when the high-risk situation has escalated to proportions requiring resolute intervention. This reverse triage process seems to be an unfortunate outgrowth of increasing caseloads, in number and severity, with a reduced number of child protective services personnel to address them.

**The Village of CHILDHELP.** Severe assault is the most common characteristic of The Village cases. As is true in the nation as a whole, mothers are the most frequent perpetrators. At The Village, they tended to range in age from 25 to 29 years but they were typically much younger when the first assault occurred, since their children often have been in the foster care system for several years before coming to The Village (see Chapter 8).

Of the children who have left the Village, nearly two thirds have returned to one of the parents who placed them. This is only one measure of the efficacy of the Village reunification program. It is also an indication of how many quite adequate parents may be helped to learn how to care for their children appropriately. Other factual information regarding The Village of CHILDHELP clients is presented in graphic form in updates of the Research Division's periodical progress reports (see Meier, 1981, 1984a; see also Chapter 8).

## *Identification and Reporting*

Identification and reporting of suspected child assault is necessary to bring cases to the attention of various authorities who can intervene on behalf of the child and the dysfunctional family. This is important, not only for secondary prevention of any further instances or episodes of child assault in a given child's life, but also as a means by which primary prevention of child assault might be effected. Since there are many sociological ramifications to proper identification and reporting, subsequent chapters each address these issues from different perspectives (see especially Chapters 2 and 4). Some very general characteristics exhibited by young assaulted children and their parents or adult caregivers are included in a Self Instructional Text for Head Start Personnel (U.S. Department H.E.W., 1975), which is one of the rare products of two government agencies, the Head Start Bureau and the Children's Bureau. (The writer was then director of these two bureaus simultaneously, and it was possible to effect such a happy marriage at that time.) Although no two assaulted children or assaultive adults are identical and no single all encompassing profile exists, there are some commonalities suggested by the preceding model.

Assaulted or neglected children are likely to share at least several of the following sometimes contradictory characteristics:

- They appear to be different from other children in physical or emotional makeup, or their parents inappropriately describe them as being "different" or "bad."
- They seem unduly afraid of their parents.
- They may often bear welts, bruises, sores, or other skin injuries.

• Their injuries seem to be inadequately treated.
• They show evidence of overall poor care.
• They are given inappropriate food, drink, or medication.
• They exhibit behavioral extremes: for example, crying often or crying very little and showing no real expectation of being comforted; being excessively fearful, or seeming to be fearless of adult authority; being unusually aggressive or destructive, or extremely passive or withdrawn.
• Some children are wary of physical contact, especially when it is initiated by an adult; they become apprehensive when an adult approaches another child; particularly one who is crying. Others are inappropriately hungry for affection, yet may have difficulty in relating to children and adults. Based on their past experiences, these children cannot risk getting too close to others.
• They may exhibit a sudden change in behavior: for example, displaying regressive behavior—pants-wetting, thumb sucking, frequent whining; becoming disruptive or being uncommonly shy and passive.
• They may take over the role of the parent, being protective or otherwise attempting to take care of the parent's needs.
•They have learning problems that cannot be satisfactorily diagnosed. If a child's academic, IQ, and medical tests indicate no abnormalities and still the child cannot meet normal expectations, the answer may well be problems in the home—one of which might be assault. Particular attention should be given to the child whose attention wanders and who easily becomes self-absorbed.
•They are habitually truant or late for school. Frequent or prolonged absences sometimes result when a parent keeps an injured child home until the evidence of assault disappears. In other cases, truancy indicates lack of parental concern or inability to regulate the child's schedule.
• They frequently arrive at school too early and remain after classes rather than going home.
• They are always tired and often sleep in class.
• They are inappropriately dressed for the weather. Children who never have coats or shoes in cold weather are receiving subliminal care. On the other hand, those who regularly wear long sleeves or high necklines on a hot day may be dressed to hide burns, bruises, or other marks of assault.

The following are some possible characteristics of assaultive parents or caregivers:
• They are isolated from usual supports, such as families, friends,

relatives, neighbors, and community groups. Moreover, they consistently fail to keep appointments, discourage social contact, and never participate in school activities or events.
- They seem to trust no one.
- They themselves were assaulted as children.
- They are reluctant to give information about the child's injuries or condition. When questioned, they are unable to explain, or they offer far-fetched or contradictory explanations.
- They respond inappropriately to the seriousness of the child's condition, either by overreacting, seeming hostile or antagonistic when questioned even casually, or by underreacting, showing little concern or awareness and seeming more preoccupied with their own problems than those of the child.
- They refuse to consent to diagnostic studies.
- They fail or delay to take the child for medical care. They may choose a different hospital or doctor each time.
- They are overcritical of the child and seldom if ever discuss the child in positive terms.
- They have unrealistic expectations of the child, expecting or demanding behavior that is beyond the child's years or ability.
- They believe in the necessity of harsh punishment for children.
- They seldom touch or look at the child; they ignore the child's crying or react with impatience.
- They keep the child confined—perhaps in a crib or playpen or in a bedroom or closet—for overlong periods of time.
- They seem to lack understanding of children's physical, emotional, and psychological needs.
- They appear to be misusing alcohol or drugs.
- They often cannot be located.
- They appear to lack control, or to fear losing control.
- They are of borderline intelligence, psychotic, or psychopathic. While such diagnoses are the responsibilities of a psychiatrist, psychologist, or psychiatric social worker, even the lay observer can note whether the parent seems intellectually capable of childrearing, exhibits generally irrational behavior, or seems excessively cruel and sadistic.

## Prognosis and Treatment

**Secondary and Tertiary Intervention and Prevention.** If a report of suspected child assault is judged to be a legitimate case, a differential diagnosis is necessary not only to arrive at a complete description of the nature and extent of the assault, but also to identify all of the preceding and attendant factors or events that contributed to the particular instance of assault. Following an understanding of the dynamics underlying the child assault should be an individualized treatment plan that would address the remediation of the pathological aspects of the perpetrator's assaultive behavior, the child's own functioning, and the ecological factors which contributed to the child assault episode. This is necessary to reduce or eliminate the possibility of future episodes.

If it is necessary for children to be removed from the custody of their parents–caregivers, necessary precautions must be taken to prevent undue additional assault from being inflicted by out-of-home caregivers and the foster care system itself. Strategies for secondary or tertiary prevention are presented and discussed in subsequent chapters of this book.

**Primary Prevention.** The foregoing model and discussion have presented a framework for understanding the complicated dynamics and interactions found in most child assault cases. It is hoped that the insights generated from analyzing the multifactorial dynamics of child assault will ultimately lead to the prevention of such trauma in the lives of all children. This model serves as a framework for defining the dimensions, reviewing some of the relevant literature, and appreciating the salient and complex considerations regarding assault against children. In subsequent chapters the next steps in identification, evaluation, intervention, and prevention are addressed.

*Chapter 2*

# Causes, Consequences, Treatment, and Prevention of Sexual Assault Against Children

## *Roland Summit*

Sexual abuse is the last frontier in the growing awareness of child abuse (Sgroi, 1975). Common knowledge, clinical traditions, and much of the current practice in dealing with child victims of sexual abuse are based on a persistent mythology that serves to minimize effective  intervention and potential recovery. The myths are perpetuated by what Butler (1979) has called a conspiracy of silence that insulates adult society against confronting the terrifying discovery that large numbers of children are molested, assaulted, incestuously exploited, and raped by their entrusted caregivers.

No one can welcome such a discovery. The most caring adult and the most dedicated clinician will cling to the mythical hope that incest is rare, that "good" families are immune, and that "normal" adults would not sexually exploit or assault children. It is easier to accept that children imagine or exaggerate accounts of sexual assault, or that the intrinsic sexuality of children makes them irresistibly seductive.

Most behavioral scientists have been trained to recognize oedipal conflicts and wish-fulfilling behaviors in children. These dynamics are accepted as normal and universal. Adult pedophilic behavior, on the other hand, tends to be defined as stereotypic and confined to specifically  disturbed perpetrators, with an implicit expectation that such character pathology would be self-revealing and readily diagnosed. When an apparently normal child shows implications of sexual involvement with an apparently normal adult, the logical conclusions are almost inescapable. Either nothing has happened (the child imagined it), or

...rmal adult has been victimized by a seductive child.

...nese conclusions are reinforced by the child's showing symptomatic behavior and by the convincing denials of the adult involved. It is not unusual for parents to retaliate against their child in defense of a trusted relative or friend. It is also common for adult offenders to rely on character witnesses, psychiatric examination, and psychological testing to prove their normalcy, whereas a clinical evaluation of the distressed child giving equivocal results is used to impeach the testimony of the child. Finally, and most unfortunately, it is all too common for the child to equivocate, to deny, or to take the blame for the sexual encounters out of fear of adult retaliation and in the scathing self-judgment and self-punishment typical of the assaulted child.

Behavioral scientists are given an awesome responsibility and exalted expectation of knowledge and competence in an area in which they have very little specific training or experience. Recognition, belief, support, and protective advocacy for the sexually abused child depend on an awareness of new, still controversial data and a willingness to question a number of cherished, very comforting levels of denial. The basic task is defined by Sgroi (1975), an internist who is one of the pioneering physicians in the field of child abuse:

> Recognition of sexual molestation of a child is entirely dependent on the individual's inherent willingness to entertain the possibility that the condition may exist. Unfortunately, willingness to consider the diagnosis of suspected child sexual molestation frequently seems to vary in inverse proportion to the individual's level of training. That is, the more advanced the training of some, the less willing they are to suspect molestation. (p. 20)

The helping professional who is prepared to believe in the realities of child sexual assault takes on the task of dealing with resistance at a personal, intrapsychic level as well as at the intraprofessional and interprofessional levels. Sgroi speaks from long and painful experience:

> Those who try to assist sexually abused children must be prepared to battle against incredulity, hostility, innuendo, and outright harassment. Worst of all, the advocate for the sexually abused child runs the risk of being smothered by indifference and a conspiracy of silence. The pressure from one's peer group as well as the community, to ignore, minimize, or cover up the situation may be extreme.
>
> (1978, p. xv)

The behavioral scientist has the opportunity for uniquely definitive intervention on behalf of mental health. Sexual assault has been called a "psychological time bomb" (Peters, 1973), which can be totally destructive to later adjustment even when the child has shown no immediate signs of emotional trauma. It is this author's belief that self-hate, self-destruction, antisocial behaviors, substance abuse, running away, prostitution, somatic complaints, sexual dysfunctions, hysterical seizures, dissociative disorders (including multiple personality states and homicidal frenzies), affective disorders, and schizophrenia all may be associated with sexual assault.

Although it is obvious that sexual assault itself is not the sole cause of every kind of identity crisis or emotional disorder, and that not all victims of sexual assault are equally disabled, recent clinical experience inspires some radical claims. There is no question that specific therapeutic resolution of incest trauma can provide dramatic remissions of major mental illness and behavior disorders in appropriately selected cases. The possibility of a single-trauma cause in these patients raises promise for primary prevention of mental illness if sexual assault crises can be resolved during childhood.

As in other forms of child assault, there is a generational bonus of prevention if a victim can be identified and reparented. In a substantial proportion of cases, today's victim is tomorrow's offender. Boy victims tend to grow up to molest other boys. Girls can become part of an "incest carrier syndrome" (Berry, 1977), unable to protect their daughters from the incest-prone men they seem compelled to select. Uncounted numbers of children in future generations can be spared the geometric chain reaction of assault for each link that can be broken through effective intervention and care.

Child sexual assault as seen by the physician or psychiatrist is a confusing and threatening enigma that invites denial, avoidance, and rejection. For the clinician with the foresight and courage to confront the problems of sexual assault and to become a part of the solution, the therapeutic and preventative rewards can be profound.

## SCOPE OF SEXUAL ASSAULT

Sexual assault is anything but exotic or rare. It is an everyday sort of experience for hundreds of thousands of children in every economic and cultural subgroup in the United States. Although other forms of child assault are nearly limited to immediate caregivers, sexual assault may be initiated by parents, live-in partners, extended family members, friends, community caregivers, even strangers.

Retrospective surveys indicate that at least 20 to 30 per cent of girls experience some sort of sexual victimization before age 13 (Finkelhor, 1979a; Gagnon, 1965; Landis, 1956). These and other studies (Benward and Densen-Gerber, 1975; Burgess, Groth, Holmstrom, and Sgroi, 1978; DeFrancis, 1969; Peters, 1976; Queens Bench Foundation, 1976; Weiss et al., 1955) are consistent in a startling observation: only 25 per cent of the offenders are strangers. A girl who has been taught to beware of strangers is totally unprepared for the three-to-one chance she will be approached by someone she has been taught to trust and obey. Forty-four per cent of all victim experiences were with family members, including 22 per cent within the child's household. Six per cent of all victimizing relationships were with fathers or step-fathers (Finkelhor, 1979a). The figures in Finkelhor's survey of college students are predictably conservative. Projecting that sample to the general population suggests that at least 9 per cent of all women are sexually victimized by an older relative, with some 2 per cent involved in sex with their fathers or stepfathers.

Numbers for males are more elusive. Boys are known to be even more reluctant that girls to admit to sexual victimization. In Finkelhor's survey (1979a) half as many males as females reported childhood sexual victimization. Only 25 per cent of the boys told anyone during the time victimization occurred, compared to 38 per cent of the girls in the same sample. There is good reason to believe that adults engage in sexual practices with boys even more frequently than with girls, since they are the preferred target of habitual pedophiles (Groth, 1978). No survey is any more dependable than the ability of the victims to define and to confide their experiences. After a concerted effort to educate Detroit school children to report sexual molestation, the ratio of boys to girls reporting rose from a base line of 1:6 to 1:1 (Groth, 1978).

Any community or clinical response system that acts to end the secrecy and denial surrounding sexual assault will be confronted with an explosive increase in the apparent incidence. Santa Clara County in California, which initiated the model Child Sexual Abuse Treatment Project, has experienced a 3,000 per cent increase in the reporting of sexual assault over the past 7 years (Giaretto, 1976).

Peeling away layers of secrecy uncovers not only unexpected numbers but also increasingly disturbing realities of the victimization process. We can no longer reassure ourselves that victims are consenting or seductive partners who share responsibility with adults. Latency age children, not nubile adolescents, are the most frequent victims. The average girl victim is eight years old at the time of initiation, and many are only two or three years old. In one nonclinical sample of 183 women who had experienced incest, 180 were under eight years old when the sexual activity began (Armstrong, 1978). The so-called seductive years are almost immune: girls over 13 rarely allow incestuous relationships. Boys are at most risk in the three or four years immediately preceding puberty, roughly nine to thirteen. These are naive children who are intimidated by the intrinsic power of an adult. The adult offers acceptance, affection, and security on the one hand and threatens rejection, punishment, and chaos on the other. Although overt violence and physical injury are the exceptions, intimidation, coercion, and threats are basic to the sexual assault against children by adults.

Nor are the sexual experiences themselves the stuff of romantic or seductive dreams. The words "fondle" or "caress" are often used to describe moves that actually are better characterized as grab, rub, probe, lick, and suck. Whenever children are given permission to break the silence and offer explicit descriptions, they talk of being used as accessories to sexual demands of adults with almost no hint of gentleness, playfulness, titillation, reciprocity, affection, or even explanations or reassurances (Burgess and Holmstrom, 1975). The eight year old girl who describes being awakened in the night to take her father's penis in her mouth, gagging on the semen and being forced to swallow it is hardly conjuring up an oedipal fantasy.

Since the girl is sexually underdeveloped and since the man generally tries to avoid physical injury of the child, vaginal intercourse is usually not the immediate goal. Manual, oral and anal containment of the penis are the "normal" activities of incestuous intercourse, as they are also for the more typically out-of-family sexual assault of boys.

Although both girls and boys may be the targets of sexual assault, the adult is almost invariably male. Whereas women are at least equally capable of other forms of child assault, including physical battery, neglect and verbal and emotional abuse, they seem better able than men to respect the sexual autonomy of children in their care. This should not be too surprising, since it merely reinforces a truism in sexual perversity: compulsive voyeurs, exhibitionists, fetishists, pedophiles, rapists, sex murderers, and other mentally disordered sex offenders are nearly always males. Occasional exceptions occur, of course, and these atypical women become celebrated and immortalized in popular literature. They are the exotic exceptions that prove the rule. Sexually perverse males are not newsworthy. People seem to take it for granted that men will almost normally sexualize their need for power or subordinate others in their need for sex, no matter how eccentric or odious that need might be. Stoller (1974), one of the premier psychoanalysts in the field of gender identity and sexual behavior, believes that perverse mechanisms are almost inevitable in the development of male sexuality.

## DEFINITIONS

Sexual assault is not necessarily incest, nor is incest necessarily assaultive. Incest is a legal term defining sexual intercourse between two persons so closely related that they are forbidden by law to marry. In that narrow sense, coitus between first cousins at age 20 is incest, whereas oral copulation of a four-year-old girl by her father is not. Incest between siblings seems to be harmless in many cases, if the relationship is free from intimidation and if there is no punitive discovery by adults. As a clinical issue, then, the concern here is not with consanguinity as much as with age-power relationships and the betrayal of a trusted, caregiving role. In addition, the concern is less with technicalities of penetrations or genital touching than with the child's sense that he or she has been sexually violated.

Sexual assault in the context of the present discussion is defined as the involvement of a child in specifically sexual activities with an adult. Although it is generally believed that such involvement is likely to be harmful, it is not necessary to demonstrate immediate damage in the child or even to prove that all intergenerational sexual contact is ultimately harmful. It should be enough to understand unequivocally that sexualization of a childcaring relationship is, in itself, a violation of ethics. As Finkelhor argues so simply and yet so eloquently, a child is incapable of informed consent with a controlling adult (1979b). The child has no power to say no and has no information on which to base a decision. Since the long-term psychological effects are so uncertain, and since the adult has such a vested interest in minimizing those risks, no modern concept of ethics, liability, or consumer protection could ever endorse such a lopsided contract. The child is just as powerless within the intimidating or ingratiating relationship as the adult rape victim would be at the point of a knife.

## PATTERNS OF SEXUAL ABUSE

Motivation for sexual assault against children ranges from trivial impulses to ritualistic compulsions (Summit and Kryso, 1978). No single clinical paradigm can be defined. Most offenders are relatively indifferent to the needs and feelings of children, even though the adult may see himself as uniquely caring and devoted to his child love. Many of the categories in the clinical spectrum differ from one another largely in the degree of power, punishment, and perversity imposed on the child. These variations in parental motivation and behavior are discussed more thoroughly by Summit and Kryso (1978). The most important distinction for treatment planning and estimation of prognosis is the differential diagnosis between pedophilia and endogamous incest and whether the perpetrator is what Groth (1978) defines in a very practical and consistent dichotomy as either a fixated or a regressed offender.

## The Fixated Offender–Perpetrator

The fixated offender remains fixed at a preadolescent level of sexual choice. He fails to find comfort or confidence in sexual relationships with age mates beyond puberty. Immature partners provide a continuing attraction, which typically comes to resemble a compulsion or addiction.

Such a fixation can result from trauma, as in a preadolescent sexual assault, or from excessive stimulation, such as an affectionate childhood relationship with a pedophile. In other cases there is no discernible basis for the fixation. As with other types of sexual paraphilias, theories of causation remain diverse and controversial. Whatever the causes may be, it is important to recognize that pedophilia can exist as a disorder of sexual object choice, without associated disorders of thought, affect, or behavior.

In addition to the compelling erotic appeal, the fixated offender sees children as preferred objects of companionship and love. Most such men are kind and indulgent in the extreme with their partners, never resorting to physical force or injury. They may spend years developing an affectionate, trusted relationship with the child and the parents. Children and their adult caregivers are disarmed by the uncommon interest and empathy offered by these men, who may also gain occupational positions of unquestioned trust and authority with children. A fixated offender may function very effectively as a physician, police officer, minister, youth worker, teacher, coach, or "good neighbor Sam." Although offenders studied in prison populations tend to be ineffectual and poorly socialized, there are large numbers of lifetime pedophiles who are never reported, convicted, or even suspected by friends and neighbors. They may be married (preference for children does not rule out a capacity for genital performance with adults), highly respected, well employed, and completely reliable and ethical in all outward appearances.

The fixated offender has a lifetime to accommodate to his affiliation with children, and he may escape any feelings of guilt or remorse. He tends to develop an eccentric rationalization that children desire and need his love, and that he has a mission to rescue them from the distant, uncaring world of ordinary adults. His child partners often reinforce this view, since he seeks children who are starved for attention and affection (Martin, personal communication). Such needy children may accommodate with active curiosity and without complaint to the sexual games introduced by their special friend.

Although the rationalization of guiltlessness may be defined as sociopathic, it can also be seen as analogous to the eccentric mores that are vital for the survival of any persecuted minority group. For instance, otherwise ethical persons involved in political terrorism, assassination, execution, war, and euthanasia can view themselves as having permission to kill other people. The fixated offender presents an impossible dilemma to any rigid diagnostic scheme. Any clinician who insists that an offender against children must be sociopathic, psychotic, antisocial, or sadistic will simply refuse to recognize the well-adjusted, beguiling, professional molester of children. The "well-adjusted" pedophile can elude any clinical measure of psychopathology. Clinical interviews, mental status testing, standardized testing, projective testing, and even polygraph examination will give no hint of emotional discomfort or psychopathology.

The fixated offender, or habitual pedophile, tends to be fixed to the sexual object most characteristic of preadolescence: his male playmates. The vast majority of habitual pedophiles are attracted exclusively to boys. A small minority seek girls exclusively. Ambisexual pedophilia is relatively rare. This predominant attraction to boys should not be confused with homosexuality. When the so-called boy lover has any interest in an adult, the age mate will be a woman. None of the men in Groth's (1978) sample had had any adult homosexual experience.

Those fixated offenders who prefer young females have restricted opportunity for unchallenged association with girls. Since an unrelated male is less likely to be trusted as a coach or other group caregiver of girls, the typical mode of operation for the female-attracted pedophile is to seek out lonely, vulnerable mothers who are looking for a father-figure for their daughters. Finkelhor (1979b) found that girls who had stepfathers were five times more likely than average to be victimized sexually. In fact, fully 50 per cent of the stepdaughters in the sample acknowledged child victimization. The sexual contact was most often not with the stepfather himself but with more transient predators who capitalized on the vulnerability of the broken family. Like the well-adjusted boy lover, the habitual molester of girls tends to be highly gifted in inspiring trust and gratitude in beleaguered mothers. It is not uncommon for mothers to send their daughters on day-long and even overnight excursions with a prospective stepfather, as if to test and ensure their compatibility.

The fixated offender tends to have a rather narrowly circumscribed age preference range. He knows that his love affair with a given child is time-limited, and that his compelling sexual attraction will turn to indifference or even repulsion within a few years. The appearance in the child of secondary sexual characteristics is like the stroke of midnight for Cinderella. The experienced pedophile learns to replace the fading attractions of each relationship with a succession of younger initiates. An active pedophile may have contact with hundreds, even thousands, of children within his lifetime (Martin, personal communication).

## The Regressed Offender–Perpetrator

This category defines the typical incest offender. The individual has followed a normal progression of adjustments to agemate sexual partners. He was not aware of selective fantasy or sexual attraction related to children. Neither does he have any particular interest in or empathy with the world of children. When conflicts develop in habitual and preferred adult relationships or when he feels threatened and ineffectual in his adult adjustment, he is likely to seek endorsement and a sense of importance through the sexualization of a relationship with a more available, more subordinate, and less threatening partner. The man rather suddenly and unexpectedly may find his child irresistible for a variety of reasons: (1) the child is available in a preexisting, totally subordinate, intimate relationship; (2) the child is affectionate, trusting, and attentive—eager to gain more acceptance, endorsement, and affectionate expression from the father; (3) the child embodies many of the mannerisms and appearances typical of the mother at an earlier, more idealized stage of the marriage—a kind of reincarnation of the breathless, responsive, adoring partner in adolescent courtship relationships; (4) the child, as a part of the mother, is an attractive foil for punishment and revenge in the frustration of the marital relationship; and (5) the potential for sexuality in the child is seen by the father as a threat to innocence and the beginnings of degradation and rebellious alienation from parental control. This fear of eventual autonomy of the child and the dread of out-of-family seduction seem to prompt extreme possessiveness and a compulsion for extraordinary measures of control, including perverse examples of hands-on "sex education."

These factors, and many other more idiosyncratic variables, are most selective for the female child as a surrogate for and a target of regression from the previous adjustment with a female agemate. The regressed offender will be involved less often with boys, and least often with both girls and boys (Groth, 1978).

The initial regressive experience or attraction is often experienced as overwhelming and beyond the conscious wish or control of the offender. The attraction does not make sense to him, and his conscious defenses are dominated by denial, projection, and dissociation. He may also be depressed, desperate, and relatively uncaring. His need for assurance of his adequacy tells him that there is no crisis he cannot control, so he avoids confiding in anyone for help. He tends to believe that he is responding appropriately to the seduction and provocation of a willing partner.

Dissociative aspects are quite variable, allowing for a suspension of prevailing roles. The man in the process of regression acts as if he were young and powerful again, smitten with an exciting youthful partner. He sees the child as old enough and in need of sexual attention, no matter what her actual age or level of development. He may see a daughter as the direct embodiment of her mother or some other lost love-object. Alternatively, he may conceptualize his sexual coercion as not at all sexual but rather as necessary parental exercises in education or discipline. There is a fine line here between regression, dissociation, distortion, delusion, rationalization, and plain, old-fashioned self-justification. Whatever the relative mix of psychodynamic and psychopathological variables, the most regressed offenders do not test out clinically as psychotic, borderline, hysterical, sociopathic, or sexually deviant. In terms of measurable psychopathology, the regressed offender is technically normal.

After a sexual encounter the offender may be filled with guilt, remorse, fear, and anger, and he will tend to blame the child for his distress. Because of the inherent conflicts and the essentially ego-alien nature of the attraction, the regressed offender has little capacity to invite friendly, leisurely, potentially gratifying peer-level relationships with the child. He forces the children into adult styles of behavior and holds them to adult levels of accountability and responsibility. Control and submissiveness are inherent in the preexisting parent-child relationship, so he ensures silence more often by intimidation and threat than by ingratiation.

Once the taboo against incest and adult-child sexuality has been broken, and once the offender is plagued with a recurring cycle of need, arousal, gratification, and punishment, the behavior may become habitual and compulsive. Although the regressed offender is unlikely to premeditate and create new sexual relationships with unrelated children, any children within his sphere of authority may be at risk once the pattern is established. The regressed offender who serially involves his younger children and eventually his grandchildren will rarely attempt contacts outside the family.

Some regressed offender–perpetrators find their initiation outside of a parental controlling relationship, being attracted to a child who is a close family friend or a devoted student. Therefore, not every teacher, clergymen or coach who molests a child is a fixated or habitual offender. Conversely, not every predation within a family represents a regressive response to a crisis in adult adjustment. Seduction of a family member may be part of a long-term pedophilic compulsion. There is no blood barrier to pedophilic intrusion. Differential diagnosis depends on an accurate assessment of the lifetime adjustment patterns of the perpetrator.

The clinical assessment of anyone accused of sexual assault of a child must draw on every possible source of collateral data, including marital, employment and arrest records. The history presented by the offender–perpetrator has no bearing on any behavior that he may choose to conceal. Although this fact should be obvious, it is ignored again and again in clinical evaluations that rule out pedophilia and that declare that a man is normal because he says that he has never been attracted to children.

## PROGNOSIS FOR FIXATED VERSUS REGRESSED OFFENDERS–PERPETRATORS

Accurate assessment of the perpetrator is of more than academic interest. Prognosis for treatment and control of pedophilic behavior are diametrically opposed in the two groups. Despite the hopes of penologists and therapists, there is no responsible documentation that treatment can realign the sexual preference of the fixated pedophile or gain any protection for the children at risk. Since the well-adjusted pedophile typically finds an unrestricted supply of noncomplaining partners, there is no means short of 24 hour supervision to monitor the effectiveness of any outpatient treatment model.

Finally, the lifetime pattern of ego-syntonic adjustment, missionary enthusiasm, and pressure for survival give intense energy to an illicit pedophile subculture. The pedophile underworld has its own literature, communication network, economic vested interests (child pornography and prostitution), and elitist philosophies. The pedophile subculture serves not only to reinforce the safety and comfort of pedophiles but also to minimize public concern for the protection of children and for the need for more effective control and treatment of pedophilia. Naturally, the overt and covert political efforts of such organizations as the North American Man-Boy Love Association (NAMBLA) rally in support of the most ineffectual, least repressive control and treatment programs, and graduates of the treatment programs are profuse in their praise and gratitude for their "recovery." In summary, there is little theoretical hope for treatment and no objective measure of treatment outcome for the fixated offender.

In contrast, the regressed offender has an excellent prognosis and a vital need for the specialized treatment that can provide total recovery. Treatment results can be monitored through follow-up within the predictable scope of potential victims. Rehabilitation is facilitated by reinforcement of preexisting family resources and appropriate adult sexual relationships, especially since the typical regressed offender is so intensely motivated to recover those resources and relationships. Since a familial bond defines most of those relationships, the treatment program has access to all parties to the sexual disturbance, with the opportunity for parallel treatment, peer-group reinforcement, and resocialization of the individuals as well as the family units. Since there is little subcultural organization or support for incest, and since accommodation to child sexual objects has been more recent and more ego-dystonic for the offender–perpetrator, conventional ethics and societal mores can be drawn upon to reinforce child-protective and adult-developmental values within therapeutic groups. Even if there were only minimal growth and recovery in the perpetrator, child victims and their mothers can be so strengthened through treatment that they will no longer tolerate sexual exploitation and assault. Therapy for the regressed offender is theoretically justified and has also been empirically demonstrated to be efficacious. Most important, therapy can be objectively monitored and extended in preventive continuity to potential victims.

It should not be assumed that offenders of either type will present themselves willingly or openly for diagnosis, or that they will voluntarily seek treatment. The regressed offender will mobilize every available dodge and alibi to evade personal, professional, or public recognition of his problem. The potential for recovery can be realized only within the context of absolute prohibition of any sexual access to children, with enough coercive leverage to overpower any hope of hiding or of continuing regressive and exploitive–assaultive sexual relationships. The structures and techniques of this delicate balance of coercion and support will be further explored in the section on treatment.

## ROLE OF THE CHILD IN SEXUAL ASSAULT

The normal behavior of a child caught up in sexual assault creates alienation and prejudice in potential caregivers. These normal

adjustment patterns must be understood before the clini
effective advocate for assaulted children. Since a ful
accommodation is most characteristic of incest, a fs
paradigm will be described. (Descriptions relating to the ...
be included where relevant.) Many of the same reactions can be seen
in ongoing out-of-family molestations as well. The child sexual assault
accommodation syndrome includes five characteristics: secrecy,
helplessness, accommodation, delayed disclosure, and retraction.

## Secrecy about Sexual Assault

Children rarely tell anyone, especially when they are first assaulted
(Finkelhor, 1979a; Burgess and Holmstrom, 1975). The child typically
feels ashamed and guilty. She fears disapproval or punishment from
her mother (most of the girls in Finkelhor's sample [1979a] who told
their mothers found that their worst fears were justified), retaliation
or loss of love from the offender, and, most profoundly, loss of
acceptance and security in the home. These fears are often suggested
and reinforced by direct threats from the offender–perpetrator.

The emphasis on secrecy and the fearful isolation from the mother
define the sexual activity as something dangerous and bad, even if the
child is too young to understand the societal taboos involved. Even if
the child is carefully and affectionately seduced without fear or pain,
the conspiracy of silence stigmatizes the relationship.

## Helplessness in Sexual Assault

The child feels obligated and overpowered by the inherent authority
of the trusted adult, even in the absence of physical force or threats.
Helplessness is reinforced by the sense of isolation, secrecy, and guilt,
as well as by the child's inability to make sense out of her father's
behavior or to find any acceptable way to describe the bizarre
relationship to others.

Helplessness is often expressed by immobility. If a young girl is
molested during sleep she will typically "play possum." She will not
resist or cry out, even though her mother may be in the next room.
A sibling in the same bed may also feign sleep, afraid to become
involved.

The natural inability to cry out or to protect herself provides the core
of misunderstanding between the victim and the community of adults,

as well as the breeding place for the child's later self-reprisals. Almost no adult seems willing to believe that a legitimate victim would remain still. She is expected to react with kicks and screams. Attorneys and the offender–perpetrator easily humiliate and confuse the child victim or child witness and prejudice the jury with demands for a "normal" protest. Expert testimony on these points is crucial, both to vindicate the credibility of the child and to help prevent continuing self-condemnation.

With repeated intrusions the assaulted child may lie awake in fright long into the night. Yet, if approached, she will remain motionless in a pathetic attempt to protect herself, much as she has learned to hide beneath the covers from imaginary monsters. Violation of a person's most secure retreat overwhelms ordinary defenses and leads to disillusionment, severe insecurity, and a process of victimization. Well-adjusted adults report lingering terrors and loss of basic well-being after a rape or even a robbery within their bedrooms. Children, who have few defenses at best, are even more vulnerable than adults to the invasion of their beds.

Finally, it must be remembered that the normal child has no real power or voice apart from the enfranchisement given by her parents. These are not older children or adolescents with strong institutional or peer-group support. How can a third-grader feel anything but helpless in confronting a sexually insistent father or stepfather? And how can such a small child blame herself for inviting his attention or for her failure to forcibly abort his intentions? For a child of eight (or three, five or eleven, as the case may be), self-blame is intrinsic to the accommodation process, unless her mother or some alternate caregiver can give her the power to stop the sexual entrapment.

## Entrapment and Accommodation

The process of helpless victimization leads the child to exaggerate her own responsibility and eventually to despise herself for her weakness. The child is confronted with two apparent realities: either she is bad, deserving of punishment, and not worth caring for, or her parent is bad, unfairly punishing, and not capable of caring. The young child has neither preparation nor permission to believe in the second reality, and there would be no hope for acceptance or survival if it were true. Her inevitable choice is to embrace the more active role of being the one responsible, and to hope to find a way to become good and worthy of caring. This self-scapegoating is almost universal for victims of any forms of parental assault. It sets the foundation for self-hate and what Shengold (1979) describes as a vertical split in reality testing:

> If the very parent who abuses and is experienced as bad must be turned to for relief of the distress that the parent has caused, then the child must, out of a desperate need, register the parent—delusionally—as good. Only the mental image of a good parent can help the child deal with the terrifying intensity of fear and rage which is the effect of the tormenting experiences. The alternative—the maintenance of the overwhelming stimulation and the bad parental image—means annihilation of identity, of the feeling of self. So the bad has to be registered as good. This is a mind-splitting or a mind-fragmenting operation. (p. 539)

The sexually assaultive parent provides graphic example and instruction in how to be good: the child must be available without complaint to his sexual demands. There is an explicit or implicit promise of reward: if she is good and if she keeps the secret, she can: (1) protect her siblings from sexual assault ("It's a good thing I can count on you to love me; otherwise I'd have to turn to your little sister"); (2) protect her mother from disintegration ("If your mother ever found out, it would kill her"); (3) protect her father from temptation ("If I couldn't count on you, I'd have to hang out in bars and look for other women"); and (4) most vitally, preserve the security of the home ("If you ever tell, they could send me to jail and put all you kids in an orphanage").

In the classic role reversal of child assault, the child is given the power to destroy the family and the responsibility to keep it together. The child, not the parent, must mobilize the altruism and self-control to ensure the survival of the others. The child, in short, must secretly assume many of the role-functions ordinarily assigned to the mother.

There is an inevitable splitting of conventional moral values; maintaining a lie to keep the secret is the ultimate virtue, while telling the truth would be the greatest sin. A child thus victimized will appear to accept or to seek sexual contact without complaint. As Ferenczi discovered over 50 years ago, "The misused child changes into a mechanical obedient automaton" (1933, p. 163).

Effective accommodation, of course, invalidates any future claims to credibility as a victim. It is obvious to adults that if the child were sexually assaulted as she claims, she must have been a consenting and probably seductive partner. Otherwise, she would have told right away. Either she is lying in her eventual complaints or she lied and conspired with her "lover" in her earlier coverup. In either event she has no credibility in a criminal court. Again, only expert testimony can translate the child's behavior into concepts that other adults can accept.

Since the child must structure her reality to protect the parent, she also finds the means to build pockets of survival where some hope of goodness can find sanctuary. She may turn to imaginary companions for reassurance. She may develop multiple personalities, assigning helplessness and suffering to one, sadness and rage to another, sexual power to another, love and compassion to another, and so forth. She may discover altered states of consciousness to shut off pain or to dissociate from her body, as if looking on from a distance at the child suffering the assaults. The same mechanisms that allow psychic survival for the child become handicaps to effective psychological integration as an adult. Victims at any stage of the accommodation deserve sympathetic professional understanding and assurance that their reactions are understandable, psychophysiologic, and reversible, rather than indications of poor reality testing and continuing psychopathology (Reagor, personal communication).

If the child cannot create a psychic economy to reconcile the continuing outrage, the intolerance of helplessness and the increasing feelings of rage will seek active expression. For the girl this is most often self-destructive and reinforcing self-hate; self-mutilation, suicidal behavior, promiscuous sexual activity, and repeated running away are typical. She may learn to exploit the father for privileges, favors, and material rewards, reinforcing her self-punishing image as a whore in the process. She may fight both parents, but her greatest rage is likely to focus on her mother, whom she blames for driving the father to her bed. She assumes that her mother must know of the sexual assault and is either too uncaring or too ineffectual to intervene. The failure of the mother-daughter bond reinforces the young woman's distrust of herself as a female and makes her all the more dependent on the pathetic hope of gaining acceptance and protection with an assaultive male.

The male victim of sexual assault is more likely to turn his rage outward in aggressive and antisocial behavior. He is even more intolerant of his helplessness than the female victim, and more likely to rationalize that he is exploiting the relationship for his own benefit. He may cling so tenaciously to an idealized relationship with the adult that he remains fixed at a preadolescent level of sexual object choice, as if trying to keep love alive with an unending succession of young boys. Various admixtures of depression, counterphobic violence, misogyny (again, the mother is seen as noncaring and unprotective), and rape seem to be part of the legacy of rage left in the sexually assaulted boy.

Substance abuse is an inviting avenue of escape for the victim of either gender. As Myers (1981) recalls:

> On drugs, I could be anything I wanted to be. I could make up my own reality: I could be pretty, have a good family, a nice father, a strong mother, and be happy . . . . Drinking had the opposite effect of drugs . . . . Drinking got me

back into my pain; it allowed me to experience my hurt and my anger. (pp. 98–101)

All of these accommodation mechanisms—domestic martyrdom, splitting of reality, altered consciousness, hysterical phenomena, delinquency, sociopathy, projection of rage, even self-mutilation—are part of the survival skills of the child. They can be abandoned only if the child can be led to trust in a secure environment that is full of consistent, noncontingent acceptance and caring. In the meantime, anyone working therapeutically with the child (or the now grown up, still shattered victim) will be tested and provoked to prove that trust is impossible, and that the only secure reality is negative expectations and self-hate. It is all too easy for the would-be therapist to join the parents and all of adult society in rejecting such a child, inferring from the results of assault that such an impossible wretch must have asked for and deserved whatever punishment has occurred, if indeed the whole problem is not an hysterical or vengeful fantasy. This difficulty is discussed more fully later in this chapter.

## Delayed, Conflicted, and Unconvincing Disclosure of Sexual Assault

Most ongoing sexual assault is never disclosed, at least not outside the immediate family (Gagnon, 1965; Finkelhor, 1979a). Treated, reported, or investigated cases are the exception, not the norm. Disclosure is an outgrowth either of overwhelming family conflict, incidental discovery by a third party, or sensitive outreach and community education by child protective agencies.

If family conflict triggers disclosure, it is usually only after some years of continuing sexual assault and an eventual breakdown of accommodation mechanisms. The victim of incest remains silent until she enters adolescence, when she becomes capable of demanding a more separate life for herself and of challenging the authority of her parents. Adolescence also makes the father more jealous and controlling, trying to sequester his daughter against the "dangers" of outside peer involvement. The corrosive effects of accommodation seem to justify any extreme of punishment. What parent would not impose severe restrictions to control running away, drug abuse, promiscuity, rebellion, and delinquency?

After some especially punishing family fight and a belittling showdown of authority by the father, the girl is finally driven by anger to let go of the secret. She seeks understanding and intervention at the very time she is least likely to find them. Authorities are put off by the pattern of delinquency and rebellious anger expressed by the girl. Most adults confronted with such a story tend to identify with the problems of the parents in trying to cope with a rebellious teenager. They observe that the girl seems more angry about the immediate punishment than about the sexual atrocities she is alleging. They assume there is no truth to such a fantastic complaint, especially since the girl did not complain years ago when she claims that she was forcibly molested. They assume that she has invented the story in retaliation against her father's attempts to achieve reasonable control and discipline. The more unreasonable and abusive the triggering punishment, the more they assume the girl would do anything to get away, even to the point of falsely incriminating her father.

Unless specifically trained and sensitized, the average adult, including mothers, relatives, teachers, counselors, doctors, clergy, psycho-therapists, investigators, prosecutors, defense attorneys, judges, and jurors cannot believe that a normal, truthful child would tolerate incest without immediately reporting it, or that an apparently normal father could be capable of repeated, unchallenged sexual molestation or assault of his own daughter. The child of any age faces an unbelieving audience when she complains of ongoing incest. The troubled, angry adolescent risks not only disbelief, but scapegoating, humiliation, and punishment as well.

Not all complaining adolescents appear angry and unreliable. An alternative accommodation pattern exists in which the child succeeds in hiding any indications of conflict. Such a child may be unusually achieving and popular, eager to please both teachers and peers. When the honor student or the captain of the football team tries to describe a history of ongoing sexual involvement with an adult, the adult reaction is all the more incredulous. How could such a thing have happened to such a fine young person? No one so talented and well-adjusted could have been involved in something so sordid. Obviously, it did not happen, or, if it did, it certainly did not harm the child. So there is no real cause for complaint. Whether the child is delinquent, hypersexual, countersexual, suicidal, hysterical, psychotic, or perfectly well-adjusted, and whether the child is angry, evasive, or serene, the immediate affect and the adjustment pattern of the child will be interpreted by adults to invalidate the child's complaint.

The target of the boy love is especially misunderstood. He is likely to be regarded as "queer" or sick. Adolescence has forced a crisis of rejection; the boy has outgrown the age preference of the pedophile. Sometimes the boy is hurt and angry enough to speak out, but more often he will try to cope with his betrayal silently and alone. If he does complain, it is not unusual for parents and others to reject the complaint in defense of the trusted neighbor or colleague.

Contrary to popular myth, most mothers are not aware of ongoing sexual assault. Pedophilic relatives and friends have a way of inspiring trust and gratitude while they offer love and care for the child. Marriage demands considerable blind trust and denial for survival. A woman does not commit her life and security to a man she believes capable of molesting or assaulting his own children. That basic denial becomes more exaggerated the more the woman herself has been victimized and the more she might feel helpless and worthless in the absence of a protective, accepting male. The "obvious" clues to sexual assault are usually obvious only in retrospect. Our assumption that the mother "must have known" merely parallels the demand of the child that the mother must be in touch intuitively with invisible and even deliberately concealed family discomfort.

So the mother typically reacts to allegations of sexual assault with disbelief and protective denial. How could she not have known? How could the child wait so long to tell her? What kind of mother could allow such a thing to happen? What would the neighbors think? As someone substantially dependent on the approval and generosity of the father, the mother in the incestuous triangle is confronted with a mind-splitting dilemma analogous to that of the assaulted child: either the child is bad and deserving of punishment or the father is bad and unfairly punitive. One of them is lying and unworthy of trust. The mother's whole security and life adjustment and much of her sense of adult self-worth demand a trust in the reliability of her partner. To accept the alternative means annihilation of the family and a large piece of her own identity. Her fear and ambivalence are reassured by the father's logical challenge: "Are you going to believe that lying little slut? Can you believe I would do such a thing? How could something like that go on right under your nose for years? You know we can't trust her out of our sight anymore. Just when we try to clamp down and get a little tough with her, she comes back with a cock and bull story like this. That's what I get for trying to keep her out of trouble."

Among the small proportion of incest secrets that are shared, most are never divulged outside the family. Now that professionals are required to report any suspicion of child abuse (see Chapter 3), increasing numbers of complaints are investigated by protective agencies. Police investigators and protective service workers are now more likely to give credence to the complaint, in which case all the children may be removed immediately into protective custody pending hearing of a dependency petition. In the continuing paradox of a divided judicial system, the juvenile court judge is likely to sustain out-of-home placement when the "preponderance of the evidence" indicates that the child is in danger, whereas the adult court takes no action on the father's criminal responsibility (see Chapter 4 for more detail). Attorneys know that the uncorroborated testimony of a child will not convict a respectable adult. The test in criminal court requires specific proof "beyond reasonable doubt," and every reasonable adult juror will have reason to doubt the child's fantastic claims. Prosecutors are reluctant to subject the child to humiliating cross-examination, just as they are loath to prosecute cases they cannot win, so they typically reject the complaint on the basis of insufficient evidence. Defense counsel can assure a father that he will not be charged as long as he denies any impropriety and as long as he stays out of treatment.

Out-of-family pedophiles are also effectively immune from incrimination if they have any amount of prestige. Even if several children have complained, their testimony will be impeached by trivial discrepancies in their accounts or by the countercharge that the children were willing and seductive conspirators.

The absence of criminal charges is tantamount to a conviction of perjury against the victim. "A man is innocent until proved guilty," say adult-protective relatives. "The kid claimed to be molested but there was nothing to it. The police investigated and they didn't even file charges."

Outrageous as it might seem, there is an open season on children for the sexual predator. Unless children can be encouraged to seek immediate intervention and unless there is expert advocacy for the child in the criminal court, the child is abandoned as the helpless custodian of a self-incriminating secret that no responsible adult can believe.

The physician or professional has a crucial role in both early detection and expert courtroom advocacy; he or she must help mobilize skeptical caretakers into a position of belief, acceptance, support, and protection of the child. The professional must first be capable of assuming that same position in diagnostic statements and court testimony. Even so, the expert on child assault dynamics, who learns to accept the secrecy, the helplessness, the accommodation, and the delayed disclosure, may still be alienated or totally compromised by the fifth level of the accommodation syndrome, namely retraction.

## Retraction of Complaint

Whatever a child says about incest, she is likely to reverse it. As a young child she may deny incest when questioned, yet later she may make criminal complaints when moved by anger. Beneath the anger remains the ambivalence of guilt and the martyred obligation to preserve the family. In the chaotic aftermath of disclosure, the child discovers that the bedrock fears and threats underlying the secrecy are true. Her father abandons her and calls her a liar. Her mother doesn't believe her, or she decompensates into hysteria and rage. The family is fragmented and all the children are placed in custody. The father is threatened with disgrace and imprisonment. The girl is blamed for causing the whole mess, and everyone seems to treat her like a freak. She is interrogated about all the tawdry details and encouraged to incriminate her father, yet the father remains unchallenged, remaining in the home if the dependency petition is sustained.

The message from the mother is very clear, often explicit: "Why do you insist on telling those awful stories about your father? If you send him to prison we won't be a family anymore. We'll end up on welfare, with no place to stay. Is that what you want to do to us?"

Once again, the child bears the responsibility of either preserving or destroying the family. The role reversal continues, with the "bad" choice to tell the truth, or the "good" choice to capitulate and resort to a lie for the sake of the family.

Unless there is special support for the child and immediate intervention to force responsibility on the father, the girl will follow the "normal" course and retract her complaint. The girl "admits" she made up the story: "I was awful mad at my dad for punishing me. He hit me and said I could never see my boyfriend again. I've been really bad for years and nothing seems to keep me from getting into trouble. Dad had plenty of reason to be mad at me. But I got real mad and just had to find some way of getting out of that place. So I made up this story about him fooling around with me and everything. I didn't mean to get everyone in so much trouble."

This simple lie carries more credibility than the most explicit claims of incestuous entrapment. It confirms adult expectations that children cannot be trusted. It restores the precarious equilibrium of the family. The children learn not to complain. The adults learn not to listen. And the authorities learn not to believe rebellious children who try to use their sexual power to destroy well-meaning parents. Case closed.

## PSYCHODYNAMIC DETERRENTS TO RECOGNITION

Now that some of the myths and enigmas of sexual assault have been discussed, it is worth repeating Sgroi's cardinal rule of recognition, "Recognition of sexual molestation of a child is entirely dependent on the individual's inherent willingness to entertain the possibility that the condition may exist," and its companion statements, "Unfortunately, willingness to consider the diagnosis of suspected child molestation seems to vary in inverse proportion to the individual's level of training" (1975, p. 20). Behavioral scientists are schooled to be skeptical of children's accounts of sexual activity.

Enlightenment in the complexities of psychosexual development and oedipal psychodynamics tends to create a bias toward finding a fantasy basis rather than reality when evaluating a child's memories of sexual experiences with caring adults. This bias follows the precedent set by Freud himself in confronting the dilemma of fantastic-sounding complaints. As Freud wrote in 1933, "Almost all my women patients told me that they had been seduced by their father. I was driven to recognize in the end that those reports were untrue and so came to understand that the hysterical symptoms were derived from fantasy and not from real occurrence" (p. 584).

As early as 1892, Joseph Breuer and his pupil, Sigmund Freud, published in the Studies on Hysteria the first reported observation that childhood sexual trauma could lead to symptoms of hysteria. As Freud developed his techniques of psychoanalysis, he was troubled by the persistent implications of sexual assault he found in each of his patients with hysteria. His conclusion that childhood seduction was the basis for hysteria led to scathing criticism from both of his teachers, Charcot and Breuer, as well as most of his other colleagues in the Doktorenkollegium. The troubling implications of widespread parent-child sexuality seem to have driven Breuer from psychology back into the safer, more socially acceptable study of pulmonary physiology (Peters, 1976). Freud sought to minimize professional outrage on behalf of respectable fathers by documenting less controversial relationships. He acknowledged 30 years later that two of the patients described in Studies on Hysteria (1896) had been seduced not by their uncles, as originally described, but by their fathers (Peters, 1973). Outrage increased, however, in response to Freud's determined assertion of his seduction theory in "The Aetiology of Hysteria" (1896), in which he concluded, "I therefore put forward the thesis that at the bottom of every case of hysteria there are one or more occurrences of premature sexual experiences, occurrences which belong to the earliest years of childhood" (1896, p. 203).

The Oedipus complex offered not only the attraction of universality, but it also served as a fortuitous, adult-reassuring alternative to the seduction theory. Children, not their fathers, were responsible for the allegations of sexual assault. It was the perverse needs of the child that scapegoated adults with undeserved accusations. Finally, whatever children (or adults) chose to say about sexual experiences with their parents, it must be assumed to be wishful fantasy unless proved otherwise.

Freud's early discovery was therefore an idea ahead of its time. Neither Freud nor the adult-protective world of that time was ready to explore or to validate the implications of the seduction theory. Not only was the theory discredited; worse than that, the adult-protective reaction served to discourage and delay any subsequent reappraisal of that discovery. Freud's precocious, outrageous early speculation led him and many of his followers to arm themselves with a dogma of disbelief. The messenger of incest risks not only provoking ordinary, common sense denial but also inviting charges of heresy among the most highly trained and sophisticated professionals.

Peters (1976) combined his experience as Director of the Sex Offender and Rape Victim Center, Philadelphia General Hospital, with his sensitivity as a practicing psychoanalyst to propose a new look at Freud's shift from the seduction theory to the Oedipus complex. In a paper written in 1976, he reviewed the impact of that shift on psychiatric thought:

> After 1924 the notion that hysterical symptoms were based upon actual events, real sexual assaults upon children, fell increasingly out of favor. Psychoanalysts abandoned the search for a distinction between actual childhood sexual trauma and children's fantasies. In the Freudian theory of psychoneurosis, the fantasies became as important as real events. Since Freud's thinking developed in this way, his earlier followers were relieved from facing the fact that patients sometimes had been real victims of sexual assault . . . . It is my thesis that both cultural and personal factors combined to cause everyone, including Freud himself at times, to welcome the idea that reports of childhood sexual victimization could be regarded as fantasies. This position relieved the guilt of adults. In my opinion, both Freud and his followers oversubscribed to the theory of childhood fantasy and overlooked incidents of actual sexual victimization in childhood. [p. 401] In their aversion to what are often repulsive details, psychotherapists allowed and continue to allow their patients to repress

emotionally significant, pathogenic facts . . . . In addition, it is important to note that because the reported offender was frequently the patient's own father, in order to avoid the fact of incest, my colleagues seized upon the easier assumption that the occurrences were Oedipal fantasies. [p. 402] . . . Relegating these traumas to the imagination may divert treatment into a prolonged unraveling of natural developmental processes in which fantasy is a component. Furthermore, unsuccessful psychotherapeutic evaluation opens the way for prescribing . . . antipsychotic drugs and electroshock. The treatment may compound the patient's original psychological problems. Ascribing these events to psychological fantasy may be easier and more interesting for the therapist, but it may also be counterproductive for the most efficient resolution of symptoms. [pp. 407–408] . . . An immediate supportive response by parents, criminal justice personnel, doctors and nurses is crucial to preserve the emotional integrity of the child. Particularly when the offender is a member of the family, care must be taken by service personnel to ensure that the child's needs are put first. (p. 421)

Rush (1977), writing from a feminist perspective with scholarly documentation from the psychoanalytic literature, challenges Freud's shift to the Oedipus complex, especially in the concepts of penis envy and the universal wish of little girls to possess their father's penis.

As he approached the source of the neurosis, and evolved the now-famous Oedipal complex, Freud freely applied his particularly personal discovery to everybody; to all cultures, and to females as well as males. [p. 37] The seduction theory maintained that hysteria was a neurosis caused by sexual assault, and it incriminated incestuous fathers, while the Oedipal theory insisted the seduction was a fantasy, an invention, not a fact—and it incriminated daughters . . . . However, one must remember that when Freud arrived at the seduction theory, he did so by listening carefully and intently to his female patients; when he arrived at his Oedipal theory, he did so by listening carefully and intently to himself . . . . Freud therefore cautioned the world never to overestimate the importance of seduction and the world listened to Freud and paid little heed to the sexual abuse of children. [p. 39]. The reason is illogical. It categorically assigns a real experience to fantasy, or harmless reality at best, while the known offender—the one concrete reality—is ignored. With reality sacrificed to a nebulous unconscious, the little girl has no recourse. She is trapped within a web of adult conjecture and is not offered protection but treatment for some speculative ailment, while the offender—Uncle Willie, the grocery clerk, the dentist, or the little girl's father—is permitted further to indulge his predilection for little girls. The child's experience is as terrifying as the worst horror of a Kafkaesque nightmare: her story is not believed, she is declared ill, and, worse, she is left at the mercy and the "benevolence" of psychiatrically oriented child experts. (p. 40)

It is indeed strange how psychology is used not to help, but to trap and ensnare the female. The myth of consent—that is, the female desire to get a man, to have a penis—is used to explain victim participation and therefore accepts as inevitable the sexual abuse of children. The tragedy is that the myth is believed and that so often the victims are punished. Once a child has been raped or molested, no matter how impressive the psychological nomenclature describing her plight or how sophisticated her caretakers, the little girl is an outcast, a nymphomaniac, a "whore." (p. 41)

The little girl, then, with her innate passion for a penis, is—as in Christian doctrine—the temptress Eve, and, if she is violated, the nature of her sexuality renders her culpable. Any attempt on the part of the family to expose the violator also exposes her own alleged innate sexual motives and shames her more than the offender; concealment is her only recourse. The dilemma of sexual abuse of children has provided a system of foolproof emotional blackmail; if the victim incriminates the abuser, she also incriminates herself. The sexual abuse of the child is therefore the best-kept secret in the world. (p. 45)

There are many other factors, of course, besides psychoanalytical concepts that stigmatize the child victims, and many of them penalize the boy as well as the girl. Psychoanalytically oriented professionals are likely to be offended by the angry edge of Rush's attack on "child experts." The lengthy quotations from her thoughtful and thought-provoking article are included here not to alienate mental health specialists nor to widen the feminist-Freudian schism, but to illustrate two current clinical realities. First, rape crisis services, abused women's shelters, incest survivors' groups, and other feminist-oriented resources that do active case finding in sexual assault typically will not refer clients to psychoanalytically oriented treatment centers. A potentially vital link in the hospital-community network is broken, unless there can be active efforts to develop shared priorities and values. Second, although not all mental health specialists stigmatize victims with prejudicial interpretations and labels, many do. Sexual assault treatment networks have to search for professionals who can "believe in" child sexual assault and who are also willing to appear in court to help offset the inevitable "child fantasy" or "seductive child" expert opinion provided by defense.

Mothers who leave sexually assaultive husbands may go bankrupt trying to buy testimony that will challenge the father's demands for child custody. If a woman allows sexual assault to occur under her roof, she is accused of setting up the assault. If she separates from the husband with her children, she is accused of inventing prejudicial stories to block her estranged husband's legitimate access to his children. Clinical evaluation of both the disputing parties and of the children provides the major evidence in such suits, and the "objective" evaluation almost invariably faults the woman. The man is evaluated as normal if he is sufficiently self-assured and if his testimony is no more conflicting than that of the average unemotional, well-defended male. The woman is evaluated as within normal limits, but as having marked anxieties in the area of sexuality. Projective testing is characterized by themes of loss of security, fear of attack and jeopardy and rescue of children. The woman typically will be quite candid in discussing marital discord, sexual incompatibility, and childhood family conflicts, all of which are seen in court as evidence of instability and punitive vested interest.

The keystone of the argument is the evaluation of the child. The younger the child, the more sensitive the mother has been in picking up subliminal clues to sexual assault, and the more accommodated the child has become in trying to heal the split between the parents, the more ineffectual the examination will be. The verbal, expressive child will be interpreted as fantasizing or as reflecting the anxiety and coaching of the mother. The blocked or concealing child will be written off as either untouched or noncontributory. It is not unusual to read evaluations of children in which no direct questions were asked relating to sexual material, in the belief that such questioning would be either punitive and intrusive or might fuel additional fantasy.

The following report was written by a psychiatrist evaluating the father in such a dispute. The father was suing for full custody of his three year old son and 14 month old daughter on the charge that his estranged wife was mentally unfit to care for the children. He alleged that his wife had fabricated charges against him in order to deprive him of custody; "she fabricated these charges against me, so I think she's very emotionally disturbed."

The mother had sought protective service intervention and psychiatric help for the boy, reporting he had complained of mutual masturbation and mutual oral intercourse while on visits with his father. According to the mother, the child had also demonstrated to her how his father had taught him to bend over, grasping his ankles, while his father inserted his finger and attempted to put his penis in the child's "tushy hole." She also described threats reported by the child that his father would go away and never see him again if the child told his mother. The mother had recorded in a diary from a series of hints and increasingly specific complaints made by the boy beginning about a month after the parents separated. She sought protective service intervention within two weeks of the first hint that the father might have handled the child's penis, saying that at first she had been afraid to believe such a thing could be true.

Most of the psychiatric evaluation of the father is devoted to extended verbatim quotations of the man's complaints about his wife. Of seven pages of single spaced material, there is a six line summary of sexual history: "He first had sexual relations in his early 20's; never engaged in any perverse homosexual practices, and had a good sexual relationship with his first wife before and during marriage. His second wife was very slow to arouse, but enjoyed sexual relations and usually had climaxes."

The diagnostic opinion says, in effect, that a man who presents so well in clinical evaluations could not molest such a small child, or if he did molest a child it was his wife's fault.

## Diagnostic Opinion

Defendant/subject is not mentally disordered, and there is no evidence from his history or clinical examination that he is sexually perverse or tends to pedophilia.

He has a somewhat aggressive and rigid manner, with relatively little empathy expressed in this procedure; but much of his defensiveness and criticism of his wife are appropriate to the circumstances in which his wife's charges have placed him and to other behavior on her part which he described.

His religiosity, character, history, record, concern for his children's welfare, and the tender age of alleged victim make the charges against him most unlikely to be based on facts of his behavior.

If committed, offensive acts were precipitated by loneliness, anger at his wife, and intimate circumstances, and are very unlikely to be repeated. He is not a danger, not in need of hospital treatment, and not a "mentally disordered sex offender."

Save for the charges, there appears no reason subject is unfit for child custody and to the degree his description of his wife's behavior is accurate, her emotional stability is questionable. Moreover, if her charges are found to be fabricated, she is very unstable and unreliable, and reveals her disregard for the children's need for contact with both parents.

This report is not an isolated aberration: two subsequent evaluations, one by a clinical psychologist and another by a court-appointed psychiatrist, have been similarly prejudiced against the mother's complaints. The third examiner was most outspoken in condemning the "highly emotional" and "naive" reactions of those who reported child assault:

I must say the naivete and unprofessionalism of this report shocked me. Sheldon [fictitious name] told her [the play therapist] that his father put his penis in Sheldon's mouth and his thumb up his anus . . . . I must comment that what is so remarkable and psychiatrically naive is that what Sheldon was telling [the therapist] was *undoubtedly* a fantasy. Not only is it common psychiatric knowledge that children of all ages, and especially children from the ages of 3 to 5, engage in quite intensive sexual fantasies about their own and parents' bodies but also fantasize any manner of sexuality that would be considered perverse by adults. I am not saying that I can claim with certainty that Sheldon is not reporting real events, but the distinction between reality and fantasy is not clear . . . . However, I am saying that *"perverse" sexual fantasies are to be expected at this age* and if a child did not have some of them that would be considered an abnormality . . . they are the fantasies of a child who is anxious about the affectional bonds with both his parents and is perhaps sexually overstimulated unconsciously by both of them, although *most certainly* by the mother, who is quite sexually preoccupied. What is also clear is that *Sheldon is quite turned on by women.* And although some homosexual urges toward his father are also obviously present in his fantasies, we see that even these fantasies come up only in situations where *he is being seductive* with women. An Oedipus complex at this age with sexual longings primarily for the mother but also the father has been reported by psychoanalysts from the turn of the century and it shocks me that such an elementary piece of data is ignored . . . . When Sheldon reports to his grandmother about sexual activity between him and his father, this is brought up in the context and follows trying to *seduce* his grandmother into taking a bath with him. Later *he has her* examine his penis and he gets an erection in the process. In the long note that [the mother] wrote on the police report at initial contact, she gives a similar context. "Sheldon tells me that he had to go to bed in my room" (after reporting sleeping with his father on a prior visit). At this point [the mother] asked Sheldon rather directly what was so special about going to bed with his father and Sheldon, who is *undoubtedly* still thinking about going to bed with his mother, described the things that can be done in bed . . . . Later on [the mother] says "On April 8, 1980, I was giving Sheldon his bath. I showed him how to retract his foreskin and wash his penis. He said no, my dad says you do it slow and demonstrates rubbing very slowly across the head of the penis. *Clearly* he is showing his mother what *he wants from her* and how he wants her to do it . . . . There is also abundant other data that these are fantasies that we are involved with, e.g., the theme of castration by his father. This particular anxiety is part of the growing Oedipal attachment to the mother, and the fantasy that the father is going to cut off his penis *is as predictable as the rising of the sun.*

The italics in the preceding quotation are added to emphasize the imperative terms used to demand acceptance of a theoretical oedipal, mother-stimulating and child-seductive explanation for the reported sexual material. Among 15 single spaced pages of very thoughtful and careful discussion, it is only when attacking the "emotional" involvement of those who intervened in behalf of the child's complaints that prejudicial language is used.

Did the father molest the child? It is impossible to know or to predict on theoretical or statistical grounds. But the child and a passionately protective parent must have some right to literal credibility. It is at least as logical to believe that a child overstimulated by his father would try to root out the meaning of his experiences through reenactment with maternal figures as that he fantasized experiences with his father out of a projected lust for his mother. And if a child is searching for a way to communicate confusing sexual experiences, wouldn't the bathtub be a good place to start, in the midst of touching by a safer, more trusted figure? It is difficult to imagine what a child might say or do regarding an actual sexual molestation by a parent demanding secrecy and threatening bodily harm that could not be translated into oedipal terms. How can a mother be responsive to a child's sexual distress without being labeled as sexually preoccupied or seductive? And what complaints should a therapist accept as real without being condemned as naive and unprofessional? Rush has a point.

Why should a chapter on clinical recognition and management of sexual assault be so burdened by the polemics of legal, domestic, and ideological disputes, with so much emphasis on reports and testimony in the courts? The answer is simple and vital: Advocacy for the victim is the most basic and the most challenging function any professional can perform in the area of child sexual assault. Any physician or professional who must remain adult-protective, male-protective, or self-protective, and who cannot communicate accurately and fairly with protective agencies can be only obstructive to the needs of the victim.

## CLINICAL RECOGNITION OF SEXUAL ASSAULT

Once the clinician is sensitive to the realities and patterns of sexual assault, and once there is no longer a reluctance to ask the questions and to accept the answers, sexual assault leaps to the attention with bewildering frequency. Beyond such intangibles as increased sensitivity to subliminal clues, the cardinal tool for clinical recognition is the ability to ask a simple, direct question without embarrassment or fear in every pediatric examination. The question is not "Have you ever been sexually molested?" or "Has anyone ever molested you?", both of which inspire fear and invite a hasty denial. A more congenial, more universal question might be something like, "How often do you feel icky or uncomfortable from the way someone touches you or plays with you?" Or, "Do you know any grown-ups who play secret games with children's bodies?" Or, "How many grown-ups and relatives do you really feel safe with?"

If a child seems comfortable or naively confused with the implications of such questions, there is opportunity for a preventive educational follow-up; "You're very lucky if you've never had to feel scared or uncomfortable with grown-ups. Some grown-ups, even daddies or mommies or other relatives, act like bullies sometimes and make children play with their bodies or they handle children's bodies in ways that don't feel right. Kids are usually afraid to complain or tell anyone, so they think they have to keep secrets and feel bad. If anything like that ever happened to you, I hope you'd tell me and give me a chance to help you. I promise I would understand and be on your side. I don't want any child to have to feel alone or afraid."

If there are symptoms of emotional distress or disturbed behavior indicating possible sexual assault (Table 2–1), questions should be more explicit, and should be reinforced in each successive visit. When clinical suspicion merits such concern, questions should be deliberately leading and preceded by expressions of understanding and empathy to counteract the predictable distress and fear, as well as to address the typical feelings of isolation and guilt: "Most of the girls I see with this kind of upset are afraid to talk about something very secret that is happening to them. Some grown-up like their uncle or their father or some special friend has taught them to be sexual with them. The child usually feels all alone and afraid nobody can help or understand. Lots of times they think it is their fault, or they have been told terrible things would happen if they don't keep it a secret. They do not know that men with that kind of problem need help to stop getting sexual with little kids. And they do not know that lots of kids have found help by getting someone else to stop it. I can understand things like that; it is my job. And I know other people who have special jobs just to protect kids and to help their families to take care of them. Anyway, that is the way it was with other kids, and they are glad they did not keep the secret any longer . . . . I wonder if something like that has been happening to you?"

Acknowledgment may be tentative or it may come pouring out like a flood. In any case whoever is taking the history should be rewarding and supporting of disclosure. An outstretched hand or an offered embrace will go a long way to offset the child's fear that she is making herself reprehensible through disclosure. In general, a girl will be more comfortable with a female examiner. More important than gender, though, is the level of comfort and experience reflected by the clinician.

It should be understood that the more prevalent forms of sexual abuse involve little physical trauma and no visible tissue damage. A careful and well-documented physical examination is all the more important. The child will be reassured by the physician who can say, "I've checked you over very thoroughly inside and out, and there is no sign of any damage or any kind of change in your body. Once you get help to get over the bad feelings, you'll be perfectly OK again. You don't have to worry that there's anything about your experience that shows."

The patient's chart becomes crucial evidence in subsequent court actions. The victim's statements to a clinician during the distress of initial disclosure may be acceptable as prima facie evidence despite later distortions or retractions. Statements outside clinical evaluation,

**Table 2-1. Indicators of sexual abuse***

---

A. Presumptive Indicators of Sexual Assault
1. Direct reports from children. False reports from young children are relatively rare; concealment is much more the rule. Adolescents may rarely express authority conflicts through distorted or exaggerated complaints, but each such complaint should be sensitively evaluated.
2. Pregnancy. Rule out premature but peer appropriate sexual activity.
3. Prepubescent venereal disease.
4. Genital or rectal trauma. Remember that most sexual assault is seductive rather than coercive and that the approach to small children may be nongenital. The presence or absence of a hymen is nonspecific to sexual assault.

B. Possible Indicators.
1. Precocious sexual interest or preoccupation.
2. Indiscreet masturbatory activity.
3. Genital inflammation or discharge. More often this results from masturbation or foreign body than abuse. Items 1 to 3 most often indicate a sexually stimulating environment or a sexually permissive environment, which may not be deliberately abusive or intrusive.
4. Apparent pain in sitting or walking. Be alert for evasive or illogical explanations. Encourage physical examination.

C. Behavioral and Clinical Associations—Nonspecific
1. Social withdrawal and isolation.
2. Underachievement, distraction, and "daydreaming."
3. Indications of any parental child assault.
4. Fear and distrust of authorities.
5. Identification with authorities. Too-willing acquiescence to adult demands may represent a conditioned response to parental intrusion and a high vulnerability to adult exploitation.
6. Negative self-esteem, depression, suicidal behavior, substance abuse.
7. Somatic complaints: abdominal or pelvic pain, nausea, vomiting, anorexia, dysphagia, headache.
8. Dissociative states, hysterical phenomena, multiple personality.
9. Atypical seizures.
10. Sleep disorders.
11. Normal peer appropriate behavior and achievement. Remember that many children will carefully conceal any sign of sexual victimization. Attempts at compensation may even lead to overachievement, extraordinary social skills, and model behavior.

---

*This outline is intended only as a superficial inventory of signs of potential sexual assault as they might be observed by a teacher, school nurse, parent, or physician. The list is neither exhaustive nor specific. No attempt is made to correlate these isolated signs with the clinical and descriptive information needed for the further evaluation, investigation, diagnosis, and management of sexual problems in children. This outline should be used only in conjunction with study and professional consultations in sexual problems. Any firm suspicion of sexual assault must by law be reported to the appropriate authorities.

whether to parents or police officers, are regarded only as hearsay. The child's welfare is betrayed by the offhand jargon typical of so many charts: "Child seen because of alleged sexual abuse. P.E.w.n.t. External genitalia o. Pelvic deferred. No indication of sexual activity." With explicit documentation of the child's complaints, specific description of the genital examination, and a statement that the sexual activity described would normally leave no signs of trauma, the clinical evaluation speaks for the child. As written here, the examination findings will be used to dispute the child's claims.

There should be a protocol for adequate evaluation and documentation of each child with indication of sexual assault. All clerical, nursing, social work, and medical personnel who have contact with children should be trained in appropriate response and coordination of roles for the support of the child and the family. Appendix IV of the California Attorney General's Child Abuse Prevention Handbook (Van de Kamp, 1983, pp. 47ff) serves as a helpful format for documenting sexual assault.

Recognition of sexual assault in boys is especially difficult. Clinical sensitivity must be acute, since, as mentioned earlier, boys are even less likely than girls to volunteer sexual information. Of the victimized boys in Finkelhor's sample (1979a), only about one fourth told anyone. Victimized boys tend to fall into two somewhat polarized categories: (1) forcible, often physically traumatic sexual assault, and (2) careful, premeditated sexualization of an ongoing, affectionate pedophilic relationship. The traumatized boy will avoid disclosure for fear of retaliation and from a sense of unmanliness and shame at being weak and helpless. The partner to affectionate seduction will be protective and idealistically defensive of the relationship. Boys often feel threatened by the stigma and fear of homosexuality attached to their involvement with a male. Counterphobic denial and exaggerated, macho behavior with girls may give clues to occult victimization.

Once sexual assault is properly detected and disclosed, the next step may be to involve the child and family members in a program of therapy. The issue of treatment must go well beyond the child, reaching out to families, courts, therapeutic agencies, social services, and other involved persons or agencies. Often the intervention will require an entirely new outlook on the part of the various participants (see remainder of this chapter and all subsequent chapters for intervention and prevention ideas and procedures).

# TREATMENT OF THE SEXUALLY ABUSED CHILD

Any concept of treatment of sexual assault must include a variety of resources and services beyond those ordinarily available to a hospital or medical clinic setting. The medical model is not incapable of expanding into multimodal services, but without a somewhat radical realignment of priorities there is a tendency to undervalue the child protective, law enforcement, parental support, and child reparenting aspects vital to a comprehensive program. A hospital-based or office model built on patient-initiated voluntary requests for professional services at scheduled intervals cannot meet the needs of children who are alienated from the advocacy of their parents nor the frustrations of parents who cannot be assumed to be responsible for their children. The success of the physician and any paramedical specialist will depend on the ability to develop an innovative style of interagency outreach and the willingness to share therapeutic roles with members of an extended network of community services.

At least three cherished traditions of American medicine are challenged by the interagency model:

1. *Authority.* The physician may have relatively less experience, contact, and salient data than other investigators in a given case. Clinical impressions may be overruled by police evidence or protective service findings. Alternatively, conclusive medical evidence may be ignored in court decisions. Clinicians accustomed to having the ultimate authority in management decisions will be alienated and distrustful in having to take a relatively subordinate role.

2. *Fee for service.* The private practitioner may feel in competition with publicly funded, philanthropic, or voluntary self-help aspects of an integrated program. Turf disputes and chauvinistic defensiveness on both sides may cause clients to distrust the quality of free services on one hand or the sincerity of paid services on the other.

3. *Sanctuary.* The physician shares with the priest and the attorney the carefully guarded power of confidentiality. The physician-patient relationship offers the implicit guarantee that a person in need of care will not be exposed to social or political intervention. Child abuse reporting laws are a specific and sometimes problematic exception to privileged communication. The physician finds neither precedent nor

comfort in informing police and social agencies of suspected child assault, especially when reporting violates the expressed wish of the child and parent for a confidential, clinical resolution of their "family adjustment problem." It is often tempting to avoid reporting to spare both family and physician the anxiety and uncertainties of a compromise in clinical control. Yet the success of coordinated programs contrasts sharply with the high dropout rate and limited disclosure of families who are offered clinical sanctuary (Summit, 1978). Like it or not, the physician is subject to both criminal and civil liability if reporting mandates are ignored (see Chapter 3).

Design and coordination of an effective sexual assault treatment program require experiential training, community organization, and locally adaptive adjustments, all of which lie beyond the scope of this chapter. In addition, the available models and concepts of sexual assault treatment are expanding so rapidly that no one publication can give a really timely or comprehensive appraisal of the immediate state of the art. Several excellent texts, articles and training programs are available. *Sexual Assault of Children and Adolescents* (Burgess and colleagues, 1978), Giaretto's chapter (1976) entitled "Humanistic Treatment of Father-Daughter Incest," *Sexually Victimized Children* (Finkelhor, 1979a), *Sexually Abused Children and Adolescents* (Kempe and Kempe, 1982) and "Dealing with Sexual Child Abuse" (Summit, 1978) are essential references. Textbooks should be supplemented by a comprehensive review of the current professional literature in the subject categories of child abuse, sexual abuse, incest, victimization, pedophilia, and sexual offenses. The National Center on Child Abuse and Neglect funds several regional training programs in sexual abuse management, currently including the Parents United model in Santa Clara County, California, and the Sexual Assault Center in Seattle, Washington.

Any program treating sexual assault should be closely linked with other community programs related to child assault, child development, and parent education. Lessons learned in dealing with assaultive parents provide new understanding of the essentials of positive parenting. The ideals of empathic parenting, constructive discipline, and enhancement of self-esteem are best learned by assaultive parents in association with other families with less assaultive backgrounds.

Community councils on child assault or family violence offer an exciting forum for shared development of services for children. Any person or group developing a sexual assault treatment program should work to set up such a council or to support an existing network. An excellent training film, *Child Abuse, A Chain to be Broken* (Motorola Teleprograms, 1977) describes the purposes and potentials of community networking.

# Key Elements in Specialty Treatment Programs

Sexually assaultive families have a number of special needs that must be met in the course of intervention and treatment. These factors are discussed more fully elsewhere (Summit, 1978) and are explored here only as general principles.

**Child Protection.**    The greatest single failure of traditional treatment and counseling approaches when applied to child assault is the continued reliance on the parents for child advocacy. The therapist who depends on the motivation of conflicted parents to keep appointments and to verbalize humiliating parent-child identity struggles will conclude that abusive families are untreatable. In addition, the therapist who monitors the welfare of the child only through the office descriptions of the parent is depending on the fox to look after the hen house. It must be assumed that the parents begin treatment in an inverted role, depending on children to meet their needs, and that they will be both fearful and jealous of protective attention directed to the child. Just as the parent denies and conceals any ongoing assaults, the child continues to seek security and approval by shielding the parent from discovery. In many cases the mother will be unquestionably supportive and protective of her child. In other cases the mother will require reassurance and reinforcement that the child is telling the truth and that the child is not to blame for the initiation of the sexual behavior.

Many sexually assaulted children will require initial separation from both parents. Eventual reunification must be carefully monitored to protect the child from slipping back into the inverted role of subordinating personal welfare to the needs of the parent. Children will typically echo their mother's urgent wish to patch the family again with an early return of the father, despite their own unexpressed fears and feelings of betrayal. The child's therapist must take the lead in translating ambivalent fears and tentative complaints into protective demands. It is unfair to leave to the child the choice of whether to report that the father is back home in violation of a court order, or that she feels sexually threatened by the way he holds, tickles, teases, or wrestles with her. Professionals do their child patients no favor by abdicating adult supervision too soon or by saddling the very young with the responsibility for their own survival.

Treatment staff members working in conjunction with personnel in protective services and courts must be advocates for the child's comfort despite superficial treatment gains professed by the parents. The entire treatment team must be on guard against a strong societal and professional idealism that seeks to keep families together and to preserve adult authority at all costs.

This precaution is not meant to encourage another reactive excess: a tendency to punish parents by depriving them forever of any contact with their children. In both extremes the children serve as pawns in the self-protective or punitive skirmishes of adult-oriented systems. The therapist must decide whether to report new assaults, whether to report violations of court orders, and how soon to advocate reconstitution of families. These decisions must be based not on wishful thinking, therapeutic optimism, prejudicial conservatism, countertransference issues, programmatic convenience, or blind tradition, but on a canny and realistic appraisal of what best speaks for the psychic integrity, autonomy, and identity of the child.

With experience, most therapists in specialty child assault treatment programs become more comfortable with discovering and reporting assaultive trends as part of their advocacy for the parents as well as their protection of the child. The therapist achieves a new maturity in the process of reparenting an assaultive parent. The therapist, like any effective parent, must be willing to carry the burden of defining limits and upholding discipline at the risk of being resented or considered unfair. The challenge for any therapist or parent is to define discipline in the context of growth and to apply any judgments and proscriptions of behavior upon a well-established foundation of caring and endorsement for the person.

**Court Advocacy.** Court intervention is an overwhelming fact of life for the sexually assaultive family. Fear of criminal prosecution, public disgrace, and family disruption creates a survival panic that belittles all other treatment issues.

Therapists themselves may panic in the process of identification with their patients. They may express distrust of shelter care facilities and try to sequester children from protective custody. They may feel that child-assaultive behavior is an illness and that a parent should not be punished for uncontrollable impulses. They may decide that the child must be protected at all costs from the agony of victim-witness testimony and cross examination. Or the therapist may feel helpless and ineffectual or even fearful in attempting to deal with the court system. The list goes on and on, with countless logical and self-comforting reasons to avoid dealing with court issues.

Avoidance of court involvement serves only to increase anxiety within the family and to leave courts ignorant of treatment and rehabilitation potentials. However unreliable or capricious juvenile court decisions may seem, and however punitive and damaging criminal actions may appear, the therapist must be willing to take an assertive role as an expert child advocate. While such advocacy generally speaks also for a favorable prognosis with cooperative parents, it may at times favor lifetime separation from recalcitrant offenders. Just as expert testimony speaks to the right of rehabilitation for selected incest offenders, it must also caution judges and prosecutors against unwarranted optimism for chronic sexual offenders. A treatment program with a good recovery record for incestuous fathers will be swamped with court referrals of overt and covert pedophiles unless admission criteria are repeatedly defined and strictly enforced.

Although most incest treatment programs support appropriate child protection through the dependency court, there is a sharp division of opinion regarding criminal prosecution of incestuous fathers. Many programs encourage negotiation for treatment as an alternative to criminal action. There has been a trend to decriminalize parental violence in the hope of enhancing parental self-esteem and encouraging more voluntary participation in therapy. Advocates for decriminalization argue that the victim-perpetrator model of criminal prosecution is inappropriate for complex and interdependent family relationships. There is a well-founded fear that if fathers are encouraged to seek favorable consideration by admitting to charges of incest they might be punished more severely than the treatment-resistant offender who flatly denies all charges and is believed. Finally, the cruel scapegoating and character assassination directed toward the victim-witness in an adversary proceeding are seen as more abusive to the child than the risks of nonprosecution.

Although there is ample clinical experience to reinforce distrust of the criminal justice system as a therapeutic ally, I believe that the child's hope for maximum recovery is compromised by decriminalization. There is an enormous ethical contradiction in a position that tells a man it is a criminal offense to rape a child unless it is one of his own. Moreover, how can the child be assured that it was not his or her fault if we do not empower the child to define a crime against his or her person? And how much is he or she worth as a person if such a crime is not charged? Of even more immediate consequence is the fact that most men will not submit to meaningful treatment and will not honestly examine their own culpability for incestuous assault unless coerced through the fear of inescapable criminal reckoning. Punishment alone will do little for recovery. Treatment alone has little power to require painful disclosures and drastic changes in a man's balance of power.

The fear of court involvement that tends to resonate between therapists and patients can be decreased by a more pragmatic approach to the issues, a willingness to address the problems as part of therapy, and, especially, the assumption of more active therapeutic initiative and involvement within the court system. Staff members should be trained, experienced, and confident in dealing with every aspect of the justice system. The treatment program must prepare child-witnesses for their day in court and must train prosecutors and judges to deal fairly and compassionately with children. These issues are explored by Berliner and Stevens (1979), and a training film, *Double Jeopardy*, has been developed by the Harborview Sexual Assault Center.

**Outreach and Availability.** Traditional systems of treatment assume that individuals will present themselves willingly and will confide freely whatever conflicts are troubling them. Office therapy also assumes that patients will be motivated to change their perceptions or behavior to decrease anxiety and to improve self-esteem. Traditional outpatient therapy depends on a patient's self-motivation to keep appointments and to take the risks of change. Individuals involved in sexual assault tend to be desperately afraid of discovery, judgment, further stigmatization, and exposure. The sexual assault itself tends to maintain adult control and a precarious sense of security, which depends on secrecy and isolation. Giving up the behavior, losing control, exposing feelings, exploring adult dependency needs, and learning to trust others in a position of authority are anxiety provoking rather than reassuring experiences. This is especially true for those who have been consistently assaulted by parents and who were taught to accept blame and punishment for anything they do. For the self-hating victim of child assault, whether current victim or an adult who is now a father or mother himself or herself, disclosure of assault leads not to relief or insight but to further humiliation, self-blame, and self-punishment. A person conditioned to scapegoating and unreasonable punishment simply cannot accept that he or she will not be condemned and punished by insight, and that the therapist, who seems so much like a parent, would not inevitably reject and punish anyone so patently offensive.

There is a sad irony in the reality that assaulted and assaultive individuals so often must be coerced into therapy through threat of punishment. It is additionally ironic that so many victims will distrust and try to escape from anyone who offers the hope of a benevolent and nonpunitive reception. The therapist must anticipate these problems by giving unqualified reinforcement and support to each member of the conflict while drawing on outside coercion and control to maintain contact through the predictable stresses of engagement. The treatment interface must be engaging. The style of the counselors should be engaging, open, and directly reassuring, even while requiring clearly defined limits on assaultive behavior. A humanistic faith that any individual will seek his or her highest ideals should be coupled with the pragmatic acceptance that anyone under threat will fight to avoid exposure or change. Treatment develops as a dynamic progression from fear, distrust, and hopeless avoidance to optimism, human acceptance, and enthusiastic involvement. Missed appointments cannot be tolerated, but rescheduling and unexpected crises must be accommodated without prejudice. If an appointment is missed in the midst of a transference crisis it is the responsibility of the therapist to call to reestablish contact. Whenever there is any risk of child-assaultive, self-mutilating, or suicidal behavior, there must be provision for home visits and physical intervention by program staff members. Engagement of reluctant, self-defeating, potentially dangerous individuals cannot be accomplished by the old "Take two aspirin and call me in the morning" approach. If the program presumes to understand and to care for the child-assaultive family, it cannot demand that the parents structure their needs and crises to serve the schedule and style of the therapist.

In practice, most families will avoid making unreasonable or even reasonable demands on the program. Early reinforcement of outreach availability will tend to encourage judgment and maturity in clients, allowing them to make the best use of services to avoid explosive, untimely crisis demands.

**Peer Group Contact.**    Child assault thrives on isolation and secrecy, and it carries the seeds of its own alienation and generational survival. The assaulted child learns to hide from discovery out of fear of further rejection and punishment and the related belief he or she is inherently bad and deserving of contempt. The child grows up to achieve a certain amount of adult acceptance and approval but with an inner sense of counterfeit identity: "They accept me because they don't know. They think I'm like them but there's really nobody in the world like me. If they knew how bad I am they'd hate me."

In accepting and trying so hard to hide the stigma of assault, the child abdicates an awesome power to parents and other adults, as well as the potential to claim some of that power after growing up into the role of parent. Assault survivors may be able to act as if they are comfortably adjusted while hiding enormous and often poorly acknowledged self-hate and projections of destructive power onto their own children. When they find themselves resenting, exploiting, or assaulting their children they may rationalize this as appropriate, in identification with their own assaultive parents. They can protect their image of the good, protective parent, as well as protect themselves from memories of vulnerability by overinvesting the parental role with righteousness and power. If this defensive structure is threatened, either by compassion for the feelings of the child or by insight gained through treatment, the assaulted, now assaultive parent will seem to overreact into denial, panic, or flight with the discovery of the inner destructive power and the sense of being a monster (a word heard frequently in the productions of assaulted children and assaultive parents).

Issues of smallness, helplessness, blame, guilt, pain, anger, disapproval, punishment, and rejection are so disproportionate that they tend to overwhelm the patient's transference toward an individual therapist, whatever the reality and style of that therapist. Whether male, female, gentle, directive, old, or young, the role and parental associations inherent in the psychotherapeutic process will invoke intense, defensive, often countertherapeutic parental transference in the assault-scarred patient.

Psychoanalyst Leonard Shengold writes of the challenge to the psychotherapist in treating the victims of what he calls soul murder: consistent parental deprivation or assault. "Can we help them modify their misery on the basis of a human relationship (which is what we do as analysts) if they have never had and therefore perhaps never can have a decent human relationship? . . . We require that our patients be capable of transference. Victims of soul murder may have very little that is positive to transfer . . . . We may be able to understand a good deal of how such people become what they are, but interpreting our knowledge may be of little help to them" (1979, pp. 553–554).

The compression of identity, self-worth, punishment, trust, and survival into the destructive parent-child relationship deprives the survivor of positive mirroring, either from the primary parent or from important others and peers. Since the survivor presents a counterfeit identity to others, any positive mirroring is perceived as ill-founded. (If they really knew they'd hate me). Negative reactions, on the other hand, are accepted and amplified as genuine, especially from anyone with presumed knowledge and the parental power to penetrate the "as if" facade. Ordinary social support and professional attempts at reassurance are therefore not only poorly effective; they also carry the threat of alienation and punishment whenever relationships become close or important.

Individual therapy, by itself, tends to be frustrating at best and countertherapeutic at worst. Trust and capacity for positive transference can be built only over time and in conjunction with acceptance within a genuine peer group. The isolated, poorly disguised "monster" who is so distrustful and fearful of the image reflected by mainstream society discovers an unexpected acceptance and genuineness within the reflection of others who have shared the same stigmatizing experience. The others don't look like monsters and they don't seem to be repulsed by what they see in the newcomer. As the peer group makes it clear that nothing the newcomer can present is alien to the collective experience or capability, it becomes safe to drop the facade and look intently into a new mirror.

While the metaphor of the mirror is too superficial and specifically visual to describe fully the complex benefits of a specialized peer group, it is part of the language of both group members and specialists in object relations. Within the affinity and the warm acceptance of the specialized peer group, the stigmatized victim comes to "see" and feel that he or she is not uniquely cursed and that there is hope for genuine acceptance even without secrecy and self-deception. In addition, recognition that others are capable of surviving and of dealing directly with assaultive childhood experiences builds confidence that the evils of childhood can be confronted without humiliation or annihilation. Seeing others discuss and cope with child-assaultive experience without humiliation or punishment allows the individual to challenge the self-fulfilling prophecy that anyone who knows about these experiences would react with horror. Finally the group can use its collective, emerging self-esteem to encourage individuals to present themselves to the outer society without shame and without expectations of prejudice.

Rather than preparing patients for a group through individual counseling, group involvement should be used in most cases as the first resource for crisis intervention, with individual contact used as needed to coordinate overall treatment priorities and to deal with the consequences of the group experience. The initial use of a group helps to diffuse negative transference issues and to encourage a social model of resourcefulness rather than emphasizing dependency and possible regression within a more parental model of individual care. Intensive individual therapy, with deliberate exercises in regression and abreaction, and with controlled enhancement of parental transference and reparenting may be appropriate and necessary to repair the more seriously damaged survivors of soul murder. But such volatile and demanding techniques should be applied whenever possible on a foundation of preexisting peer group identity and resources. Many who are not at first capable of trust or effective transference develop or recover enough ego strength through peer group endorsement to take on the risk of intimacy in individual treatment and the challenge of finding a peer in the person of the psychotherapist.

The benefits of peer group interaction apply also to the professional who works with the group. The leveling effects of the group as well as the prevailing candor and comfort initiate the therapist into the inside world of victims and victimizers and provide the therapist with an increased capacity for empathy. With the help of the peer group, the therapist is enabled to take on the risk of intimacy in individual treatment and the challenge of finding a peer in the person of the assaulted child or the assaultive parent.

One of the great strengths of a specialty program for sexual assault is the inherent potential for grouping of clients according to peer experience. Adult survivors, assaultive parents, passively involved mates, adolescent offenders, and recent victims in preschool, latency age, early adolescent, and later adolescent groupings all seem to benefit from peer group contact and all seem to achieve more rapid and more effective recovery than could be expected from individual therapy alone.

**Self-Help.** A logical extension of the strengths of the peer group is the encouragement of self-help. Parents United, Inc., is a modified self-help program that developed in conjunction with the vanguard Child Sexual Abuse Treatment Project in Santa Clara County, California. Organized and incorporated by the parents themselves, Parents United uses both professonal and peer counselors who lead specialized groups (orientation, men, women, couples, and women assaulted as children) as well as combining all participants in an opening and closing social-organizational gathering. Chapters also support separate groups for the children (Daughters and Sons United) and organize teams for telephone hot line service, crisis outreach, shared residence (especially for fathers who agree to move away from home in deference to their children), agency outreach (advocating more effective policies in the justice system, better support for treatment programs, and so forth), and community education. Far from being counter-professional or self-serving, the combined strength, energy, and conscience of so many participants freeing themselves from entrapment and stigma serves to endorse the importance of professional skills and the need for treatment system involvement in child-protective and law enforcement activities.

Remarkably, when incestuous fathers and step-fathers are empowered as a group to work toward preventing sexual assault, they are the first to encourage firm control and limits, including criminal investigation and prosecution. The most effective deterrent to dismissed charges, adversary deadlocks, and child-witness humiliation is the power of a fathers' crisis intervention team to prevail on a peer to plead guilty or no contest and to accept compassionate sentencing and mandatory treatment rather than protesting his innocence.

The immediate support of peers around issues of disclosure, separation, and rejection provides near-perfect protection against despondency, depression, and suicide. Fathers treated with hospitalization not infrequently leave the hospital, only to commit suicide. Yet among thousands of families in California assisted by Parents United, not one father has been lost in this way. Clinical intervention alone cannot extend support into the lonely hours when a father may be overwhelmed by loss, guilt, and hopelessness. Empathic fathers who have overcome such an experience and who feel a missionary kinship with the newly discovered offender will stay up through the night to provide companionship throughout the crisis.

The leadership and interaction of various advocacy positions within the self-help programs helps to maintain internal balance and self-government without authoritarian demands or intervention from staff. Indignant, confident wives help strengthen those who would otherwise be hopelessly disillusioned or intimidated by their husband's behavior. Women in general support one another against inappropriate or premature reconciliation with their husbands, as well as resisting the prevailing expectation on the part of fathers that everyone should reward them with immediate expiation and loving reconciliation for their willingness to admit their fault (the same narcissistic insensitivity that insulates fathers from the feeling of their children protects them also from appropriate responsibility to their wives: "Why do you keep bringing it up and punishing me? I already said I was sorry. What more do you want from me?"). If husband and wife choose to reconcile, both may tend to defend against the impact of incest on their children, including a tendency to fault the child for reporting or for inviting "the incident" (ten years of ongoing rapacious, intimidating, and thoroughly obscene behavior can be trivialized and condensed into such a term). This tendency of parental adults to gloss over assaultive behavior is offset by the presence in the chapter of another adult presence: that of the woman assaulted as a child who attends for her own recovery. These women may vary in age from newly emancipated older teens to senior citizens. Their apparent pain and their newly discovered determination to set their emotional records straight allow no room for trivialization of children's feelings or scapegoating of the children with any responsibility that belongs to the parents.

The chemistry of the large group interaction also fuels work in specialty subgroup and individualized therapy. A mature survivor who is afraid to recognize anger toward her own father may be furious with another father she hears projecting blame on his child. Her passionate recognition that the child is blameless and unfairly treated can help her to respond to assurances in the survivors' group that she is now safe and secure enough to assign a similar blame and anger to her own father. And a father who is too rigidly defended to acknowledge his daughter's pain may be moved by the obvious, adult-authenticated distress expressed by the adult survivor to understand for the first time what his own daughter has experienced.

There are potential drawbacks, of course, to building self-help concepts into an integrated professional treatment system. Professionals may be distrustful or intimidated by the shift of power and responsibility to the patients. Therapists must be mature in their experience and professional identity to allow for such a diffusion of authority. Participation within the self-help style calls for informality and self-disclosure, which may be antithethical to the training and comfort of the professional. Again, a professional person must be quite secure to maintain balance in such an unaccustomed role.

At the same time the staff must remain vigilant to protect the program against manipulative members who pretend to positions of authority. Would-be peer counselors who seek power in controlling others' decisions are a fairly obvious hazard. Charismatic sociopaths are a more difficult problem. The self-help approach tends to be self-leveling and endorsing of mainstream values as long as the fathers are dedicated to recovering age appropriate sexual partners and as long as there has not been a lifetime rationalization of sexual intimidation. If a well-defended pedophile gains access to the group he may be all too quick to recite typical incestuous conflicts and to take advantage of the optimistic prognosis afforded to incest offenders. His long-practiced skills of ingratiation and reassurance will propel him to figurehead status as the leader and a perfect example of the kind of total recovery and trust the program has afforded. Unfortunately, public testimonials ring sour and the integrity of the program is threatened when the leader is found to be molesting children or using groups to expound his views on child love and consent.

The possible idiosyncrasies and excesses of self-help zealots should not deter program planners from initiating and supporting affiliated self-help programs. Most medical programs have little precedent for active interaction with self-help groups, so the initial steps may appear intimidating. Professional responsibility, licensure, quality of care, liability, confidentiality, record keeping, fees for services, and a host of other professional considerations seem to exclude self-help involvement. Yet the experience can pay unexpected dividends if the reluctance and red tape can be overcome.

The Family Support Program at the Neuropsychiatric Institute,

UCLA Center for the Health Sciences, is a good example of triumph over tradition. The program is a specialty child sexual abuse treatment project within the Psychiatric Clinic for Children, with full professional services as well as an active chapter of Parents United. The considerable difficulties of adapting university procedure to accommodate a self-help adjunct have faded in the light of the increased effectiveness, client enthusiasm, and community impact the Parents United component has contributed.

**Rage.** Victims of sexual assault and their adult counterparts are not just ordinary people, any more than they are morally defective or constitutionally inferior. Whatever diverse factors have combined to allow for the reality of sexual assault, there is a continuing legacy of hurt and anger. As long as the anger is turned inward and contained as self-hate, there may be little outward indication of danger to others. When the child grows up the anger may explode against the child or children in the next generation, as already described in the section on peer group contact. If the victim is male, he is more likely than the female to grow up expressing his anger through violence and criminal behavior, as well as in relatively nonviolent molestation of children. Both women and men who are not ordinarily violent may be subject to dissociative states of homicidal frenzy or of carefully premeditated assassination and mass murder. The multiple personalities and the encapsulated rage states that characterize normal accommodation to sexual assault are a poorly recognized source of substantial human suffering. Suffering spills from the reservoir of silent victims to their noncomplaining assaulted children and into the isolated, apparently wanton outbursts of violence against strangers.

Whatever their capacity for outward violence, the unhealed victims of assault feel threatened by a poorly harnessed core of destructive energy. They may be passive and nonassertive for the very fear that any expression of negative feelings will erupt into a chain reaction of cosmic intensity. They tend to conceptualize themselves as a fragile layer of skin containing an expansive nucleus of indescribable badness that would contaminate and destroy anything it touched. The victim will call that core shit, scum, slime or vomit, expressing obvious linkages to pregenital concepts of dirtiness, defiance, and badness. Sometimes there are direct associations to oral incorporation of semen or to anal penetration. Whatever the symbolic origins of the introject, it is endowed with demonic power in direct proportion to the outrageousness of the original assaults and in inverse proportion to the quality of maternal care and intervention experienced by the child. Because the introjected core is seen as so potentially destructive and because it is so charged with secrecy and self-blame, the victim has no permission for any reasonable discovery or outlet of the badness. Anything that scratches the surface is regarded as a threat, and any attempt to vent any of the pressure carries the imagined risk of loss of control and catastrophic explosion. As Shengold writes,

> The most difficult task for the analyst is dealing with the patient's transference and projection. These are people whose bad expectations are of almost delusional intensity and whose rage is at a cannibalistic pitch (threatening destruction of both self and parent images as the rage begins to be felt). Fear of his rage is the greatest burden to the patient. It takes skill and empathy to help the patient in his struggle to tolerate the terrible anger, and in some cases it turns out to be too much for him to bear. And if this continues to be so, the responsible knowledge that the rage is there (even if it cannot be felt fully) enables the patient to think about it and to use it as a warning signal; this can make emotional growth possible. (1979, p. 555)

The rage must be appreciated and respected by the therapist as well as the patient. Provocative challenges and unsupported probings for what may prove to be self-destructive or homicidal memories have no place in responsible treatment. Yet when rage comes up it should not be left unrecognized or hastily covered in fear. Direct exercises in the constructive use of anger are often helpful. Role-playing and even hypnotically abreactive excursions into the actual basis for the rage and the original pressure for self-scapegoating and helplessness can be therapeutic if conducted within an environment of responsible care and support. The therapist and the supportive peer group can assume a reparenting role to give adult endorsement and a kind of secondary mirroring to the experiences that seem so totally reprehensible and devastating when seen through the eyes of the child in the absence of a redeeming primary parent. (Throughout this discussion terms and concepts drawn from several theoretical perspectives have been mixed and applied to apparently incongruous levels of development. Since the sexual trauma occurs most often in latency years with a paternal figure, the emphasis on primary identity, basic trust, individuation and other pre-oedipal, maternal issues may appear paradoxical. It can only be assumed that the betrayal of the paternal relationship and the consequent alienation and abandonment of any hope for maternal acceptance leave the child faced with a sense of annihilation that is comparable to the hungers and fears of early infant individuation and separation. There seems to be at least a fragmented or partial regression to primitive issues of survival.)

When rage is recognized, defined, and experientially rechanneled from the self and the concept of the bad child to a controlled focus on actually traumatic circumstances and actually hurtful caregivers, the patient experiences not explosion and punitive annihilation but an unaccustomed sense of release and a capacity for self-control. Associated symptoms of somatic pain, neuraesthenia, depression, and dissociative states tend to resolve with the reassignment of responsibility and anger. Conflicting personalities can be reconciled, and hallucinations, childlike fantasy states, and ideas of reference can disappear. An individual whose thinking is characterized by grandiosity, paranoia, magical thinking, and self-mutilating punishment can mature into one with realistic self-acceptance and autonomy, all with the careful resolution of assaultive conflicts within an atmosphere of responsible reparenting.

Such claims may in themselves sound grandiose and fantastic. It should be remembered that while victims of assaultive atrocities may have spectacular conflicts and graphic symptoms, they are in fact survivors who have learned to protect themselves and to adapt to unbearable hazards. Their spectacular powers for recovery should be no less surprising than their remarkable feats of survival (Reagor, personal communication).

Techniques of reparenting and optimal environments for support are still experimental, controversial, and anything but consistent, ranging from hospital programs to weekend marathons. The potentials and the limits for the most severely damaged survivors are not fully explored. There is a growing recognition that the large middle group of moderately symptomatic survivors, including most sexually assaultive parents, can make remarkable readjustments and can achieve substantial recovery within programs incorporating traditional treatment skills combined with new appreciation of child-assaultive dynamics and peer group support.

**Touch.** There has been an empirical observation among workers in child abuse programs that adult clients turn to one another and to the staff for hugging as they resolve the conflicts of their own childhood and as they seek reassurance and permission as adults to confront their own fears and discomforts. Staff members have also learned that embraces can be an appropriate celebration of progress and a refreshing expression of endorsement and caring. Programs that develop comfort in physical contact and affectional reinforcement seem to achieve better results with less attrition of clients and staff than programs that maintain more traditional distance and "adult" communication.

Child-damaged and child-damaging clients need something more meaningful than "adult" communication if they are going to learn to find trust in human contact. The vocabulary of reparenting, as with any parenting, includes the nonverbal language of touch.

The child who has enough noncontingent caring and unrestricted holding in the first few years of life learns to spend increasing periods of time apart from physical contact as long as there remains full confidence that holding is never far away. With increasing sensory and cognitive development, the child learns to respond to smiles, words, material rewards, and complex behavioral conditioning for approval, in addition to maintaining pleasure in being held. Somewhere around school age for boys, and only a few years later for girls, we begin to teach children that holding is for babies and that "growing up" requires taking pride in stoicism and self-reliance. Being held, like crying, thumb-sucking, fuzzy blankets, and teddy bears, is put aside as an unacceptable residue of childhood. After a certain age, people can be held only in the midst of pain, excitement, or, eventually, sexual arousal.

What is forgotten in this progression from closeness to distance, somatosensory to special senses, and concrete to abstract is that skin contact, warmth, and enfoldment constitute the basic human communication and the prototypic model for acceptance, affection, and reassurance. It is not so much that holding is "babyish" as that adult society tends to be "adultish"; that is, adults become progressively alienated, defensive, and distrustful of dependency, intimacy, tenderness, and affectionate expression as they communicate with increasing numbers of abstractly related individuals. Rather than preserving and celebrating our small nucleus of touchworthy intimates, adults seem to identify with the more alien society and to rely on abstract communication even within their most intimate and cherished circle of friends.

Some anthropologists and many students of family behavior believe that older children and adults develop a "skin hunger," which leaves individuals feeling vaguely unappreciated and unfulfilled and which can lead to reactive touching, such as tickling, wrestling, tussling, and fighting, as well as premature and promiscuous sexual activity.

Simon (1976) writes about this hunger for human contact as well as of the therapeutic benefits of compassionate contact. He defines the benefits of holding as "the simple but potent combination of touch itself and the human affirmation it delivers in a direct, unmistakable, nonverbal way . . . . Beyond all this, it establishes in the very young the building material for better communication in all human relationships . . . . It results in people who are more open to the experience of life itself—people who feel secure enough to ask for what they want and need and who are generous enough to give others what they want in return" (1976, p. 101).

Simon cites the primate research of Fassey and of the Harlows, as well as the human development observations of Spitz, to illustrate what should be obvious to any observant human being: physical contact is indispensable for social development and emotional survival.

Although Simon's prescription that every individual should have no fewer than three family hugs a day may seem humorous, it seems unquestionable that people who were assaulted as children and those who treat children abusively need permission and opportunity for noncontingent holding. For them, touching has become painful and possessive as often as it is protective, and caring has been dispensed only as a reward for performance or as a respite after an exhausting cycle of assault. The sexually assaulted child has a special confusion about the meaning of touch, most often concluding that she or he is not worthy of touching apart from the painful ambivalence of being possessed by a parent.

For the patient deprived of basic trust and filled with self-hate and destructive rage, no real contact is possible short of an outstretched hand or an embrace. Smiles, words, and reassurances will not offset the individual's expectation of rejection and punishment. Any physical distance in the face of verbal reassurances only affirms the conviction that the patient is in fact untouchable: too filthy, ugly, and dangerous to touch.

On the other hand, the therapist's capacity to feel and express genuine affection (token gestures are worse than nothing) through a solid hug can be redeeming and uniquely nourishing. As a patient wrote to her therapist in an incest survivor's group:

Your hugs are warm: When you hold me I feel warm and good; most importantly warm.

Your hugs are caring: They prove a person is cared for. Who can willingly hold someone they dislike or hate?

Your hugs are respectful: They start and stop on time, allowing respect for someone's choice. When you hold me I feel I have the right to say what happens to my body. Not duty bound or forced. I can say No.

Your hugs are deeply satisfying: When you hold me the pain in my chest stops and the longing is fed. They last long enough to fill the whole with your goodness.

Your hugs are full: Arms surrounding completely and just tight enough to keep the goodness in and keep it from escaping. Close enough to really feel cared for.

Your hugs are encouraging: They make me feel that the dirt doesn't show and can't be felt perhaps there is a slight doubt that it exists.

Your hugs are everything a hug should be.

Thank you for your hugs.

For the child damaged during those years when touching was the only real meaningful contact, therapists cannot offer only abstract, adult-loaded, verbal signals of acceptance and approval. If the only therapeutic support available comes from someone who must maintain a formal separation and an objective distance from the patient, it is better that the realities of incestuous touching be left buried and unexplored.

The office practitioner in individual therapy is not in a comfortable setting to provide holding, especially with adult patients of the opposite sex or wherever there is a risk of eroticized or regressive transference. Group settings are likely to be more comforting to both patient and therapist, but the psychotherapist may still prefer to maintain a more traditional and more objective distance. In any case, when the therapist does not provide the vital endorsement of holding, it is all the more important to endorse affectionate contact within an ancillary peer group. The therapist who expects the sexually assaulted child or adult patient to confine all therapeutic communication within an individual, abstract relationship, and who would reprimand the patient for "acting out" or "diluting the transference" by seeking ancillary caring and endorsement, is guilty of a form of child neglect only slightly less damaging than the original assaults.

## CONCLUSIONS

Any subject as diverse and controversial as child sexual assault can be surveyed only superficially in one brief chapter. Rather than offering the recapitulation of any specific program model or giving limited directions for complicated techniques of therapy, the author's purpose was to stress underlying principles and goals.

It should be understood emphatically that recognition and the capacity for belief are the primary requisites for any effective response. Physicians must challenge their personal adult denial and theoretical objections if they are to accomplish genuine objectivity and gain the capacity for subjective advocacy.

Reception room and emergency room recognition can be enhanced by improved diagnostic skills and protocols as noted in this chapter. Effective intervention requires also the documentation of behavioral and physical evidence as well as the willingness to report suspected assault and to enter actively into both juvenile and criminal court procedures.

Follow-up support and optimum resolution of potential emotional consequences of child sexual assault require services not ordinarily available within pediatric or psychiatric centers. A specialized, integrated program for victims and their families can be established within a medical setting if adjustments can be made for the necessary paraprofessional, self-help and community interagency networks required.

If development of a specialty program is not practical within existing clinical resources, it is all the more important to participate in community councils on child assault to encourage and support development of a free-standing sexual abuse treatment center.

Service elements and treatment philosophies for such a center are described. These elements are presented as a preliminary guide for program design and as an invitation to understand and to support such unfamiliar elements as reparenting therapies, peer group techniques, self-help programs, and compassionate holding.

This chapter includes treatment strategies for parents and for adult survivors of childhood sexual assault as well as for child victims. Consideration of adult services and the involvement with the intergenerational cycle of child assault establishes a supportive context for the immediate intervention and treatment of the child victim.

Aside from the introductory remarks concerning male victims of chronic sexual offenders, there is little reference to the treatment needs of sexually assaulted boys. While many boys and their parents seem to respond well to the general sexual assault treatment program described here, there is an obvious need for better case finding and additional clinical experience with male victims.

There is also a pressing need for better recognition and diagnostic separation of chronic pedophiles from the more treatable incest offenders. Until more sensitive clinical measures can be devised, psychiatrists and other physicians are ill-prepared to define for the public or for the courts any reliably predictive guidelines for prognosis and potential treatment of sexual offenders against children.

Although much remains to be learned, any professional participating in the recognition and reparenting of a sexually assaulted child should experience the opportunity to explore the last frontier of child assault. The last frontier offers also a new threshold for understanding, treating, and preventing a syndrome of disturbed behavior and mental illness previously considered limited to adults.

*Chapter 3*

# Assault Against Children: The Law and Its Enforcement

## *Richard D. Willey*

When babies cry, they tell the world that they are hungry, wet, tired, or just bored. Of course, it is natural for babies to cry.

Sometimes, however, a baby or an older child's crying takes on a sinister significance. Deliberately and willfully, bones are broken; burns are inflicted by scalding water, irons, flames, or lighted cigarettes; blood vessels, intestines, livers, and spleens are ruptured by kicks and blows; skin is flayed and mangled by whippings; heads are smashed and cracked open; little bodies are starved to sickness and death. For all these things, too, a child cries.

(Van de Kamp, 1983, p. 4)

## THE ROLE OF LAW ENFORCEMENT

Does law enforcement have a legitimate role in the multifaceted problem of child assault? Are we dealing with an area of criminal conduct or is child assault the overt and observable manifestation of a totally dysfunctional family unit which is more appropriately the realm of the therapist?

These, as well as innumerable other questions, have been vigorously debated among professionals in the field of child assault since Kempe and colleagues (1962) first coined the phrase, the "battered child syndrome."

This chapter presents one police officer's perceptions of the problem of child assault and why many of us feel that it is imperative that law enforcement maintain an active role in the investigation and disposition of child assault cases.

## OPERATIONAL DEFINITION: WHAT IS CHILD ASSAULT?

The definitions of child assault are as numerous and varied as the dynamics of the problem itself (Paulson and Blake, 1969; see also Chapter 1). For the purpose of this chapter child assault is defined as follows: "Any act of omission or commission that endangers or impairs a child's physical or emotional health and development" (California Commission on Peace Officer Standards and Training, 1980).

This is an admittedly broad definition but it is so dictated by the variations in the acts themselves, as well as the various degrees of social acceptability encountered within the cultural, ethnic, racial, and economic subgroupings that compose the total of our society (International Association of Chiefs of Police, 1977).

## LAW ENFORCEMENT: PROACTIVE VERSUS REACTIVE

The basic underlying goal of all law enforcement oriented activity is the protection of life and property (Los Angeles County Sheriff's Department, 1981). Should the chronological age of an individual be the determinate factor in who is protected and who is not, or should it be a combination of chronological age and the relationship of the perpetrator to the victim that decides the level of protection an individual is afforded?

> Although the right of parents to control and raise their own children is accepted as a fundamental right in our society, intervention is justified by a paramount social interest—the safety of the child. The Fourteenth Amendment of the United States Constitution states that everyone has equal protection under the law.
>
> (Van de Kamp, 1983, p. 5)

In addition to the United States Constitution, the courts in California, recognizing the necessity for law enforcement's involvement in the field of child assault and the potential gravity of the situation, have granted considerable latitude in the interpretation and application of both statutory and case law as they apply to child assault cases.

This latitude is best exemplified in the area of warrantless entries and arrest (People vs. Smith, 7 Cal.3d 282, 285–287; People vs. Roman, 256 Cal.App.2d 265,260) and warrantless entries based on hearsay evidence:

> The walls of privacy and domestic security may protect some crimes from

observation and from prevention by all who are unarmed with a warrant or probable cause for arrest, or who, even when so armed, failed to demand admittance and to explain the purpose for which entry is sought. But the rights of privacy and domestic security extend no impenetrable protective cloak against the prevention of a felonious assault upon a helpless victim whose right to physical and mental integrity outweighs the right of the aggressor to remain secure in his domestic sanctuary when used for such a purpose.

(People vs. Brown, 12 Cal.App.3d 600, 605)

In addition to the legal mandates just discussed, law enforcement also has a vested interest in the victims of child assault and their future potential impact on society.

Several recent studies have indicated a close relationship between early childhood experiences and a propensity toward adult violence (Leftkowitz, Eron, Walter, and Hensmann, 1977; McCord, 1979), an area of obvious concern to all law enforcement agencies.

The most graphic study, however, was presented at the Western Psychological Association Convention by Maurer, of End Violence Against the Next Generation, Inc. This study indicates that a high positive relationship exists between child assault, juvenile delinquency, and violent adult behavior (Maurer, 1976). While conceding that the table given indicates only a statistical relationship, Maurer is of the opinion that the findings strongly suggest the presence of a cause and effect relationship that should be pursued in further study (Table 3–1).

Legal mandates and generally applied research are not, however, the only reasons for law enforcement's involvement in the field. The logical and practical considerations of this involvement must also be addressed.

The police are the only twenty-four hour a day field service community agency with investigatory and arrest authority. By the nature of their daily work, their role in the community, and their powers, the police are in an almost ideal position to discover child abuse. More child abuse cases naturally come to their attention than to that of any other agency. They also have the perceived authority and status which induces cooperation. Compared to the personnel of other agencies such as social welfare workers, they are better trained to demand respect for constitutional rights and to handle cases through the process of the law. No other existing agency combines such training and investigative capability with the powers of law enforcement.

Additionally, while the great majority of child abuse cases may properly be viewed as presenting psychological rather than criminal problems, a properly trained police force, with carefully selected personnel and considerable discretion, might still beneficially enter these cases. Furthermore, in some cases the possibility of a criminal charge, which is suggested by police involvement, may actually provide the abuser with the necessary stimulus to change behavior or to seek help.

(Northern California Criminal Justice Training and Educational System, 1978, p. 76)

TABLE 3-1. Aftermath of Physical Punishment—Ages 1 to 10*

| | (1) | (2) | (3) | (4) | (5) |
|---|---|---|---|---|---|
| Violent inmates (San Quentin) | 0 | 0 | 0 | 0 | 100% |
| Juvenile Delinquents | 0 | 2% | 3% | 31% | 64% |
| High School Drop-outs | 0 | 7% | 23% | 69% | 0 |
| College Freshmen | 2% | 23% | 40% | 33% | 0 |
| Professionals | 5% | 40% | 36% | 17% | 0 |

(1) Never.

(2) Rare.

(3) Moderate. Includes open-hand slaps and spanks.

(4) Severe. Use of an instrument such as a belt, paddle, hairbrush.

(5) Extreme. Needing medical attention or hospitalization.

* These figures were the result of self-reports to 200 psychologists at the 1975 CSPA/CASPP Convention by 372 college freshman at University of California, Davis, and California State University, Fresno. The high school drop-outs were actually slow tract underachievers reading at a fourth to fifth grade level, whereas data on delinquents were secured by Ralph Welsh, Ph.D., from Bridgeport, Connecticut. Prisoner information was supplied by Hobert Banks.

# TOWARD A MORE PROFESSIONAL TOMORROW

Although it is suggested that not every law enforcement agency has either the necessary resources or the need to establish a separate, specialized unit to handle the investigation of child assault cases, it is strongly recommended that consideration be given to either establishing such a unit, where the resources are available, or assigning specific individuals within an existing juvenile unit to handle the investigation of all child assault cases.

Recognizing the need for a specialized unit composed of carefully selected and highly trained personnel, the Los Angeles County Sheriff's Department in 1975 established a centralized Child Abuse Detail. This Detail, which currently consists of one lieutenant, three sergeants, and 19 investigators, is charged with the investigation and case disposition of all physical and familial sexual child assault cases occurring within the Sheriff's jurisdiction, an area encompassing more than 3,000 square miles and serving a population of approximately two million citizens.

In 1983 the Los Angeles County Sheriff's Department Child Abuse Detail received 3,210 referrals resulting in 1,781 active cases. The vast majority of these referrals came directly from daily contacts with medical, educational, and social science professionals in the community. This high number of referrals is directly attributable to two main factors—first, the California Mandatory Child Abuse Reporting Law, and second, the professional credibility and case disposition policies that have been established within this Detail.

From its outset, the basic goal of the Child Abuse Detail has been and will continue to be the protection and best interest of the child and his or her siblings. The protection of the child, however, does not mean merely removing the child from that specific environment. Nevertheless, removal is generally chosen pending a thorough investigation of the incident.

In support of this course of action, Dr. James Apthorp, who heads the Child Abuse Detail at Children's Hospital in Los Angeles, has this advice for the patrol officer:

> A child does not have to have serious, life threatening injuries to be in danger. A few minor bruises that are suspicious by their pattern should indicate to you that the child may be in as much jeopardy as if he were knocked unconscious. If you can establish the trauma, you can bet that if the child stays in the environment there's a chance he may even get killed the next time around.
> (Northern California Criminal Justice Training and Educational System, 1978)

This view, which is appropriate advice for any caring citizen, was echoed by the Court in People vs. Roman: "In cases of suspected child beating, we prefer the police to consider any apparent injuries as serious ones until they have satisfied themselves to the contrary" (People vs. Roman, 256 Cal.App.2d 265, 260).

A number of factors, however, must be taken into consideration in the determination of actual child assault cases and case disposition. The actual mechanics of an effective investigation have been sufficiently documented in other works (see References). Some of the most important factors include the answers to questions such as the following:

- Is this an isolated incident or is there a history of abuse or neglect or family disturbances?
- How was the incident reported? Who reported it, if known?
- What is the emotional and mental attitude of the parents?
- What is the general condition of the home?

• Do the nature and severity of injuries indicate assault or neglect?

• What is the general behavior of parents? Are their explanations of the child's injuries unreasonable? Do they place the blame vehemently upon one another? Are they apathetic or insensitive to the child's condition?

The investigating officer will decide whether to take the child into protective custody, to arrest the parents, to seek the filing of criminal charges, or to refer the case to Probation, Welfare, Social Services, Child Protective Services, or another appropriate agency. The disposition is often made after consultation with representatives of other disciplines (California Commission on Peace Officer Standards and Training, 1980, p. 15).

It has, however, been this Detail's experience that the vast majority of cases—78 per cent in 1983—do not warrant criminal prosecution. It is our contention that by utilizing the available public and private community based support systems the needs of both the child and the family, in most instances, may be better served.

By following this basic philosophy several benefits are realized:

• Parents are placed on notice that any repeat conduct will be pursued through the criminal courts.

• The family unit is kept intact and access to community based resources is provided, or mandated, via the Dependency Court.

• All pertinent data relating to the case are entered into the State Child Abuse Register for future tracking.

• Most importantly, a resistance to reporting incidents of suspected assault by other professionals in the field is drastically reduced.

• As a result of reduced resistance, incidents are being reported at a much earlier stage, thereby allowing more flexibility in case dispositions.

In the opinion of this writer, there are four basic ingredients to the successful handling of child assault cases:

1. the establishment of a centralized unit, or specified individuals, to handle the investigation and case disposition of all child assault cases.

2. the establishment and maintenance of lines of communication and mutual cooperation among all agencies concerned with child assault in both the public and private sectors.

3. intervention at the earliest possible point in time.

4. the establishment of policy which allows maximum flexibility and latitude in case dispositions.

With these four features, today's law enforcement agencies can and will have taken large strides toward eliminating much of the criticism which has been aimed at them in the past.

As Paulson stated:

A close working liaison between community based treatment and intervention programs, law enforcement agencies, and elements of the judicial system such as Juvenile Court, Family Relations Court, and the Superior Court is imperative. Only through effective liaison can the needs of abused children and their families be met. Basic to any court justice is recognition of the rights of every citizen, including the abused child. Such rights must be defined clearly not only for the protection of those children who have already experienced the trauma of psychological and physical abuse and neglect, but for those potential victims who in the future will be the offspring of unidentified, high-risk parents.

(Paulson, 1975, p. 29)

# DISCRETIONARY CASE DISPOSITIONS

The following case studies, taken from the files of the Los Angeles County Sheriff's Department Child Abuse Detail, are offered as a representation of the latitude available to investigators in the disposition of child assault cases.

In each of these cases the resulting disposition, which was reached after consultation with other disciplines in the field, illustrates an accommodation reaching an equitable balance in the best interests of the child, family, and society in general.

The names have been changed to protect the identities of the parties involved; however, the relevant facts and the chronological order of events are accurate.

These are not atypical cases, but exemplify the wide spectrum of cases with which law enforcement agencies and personnel must cope.

## Case Study: Judy K.

| | | |
|---|---|---|
| *Child:* | Judy K. | Age: 14 years<br>Education: 8th grade |
| *Mother:* | Mary S. | Age: 35 years<br>Education: 10th grade |
| | Marital Status:<br>Divorced | |
| | Occupation:<br>Cocktail Waitress | |

| *Siblings:* | Joan K. | Age 16 years |
|---|---|---|
| | | Education: 10th grade |
| | Bobby K. | Age 12 years |
| | | Education: 7th grade |
| | James S. | Age 5 years |
| | | Not in school |
| | Michael S. | Age: 3 years |
| | | Not in school |
| | Joe S. | Age: 1 year |
| | | Not in school |
| | Sam S. | Age: 2 months |
| | | Not in school |

*Source of Referral:*    Intermediate School

For the past year Mrs. Mary S. and her seven children had resided in a two bedroom quadruplex in the suburbs of Los Angeles. In order to obtain the home, which was all that she could afford on her income, Mrs. S. had lied to the landlord about the actual number of children she had. This made it necessary to keep the three younger children inside the house most of the time.

Mrs. S. was employed as a waitress at a local bar from 4:00 PM to 2:00 AM which necessitated that the older children care for the younger children not only during Mary's working hours, but also periodically during the day while the mother slept, forcing the older children, at times, into the parental role. As a result of this situation the older children's school attendance and grades were poor, and it was virtually impossible for them to enter into, much less maintain, any friendships or social lives of their own.

At approximately 7:30 PM Tuesday evening, Mrs. S.'s only night off, the baby, who was teething, was fussy and crying as he had been for most of the past week. Mrs. S. instructed Judy to give Sam some baby aspirin and put him to bed. Judy, however, was unable to locate the aspirin. Mrs. S. then became outraged and began screaming at Judy and beating her with a plastic curtain rod. Judy was struck numerous times on the back, legs, and arms, causing a number of large red welts. Mrs. S. then grabbed Judy by the hair and pulled her into the bathroom and showed her the aspirin in a bathroom drawer.

The following day Judy's teacher, noticing some of the welts, questioned Judy about their cause. Judy was then sent to the nurse's office and both the Department of Social Services and law enforcement officers were notified. The responding investigator interviewed both

Judy and Bobby, who was also at school that day. These interviews revealed a long series of physical beatings and verbal abuse directed at Joan, Judy, and Bobby. The younger children, however, were rarely if ever disciplined in any manner. All of the older children agreed that their mother "loses her temper and doesn't know when to stop."

Bobby, who showed evidence of an earlier beating, was initially very reluctant to discuss his home situation, relating that his mother "only beats me when I've done something wrong."

As a result of these interviews, and a subsequent interview with Joan, all three older children were placed in protective custody pending a thorough investigation of the case. Interviews with and examinations of James, Michael, Joe, and Sam revealed no indication whatsoever that they were assaulted. Consequently, they were allowed to remain in the home.

On Thursday morning an interview was conducted with Mrs. S. During the course of this interview, she readily admitted that she lost her temper with the older children because "they just push me too far." Nevertheless, in her opinion, she had never been abusive to any of her children. Mrs. S. found her life and children "very frustrating," stating that she just could not continue to cope with things the way they were.

Based upon all of the facts and circumstances surrounding this case it was the investigator's opinion that the interests of the family would be best served via the Juvenile Court and the support systems available through the Department of Social Services. No criminal action was sought in this matter and, following the Juvenile Court proceedings, all of the children were returned home with follow-up case work by the Department of Social Services.

## Case Study: Patty L.

| | | |
|---|---|---|
| *Child:* | Patty L. | Age: 16 years |
| | | Education: 11th grade |
| *Stepfather:* | John M. | Age: 34 years |
| | Employed | Education: High School |
| *Mother:* | Lydia M. | Age: 32 years |
| | Employed | Education: High School |
| *Source of* | | |
| *Referral:* | School Counselor | |

Patty L. had been molested for as long as she could remember. At first her stepfather would only fondle her genital area but after a period of time he began to insert his fingers. When Patty was about 12 years of age, her stepfather began having sexual intercourse with her on a regular basis.

When Patty was 13 years old she became pregnant with her stepfather's child. She refused to tell her mother who the father of the child was, fearing it would "destroy her family." Patty had cooperated in the relationship because she "felt sorry for him," since he had both just lost his own parents and claimed that her mother could not satisfy him sexually.

It was not until Patty was 15 years old that she finally decided to confide in her mother. When confronted with the accusations, John M. readily admitted that he was having relations with Patty and promised to seek therapy for his problem. John, however, failed to follow through with his commitment.

In June, following Patty's sixteenth birthday, she confided in a school counselor, who convinced her that reporting the relationship to the authorities would be the best course of action.

Investigative interviews were conducted with both Patty and her mother, which confirmed Patty's statements to her counselor. That afternoon John M. was interviewed. John readily admitted to having a long-term relationship with his stepdaughter and also confirmed all of Patty's statements. John related that he was "glad the situation was now in the open" as he did not want to "hurt" his family but didn't know how to deal with what had occurred.

As a result of this investigation John M. was arrested and pleaded guilty to one count of "crimes against children." John was placed on five years' active probation and ordered into a court approved therapy program aimed toward family reunification.

## Case Study: Cindy M.

|  |  |  |
|---|---|---|
| *Child:* | Cindy M. | Age: 8 years |
|  |  | Not in school |
| *Father:* | George M. | Age: 36 years |
|  | Unemployed | Education: Unknown |
|  |  | Extensive criminal background, including numerous arrests for narcotics and fraud |

*Mother:*  Carol M.  Age: 32 years
Whereabouts unknown

*Source of
Referral:*  Neighbor

Cindy M. first came to our attention as a result of a "found child" call. A neighbor found Cindy wandering in her backyard and, when told that she was lost, called her local Sheriff's Station for Assistance. Cindy told the responding deputy that she had become separated from her father while at a store, and was attempting to find her way home when she became lost.

The officer placed Cindy in his patrol car and for approximately ten minutes drove her around the neighborhood attempting to locate her home. Cindy then began crying, telling the officer that she had lied to him and begging him not to beat or burn her. After reassuring Cindy that nothing bad was going to happen to her, she confided in the officer how her father had repeatedly beaten her and burned her with a fireplace poker, for any minor behavioral infractions. Furthermore, Cindy related that her father broke her teeth and usually locked her in a closet whenever he left home. However, on this day, he forgot to lock the door.

Cindy had never attended school, her father persuading her that "the school won't take me with all the scars and burns on my body."

At the officer's prompting, Cindy then took him to her home to show him the closet where she was kept as well as the fireplace poker and other items her father used on her. At home Cindy showed him the closet, which contained only a naked electric light hanging from the ceiling, a metal bedpan, and two workbooks, which her father had purchased so that she could educate herself.

Cindy then showed the officer the fireplace poker, stating that her father "ties me up with rope and then heats the poker on the stove and burns me all over my body."

Until this point the officer had no idea of the extent of Cindy's injuries, because it was during the winter months and Cindy was clothed in a long-sleeved sweater and wore pants. At this time she showed the officer her upper torso, which was covered with a mess of new and old burn marks.

Cindy was then transported to the hospital, where a thorough examination revealed the total extent of her injuries. This examination showed extensive first and second degree burn damage to her entire pelvic area, abdomen, rectum, upper legs, hands, and left upper arm. In the examining doctor's opinion, the damage to Cindy's left hand was so extensive that "even with plastic surgery it is possible she will never grip with her left hand again."

In addition to the burn damage, Cindy had sustained an old fracture to her right leg and had lost several of her permanent front teeth as a result of beatings. Cindy was hospitalized for her injuries and an immediate police hold was placed on her.

Subsequent interviews with the child abuse investigators revealed that, in addition to the physical abuse, which had been continuous for the past two years, Cindy was also subjected to nearly every form of sexual abuse imaginable.

At approximately 8:00 PM, George M. returned home and was arrested by deputies who had had the house under surveillance since that afternoon. The following day George M. was interviewed concerning the circumstances surrounding his daughter's injuries. Initially, George maintained that Cindy's injuries were self-inflicted and resulted from her playing with matches and starting fires. George denied ever having locked Cindy in the closet or ever having had any sexual contact with her whatsoever.

In follow-up interviews, however, George did admit that he once "pushed her on a fire that she started in her bedroom to punish her," and that he had touched her with the poker but that it had not been hot enough to burn her. When questioned about the massive burn damage, in varying degrees of healing, as well as the allegations of sexual abuse, George responded by asking, "What kind of an animal do you think I am?"

This case was presented to the District Attorney, who filed 14 felony counts against George M. Following a 15 day trial in Superior Court, George M. was found guilty of ten felony counts and was sentenced to 17 years in the State Prison, a term which he is currently serving. Cindy M. was placed at the Village of CHILDHELP, U.S.A.

## REVIEW OF THE CASE DISPOSITIONS

In each of these cases, even though vigorous criminal prosecution was possible, the involved investigators followed a course of action which they deemed to be most appropriate and in the best interests of the child and other parties involved.

In the case of Judy K., the entire family unit was in need of support services. As a result of the Juvenile Court proceedings the family was networked into a community based support program that not only is helping to meet the needs of this family but also is assisting Mrs. S.

in learning to cope in alternative ways with the daily frustration she encounters.

Patty L. and John M., on the other hand, found themselves in a situation from which they could not extricate themselves. Patty, victimized by her stepfather, found no support from her mother. John, following a confrontation with his wife, had little if any need either to address or to alter the situation, even though he regretted being a party to it.

Through the Juvenile and Criminal Court process both Patty and John are now actively involved in a therapeutic program aimed at reunifying this family. Based upon John's failure to meet past commitments, had it not been for the Court's action and the threat of five years in State Prison if he failed to comply with the conditions of his probation, it is unlikely that he would ever have voluntarily entered into any type of treatment program.

Cindy and George M.'s case, however, presents a totally different set of dynamics. It was only through the total separation of father and daughter that Cindy's safety could be assured and, for that matter, her life protected. George M., who was nearly lacking in socially redeeming graces, received a comparatively light sentence considering the fact that Cindy must live and learn to cope with the results of his barbarism for the rest of her life.

## CHILD ABUSE AND THE LAW

Without the active support of the state legislature, neither law enforcement agencies nor the Department of Social Services, the courts, or other organizations can adequately address the problem of child abuse and neglect.

Recognizing this fact, the California state legislature drafted what many see as a model Child Abuse Reporting Law. These sections, the full text of which may be obtained by writing to the office of the Attorney General of the State of California, Sacramento, were signed into law by the Governor, and became effective January 1, 1980.

The following excerpts and summaries of the statute are quoted from the California Child Abuse Prevention Handbook (Van de Kamp, 1983):

## Reporting Child Abuse

While everyone should report suspected child abuse and neglect, Article 2.5

of the Penal Code provides that it is a crime for certain professionals and laypersons who have a special working relationship or contact with children not to report suspected abuse to the proper authorities.

Any child care custodian, medical practitioner, nonmedical practitioner, or employee of a child protective agency who has knowledge of or observes a child in his or her professional capacity or within the scope of his or her employment, whom he or she knows or reasonably suspects has been the victim of child abuse, shall report the known or suspected instance of child abuse to a child protective agency immediately or as soon as practically possible by telephone, and shall prepare and send a written report thereof within 36 hours of receiving the information concerning the incident. For the purposes of this article, "reasonable suspicion" means that it is objectively reasonable for a person to entertain such a suspicion, based upon facts that could cause a reasonable person in a like position, drawing when appropriate on his or her training and experience, to suspect child abuse. (Penal Code Section 11166)

Failure to report by telephone and in writing within 36 hours is a misdemeanor punishable by six months in jail or a $500 fine, or both. (For those required to report who do not do so, there may also be civil liabilities . . . ). Basically, this penalty ensures that those required to do so will report all suspected incidents of child abuse immediately to a child protective agency (the local police authority, sheriff's department, juvenile probation department or the county welfare department).

Those required to report should be aware that mere reporting does not always mean that a civil or criminal proceeding will be initiated. However, all reports are investigated.

Those agencies to whom reports are made are obligated to follow procedures in the reporting law which ensure that all reports of suspected abuse or severe neglect reach the Department of Justice statewide central index.

Not all counties are alike in their make-up, size, etc. Therefore, it should be noted that there will be some differences in how each county implements the reporting and handling of child abuse and neglect cases.

It is important to note that reporting under the law is an individual statutory responsibility, and that no one should in any way interfere with an individual's legal obligation to report. Additionally, no individual required to report is relieved of his or her obligation by depending on another person or a supervisor to report the suspected incident.

Those professionals required to report by Penal Code Sections 11165 and 11166 are:

• "Child care custodian" means a teacher, administrative officer, supervisor of child welfare and attendance, or certificated pupil personnel employee of any public or private school; an administrator of a public or private day camp; a licensed day care worker; an administrator of a community care facility licensed to care for children; Head Start teacher, licensing worker, or licensing evaluator; public assistance worker, employee of a child care institution including, but not limited to, foster parents, group home personnel of residential care facilities; a social worker or a probation officer, as well as others.

• "Medical practitioner" means a physician and surgeon, psychiatrist, psychologist, dentist, resident, intern, podiatrist, chiropractor, licensed nurse, dental hygienist, or any other person who is currently licensed under Division 2 . . . of the California Business and Professions Code. Physician and psychotherapist privileges are inapplicable. The doctor or psychotherapist must file a report as mandated even if the patient does not want him to. For example, if a patient tells a doctor or psychotherapist that his or her spouse is abusing their child, but the patient would like this fact to be kept in strict confidence because he or she does not want the spouse arrested, the abuse must be reported in any event. The same is true if a child patient makes a statement about abuse of a sibling or of himself or of herself.

• "Nonmedical practitioner" means a state or county public health employee who treats a minor for venereal disease or any other condition; a coroner; a paramedic; a marriage, family, or child counselor; a religious practitioner who diagnoses, examines, or treats children.

• "Child protective agencies" are police or sheriffs' departments, county probation departments, and county welfare departments.

• "Commercial film and photographic print processors" means any person who develops exposed photographic film into negatives, slides, or prints or who makes prints from negatives or slides, for compensation. The term includes any employee of such a person; it does not include a person who develops film or makes prints for a public agency.

Persons required to report are not liable either in civil damages or for criminal prosecution as a result of making a report. Other persons are not liable either civilly or criminally, unless it can be proved that a false report was made and that the person knew or should have known that the report was false.

When making suspected child abuse reports, the following information is to be provided:

• name of the child;
• whereabouts of the child;
• character and extent of injuries–or molestation, and any other information which led the person to suspect child abuse;
• age of child; and
• address of the child and parents.

Additionally, as authorized by law . . . the Attorney General has adopted a special, uniform reporting form entitled "Medical Report—Suspected Child Abuse," which medical personnel are required by law to complete, even without the consent of the child's parent or caregiver.

This reporting form was designed to elicit a sufficient amount of data concerning suspected child abuse, but at the same time not to be unduly burdensome to the reporting medical personnel, thereby discouraging its use. The form is also designed to be educational for medical personnel who come in contact with possible child abuse. The form is printed by the state government, and copies are available through county welfare departments and law enforcement agencies.

# What Happens to the Reports?

Reports are investigated by either the local law enforcement agency or the county children's protective services agency assigned to handle dependency cases (the welfare department or juvenile probation department). If the investigation reveals evidence of criminal child abuse, the local law enforcement agency has the authority to take the following actions: take the child into protective custody, file criminal charges against the parent(s) or responsible parties, and to refer the case to probation, welfare, or another service agency (counseling, church, etc.). Ideally, this decision is made after consultation with representatives from other disciplines.

If an investigation does not reveal evidence of criminal child abuse but suggests that other family problems or a potential abuse situation exists, the children's protective service agencies can attempt to intervene and provide appropriate services to prevent the crisis before it happens.

Copies of all written reports received by welfare and probation agencies are filed immediately, or as soon as possible, with the local law enforcement agency having jurisdiction. Law enforcement officers are also required to report immediately, or as soon as possible, to the agency responsible for such investigations (welfare or probation). Essentially, therefore, the reporting law is designed to ensure that local law enforcement and county social service agencies receive all reports (except of general neglect), whether initially reported to them or to an alternative agency.

In turn, all child protective agencies (law enforcement, welfare and probation) are required by law to file their reports with the Child Abuse Unit in the Bureau of Identification, State Department of Justice. The Unit then enters the report into the statewide central index and analyzes and compares all reports to determine whether there is a record of prior abuse, neglect, or molestation. The reporting law enforcement agency or local juvenile probation or welfare department is notified immediately if the Child Abuse Unit's records reveal any previous reports of suspected or actual infliction of physical injury, physical pain or mental suffering, or sexual molestation, concerning the same victim, family, or suspected abuser.

A history of abuse is not easily spotted because child abusers tend to be recidivists who take their children to different doctors or hospitals for treatment of each new injury. Therefore, the index is vital to investigatory agencies to provide information on prior incidents for purposes of early identification and prevention.
(Van de Kamp, 1983, pp.19–21)

## SUMMARY

Law enforcement agencies, in and of themselves, will never be able to address adequately the problem of child assault. They are only one component in the total service system currently involved with the assaultive family. What is imperative, however, is that every person, in both the public and the private sector, must become an informed and aggressive child advocate.

Through this dedication the territorial barriers so common among today's service agencies can be eliminated, and open lines of communication and cooperative problem solving can be established. It is only through the cooperative effort of all the agencies and professions involved in this area that the problem of child assault will be ameliorated.

This is not to say that law enforcement agencies cannot take steps to improve their performance or credibility as a single entity within the professional sector. As discussed earlier, the establishment of specialized units, staffed by highly trained investigators who are allowed maximum flexibility in their case dispositions, can certainly help to eliminate much of the criticism historically leveled at the involvement of law enforcement personnel in child assault cases.

The key to the successful management of any child assault case lies in the infusion of both public and private sector resources acting in concert, at the earliest possible time. This can only be accomplished if all professional and laypersons begin to act as child advocates and report any incident of child assault as soon as it is witnessed or suspected.

Finally, although each of the 50 states now has laws prohibiting child assault, much still remains to be done in the areas of statutory refinement, modification, and legislative lobbying to ensure that each child is legally guaranteed the right to a safe and secure home.

*Acknowledgment.* Grateful acknowledgment is given to Sheriff Sherman Block for written permission for Lieutenant Willey to prepare and submit this chapter.

*Chapter 4*

# Sociolegal Approaches for Helping Assaulted Children and Their Families

*Diane Gallinger,*
*John H. Meier,*
*and Joan Carney*

Once child assault has been discovered and appears to be substantiated, a flurry of activity begins to take place among the legal and social service professionals. Social workers, who by this time have already become involved in the case, must fully investigate and document the assaultive incident(s) and prepare recommendations for the court. Lawyers must be assigned to any party whose legal rights include representation if this party has not yet found or cannot afford a lawyer. As will be seen later, children may be represented by someone other than a lawyer. Once assigned to any client from a child assault case, the lawyer's role is basically predetermined. Jurists must begin preparing to make some very difficult decisions using the data reported to them by social workers and other designated representatives and evaluating the proceedings that take place in the courtroom. Generally speaking, jurisdictional issues may not be terribly difficult; however, the question of removal of child victims or adult perpetrators from their families is an agonizing dilemma for the court and everyone involved.

Since the early 1970s, there has been a push to reform the approach used in cases of child assault. In the opinion of some authorities, this reform must begin at the birth of the child and the changes that need to occur involve every possible system—the family, the educational system, the community (social and occupational networks), the government, the church, and, particularly, the system that provides children's services (Whittaker and Garbarino, 1983). For others, the necessary reforms are more specific and include changes mostly in the delivery of children's services, in the degree of interagency support and communication, and in the basic attitude toward resolving the issues of child assault. These reformists do not necessarily agree and, at times, their suggestions are economically or physically prohibitive for universal implementation; nevertheless, their ideas are presented in this text where appropriate.

## THE LONG ARM OF THE LAW REACHES OUT TO ASSAULTED CHILDREN

Before an assault case ever appears on the courtroom agenda, it has begun to be affected by current legislation. One of the most important laws currently governing child assault cases is the national Child Abuse Prevention and Treatment Act (CAPTA, Public Law 98-457). The main goals of this piece of landmark legislation are the following: to establish and appropriate funds, create a National Center on child abuse, study existing laws, establish "demonstration programs," mandate reports of child abuse, set up requirements for states in order to receive federal funds, require counsel for parents, and define the terms *child abuse* and *neglect* for governmental purposes. This bill became law in January of 1974 following the realization that the funding and treatment of child abuse at that time was sorely lacking (Senate Report 93-308, 1973). The National Child Abuse Coalition, comprised of several national organizations serving assaulted children and their families, is actively and at this writing successfully seeking increased support (upwards of thirty million dollars for fiscal year 1984-85) for CAPTA (American Humane Association, 1984).

The Adoption Assistance and Child Welfare Act of 1980 (PL 96-272) encourages maintaining the child in the home whenever possible and promotes the provision of the required services directly to the family to avoid the removal of the child (victim) or adult (perpetrator). The premise on which this law is based is that keeping the child at home is the most cost-effective and least disruptive alternative for all involved. This, then, becomes the main duty for the social worker. Using the accumulated case data, an initial decision must be made about whether any given family may be immediately restored to a functional level with the aid of emergency services or whether the dysfunction at the current time is so great that assault of the child is likely to continue. If preventive measures appear to be workable, the social worker must determine which services (e.g., day care, parent aide, homemaker services, etc.) will be most beneficial.

Although there is no specific unified approach to cases of child assault across the nation, a number of states are attempting to develop legislation that enhances their ability to comply with PL 96-272.

Reformists in this area have tended to criticize the attitude employed by legislators. For example, some authors have suggested that more attention should be paid to psychological factors of the family and that the primary focus should be on maintaining biological ties and seeking treatment for the entire family (Bryce and Lloyd, 1981; Colon, 1978; see also Chapter 6). Besharov (1983) argues that social and legal professionals must combine their efforts to create laws that "could help protect caseworkers from unfair criticism and, thus, help caseworkers to withstand the pressures toward defensive social work" (p. 4033). Since social workers can be prosecuted for supposed negligence in child abuse cases (see Besharov, 1983, for case examples), they tend to err on the side of overinvolvement, which is as heavily criticized as underinvolvement. Besharov believes that law can set the ground rules for decision making and can specify when child protective intervention should occur and when it should not occur. He goes on to present a hypothetical model for what to include in such legislation. Other reformists (e.g., Lindsey, 1982) suggest that research efforts must be increased to discover which new treatment approaches are most successful and to review past research data to discover what procedures have already achieved some success. These potentially successful treatment approaches can then be researched and tested more widely, and, if outcomes are positive, be considered for implementation on a legislative level.

# CHILD ASSAULT CASES IN THE COURTROOM

If the social worker(s) involved in investigation and treatment of the child assault case determines that the best recommendation is to have the child removed from the home, the case proceeds to the courtroom. At this time there are no nationwide criteria regarding which factors need to be present for children to be removed from their own homes. States may attempt to create laws that outline such criteria, but they are often open to interpretation and cannot possibly make provisions for every unique case that comes to the attention of authorities (Besharov, 1983; Goldstein, Freud, and Solnit, 1979; Katz, McGrath, and Howe, 1976; Wald, 1975).

For example, California case law guidelines (such as "a finding of immediate or urgent necessity for the protection of the minor," or "clear and convincing proof that the minor's best interests are served by being removed," or "a finding that all reasonable alternatives to removal have been exhausted") create a situation in which jurists are forced to make educated guesses as to whether a child still remains at risk of assault if left in the home. In one study (Phillips, Shyne, Sherman, and Haring, 1971), 94 cases in which the question of removal was pertinent were presented to three judges. The judges agreed in only 48 per cent of the cases as to the issue of removal and, even when they agreed, the reasons given for their decisions were often remarkably dissimilar. Research on the decision-making process among social workers has yielded similar ambiguous results (Shinn, 1968). Nonetheless, jurists, social workers, and law enforcement personnel must make such extemporaneous judgments and establish their own reasonable criteria for deciding when to remove a child in an assault case (De Francis, 1975).

From the personal viewpoint of one of the authors of this chapter (Carney)—a Los Angeles County jurist who for nearly 20 years presided over literally thousands of cases of assault against children—the most important considerations to weigh in deciding whether or not to remove the child are the following: (1) What is the extent of physical or psychological injury? (2) Was the child abuse the result of a deliberate action or of ignorance? (3) What are the parents' perceptions of their actions? (4) Does the child want to return home? (5) Is each parent capable of insight into his or her own behavior? (6) Is the parent or adult perpetrator amenable to counseling? This latter concern is of great importance because of the need for the jurist to be able to distinguish those parents who mean what they say from those who are mouthing platitudes simply to get their child back.

At this time, if a child abuse case gets to court, the child, the parent, and the protective services agency are all entitled to legal representation (Duquette, 1981). In the case of the child, special provisions are necessary, since the child's rights are not always the same as those of the adult; thus, the role of attorney is embodied in a guardian ad litem. It is this person's job to act in the child's "best interests," not necessarily as an advocate, but more as a technical watchdog, deciding independently what he or she believes to be best for the child (Duquette, 1981). This guardian ad litem may or may not be a lawyer and may have very little training in the area of child welfare. The attorney for the parent has the duty to "minimize the effects of state intervention on the family," while the protective services' lawyer attempts to "prove and present" his or her client's case, "understand and embrace the social goals of the client agency and prepare his/her client agency for ongoing court review" (Duquette, 1981). In addition to the information presented and uncovered by legal representatives, social workers must deliver their written reports and may be required to go on the witness stand to discuss their findings. At this point in the process, the social worker has begun treating the entire family and has been able to evaluate the family and report to the court both on the family's ability to accept and make use of services and on its capacity for eventual self-sufficiency. Jurists will then assemble all evidence and pertinent information in an attempt to make the most appropriate decision, all things considered.

Reformists have made a number of suggestions with regard to changes they feel are necessary when questioning the removal of an assaulted child from his or her home. As mentioned earlier, some complain that removal takes place without sufficient attention paid to the maintenance of family ties (Colon, 1978). Others have indicated that there needs to be greater interagency communication so that the most appropriate decision can be made (Besharov, 1983; Friedman, Baron, Lardieri, and Quick, 1982; Lindsey, 1982). Research is needed to evaluate better what sort of decisions are most helpful in which kind of cases. This sort of information, along with the impressions and opinions of social workers, lawyers, and jurists, needs to then get back to legislators so that the rules governing removal of the assaulted child(ren) are the ones that will meet with the greatest success (Besharov, 1983).

Suggestions have also been made for ways in which to improve the roles played by lawyers and jurists when a case of child assault comes before the court. It has been proposed that systems of accountability be developed among legal representatives so that children are not misrepresented and so that funds are appropriately allocated (Bross and Munson, 1980). These same writers have suggested four alternative models, one or more of which might replace the current legal approach used in child advocacy cases. Included are the employment of ad hoc appointments, panels, legal clinics, and public officials. Lawyers, too, have recommended greater communication and support among involved agencies (National Legal Resource Center for Child Advocacy and Protection, 1979). Lawyers must, after all, rely heavily on the impressions and opinions of law enforcement, social services, and medical and mental health professionals.

Probably the most frequent request made of jurists in terms of reform is that they develop more educated and consistent methods for deciding when to remove a child from his or her home. Los Angeles County has attempted to develop a system that seems to have met with some success. In this particular system, seven jurists in the Juvenile Court have been assigned to a separate Child Abuse Court. This creates specialization and expertise in the field of child assault. It also allows these particular jurists access to one another to share cases and other information. Consequently, the judges presumably are more likely to react in accord with one another. Attorneys have expressed the view that they also feel that there is a high degree of consistency among the Los Angeles County child assault jurists; consequently, the attorneys believe that they are often able to predict the outcomes of the trials in which they are involved. Needless to say, this is not a field for amateurs or jurists who are passing on their merry way to "higher" benches, although that is regrettably what often happens.

In addition, these jurists keep their own cases, which increases their familiarity with the individuals involved and allows them to track the progress made by the families. Thus, the jurists are able to give specific assignments to parents who want to keep their children, to let their expectations be known to these parents, and then to follow up periodically on the results of these various requests. This integrated county court system also enables jurists to work closely with and to perform group evaluations of various treatment programs available. With the proliferation of treatment programs now available, it is not too difficult to direct the parents to a program that will deal appropriately with their problems. This is another advantage the Los Angeles court has in that there is a considerable amount of interaction between the court and various treatment programs so that communication is open and ongoing. Not only are the jurists in Los Angeles well aware of what the county has to offer but they also actively support funding for these programs and are available to assist when problems arise (Carney, personal communication).

Of course, any program that proposes new approaches to child assault cases needs to be fully studied and evaluated to determine its usefulness. Thus, systematic program evaluation research must be included among the reform strategies. Better methods of sharing the findings from such research is, of course, also necessary.

## AFTER REMOVAL OCCURS

If the choice is made to remove the child, there are several possible alternative placements, including a foster home, a large foster care residential center, a state hospital, a relative's home, the care of a guardian, or an adoptive home. Adoption is not a choice that is immediately available because of further legal requirements (discussed later in this chapter). According to one 1981 Los Angeles County study, 42 per cent of the children who were seen in child abuse court were placed in group or individual foster homes, 33 per cent were placed back in their parents' home, 19 per cent went to relatives, and 6 per cent were sent to state hospitals or unrelated other adults (Elias, 1982). Through the passage of the Adoption Assistance and Child Welfare Act of 1980 (PL 96-272), the federal government has placed heavy emphasis on achieving permanency in the child's placement (Cutler and Bateman, 1980). Thus, no matter where the child is placed initially, every effort is made to decide the most appropriate long-term environment for each individual child as soon as possible.

More specifically, PL 96-272 establishes the following: (1) federal aid for the adoption of older, handicapped, minority, and other children with special needs; (2) the development of an adoption assistance program by all states; (3) services to prevent the need to remove a child from his or her family; (4) increased services for permanency planning; (5) a change of direction in child welfare programs from a placement to a family orientation; (6) a system that keeps track of children in foster care; and (7) funds for assisting families in need of placement or preventive services without a formal court hearing. For children in foster care, the hope is that PL 96-272 will provide a shorter time in foster care, fewer disruptions in living arrangements and placements, earlier return to their own homes, more rapid placement with an adoptive family, or some other long-term living arrangement. It should also lessen the dramatic increase in the number of children entering foster care, which rose from 177,000 in 1961 to 503,000 in 1977 and is projected to continue rising. This new law also requires greater governmental accountability in the form of reports, evaluations, and tracking systems in the area of child permanency planning.

Legislatively, PL 96-272 requires that for any state to receive an increase in funds appropriated for social services to children and their families, the following safeguards and services must be put into operation: (1) the location and status of all children who have been in foster care for over six months must be determined; (2) a more complete and updated record keeping system must be used for these children; (3) a written case plan must be prepared for each child for whom family-like placement is chosen, a placement that preferably is close to the parents' home and is, at the same time, in the child's best interest; (4) a case review system should be devised for foster children along with provision for a semiannual court or administrative hearing, and a dispositional hearing once a child has been in placement for 18 months to determine when the child will be placed permanently and in what type of environment; (5) certain safeguards for parents as to the removal, changes in location, or changes in visitation of their children should be provided; and (6) a service program to help children return home or be placed in adoptive homes should be developed.

PL 96-272 also encourages the permanent placement of children in foster care by placing a ceiling on the Aid to Families with Dependent Children (AFCD) foster care funds available to families, and by stipulating that any states desiring to receive these latter federal monies must develop a foster care and adoption assistance plan that has been approved by the Department of Health and Human Services. Finally, PL 96-272 specifies that states receiving federal funds for child welfare assistance will be required to establish a maximum number of children who will be held in foster care beyond two years and also to develop a plan for reaching this goal.

This law has greatly increased the responsibilities of social workers and jurists. However, PL 96-272 is designed to ensure that children will not become stuck in a series of temporary out-of-home placements (a form of systematic abuse addressed in Chapter 8). It also pushes parents to respond more quickly and more fully if they wish to regain physical custody of their children and avoid possible relinquishment procedures. In the past, parents had been able to retain legal custody by making the smallest effort on a very occasional basis, such as an annual phone call, post card, or other fleeting contact. This not only greatly frustrates social workers and jurists, whose ongoing plans are repeatedly disrupted, but also maintains the status of the child in a series of temporary, transient placements. The apparent solution to making PL 96-272 best for all involved is to increase the number of social workers and jurists. Unfortunately, this is not economically a priority for most states; however, some social workers predict an eventual decrease in their workloads due to PL 96-272.

Out-of-home placement may only be required for a short interim while parents recover from a crisis or begin to develop the skills they need to care more properly for their children and to run their households more effectively. However, when assaultive parents are found to be incorrigible for one reason or another, lengthier placements must be available for the children. This chapter examines the placement options, including small, individual foster homes (which might include other relatives of the assaulted child) and large, institutional foster homes (including state hospitals). If assaultive parents are eventually determined to be essentially unresponsive to available intervention–prevention efforts, alternative permanent placements must be found. Thus, adoptive homes are also addressed here. Advantages and disadvantages inherent in each type of out-of-home care are discussed. Also, several reformist ideas are also examined.

For a child to be placed in a group or individual foster home the decision must be ordered by the presiding jurist. Foster care centers that house a number of children are controlled by laws, are monitored by regulating agencies, and must perform certain administrative functions. In the case of individual foster homes, certain specific requirements are made of the prospective foster parents before they may be licensed. In most instances these requirements include filling out application forms, complying with a home inspection, and cooperating with a background study and interviews to determine what sort of children are most appropriate for the parents concerned. Not only is this an attempt to screen out unacceptable candidates, but it is also aimed at gaining the information necessary to match children in need to acceptable foster parents. Social workers are responsible for continually monitoring such homes to estimate the quantity and quality of care and to be able to document and report on the child's reaction to the home and whether it has been and continues to be an appropriate placement.

Even when a large foster care residential home is the chosen placement, an attempt is made to match the child to the home. Some children may need intense treatment (e.g., medical care, therapy, on-grounds schooling, continuous supervision) and, therefore, require hospital-type care, whereas others may simply need residential placement until their lives are more in order. The residence will also have some guiding principles to help choose appropriate clients, depending on how they are financed and which children they are prepared to handle best. Residential centers are also controlled by certain regulations, and there are specific government agencies assigned to carry out supervisory activities. Unlike screening precautions that guide in the selection of small foster homes, these regulations are less concerned with who is caring for the child (the home administrators can monitor this) and more concerned with appropriate standards of cleanliness, diet, safety, and other administrative and treatment-oriented issues.

Since foster care is considered to be only temporary, it may seem that the most reasonable solution is to make the child available for adoption as soon as possible so that permanent ties can be established. However, this solution is more difficult than it may appear on the surface. First, a child may seem unable to form a bond readily with adults and so may not yet appropriately be considered a candidate for adoption. The child may be unmanageable or may simply be unwilling or unable to relate to others in a meaningful and mutually satisfactory way. A second major hindrance to adoption is that biological parents are usually resistant to letting their child go. For a child to be released for adoption either the natural parent(s) must agree to legally terminate the relationship or the courts must decide to legally remove the child from parental custody. The child–parent relationship is typically severed only under the most extreme conditions (Slader, 1978); however, there are those who believe that the relationship is frequently ended too easily and possibly for reasons not necessarily in the best interests of the child (Aber, 1980).

According to Kempe (1979), if a social worker, pediatrician, psychiatrist, or psychologist documents thoroughly any one of the following, termination of the child–parent relationship is almost always decided on and not overturned: (1) particularly brutal or sadistic child assault, imprisonment, or abandonment for a period of six months or more; (2) serious, incurable psychopathology of the parent that places the child in immediate danger; or (3) failure of a serious effort at treatment, following which the court no longer feels the child may be raised successfully in the child's biological family. Still, relinquishment is not a step lightly or easily taken, and children can often be left hanging in a series of temporary placements while the final decision is being made. This, in turn, creates a Catch-22 situation in which a child is shuffled around so much that forming bonds becomes impossible—yet the ability to form such bonds continues to be a necessary requirement for the child to be considered adoptable.

Even if adoption is accomplished, there is no guarantee for its success. Although no one can ensure that a particular child is going to fit a particular family or that the parents will truly be able to handle the adopted child once the situation becomes a final and formal reality, attempts are certainly made to prepare the potential adoptive parents for the tasks they will face. Adoptive parent applicants typically face the following: a long wait before the process starts; a need for education in certain areas; a background study; home visits; therapy that continues until their own issues are worked out; and, all too often, more waiting. If all has gone well, the child begins a series of visits which progress in length as time goes on (this is an optimal situation since, in some instances, an adoptive placement is required almost immediately). In the best of all possible situations, the adoption process proceeds at a rate most beneficial to the child and the adoptive parents. This process may be halted at any point, which is determined by either the parents or the adoption worker.

# ALTERNATIVE PLACEMENTS: ADVANTAGES, DISADVANTAGES, AND SUGGESTED REFORMS

Each placement option available to an assaulted child who has been removed from his or her natural home has its own particular advantages and disadvantages. The positive and negative qualities of each type of placement are now examined. Particular emphasis is placed on large foster care–residential treatment centers for two reasons. First, many assaulted children need the services offered by a residential treatment-type setting, and so this sort of placement is of particular concern. Second, in the last few years, large scale foster care has come under severe attack in the literature, and it seems important to balance the scales properly in terms of benefits and drawbacks. For each placement option, there are also certain suggested reforms, which, if implemented, would provide additional advantages and greater probability for long-term success. Although it certainly is not possible to present an exhaustive list of all advantages, disadvantages, and suggested reforms for all placement options, it is possible to present some of the more chronic critical concerns.

## Reunification

Placement of the assaulted child back in his or her home with the family of origin is the option most vigorously sought by social and legal professionals when it appears to be safe and feasible. Perhaps the greatest advantage of reunification is that it is the least disruptive option in terms of maintaining family ties and in terms of limiting the total number of placements experienced. Children desperately need to have a sense of belonging and, if it can be safely worked out, this can probably be best achieved in the original family home, even if the children had previously been assaulted there. Also, reunification provides the greatest opportunity for permanence with the fewest legal complications; the parents are already the lawful custodians, and no legal procedures are needed to establish this fact. Another advantage of reunification is that it enables the family members to face their problems together and to deal with them directly (Bryce and Lloyd, 1981). Each member of the family is bound to feel some degree of pain, fear, and anger, and working through these feelings helps bring the family closer together. Finally, reuniting assaulted children with the biological family is the placement option that is usually the most financially advantageous for the child welfare system and society at large. Although the reunified family in poverty might require larger welfare payments and may need to retain certain government-provided services, it is unlikely that these costs would ever equal, let alone exceed, the cost to society for maintaining the child in an out-of-home placement.

Clearly the strongest disadvantage of reunification is the risk that the child will again be assaulted. Although every precaution may be taken, there can never be total assurance that assault against children in a given family will not recur (Besharov, 1983; Schmitt, 1978). Another disadvantage in reuniting assaulted children and their families is that the children, their parents and siblings may not sufficiently benefit and improve from the intervention–prevention services provided to them after experiencing such a family trauma. Although the full gamut of intervention–prevention services (see Chapter 5) could be offered to the reunified child and family, there is a marked tendency for reunified families to be ignored and not receive any follow-up or after-care intervention–prevention services once reunification has occurred (Hightower, 1982; Jones, 1976; Meier, 1984c). Funds tend to be more readily allocated to children in placement because of society's responsibility for the instability of their situation.

Reformists believe that family ties are emphasized either too strongly (Jones, 1977) or not strongly enough (Bryce and Lloyd, 1981; Colon, 1978). There are those who argue that some form of contact must remain between the child and the biological parents, even if it is only in the form of a photo album kept for the child until adulthood (Colon, 1978). Others contend that if the biological parents received appropriate aftercare services once they were reunified with their child, their chances for success would be strengthened (Jones, 1976; Meier, 1978, 1984c; Chapters 5 and 8). This, in turn, would ameliorate the present rather skeptical attitude on the part of the sociolegal professionals toward reunification as the optimal placement. Some reformists even suggest that the biological parents should receive added monetary support (using money that might have gone towards out-of-home care) to supplement the reunification process (Bryce and Lloyd, 1981). One change that could be beneficial immediately in this regard would be to have more and better trained human services workers available throughout the placement procedure to help the family identify and utilize necessary resources. Of course, such expanded services require additional support on the part of lawmakers and policymakers whose current inclinations seem to lean away from, not toward, supplying the human services work force with enough workers to meet their current obligations satisfactorily (Besharov, 1983; Delaney, 1976). This is one of many places in which private sector efforts such as CHILDHELP (see Chapter 8) programs can meaningfully augment public sector performance. Finally, there is a need for more thorough research and careful analysis of the entire reunification procedure to provide a step-by-step plan for more successful services and resultant permanent placements.

# Adoption

Next to reunification, adoption is usually seen as the most permanent of the remaining placement options, although it is often difficult to achieve. In fact, permanency is probably the greatest advantage that adoption offers. Plumez (1982) points out that, contrary to what may be believed, "recent and reputable research shows that adoption is an extremely positive experience for the vast majority of parents and children" (p. xii). She further states that the number of adoptive families reporting satisfactory parent–child relationships is about the same as that of biological families. Plumez also addresses the plight of the unwed mother and the advantages that adoption might offer a woman who faces having to unwillingly raise a child alone. Statistics show that most unwed mothers remain uneducated, unemployed, impoverished, and consequently more likely to assault their children than are married mothers (Teenage Pregnancy, 1981). Advances in adoption procedures in recent years have assisted agencies in matching children to adoptive parents, a systematic procedure which is a giant step forward in creating successful adoptive experiences (Lawder, Lower, Andrews, Sherman, and Hill, 1969). Some encouraging studies (Plumez, 1982) have shown that adoptive children often emulate the traits of their adoptive parents. For couples unable to bear children, adoption provides a mutually beneficial means to create a desired family. Finally, the financial burden to society tends to be less when adoption is the chosen out-of-home placement option because the adoptive parents take on the financial responsibility for the child. Although it is certainly possible that some adoptive parents may receive monetary assistance from the government as an additional incentive to assume care for especially difficult children, again it is unlikely that this aid will equal, much less exceed, the amount which would otherwise have to be paid for foster or residential care.

Paradoxically, one of the biggest disadvantages to adoption is in direct opposition to its greatest advantage. Because adoption is approached as a permanent placement, both children and parents work on developing strong bonds and close ties. If, for any reason, adoption eventually fails, those involved are likely to suffer tremendously. For assaulted children who have already been removed from at least one home environment, this failure is just one more indication that they are not worthy of parental love, care, and affection. Some of the other drawbacks for adoption are similar to those for reunification. In both placements, the child's condition is seen as stabilized and, therefore, the child is not considered to be of high priority in terms of needing further government-funded intervention–prevention services. Adoption is also frequently complicated by numerous legal difficulties. As mentioned earlier, for a child to become eligible for adoption, either the biological parents must agree to give up their legal custody or relinquishment has to be decreed by the courts.

Severing the legal ties does not ensure that a child will be adopted. Numerous factors may render children difficult to adopt and render them "unadoptable." Probably the most common characteristics of children that compromise their adoption prospects are an inability to bond, physical disabilities, mental retardation, emotional disturbance, severe behavior disorders, and being too old. Even if a given child is determined to be adoptable, other factors frequently contribute to the failure of an adoption. Adoptive parents, although thoroughly screened, may not be able to appropriately and satisfactorily care for the child, and unforeseen difficulties may arise within the dynamics of the new family relationships. Plumez (1982) notes that adoption is seen as "unnatural" and may, therefore, be frowned upon by those in the community and in the government agencies. If this attitude is communicated to the adoptive family, it creates additional stress and contributes to the defeat or dissolution of an adoptive placement (see Chapter 1 for discussion of these and other factors that might contaminate an adoptive effort).

Reformists suggest that attitudes toward adoption expressed by sociolegal and government personnel need to become more positive (Bytner, Griffin, Jenkins, and Ray, 1979; Plumez, 1982). These authors believe that current relatively negative dispositions, much as other self-fulfilling prophecies, reduce the number of adoptions that are attempted or hinder the potential success of adoptions that are consummated. Adoption is on the decline, especially in the case of unwed mothers, who now more than previously are choosing to keep their babies (Teenage Pregnancy, 1981). Plumez (1982) suggests that the socially unacceptable act of relinquishment is at least subtly communicated to many unwed mothers, who then choose to raise their children alone because it is more acceptable, even when they are unprepared and reluctant to do so.

Most suggestions as to how to reform adoption procedures fall into the category of anticipating and easing the burdens that adoptive parents are likely to encounter. Greater contact has been urged between agencies and adoptive parents to help placement proceed as smoothly and successfully as possible (Jones, 1977; Lawder et al., 1969). Potential adoptive parents need information and training that tells them what to expect from an adopted child and counseling as to how they might deal with difficult situations that inevitably arise (Lawder et al., 1969). Once adoption has occurred, it may be unwise to ignore the adoptive family; parents often require help and someone who can empathize with their feelings and understand their problems (Meier, 1984c; Plumez, 1982). Changes have also been suggested in terms of how to work with the biological parents; certainly they should not be made to feel guilty about their choice to relinquish the child (Gill, 1979). Plumez (1982) states that the unwed mother (or birth parents, as the case may be) should be presented with the pros and cons of all options. Her decision should then be respected. If she chooses to relinquish her child for adoption, she might be allowed to have some input as to the characteristics of the adoptive home and should be helped to get back on her feet financially (giving up her child causes her to lose possible funds from AFDC) through educational or vocational counseling and training. Other suggested reforms include the following: (1) choices must be broadened both in terms of who is considered to be an adoptable child and who are considered to be potential adoptive parents (Donley, 1979); (2) those who are in the position to evaluate potential adoptive placements should be aware of facts, figures, and past research that might influence such decisions (Plumez, 1982); (3) more research must be carried out to determine what makes a successful adoption and what barriers are currently present to carrying out adoptions; (4) agencies should make greater use of photo listings, which can be a useful initial screening device (Plumez; 1982); (5) laws need to be updated to reflect recent research findings and current thinking; and, finally, (6) the most popular reform suggestion to have arisen in the last several years is that when adoption appears precarious, "risk" adoption or foster-adoption should be sought (Gill, 1979; Gill and Amadio, 1983; Lee and Hull, 1983). Because this concept has received so much attention in the recent literature and seems particularly germane to assaulted children, it is treated here as a separate placement option.

## Foster–Adoptive Care

"Risk" adoption is basically a foster care placement that has adoptive potential. Usually the child in this situation is in legal limbo, awaiting the completion of the relinquishment process, and the placement is used as a "trial-run" adoption during which the parents, the child, and the social or adoptive workers evaluate its potential for success. "Foster-adoptive" placement shares many of the benefits of both foster care and adoptive care, with the hope that it is not as temporary as foster care and, at the same time, that it does not ignore the child's need for some semblance of continuity and permanency during the months or years which may elapse while awaiting relinquishment (Gill and Amadio, 1983). Foster-adoptive care encourages the legal professionals involved in the child's case to recognize the adoptive potential and, therefore, to move more quickly and adamantly toward relinquishment (Gill, 1979; Gill and Amadio, 1983). Gill and Amadio claim that biological parents appear to be more amenable to severing legal ties with their children if they know that the child is being cared for by parents who are willing, eager, and able to adopt the child. Because the final goal for "risk" adoption is regular adoption, foster parents in this situation tend to be highly committed to the child and to working through the foster-adoptive experience (Gill and Amadio, 1983).

One of the drawbacks to "risk" adoption is implied by its name—it contains an incalculable risk of failure. Although it may initially appear that adoption will be secured, plans and circumstances may change. Biological parents may decide to reestablish contact with their child on a more pervasive and permanent basis. Children may begin to act out and become confused regarding their feelings for their foster-adoptive parents, who may, in turn, begin to question their own needs and commitment. If adoption is ruled out for any reason, the "risk" adoption becomes another potentially traumatic separation and failure experience. Lee and Hull (1983) point out that, just as parents and children may become overinvolved in this situation, so may professionals, who must be cautious not to become biased or neglectful of their responsibilities to all parties involved. Although "risk" adoption starts out as foster care, it must eventually jump all of the necessary legal hurdles to become adoptive care; this can be a very strenuous process for all involved.

Reformists (Gill, 1979; Gill and Amadio, 1983; Lee and Hull, 1983) suggest that greater use be made of foster-adoptive programs with some warnings kept in mind. These writers tend to agree that preparation and honesty are the keys to success. Gill and Amadio (1983) propose that a positive foster-adoptive care experience is likely to occur if sociolegal professionals can work together to do the following: (1) educate potential families regarding legal realities and child welfare principles; (2) have legal counsel available early to clarify all issues; (3)

fully assess potential families; (4) prepare those involved for postplacement problems; (5) be honest; (6) use care to develop a realistic adjustment plan and put it in writing if necessary; and (7) allow those involved to make their own decisions and be responsible for the outcome. Biological parents, potential adoptive parents, and the involved children must all understand their roles and functions as individuals and in relation to one another at each step in this lengthy and complex procedure.

## Foster Care

Foster placement can provide temporary care until a crisis within the family of origin is resolved or until more permanent arrangements can be made. Both parents and children are helped to understand the temporary nature of the placement. Felker (1974) identified several positive aspects of temporary care. Foster parents are less likely than biological parents to see children as extensions of themselves and may, therefore, be more able and willing to allow the children to be themselves and dream their own dreams. Also, properly trained foster parents do not become so overinvolved that when a child leaves their lives seem deflated or destroyed. Felker further believes that the temporary nature of foster care emphasizes the importance of each day. Foster care can provide a family environment that may be less intense and structured than residential or hospital care and may be more personalized (Linn, 1981; Linn, Caffey, Klett, and Hogarty, 1977). If the foster parents are willing and the child is in need, foster care should be a rehabilitative experience (Cautley, 1980). Social workers can supply foster parents with available resources that may be used to provide appropriate treatment, and some forms of treatment may be extended into the foster home. Linn (1981) suggests that foster care has not yet become overly regulated by the government, which helps to keep costs down and to maintain a family atmosphere. Although foster and biological parents may have little or no contact, Felker (1974) believes that the temporary availability of multiple parents can be seen and used as a real asset in helping disenfranchised children and disintegrated families put their lives back together.

The strongest disadvantage to foster care is its temporary and unstable nature (Cautley, 1980; Elias, 1982; Plumez, 1982). As already mentioned, children all too often get caught in a series of unsuccessful placements while their status hangs in legal limbo (Gruber, 1978). It has been shown that "early emotional and academic gains following foster placement quickly erode as time in care and number of placements increases" (Elias, 1982). If children never feel safe and secure enough to develop trust, they will not be able to establish mutual attachment and bonding; ironically, as mentioned earlier, the inability to bond can cause a child to be labeled "unadoptable." Foster parents are sometimes unprepared for the responsibilities and problems they may encounter (Jacobs, 1980). They often lack appropriate training and skills, feel unsupported by social services personnel and by others in their environment (e.g., neighbors and teachers), have unrealistic expectations of themselves, have little contact with other foster parents, and feel isolated and powerless. It has also been observed that some foster parents see their role as that of paid employees and may not be motivated to carry out the tasks necessary to care for a foster child properly. Finally, there tends to be a high turnover rate among social workers who monitor foster home placements, which in turn creates inconsistency and confusion for both foster parents and children (Gruber, 1978).

Reformists propose that past research be reviewed and new research be conducted to discover what should be done to encourage more successful and more enduring foster care placements. Many researchers who have published their findings from foster care studies have also drawn some conclusions and listed suggestions to improve the system. More clearly defining various roles is proposed as a step in the right direction. Foster parents need to know what their functions and expectations should be, whereas researchers must better determine what it is that foster parents can do to make a placement more potentially successful (Fanshell and Shinn, 1978; Gruber, 1978; Meier, 1984c; Vasaly, 1976). Social workers must also have their roles defined and know what is expected of them so that they can function more effectively within the realistic constraints of the time and energy available (Cautley, 1980). There needs to be some room for social workers to prioritize their schedules so they do not feel overwhelmed or do not burn out, which in turn, would help to reduce the high turnover rate (Freudenberger, 1974; Gruber, 1978). Felker (1974) encourages a more positive and compassionate attitude toward biological parents, foster parents, and social workers—each performs an important function and each needs to be able to work with the others. Biological parents need to know that they have not been forgotten and to be assured that some sort of contact will persist, whatever is determined to be in the child's best interests (Colon, 1978; Felker, 1974; Goldstein et al., 1979). They may also need services to become emotionally and financially stable (Gruber, 1978). In terms of the foster parents, it has been shown that when they were given appropriate training, the number of failed placements decreased, the number of successful placements increased, and more of the trained than untrained foster parents were able to remain licensed (Boyd and Remy, 1978). Foster parents, too, need to know how to obtain available ancillary services when they are needed (Felker, 1974). A social worker's time is very limited and should not be entirely consumed administering to a group of foster placements that have become unduly dependent. Finally, current legislation needs increasingly to reflect the most salient current research findings. The promising new legislation, particularly the Adoption Assistance and Child Welfare Act of 1980 described earlier, addresses the most pertinent issues, with permanency being at the top of the list. This revised focus, then, reverts to the intermediate compromise of the foster–adoptive placement with its many possible advantages over both foster and adoptive care.

## Residential Care

Although residential care is seen by some to be a last resort, it has many advantages for some children who are in dire need of its comprehensive and intensive services. In many ways, residential care could be likened to a hospital for the severely emotionally disturbed. Intervention–prevention may be provided anywhere along a continuum between outpatient and intensive inpatient care, and service providers may range from volunteer lay persons to highly trained professionals. The amount of structure provided may also vary depending on the resident's needs (Keith-Lucas and Sanford, 1977; Lamb, 1981). The range of services provided by a comprehensive residential treatment center may be almost unending, and this is why these settings become so necessary when an assaulted child has been removed from the home. In some cases the child has already experienced several unsuccessful foster home placements and clearly needs more intensive care than was previously delivered. In other cases, the degree of damage done leaves the child unable to cope in any normal or regular foster family environment. Still others may be able to handle a less intense setting but need the care of trained professionals who can better understand and meet their many complex needs. Certainly one of the greatest advantages, then, of residential care is the opportunity to match the child to one of many possible homes, depending on a thorough evaluation of individual needs (Bachrach, 1980; Dubin and Ciavarelli, 1978; Keith-Lucas and Sanford, 1977; Segal and Baumohl, 1981).

What are these needs that residential care may satisfy? Keith-Lucas and Sanford (1977) have categorized the services of residential care into seven major subdivisions. First, residential care staff members can work together to help plan for the child's future. Each child's needs must be individually assessed and reassessed at appropriate and regular intervals. The biological family may be asked to participate in this planning when it is time for them to do so. Second, the child's mental and physical health must be maintained. A therapeutic milieu is provided in which every attempt is made to meet the needs of each individual child and to respect his or her rights. Rules must be consistent and life should feel stable and comfortable. All necessary medical care should be provided; medication effects should be assessed periodically and diets should be appropriate. The third service provided by residential care is the development of an individualized educational plan, which may include regular school curriculum, remedial work, or special classes provided either by local public schools or in an on-grounds school program (Lamb, 1981). It is important that child care workers maintain contact with teachers and other school officials to reinforce and maintain the learning. Group care is the fourth service offered by residential homes. If used appropriately, group living can be very advantageous. Unit populations may be assembled so that the children are all working on the same particular skills or in which the children complement each other and are able to offer one another assistance; a more heterogeneous family atmosphere may be created for those children who are prepared for such a setting. By making use of the group living arrangement, social skills may be improved (Bachrach, 1980; Lamb, 1981), and children may be able to begin to work on sibling and parental issues. The fifth service provided by residential treatment centers is expert counseling. If clients can learn to make use of resources while in residential care, they may become more willing and able to seek help in the future when otherwise unmanageable problems arise. In addition, appropriate guidance helps these assaulted clients to cope with their problems more effectively on their own. Therapy (see Chapter 5) is the sixth service. Providing a constant therapeutic milieu in which trained staff are sensitive to and aware of each child's needs is certainly beneficial; moreover, most, if not all, assaulted children require intensive, individual psychotherapy. Family therapy is also in order, especially if reunification is intended (Lamb, 1981; see also Chapter 6). Finally, residential care provides services that ensure that the child's rights are communicated, respected, and upheld.

It has been countered that, with appropriate guidance, foster, adoptive, or biological parents could offer their children these same advantages. However, good residential programs have these services immediately available and usually on the grounds. Furthermore, and perhaps most important, the staff members are appropriately trained. Competent child caregivers have degrees and experience in the areas of child development, sociology, or psychology plus considerable on-the-job training.

The benefits of residential care are greatly enhanced by team work. Staff members can share important information, combine efforts to develop the most appropriate goals and treatment for each child and jointly participate in the hiring and training of staff, making use of the expertise of the interdisciplinary team members (Bachrach, 1980; Budson, 1981; Dubin and Ciavarelli, 1978; Keith-Lucas and Sanford, 1977; Lamb, 1981).

The residential treatment center idea of unifying the efforts of several specially trained individuals to achieve centralized goals and expectations for residents is similar to that of the kibbutz (Beit-Hallahmi and Rabin, 1977; Devereux et al., 1974; Kahane, 1975), although assaultive parents do not "choose" to involve their children in residential care and there is not a shared sociopolitical ideology. The kibbutz reportedly has been quite successful in meeting many of its humanistic and self-actualization goals (Beit-Hallahmi and Rabin, 1977; Kahane, 1975); this suggests that the use of trained caregivers and collective and intensive provision of care, focused on uniform treatment goals, are characteristics of a successful kibbutz (and residential program). In the past, the kibbutz children spent little time with their biological families, which allegedly tended to increase their enjoyment of and positive attitudes toward their parents (Beit-Hallahmi and Rabin, 1977); however, more recently, the kibbutz has been involving parents to a greater degree, as the proponents become more accepting of Western ideas (Beit-Hallahmi and Rabin, 1977; Devereux et al., 1974). This suggests that residential treatment centers should also increase family involvement (Keith-Lucas and Sanford, 1977). Staff members could assist in family contacts, help residents work through unsatisfactory visits and "no-shows," provide some family therapy (Lamb, 1981), help to ease the transition from the center to the home when reunification is the goal, and participate in a system whereby follow-up and after-care are provided (Meier, 1984c).

One final advantage of residential care is the degree to which its services are monitored by licensing agencies enforcing government regulations (Dubin and Ciavarelli, 1978; Lamb, 1981). Periodic checks are made and, it is hoped, inappropriate practices are discovered and discontinued. Bachrach (1980) and Meier (1983c) suggest that existing successful programs have systems of internal evaluation that provide continuous self-monitoring more quickly and more thoroughly than formal regulating systems (see also Chapter 8).

Residential care shares most of the disadvantages of foster care (see preceding section on foster care). Some drawbacks are more peculiar to the residential setting, including the following: (1) bureaucratic and monetary concerns that sometimes compromise the quality of care (Lamb, 1981; Segal and Baumohl, 1981); (2) poor community reaction to having an institution located nearby (Baron and Piasecki, 1981; Segal and Baumohl, 1981); (3) the label of "last resort" (Keith-Lucas and Sanford, 1977; Wolfensberger, 1971); (4) population and attendant problems of overcrowding; and (5) an institutional environment that may prevent family-type interactions and which may instead contribute to institutional behavior (e.g., acting out to receive individual attention). The remaining disadvantages to residential care tend to be the byproducts of a poorly run organization, such as underqualified and undertrained staff; high employee turnover; a tendency to overmedicate residents; poor supervision; unclear standards and guidelines; too much or too little structure; a lack of necessary services; the absence of interdisciplinary team work; inadequate screening procedures for hiring staff; ignorance of the need for total family involvement in preparation for reunification and aftercare; poor community relations; and few internal regulatory devices (Blatt and Kaplan, 1974; Keith-Lucas and Sanford, 1977; Wolfensberger, 1971).

Reformists tend to agree that more research is needed to determine which children require residential treatment and what type and size of center provides the best care for what sort of child (Bachrach, 1980; Budson, 1981; Lamb, 1981; Segal and Baumohl, 1981). Some residential centers are carrying out their own research and are greatly benefited by this type of self-monitoring and feedback (Meier, 1983c; also see Chapter 8 on The Village of CHILDHELP). Before such comparative research can be conducted, a better system of classifying homes, services, and residents must be developed (Budson, 1981; Segal and Baumohl, 1981). When a good fit is found between center and resident, the level of the intensity of training and supervision matches the needs of the child (Dubin and Ciavarelli, 1978). Since interdisciplinary team work provides many client and staff benefits, many reformists encourage greater intercommunication and more unified efforts (Budson, 1981; Dubin and Ciaverelli, 1978; Keith-Lucas and Sanford, 1977; Lamb, 1981). Regular and goal-oriented meetings can help maintain staff communication and integration (Dubin and Ciavarelli, 1978). Appropriate senior staff members should be involved in hiring and other administrative decisions to keep them more involved and to help them to understand various bureaucratic and monetary concerns (Lamb, 1981). This helps to keep the clients' needs first and encourages the staff to see itself as more important and esteemed (Keith-Lucas and Sanford, 1977). It may also encourage the provision of services and benefits that will inspire staff to stay with their jobs longer, increasing the continuity of care to residents. Most residential treatment centers would be improved by more thorough internal monitoring systems both for services (social, physical, educational, psychological, and medical care) and for staff (screening, training, and evaluating) (Bachrach, 1980). Some reformists are suggesting more family-like atmospheres and greater family involvement (Budson, 1981; Keith-Lucas and Sanford, 1977; Van Hagen, 1983). This may enhance the ability to transfer the child smoothly and effectively from the residential placement to the biological or foster–adoptive home. Finally, reformists encourage more communication and greater cooperation between the residential center and the community (Bachrach, 1980; Baron and Piasecki, 1981; see also Chapter 7). The members of the community often have misconceptions about residential care, which may cause them to limit resources, services, and support to residential programs; this must be overcome by improved education and communication (Baron and Piasecki, 1981; Goldberg and Dooner, 1983).

In conclusion, sociolegal professionals play crucial roles at every step in the process of dealing with the assaulted child. Even before assault has occurred, laws reflect society's definition of reportable assault. In the case of a verified report, the decision must be made immediately by the investigating law enforcement officer or social worker whether or not to take temporary custody of the children, and subsequently the courts must decide whether the child needs to be removed from the home for longer term care or whether services can satisfactorily be provided to maintain the child in the home. If removal occurs, several alternative placements are available. Fortunately, the choices are varied enough to provide a setting that, it is hoped, best serves each individual assaulted child. The various placements must be considered, with the goal of permanency always kept in mind. Treatment may be minimal or intensive, and care providers may range from untrained lay persons and foster–adoptive parents to trained child caregivers and interdisciplinary professional teams. With continuing appropriate reform, based on careful research evaluations and resultant recommendations, these various placements can provide assaulted children and their assaultive families with the intervention–prevention services they so desperately need. The sociolegal personnel are critical interdisciplinary professional teams. With continuing appropriate reform, based on careful research evaluations and resultant recommendations, these various placements can provide assaulted children and their assaultive families with the intervention–prevention services they so desperately need. The sociolegal personnel are critical links in the chain of events that rescue and rehabilitate the very citizens who will become integral parts of the adult society, which in turn will develop and enact further legal reforms necessary to ensure the optimal development of subsequent generations.

*Chapter 5*

# Intervention–Prevention Approaches for Assaulted Children and Their Assaultive Parents and Families

## *John H. Meier*

This chapter presents a comprehensive view of useful and promising modalities and disciplines for providing interdisciplinary intervention services to the victims and perpetrators of assault against children, along with suggestions for preventing such assaults. To reflect an interdisciplinary (multimodality) perspective, a wide variety of useful intervention–prevention modalities and disciplines are presented and discussed. The more traditional and well-established disciplines are only briefly mentioned, since there are extensive treatises on them available elsewhere. However, the newer and less well-known disciplines and modalities are given more detailed attention to help the reader become more familiar with and accepting of them.

The terms *discipline* and *modality* are used somewhat interchangeably, although the former typically refers to a formalized body of theory and practice applied by degreed, certified, or licensed professionals, whereas the latter typically is a specific methodology or therapeutic procedure that may be evolving into a full-fledged discipline, such as art therapy, family therapy, occupational therapy, and recreational therapy, to name a few current and relevant examples. Thus, for assaulted children and assaulting parents and families, the following sections present intervention–prevention approaches from numerous interdisciplinary perspectives; any one approach or various combinations of compatible approaches may be used in providing a comprehensive service for a given case of child assault and would contribute to a comprehensive intervention–prevention program.

To reflect the interdisciplinary parity principle, whereby each discipline has equal status on an interdisciplinary team (Meier, 1976a), the disciplines and modalities are presented in alphabetical order. The integrated diagnosis and treatment planning done by an interdisciplinary team requires a case coordinator or manager based on the extent of a given discipline's or modality's responsibility toward and involvement with a given client. In some settings, the coordinator role is assigned on a rotational basis, which is usually less satisfactory, since responsibility and authority are not in accordance with the relative investment of time and effort required from the lead discipline or modality.

Individual integrated treatment planning and implementation by an interdisciplinary team is quite demanding, complex, and often difficult to orchestrate. Various in-home and out-of-home options are noted and cross referenced with other chapters in this book that address particular options in greater depth. Since there are several useful family treatment approaches, of which Chapter 6 is only one example, a brief description is included in this chapter to acquaint the reader with some of the other representative and useful family treatment approaches. Some discussion about and examples of the relationship between intervention and prevention are presented to illustrate the overlap between secondary prevention and primary intervention, tertiary prevention and secondary intervention, and so forth. The terms *intervention* and *treatment* are used almost interchangeably, except that the former connotes a broader effort and goes beyond the narrower medical model. It should be noted at the outset that the combination term intervention–prevention is used deliberately to indicate the overlap of the two concepts; this is clarified by the following definitions of the "three phases of prevention" (Meier, 1983a):

**Primary Intervention–Prevention.** All forms of assault against children (the target condition) are prevented from occurring in the first instance due to anticipatory actions of controlling or eliminating their basic causes, as enumerated and described briefly in Chapter 1.

**Secondary Intervention–Prevention.** Various forms of assault against children occur but are identified and reported, it is hoped before too much damage is inflicted and in time for appropriate measures to be taken to prevent further episodes and after-effects (sequelae), which predictably are inevitable without proper intervention–prevention.

**Tertiary Intervention–Prevention.** Assaults against children (and some sequelae) do occur; secondary intervention–prevention itself may cause additional problems similar to iatrogenic diseases gotten from hospitals (the "cure" becomes worse than the original illness); for example, further psychic or behavioral deterioration, or both, results from chronic confinement in traditional institutional or other systemic "treatments" (Meier, 1984c; see also Chapter 4).

Clearly, prevention does not just happen, even at the primary level, since some active intervention and change must occur within the child, parent, and environment to reduce the risk of assault from ever happening in the first instance. The term intervention is somewhat broader than the more traditional term treatment and is used to connote a more comprehensive modification of all of the tripartite dimensions (victim–perpetrator–ecology; see Chapter 1) usually involved in cases of assault against children.

## FROM THEORY TO PRACTICE

As pointed out in Chapter 1, a theoretical model is useful not only in conceptualizing the multiple and complex dynamics contributing to assaults against children but also and more importantly, it informs efforts toward the intervention–prevention of assaults against children. In *The Mikado*, the Gilbert and Sullivan operetta, it is stated that the punishment must fit the crime; similarly, in the case of the crime of child assault, it is important that the intervention–prevention fit the underlying causes and consequences to ensure lasting results. Thus, the model depicted in Chapter 1 serves as a checklist for intervention–prevention planning, evaluation of progress from intervention–prevention efforts, and the planning of comprehensive intervention–prevention programs. This simply underscores the necessity for carefully selecting and meshing intervention–prevention techniques specifically to alleviate and ultimately to eliminate each of the contributing factors, or at least enough of them to reduce significantly the probability of any first offense or certainly any repetition (recidivism) of child assault.

Of course, since the three major ingredients—namely, the child (victim), the parent or adult (perpetrator), and the circumstances (ecology)—are in a dynamic state of continuous interaction and change, intervention–prevention efforts must be sufficiently flexible to address spontaneously the dynamics and changes as they arise. In fact, the very process of intervention–prevention is diagnostic in itself, since the victim–perpetrator–environment's response to the procedures either confirms or denies that the intervention–prevention techniques selected are appropriate; this feedback loop is an essential part of any scientifically based intervention–prevention effort. In cases of child assault, it refines the process step-by-step as new hypotheses about causes and remedies are developed and empirically tested and evaluated, in turn leading to next steps, and so on.

Beery (1967) referred to this feedback loop in educotherapy as the diagnostic-remedial approach. It is consistent with the cybernetic information processing model advanced by Meier and Malone (1979) for facilitating optimum child development within developmentally disabled children, who present many similar challenges to the community intervention–prevention specialists (Meier and Sloan, 1983). Such a feedback loop should be included in any effort to remedy or change a client's learning and behavior so that, in a very pragmatic fashion, that which works is continued and perhaps intensified as indicated, whereas that which does not yield desirable results is modified or discarded and replaced by that which is more appropriate or responsive to the new information. This means that treatment planning is an ongoing process and that neither a diagnosis nor a treatment plan remains static, since the client is a constantly changing dependent variable, being affected by a variety of independent and changing variables.

It should also be borne in mind that the multifactorial model provides numerous points of entry into the intervention–prevention process. Thus, the term client may be construed to refer to the assaulted child, the assaultive adult (who frequently proves also to have been a victim just a short generation ago), and the assault-ridden environment, which passively permits if not actively provokes and encourages violence within its sphere of influence. This chapter focuses primarily on intervention–prevention for the assaulted child, whereas other chapters reveal promising family–based (Chapter 6) environmental, community-based (Chapter 7), and comprehensive (Chapter 8) modifications and approaches necessary to arrest and eliminate this cancerous and vicious cycle of child assault, which is presently ravaging millions of children, their families, and indeed their civilized (?) societies.

It has also been observed that the cumulative impact of numerous contributing factors not only leads to escalation in severity, frequency, and complexity of assaultive episodes but also suggests a more guarded prognosis and longer rehabilitation period, since it ordinarily is not possible to deal satisfactorily with all contributing factors simultaneously. In fact, the individual therapists, or preferably interdisciplinary treatment planning team members or intervention–specialists, engage in a kind of triage procedure in conducting an evaluation and analyzing the diagnostic findings in such a manner that the most severe and life-endangering factors are given immediate attention, and the less serious factors are reserved for subsequent attention. The aforementioned model is helpful in this regard as well, since it helps to keep track of the factors that are being dealt with and those that have been put on the "back burner" until the more pressing immediate issues and contributing conditions are addressed and resolved.

For example, although a given assaultive parent was herself sexually assaulted as a child by her own brother, is an unwed teenager, is unemployed, lives in a violent neighborhood, and feels overwhelmed by the demands placed on her by two children under three years of age who seem to be somewhat developmentally delayed, she must first learn simply to stop hitting and yelling at (verbally assaulting) her infant when the child cries in the middle of the night. Thus, the first priority is the immediate elimination of violent childrearing behavior on the part of the responsible adult, to be followed (it is hoped) by training in anger reduction techniques and ultimately more facilitative interaction patterns with her child. As time and resources permit, attention then can be focused on helping this distraught mother strive to accomplish such goals that will improve her own sense of self-esteem, to learn marketable job skills to make her employable, to deal with her resentment and distrust of other adults, especially men, all of which will eventually enable her to get gainful and meaningful employment, to afford to live in better circumstances, to get some assistance with raising her children, and perhaps to strike up more meaningful relationships with other adults, whether as helpmates in childrearing or as loving companions to share in coping with life's vicissitudes and enjoying its pleasures.

Eventually, attention must be given to modifying the environment that surrounds and supports violence as a way of life. The marshaling of community resources to support families, renewing of deteriorated urban life circumstances, providing appropriate job training and employment opportunities, and even redefining value systems to be more humanly fulfilling, are all examples of long-range items on a comprehensive intervention–prevention agenda addressed in greater detail in subsequent chapters of this book.

## INTERDISCIPLINARY MULTIMODALITY INTERVENTION–PREVENTION

The disciplines and modalities germane to intervention–prevention of assault against children are listed in alphabetical order, although the actual order of preference and influence is highly variable, depending on the following factors: (1) the relative extent of a given discipline's involvement required by the treatment plan; (2) the strength and status of any given discipline or modality within an organization; (3) its representation (or absence) by a specialist on a diagnostic and treatment planning team; and (4) the competence, charisma, and power of its spokesperson(s).

## Art Therapy

Art therapy is a diagnostic–treatment modality that is rapidly becoming established as a separate and creditable discipline; since this modality is relatively new, is exemplary, is first on the alphabetical list, and lends itself to visual display, somewhat more space and attention is given to it than to some of the more established and traditional disciplines or modalities. A national organization has recently established criteria for becoming a registered art therapist (ATR).

Art therapy has many facets, including the following: (1) the free, nonverbal expression of one's self-concept through techniques such as "Draw-A-Person" (Goodenough, 1926; Harris, 1963); (2) a symbolic revelation of the client's perception of family dynamics through a similar "Draw-A-Family" procedure; (3) reproduction of structured stimulus symbols to evaluate some aspects of brain maturation and function (Beery, 1967; Bender, 1956); and (4) the release of sheer emotion or progressive relaxation through art and handicraft media, such as fingerpainting, clay building, knitting, leathercraft, jewelry making, and so forth.

Many assaulted children have learned that certain spoken words can be very dangerous and that to survive they must not say the inflammatory things out loud. Consequently they develop a reluctance to communicate verbally and openly with anyone. To work effectively with assaulted children, several nonverbal modalities are included as part of a multidisciplinary approach to diagnosis and intervention–prevention. In the developmental progress of a child, the use of symbols, drawings, and patterns often precedes and usually accompanies verbal communication. Art therapy, therefore, has become one of the more basic ways of entering the child's world and communicating with the child in a nonthreatening manner. Emerging through the children's drawings are certain patterns, which frequently are graphic indicators of the assault they have suffered.

Art therapy may be used for different purposes and in different settings even within the same intervention–prevention program. It provides helpful diagnostic procedures for nonverbal children who do not respond to or trust the more traditional verbally loaded testing. The first purpose of an art assessment is to help evaluate the current status of the client and to help formulate an individualized treatment plan. Along with the traditional House-Tree-Person, Draw-A-Person, and Kinetic-Family Drawing, children should also be asked to create a spontaneous free drawing—one that they wish to do. Not only can problems be identified from the drawings, but the children's strengths, interests, and developmental level can be estimated. Art evaluations may be repeated before case reviews and also at termination of a given therapeutic relationship to help monitor and document change.

The art therapy modality facilitates evaluation of the family as well. Developed by Kwiatkowski (1978), the family art evaluation reveals to the therapist and to the entire family some of the underlying family dynamics, some of which were not apparent until seen in graphic form.

After a diagnostic art workup has been completed, if the treatment plan specifies art therapy, an appointment is made with the therapist providing the specified type of therapy, whether individual, group, or family. In a typical art therapy session, primary focus is on dynamically oriented art therapy, pioneered by Naumburg, who states:

> The process of art therapy is based on the recognition that one's thoughts and feelings are derived from the unconscious and often reach expression in images rather than in words. By means of pictorial projection, art therapy encourages a method of symbolic communication between client and therapist. Whether trained or untrained in art, every individual has a latent capacity to project his inner conflicts into visual form. As patients picture such inner experiences, they frequently become more verbally articulate. When spontaneous images are created by the client, he is encouraged to supply free verbal associations to the image. He comes to recognize the symbolic significance of his work, being a kind of mirror which reflects what is taking place in his unconscious. (1966, p. 137)

Most importantly, the art therapist does not interpret the art expression but merely encourages the client to discover the meaning of the art production. This free association process is provided in a characteristic therapeutic session, which may use a variety of media. Expression of repressed feelings is extremely important in the treatment of assaulted children and their families. The art therapist might propose that clients use a clay board, at which they are encouraged to throw clay as hard and as long as they wish to do so. When an image begins to take shape in the clay, the clients are asked to finish the image. Thus, the expression of a client's repressed anger, for example, can lead to something that is creative rather than something that is destructive.

Group art therapy may be held in a variety of settings. The goal of this approach is to facilitate peer interaction and communication as well as to promote interpersonal problem solving within the family, whether it is the biological, foster, adoptive, or residential treatment center family. Just as an assaulted child can become trapped in a world of noncommunication, so can the members of a family find themselves ensnared in a conspiracy of silence and consequently not relating effectively to one another. To illustrate this lack of communication and to begin to compensate for these individual feelings of isolation, art therapy emphasizes communicating, understanding, and clarifying relationships within the family group.

A significant component of a complete art therapy program is the art studio–gallery. The art studio concept follows that of Erickson (1963) and is product-oriented, especially designed to meet the children's needs for increased self-esteem and possibly vocational preparation. Not all clients who have a need to express their creativity have a clinical need for formal art therapy. The studio–gallery helps clients to develop and realize their creative potential for its own sake. In addition to the major difference between the product versus process approach, the art studio–gallery experiences and art therapy sessions differ in the concept of "hours of operation." Unlike the formal art therapy session, which is an individually appointed block of time, the studio is open at regular hours and the clients may participate as often and as long as they like. The studio includes an art gallery, where the artwork products are displayed in a professional manner (e.g., matted, framed) to enhance the artisan's pride and self-esteem. Clients with a desire for vocational training have the opportunity to learn the various fields of design and production.

In an effective art therapy program there is a delicate balance between the therapeutic process and the artistic product. The studio focuses on art production and the artist's developing talents while the art therapy session focuses on the clinical process and the client's perceptions and feelings. The training of interns in art therapy involves the disciplines of both psychology and the creative arts. The program is structured in that it is organized to meet the needs of many children, but not so rigidly run that it discourages imagination and originality. An important goal of the art therapy program is that it remain flexible enough to encourage the flow of ideas, productivity, and creativity.

Another aspect of the art therapy program is that of research. Research supports the hypothesis that creative expression is a very positive deterrent to delinquency, depression, and mental illness (Hunner and Walker, 1981). At the Village of CHILDHELP and in other research-oriented intervention–prevention programs, psychometric tests of intelligence reveal that the majority of assaulted children get lower scores on verbal scales than on performance scales (see Chapter 8). These clients and often their assaultive parents reveal a tendency to act out their emotions—that is, they physically manifest their affection, anger, fear, and other feelings rather than expressing them verbally. Art therapy can help to bridge these communication gaps within individuals themselves, between parents and children, between families and larger groups, and, ultimately, between groups and society. The following questions are being asked as a basis for future research studies using art therapy as a diagnostic–treatment modality: (1) Are there specific assault indicators in art? (2) Can behavioral and emotional change be monitored through art? (3) Can a different quality and greater quantity of information be derived from free art expression to complement more structured psychometric tests and procedures (R. Meier, 1984)? (4) Does art therapy help to improve communicative and expressive skills in previously nonverbal children? (5) What relationship is there between the improvement of communication and the development of creative potential?

During the past six years at The Village of CHILDHELP thousands of drawings have been produced by assaulted children for the purpose of conducting an in-depth study of specific indicators of assault and violence in children's art. Thus far, it is possible to present a series of observations and cautious generalizations based on many individual forms of expression; however, no conclusions have yet been derived from a quantified statistical analysis of group trends and correlations. When the drawings of clients are reviewed, two principles should be considered: (1) there are developmental stages of children's art; and (2) children draw as they perceive things to be, not as things really are (Kellogg, 1967; Lowenfeld, 1954).

In the self-portraits drawn by assaulted children, the following characteristics are frequently found: (1) arms are missing; (2) the self is sometimes pictured as relatively very small in a very large space; and (3) the assault is sometimes graphically drawn or indicated by omission (e.g., sexually assaulted children often fail to include the lower half of their bodies). In the family portraits, the dominant feature is that of isolation. Not only is the family isolated as a group, but also the individuals within the family are isolated from one another. The assaulted child frequently leaves himself or herself out of the family portrait. The spontaneous drawings contain numerous symbolic elements, often depicting raw emotions (such as anger and fear), presented in an atmosphere of turmoil and confusion. At the end of this chapter are some representative examples of art work produced by assaulted children with accompanying descriptive and partially interpretive captions.

## Audiology

When it is known that a child has suffered physical assault, it is wise there is any measurable hearing loss at various sound frequencies. Being hit on the head can often induce such hearing losses, which in turn lead to a child's inability to follow directions from adults who, in a state of exasperated frenzy, may strike out and hit the child across the side of the head again, only to exacerbate the original problem. Such a vicious cycle is extraordinarily confusing to the child, who did not even hear at the outset why he was being punished so wantonly and capriciously, at least as he perceived it. Since hearing deficits are not as readily observed as orthopedic or visual handicaps, they may go undetected, not only contributing to the aforementioned vicious cycle but also underlying subsequent communication and learning disorders.

It must be borne in mind that many physically assaulted children have mild to severe hearing losses that would compromise their ability to satisfactorily understand the spoken word and subsequently to reproduce it intelligibly. An informal study of assaulted children at The Village of CHILDHELP (see Chapter 8) revealed an unusually high incidence of audiological defects (Billingslea, 1979), which were in part responsible for the even higher incidence of speech defects among these severely assaulted children. Of course, once the auditory defects are identified and treated as well as the state of the art and science will permit, it is necessary to institute an extensive and intensive speech therapy program to help compensate for the child's loss of time and experience with the spoken word during previous critical and formative years (see later section on Speech Therapy).

## Dance Therapy

The therapy and relaxation derived from rhythmic movement of the body are evident throughout the history of mankind. For some assaulted clients dance may become a pleasant means for developing better coordination and general fitness while expending physical energy in a pleasant and calming manner, instead of resorting to the violent, counterproductive physical expression of fighting. Victims of assault are known to harbor deep feelings of resentment and rage over past events. This anger gives rise to considerable agitation and evokes the fight-or-flight response, which is often chronically repressed in the form of agitated depression and thinly veiled hostility, which may erupt with the slightest provocation. In addition to the physical therapy of dancing instead of fighting (making love instead of war), a treatment plan may include a program of jogging alone or with a group instead of running away to reduce free-floating anxiety and depression (see Recreational Therapy later in this chapter).

# Educational Therapy

Education is a generic term, which in this context refers to all formal school-related activities from preschool programs like Head Start and therapeutic nursery schools to regular elementary school mainstreaming provisions. It also includes the many special public and private school programs for children with special needs, depending upon the nature of their developmental or learning disabilities. New materials and guides are becoming available specifically for teachers to understand assaulted children and better manage them in their classrooms (Tower, 1984; Van de Kamp, 1983).

Assaulted children are frequently "special needs" children in many respects and it is frequently necessary to provide special educational experiences and settings to enable them ultimately to benefit from regular formal schooling. *The Educateur Model* (Goocher, 1975; Linton, 1971) is a highly touted individualized education process essentially based on a remedial diagnostic approach to helping children learn various academic skills. The whole of child development is indeed a learning process, which can be impaired by the trauma and sequelae of child assault. Whether or not there is actual neurophysiological damage impairing a child's ability to receive, process, and express information, various psychological impairments may make it difficult or impossible for the child to risk new experiences which are essential for continual and optimal learning and development. This author, with several colleagues, pioneered an *autotelic responsive environment* for very young, deprived, and disturbed children, and such an approach has proved to be quite helpful in a variety of therapeutic nursery and day care settings for young learning disabled and disadvantaged children (Meier, 1970; Meier and Malone, 1979; Nimnicht, McAfee, and Meier, 1969). However, any special educational setting requires specially trained professional and paraprofessional personnel who are able to understand and accommodate the individual differences and behavioral disorders of developmentally delayed and disturbed children. They must be able to manage difficult child behavior without resorting to corporal punishment or other forms of cruel discipline, which unfortunately are still legal forms of child assault in our society and must be replaced by better alternatives (Dubanowski, 1983; Hyman and Wise, 1979; Meier, 1982).

Individually prescribed instructional opportunities should be a part of any interdisciplinary treatment plan for assaulted children, who often qualify for placement in classes for severely or moderately emotionally disturbed or educable mentally retarded children, and are thus covered in the public schools by the provisions of the Education for All Handicapped Act (PL 94-142), which requires that each child have an individualized educational program designed by an interdisciplinary team.

The concept of mainstreaming also is important with assaulted children, since frequently they believe not only that they are different from other children but also that they are somehow unworthy of participating in the normal curriculum and extracurricular activities available in regular schools. Thus, although it is often beneficial for assaulted children to be available to one another, to mutually share tragedy and triumph, and to be clustered for various group therapy experiences, it is also important that they mingle with nontraumatized, normally developing children to realize that they are much more like them than different from them. Many learning disabilities have their roots in prior developmental disabilities, which result from compromising acts of God or rites of families (Meier, 1976a; Meier and Sloan, 1984).

## Family Therapy

The inclusion of the entire family system is exigent for any intervention–prevention efforts to have the long-term effects of eliminating assault against children. As stated in the Preface, a major legacy of this writer's service with the federal government was to broaden the name and function of the U.S. Office of Child Development to include the family, which led to the substituted and enlarged Administration for Children, Youth, and Families. In a 1976 keynote address to the National Association for the Education of Young Children, a national network of family development centers was proposed (Meier, 1978) to build upon the growing conviction that in order to support and change individuals it is necessary to support or change the ecological system (Part III of the Multifactorial model in Chapter 1) in which the individuals live (Mora, 1974). With the appearance of a spate of theoretical and practical textbooks on family therapy (Ackerman, 1966; Ackerman, Lieb, and Pearce, 1970; Bowen, 1978; Foley, 1974; Framo, 1977; Guerin, 1976; Haley, 1971; Minuchin, 1974; Papp, 1977), plus numerous accounts of its successful application to a wide variety of dysfunctional families, the past decade has demonstrated the importance and efficacy of dealing with the entire family constellation as the client in order to have a lasting impact on its individual component stars.

Rather than attempt to review the multiple contemporary approaches to family therapy now being applied to assaultive families, it was decided to present one representative approach (Chapter 6), which embodies most of the common principles and practices; Chapter 6 also provides the reader with additional references for further reviewing this burgeoning field.

Family therapy (much like art therapy, occupational therapy, and recreational therapy, to name a few) has emerged as a discipline on its own; members in this field are granted certificates in marriage and family counseling (MFCC) after completion of a prescribed course of graduate study at the master's degree level and at least 2000 clock hours of satisfactory supervised clinical experience. The medical realm has also recently reacknowledged the importance of the family by instituting the specialty of Family Practice, which is a refined version of the revered family physician in general practice. Two pioneering physicians (see Acknowledgments) edited a fine source book focused on the importance of the family and community in treating child assault (Helfer and Kempe, 1976).

## Legal Involvement

Obviously, the most immediate and often dramatic intervention in a case of child assault is the removal of the child from the custody of the assaulting adults or, with increasing frequency, the removal of the assaultive adult from the home. Since the process of search and seizure, as well as many other related legal domestic actions, is typically fraught with profound emotional or even dangerous violent reactions, it is necessary for well-trained law enforcement persons to be involved (Bross, 1984; Kean, 1984, Mele, 1984; Stone, Tyler, and Mead, 1984; Tyler and Brassard, 1984). The serious action of removing child assault victims or perpetrators from their homes also serves to prevent recidivism in the future, since such removal is frequently accompanied by considerable inconvenience, embarrassment, and awkwardness, which most adults are reluctant to experience more than once. More is said about this procedure and its many ramifications in Chapter 3.

Since there are numerous legal implications in the disruption or disintegration of any family unit, the collective wisdom and time-tested protocol of the entire judiciary system must be utilized in the interruption and redefinition of custody. In true interdisciplinary spirit, Besharov (1983) suggests some constructive ways in which the law can help social work accomplish its child protective work more easily and effectively. Such concerns as parents' rights, children's rights, and the use of guardians ad litem and other child advocates are all concerns that are dealt with in Chapter 4. Because of the many complex and potentially compromising issues raised by legal technicalities, it is highly desirable to have a lawyer who is well versed in these matters readily available to the team or actually serve as a member of a comprehensive interdisciplinary treatment team.

## Milieu Therapy

Milieu therapy is a somewhat imprecise term referring to all of the specific provisions made within a therapeutic environment designed to facilitate growth, development, and healing within the clients who are in that environment or milieu. For severely assaulted children in out-of-home placement, the entire living environment is critical for supporting the more intensive psychotherapy and related therapies that the clients receive during each day. This underscores the importance of the child's caregiver and relates back to the notion of the autotelic responsive environment (Meier, 1970) and the facilitation of normal growth and development (Meier and Malone, 1979). Chapter 8 describes in greater detail a model residential treatment program operated at The Village of CHILDHELP.

The parenting received by an assaulted child (and usually by the assaultive parent also) is fundamentally neglectful, defective, or violent, causing the child's removal from a family situation that is life-endangering or at least requiring prompt and radical modification. The quality of the interaction between clients and parent surrogates becomes a critical element in any out-of-home intervention–prevention program for helping the clients (both child and adult victims). The term "caregiver" is deliberately chosen, as distinct from "caretaker" or "careworker," to create an image of giving care to their clients in a pleasant, purposeful, and professional manner, as opposed to taking care from their clients or having to work at caring in a laborious and grudging fashion. A caregiver can create and indeed be an integral part of a therapeutic milieu in which the children are enabled to heal physical and psychic injuries and are helped to grow and develop in a normal and supportive environment conducive to realizing their full human and humane potential. Caregivers (milieu managers), then, are first and foremost models of good parenting as they attend to the daily living needs and demands inherent in growing and developing clients. In addition to this challenging role, a trained caregiver must have finely tuned skills and knowledge for anticipating and meeting a variety of idiosyncratic developmental needs on the part of each disturbed child within a group of disturbed children; this is also true of a caregiver working with assaultive adult clients, who frequently were assaulted as children and need reparenting and redevelopment (the term *habilitation* may be more accurate than *rehabilitation*, which implies that a previously satisfactory status existed and should be restored).

The accomplished caregiver anticipates and meets the complicated daily living needs of individual clients whose previous adverse experiences or lack of experiences may cause them to be what has been referred to as "Swiss cheese" persons. Ideally, the caregiver creates an enriched responsive environment (Meier, 1970) designed to fill those holes in the client's experience and learning in accordance with the individualized treatment plan derived by the interdisciplinary planning team. This person needs to be skillful at the application of behavior modification principles with an accent on "catching clients being good" (as opposed to catching them being bad) and systematically rewarding their desirable behaviors rather than being preoccupied with punishing undesirable behaviors. Chapter 8 briefly describes a progressive development system for monitoring and evaluating client habilitation.

The art and science of effective caregiving for other people's children in foster homes or residential treatment centers is itself a growing and developing discipline, which can make or break the efficacy of the other intervention–prevention efforts, since it is the caregiver with whom clients spend most of their other 23 hours (Wineman, 1969). Various recruitment, training, and evaluation projects have been attempted to upgrade the quality of caregivers (see Chapter 8), but the answers and guidelines are by no means all available yet on this perhaps least well defined, albeit crucial discipline in the therapeutic continuum. Additional research on the recruitment and training of excellent caregivers with a formal credentialing system, similar to that of the Child Development Associate (Klein, 1973) is indicated to elevate these people to a peer status (interdisciplinary parity principle) on the treatment team. The identification of desirable caregiver characteristics to avoid their assaulting children (Haddock and McQueen, 1983) or burning out on the job (Freudenberger, 1974) is a serious current research challenge. The caregiver training curricula offered by Abrams, Naehring, and Zuckerman (1984) and by the U.S. Department of Health, Education, and Welfare (1975) are steps in the right direction. The burgeoning literature on parenting education (see section on paraprofessionals later in this chapter) is also germane to the preparation and continuing on-the-job training and education of child caregivers.

One caveat to be considered by child caregivers, especially with regard to interacting with sexually assaulted children and assaulting adults, is the psychoanalytic phenomenon of transference (Pawl, 1984). Although the phenomenon occurs in most effective therapeutic relationships, it can be especially trying for the caregiver who lives with assaulted children. As mentioned earlier, these children often become exquisitely sensitive to persons around them and are quite accomplished at testing each new person and situation to determine how trustworthy or unstable they are. This testing takes the form of deliberately provocative displays of hostility and aggression of a verbal or physical nature or may be veiled in various indiscriminate pseudo-affectionate and intimate statements and behaviors. For example, children at The Village have mastered performing spontaneous temper tantrums or proffering almost instant and profound love, to see just how far the adult target can be led astray—or, on the other hand, how far that adult can be trusted to be genuine in interacting with the child. The children have learned how to find the raw nerve endings in each adult and to push these buttons accordingly, thereby revealing to other children and staff the vulnerabilities within the adult group.

In addition to the quite natural feelings of affection and disaffection flowing between caregivers and clients (forms of transference and its corollary, countertransference) the clients may elicit inappropriate or uncontrollable reactions from their caregivers. For example, child clients have reported that a male caregiver likes to have them sit on his lap until he becomes "hard down there" and then encourages them to wriggle about, thereby giving him erotic pleasure and causing considerable anxiety in the clients, who are once again faced with the unspeakable dilemma of enjoying the physical contact with an adult but fearing any progression to more serious sexual exploitation or molestation. Naturally, female caregivers are not immune to such erotic stimulation and consequent inappropriate physical or sexual interaction with children. On the other hand, it is not uncommon to observe how caregivers deny their feelings of affection and pleasure or express their countertransference toward certain clients by being unduly harsh toward them. For example, systematic observation of milieu management may reveal that certain child caregivers resort to the overuse of such behavior modification techniques as "time out" (removing and isolating a client from other people and activities, which frequently is interpreted as quite severe punishment and rejection by a client who has already experienced a great deal of rejection), or they may be overzealous in the application of various authorized restraining procedures, which may be thinly veiled masks for aggressive or erotic interaction with an undeserving or unsuspecting and relatively powerless client.

Certainly caregiver training must address these and many other related psychodynamic issues if the daily living milieu (cottage, foster, or adoptive setting) is truly to be an adjunct to and not a deterrent from therapeutic progress with assaulted children. Similarly, all persons interacting with either assaulted children or assaulting adults in a therapeutic relationship must acknowledge and appropriately deal with their feelings of transference and countertransference toward their clients (Yalom, 1975). The current literature is replete with studies and guidelines regarding appropriate clinical behavior, and it is incumbent upon the more sophisticated and experienced clinicians to translate the relevant caveats and procedures into acceptable practices by the many paraprofessional and less technically trained professionals who interact with their clients on a daily basis, often over a prolonged period of time. This is to ensure that all adults in the therapeutic environment are contributing to client progress and not compromising the entire intervention–prevention process with sometimes inadvertently exploitative or counterproductive interaction. These observations apply across all intervention–prevention modalities and professional disciplines participating in the treatment process; when followed, they will contribute substantially to the long-term preventive process by supporting the immediate healing and by preventing the iatrogenic complications sometimes created by avoidable inappropriate events and dynamics in the treatment process itself.

In addition to the human elements in the milieu, careful consideration should be given to all of the other animate and inanimate characteristics of the living environment, including food, air temperature and quality, furnishings, domestic animals, plants, toileting and bathing provisions for hygiene and privacy, soothing sound levels and acoustics, proper lighting, general orderliness, and so forth; some of these characteristics are addressed in this and subsequent chapters. For example, success has been reported for using a particular shade of "shocking pink" on the walls of small temporary holding tanks to quiet violent criminals and other agitated persons. Such a color scheme may be appropriate for time-out or other isolation settings for clients whose anger is apparently overwhelming them (and others) and interfering with therapeutic access and progress. This notion underscores the ecological fact that multiple stimuli are continually being received from the environment by all sense modalities of the peripheral nervous system and have important effects on the person (Component III in the multifactorial model in Chapter 1). Some stimuli (colors, sounds, textures, and so forth) have quieting effects on most people; however, "different strokes for different folks" pertains here as well as elsewhere, since idiosyncratic associations may make some colors pleasant and others objectionable for certain individuals. Nevertheless, some commonly soothing color schemes can consciously be included in an environment designed to help clients focus and get themselves under control; other color schemes may be employed for other purposes.

## Laughter Therapy

A sense of humor and ability to laugh is a distinguishing characteristic of the human species and is increasingly being emphasized as a therapeutic adjunct to healing (Cousins, 1979). Most healthy families have a shared sense of humor, which often is used to defuse potentially explosive feelings and situations (Curran, 1983). Unhealthy families often resort to verbal assaults in the form of not-so-funny sarcasm, which is verbal sadism, or hurtful insults and innuendos.

## Music Therapy

Just as the aforementioned art and dance therapies serve as media for expression and communication so, too, can music serve this therapeutic purpose. The active creation and participation in musical production is quite satisfying to many children; even the passive listening to peaceful sounds may soothe the "savage beast" lurking within the violated and consequently violent human being. Listening to familiar or pleasing melodies can also have a reassuring and in some cases uplifting effect on the human spirit, thereby contributing to the healing nature of the aforementioned milieu by setting various moods of either an uplifting, up-beat, or quieting quality. The behavioral effects of such alterations in the sound environment become apparent when comparing the frantic activity at a local disco with the solemn behavior at a funeral service in a cathedral.

## Neurology

When a child is suspected of having sustained damage to the brain or peripheral nervous system, it is standard practice to schedule a neurological consultation in order to rule in or rule out various types of brain dysfunction that may adversely affect gross motor and fine motor functioning, learning and behavior. As mentioned in Chapter 1, there are many soft neurological signs manifest in minimal brain dysfunction or postconcussion syndromes that may contribute to the dynamics of child assault.The examining family physician, pediatrician, or emergency room personnel dealing with assault usually make such referrals to their neurologist colleagues who are now becoming increasingly sensitive to and knowledgeable about these subtleties of child assault.

## Nursing

In schools, in residential facilities, and now increasingly in pediatric practices, a nurse or pediatric nurse practitioner is the first medically trained person to meet and perhaps perform a physical examination on a child. A nurse, who is traditionally more likely to be female, may be especially suitable for investigating suspected sexual assault in young female victims, since she may be less threatening and consequently more likely to enjoy more open communication regarding suspected physical and particularly sexual assault. However, the nurse must be trained to identify and differentiate accidental injuries from suspected child assault and to pursue suspicions with perceptive and effective questioning. As is being repeatedly pointed out (Cantwell, 1983; Groth, 1978; Sgroi, 1982; and others; see also Chapter 2), it is critical that questions regarding inappropriate sexual experiences by young boys and girls be asked directly by trusted examining persons. To ensure that no critical areas are overlooked, it is probably wisest to have an interview outline that includes specific questions not only about physical and psychological assault but also concerning any sexual exploitation and assault. If the nurse is not the initial point of contact for a medical workup, he or she should make it a point to obtain the necessary information to complete a medical history for a child's chart, whether it be in an institutional, school, or private practice setting. As a person whom most children have been trained to trust, a nurse should be alert to any other spoken or unspoken signs of various types of assault and report these to the interdisciplinary team for inclusion in or updating of their treatment plan. The nurse, by attending to such seemingly perfunctory matters as routine height and weight measurements, should also be alert to any nutritional or medicational undesirable effects and other potential health needs or hazards in a given child's living circumstances.

# Nutrition

Although the literature is periodically clouded by numerous unscientific and unsubstantiated claims about the effects of diet on physical, mental, and emotional status and behavior, there is a growing body of literature that supports the notion that the quality and quantity of food consumed by a person does affect brain and general body functioning, which in turn impacts on mood, alertness, memory, perception of stimuli, and general sense of well-being. The current research on the effects of various food substances on the production and maintenance of at least thirty kinds of neurotransmitters is showing increasing promise for chemically modifying physical and behavioral functions. The major challenge remains that of empirically separating fact from fiction about the effects of food on one or more of these neurotransmitters and their subsequent effect on human behavior, growth, and development. The critical intrauterine period and the first few months of life seem to have the greatest impact on brain development; a balanced diet with adequate protein is clearly essential. Subsequently, nutrients, including so-called junk food and mislabeled "empty calories" do seem to have differential effects on individual children, giving rise to numerous controversial theories about dietary management to alleviate such behavioral disorders as hyperkinesis (Connors, 1980; Feingold, 1975; Lipton and Mayo, 1983; Weiss, 1982), aggression (Campbell, Cohen, and Small, 1982), violence (Meier, 1984d; Walsh, 1983), and depression, poor memory, and impaired learning ability (Ellman, Silverstein, Zingarelli, Shafer, and Silverstein, 1984; Swanson and Kinsbourne, 1980).

The Institute of Toxicology in the School of Pharmacy at the University of Southern California has addressed other pharmacological contributors to criminal behavior, allergies, and general well-being, all of which have some promise for managing diets and consequent behavior in difficult child and adult populations. Schoenthaler (1983) has reported encouraging results from nutritional managements of incarcerated juvenile and adult offenders resulting in significant reductions of antisocial and riotous behaviors, primarily due to radically reducing the amount of refined sugars in their diets. Unfortunately, more carefully designed and controlled studies must be performed before any firm conclusions and definite nutritional regimens can be confidently recommended to alter function or behavior in the desired manner (Swenerton and Jarvis, 1983).

# Occupational Therapy

Occupational therapy is a relatively recently defined discipline with registered practitioners (OTR, or Occupational Therapist, Registered) whose training prepares them to provide a variety of therapeutic and learning experiences for enabling their clients to develop or relearn practical living skills, such as eating, drinking, dressing, and so forth. At one time, as an adjunct to more basic physical therapy, occupational therapists helped victims of stroke, spinal cord injuries, and similar trauma to become rehabilitated and retrained for various appropriate occupations, hence their title. Clients were helped to relearn practical skills requiring, for example, complex eye-hand coordination, through specific exercises and such activities as handicrafts, to help prepare them for returning to the world of work and, it is hoped, remunerative occupations. More recently, occupational therapists have extended their work with developmentally disabled children to enable them to approximate normal growth and development more closely including not only refining their basic survival skills to eat, drink, and move around but also to enhance the development of other skills on which such learning tasks as speaking, reading and writing are dependent. Some occupational therapists (e.g., Ayres, 1966; Bobath, 1963) have become concerned with fundamental child growth and development and have contributed to explorations into innovative infant stimulation and related compensatory efforts to retrain developmentally disabled children (Meier and Malone, 1979; Tjossem, 1976) and to enrich the experiences of disadvantaged and even normally developing children.

# Ophthalmology

A child's ability to see normally is critical in a world so loaded with visual cues, symbols, and information. An optometric screening should be provided for all children who seem to have any difficulty seeing to be sure that they have as close to normal vision as possible, with or without correction. Since many physically assaulted children have blackened eyes as a result of blows on the face and head, it is possible that they have sustained damage to their eyes and brains, which must be identified and remedied whenever possible. Ophthalmologists are medically trained (MD) specialists who are experts on diseases of the eye and visual systems; they must treat such conditions as detached retinas. Most physicians can also be very helpful in checking for suspected brain damage by looking with an ophthalmoscope into the eyes, which are almost like windows into the brain for the trained and experienced practitioner.

## Paraprofessional Aides

The use of paraprofessionals for intervention–prevention service delivery systems is not new. Paraprofessionals are trained aides who work with professionals. Many agencies have found that the use of paraprofessionals increases the efficiency of professional staff members and allows them to serve more clients. Paraprofessional aides have functioned under a variety of titles, which reflect different orientations and emphases in their backgrounds, training, and roles; they have been called lay therapists (Alexander, 1980), lay health visitors (Haynes, Cutler, Gray, and Kempe, 1984; Kempe, 1976), foster grandparents (Barbour, 1983; Reagan, 1982), and parent aides (Gifford, Kaplan, and Salus, 1979), to name some popular labels. The opportunity for using paraprofessionals exists in every community, and the possibilities are enormous. Paraprofessional aides may be either volunteer or paid workers; the terms "lay," "layperson," and "laity" are somewhat misleading, since paraprofessionals are trained in their roles but do not ordinarily have degrees in any of the helping professions. Families who are experiencing domestic violence and child assault problems often lack support, warmth, and understanding from their families and friends. Out of frustration these parents may look to their children for the warmth and understanding they need. Children, however, are not always able to meet the needs of their parents and may become the targets of parental assault, ironically by the frustrated adults who expect too much from their children.

In their role as "special friends," paraprofessional aides enable assaultive parents to experience emotional support and acceptance and at the same time provide these parents with a model for change by acting as warm, understanding adult friends and gentle, nurturing parental surrogates for their children. The parents gradually begin to lean more on the adult aide than on their children for support in childrearing and general survival.

Since assaultive parents generally have suffered physical and emotional assault themselves as children, they need to experience a reparenting or perhaps a shared-parenting relationship (Gabinet, 1983; Meier, 1984b, c) in which their own dependency needs are met, they are accepted as worthwhile individuals, they are able to establish trust in another adult person, and they are helped ultimately to achieve mature independence. A well-trained and supervised paraprofessional can provide this type of therapeutic and facilitative reparenting or shared parenting relationship. The major emphasis of most paraprofessional aide programs is on the development of this type of nurturing relationship. Relationships between parents and paraprofessional parent aides are informal and long-term, generally lasting between 12 and 24 months. This relationship, once developed, can be used as a vehicle for resolving multiple family problems, such as inappropriate child rearing practices.

The relationship that develops between clients and paraprofessional aides is the most important factor in the success of such a program. This relationship passes through a number of stages, including (1) a development stage; (2) a transition stage; (3) a partial dependency stage; and (4) a stage of independence, ending with the termination of the formal relationship (Lieberman, 1979).

Abusive and neglectful families are repeatedly in a state of crisis. The crises may result from minor or major problems but, because these families have so few resources to call upon, they very seldom resolve crises successfully. Parents believe they have failed when they are unable to resolve crises, and this feeling of failure may lead to various forms of assault against their children.

Paraprofessional aides act as friends to assaultive parents, who often have no one else to befriend them. But there is a unique characteristic of this friendship; it is largely one-sided. The paraprofessional aide typically will be doing all of the listening, sympathizing, and initiating of contacts. The aide can help parents explore possible solutions to problems, develop confidence in themselves and responsibility for their own decisions, and become aware of community resources that might be of help to the parents over time (Schmitt and Beezley, 1976).

How do assaultive parents typically react to parent aides? At first, parents may have difficulty trusting paraprofessional aides—or any other adult for that matter. They may see the aides as just another authority figure there to criticize them. The parents may deliberately arrange not to be at home when the aide comes. Alternatively, they may test the aide's sincerity and commitment by calling at inconvenient times to complain about their children. Nonetheless, eventually the parents begin to trust and rely on the parent aides. They realize that the aides are their friends, that the aides are spending time with them because they care about the parents as individuals. As the parents begin to trust and to lean on the parent aides, the pattern of relying on their children to meet their needs is gradually replaced by a more nurturing and mature parent–child relationship.

In the past, professional constraints, such as high caseloads and the standard formality of the worker-client relationship, inhibited the development of this kind of dependent and friendly relationship. Paraprofessional aides, on the other hand, can be trained in sufficient numbers to work on a one-to-one basis with individual parents and families. In addition, the informality of the relationship allows them to become real friends to and supportive of all the family members.

In addition, paraprofessional aide programs are a cost-effective means of providing treatment to assaultive families. As volunteers, paraprofessionals receive little or no remuneration except possibly reimbursement for expenses, such as gasoline or special gifts they buy for clients. On the other hand, indigenous, nurturing individuals, who cannot afford to volunteer their time as paraprofessional aides, should be paid at least a minimum wage. Paraprofessional aides can be trained and supervised with a minimal cost to the agency providing the service; however, it is absolutely necessary that preservice and ongoing inservice training and support be provided to the paraprofessional aides by competent and motivated professionals.

The primary goal is to help assaultive parents change their unhealthy patterns of interpersonal behavior toward their children to interactions that will enable them to thrive as a healthy, functioning family unit. The success of these programs throughout the United States has been documented repeatedly (Cohn, Ridge and Collignon, 1975). The writer would add positive personal testimony to the efficacy of paraprofessional parent aide efforts based upon observations of his wife, who was one of the first lay therapists at the C. Henry Kempe National Center for the Study and Prevention of Child Abuse and Neglect in a program that began some 14 years ago; she still gets some psychic dividends from clients of 10 years ago, proudly reporting their continuing coping and achievements as parents.

Another task in intervening with assaultive families and preventing child assault in nonassaultive parents is that of formal parenting education. Several programs, such as Home Start (O'Keefe, 1974), the Mother-Child Home Program (Madden, O'Hara, and Levenstein, 1984), Parents Group Workshop Kit (Faber and Mazlish, 1980), Systematic Training for Effective Parenting (Dinkmeyer and McKay, 1982), and Education for Parenthood (Morris, 1977) have made substantial contributions to parenting education courses for new parents and even parents-to-be as early as in their junior high school years. Bavolek, Comstock, and McLaughlin (1983) have developed what they call The

Nurturing Program specifically for dysfunctional families who either have assaulted their children or are at high risk of doing so; four major parent-child interaction difficulties are identified to be reduced: (1) inappropriate developmental expectations of children; (2) lack of empathic understanding of children's needs; (3) strong belief in the use of corporal punishment; and (4) parent and child family role reversals. As pointed out in Chapter 8, CHILDHELP, U.S.A. has underwritten several research projects across the United States, and intends to use the findings to inform a parenting education program to treat or prevent child assault; many of the empirically validated aspects of the above-mentioned programs plus new materials on sociomoral reasoning will constitute the program. A pilot program employing retired elderly persons as volunteer parent aides to work with parents at high risk for child assault is being initiated at this writing (Meier, 1984c).

## Pediatrics

The pediatrician is a medically trained person (MD) who has specialized training and knowledge about childhood diseases and disorders. Consequently, a pediatrician is expected to be and frequently is consulted by others to differentiate between accidental and nonaccidental injuries and disease processes in children and teenagers. Also, since the pediatrician is often the first professional to see an infant, it is important that any incipient, potentially assaultive relationships be detected and dealt with at the outset (Parmalee, 1984; Pawl, 1984). Taking cues from others who have talked with and perhaps examined the child (see section on Nursing earlier in this chapter), the pediatrician may pursue a number of behavioral and biological clues in greater depth, requesting careful observations of interaction and specimens as needed to rule in or rule out a variety of physical trauma and disease processes (Haynes et al., 1984); books edited by Ellerstein (1981), Helfer and Kempe (1980), and Newberger (1982) are especially useful for medical specialists suspecting or investigating assaults against children. In addition to investigating for the more usual childhood afflictions, whenever sexual assault is suspected the physician inspects for several sexually transmitted diseases, including syphilis, gonorrhea, chlamydia infection, and other, less frequently occurring venereal conditions, such as herpes and AIDS, which may be transmitted to infants and toddlers through inappropriate sexual contacts with infected adults or other children. Besides differentiating accidental from nonaccidental injuries and diseases of all kinds (including nonorganic failure-to-thrive—Haynes et al., 1984), the pediatrician must often consult with colleagues in neurology, radiology, gynecology, endocrinology, and other specialties as needed, to rule in or rule out other suspected damage and complications not typically diagnosed by pediatricians. Since the pediatrician is frequently called into court as an expert witness or to give professional testimony regarding a given case, it is essential that complete and comprehensive social and medical histories and examination protocols be available. These histories may also be quite valuable in helping to make subtle differential diagnoses, such as the whiplash shaking syndrome (Carter and McCormick, 1983) or the postconcussive syndrome (Hanley, 1984), and others.

## Pet Therapy

The American Veterinary Association has expressed considerable interest in the therapeutic adjunct of animals as very important companions to elderly people and to children who are lonely or cannot yet interact satisfactorily with other human beings (Daniels, 1980; Dishon, 1970; Levinson, 1969). Assaulted children, who often refuse or are unable to relate to other children or people in general, occasionally confide in a pet dog, cat, horse, goat, pig, bird, rat, snake, fish, or other animal. The unconditional affection, stimulation, and even protection received from some animals can help overcome feelings of isolation, rejection, low self-esteem, and worthlessness in children and adults alike. The responsibility for the animal's well-being can give the client a loving and grateful sense of purpose. Ironically, the American Humane Association (AHA), which was originally founded to prevent cruelty to animals, prior to a few decades ago was the only place to which child assault could be reported. AHA now has a Children's Division, which has also expressed interest in the use of pets in a therapeutic fashion. Pet animals and even other living things, such as plants, seem to provide solace to some humans. They have even become the target of human anger, in the familiar scenario in which the father is reprimanded by his boss, returns home to attack his wife, who in turn passes violence on to a youngster, who then attacks the family pet.

## Physical Therapy

Physical therapy is a well-established discipline that provides much of the painstaking rehabilitation necessary for a wide range of physical injuries, focused on enabling the patient to recover basic reflexes and other critical motor and sensory functions involved in walking or grasping; many times the patient is dealing with healing limbs or with artificial limbs that replace those amputated as a result of disease or accidents. The RPT (Registered Physical Therapist) is frequently found in medical settings in which victims of strokes, severe illnesses, accidents, and assaults require extensive and intensive rehabilitation. The physical therapist can be quite helpful to assaulted children in enabling them to function more satisfactorily with various prosthetic devices, such as artificial limbs, wheelchairs, and so forth; the physical therapist may also assist in cases of blindness, deafness, and other neurological damage by helping the clients to learn how to function as independently as possible regardless of their injuries and disabilities.

## Psychiatry

Since specialists in child psychiatry are scarce and their time quite expensive, they are seldom used to provide routine psychotherapy, particularly over a long period of time, for assaulted children or their families. Nonetheless, child psychiatrists are well versed in helpful interviewing principles and practices (Jones, 1984) and the appropriate use of various psychotropic medications which by definition alter various mental, temperamental, and concomitant behavioral functions. Moreover, since psychiatrists have a doctorate in medicine (MD), they are concerned with any organic manifestations of psychic disturbances, as well as psychic manifestations of organic disorders; hence, they are particularly sensitive to psychosomatic symptoms and disorders that may be arising from various combinations of physical and psychological trauma found in child assault.

Child psychiatry typically concerns itself with the impact of early childhood experiences on subsequent growth and development. The burgeoning literature on the developmental sequelae of separation (Akins, Akins, and Mace, 1981) is an example of the way in which psychiatric attention given to the importance of children's early experiences has led to a plethora of research studies and findings. Thus, from the early work of Spitz (1946)—who, as professor emeritus at the University of Colorado School of Medicine, was a great inspiration to this writer and all who knew him—the recent psychophysiological investigations into childhood depression caused by maternal separation have evolved. Of course, the discipline of child psychiatry has evolved considerably from its early days of preoccupation with Freudian psychoanalytic theory and practice (Rush, 1977; see also Chapter 2), to a more broadened scope expressed in the monumental and classic synthesis by Erikson (1950), to the contemporary and controversial, although refreshing, treatises on general child psychopathology written by such interdisciplinary luminaries as Chess (1960) and Emde and Brown (1978), as well as insights on child assault offered by Green (1980), Martin (1976, 1984), and Steele (1976). In addition to analyzing the child's developmental status from a psychoanalytic point of view, these contemporary psychiatrists are able to weave in the best of other disciplinary points of view to generate meaningful evaluations and to effect desirable changes in children's physical and mental status.

Psychiatry is also concerned with the treatment of adult psychopathology. As observed by Steele (1975), parents or adults who assault children are seriously disturbed people who may have many other problems, too. Patterns of immaturity, excessive defensiveness and dependence, lack of cooperative response to help, free-floating hostility, diminished ability to enjoy life, and other, related problems make these adults quite difficult to work with, and the prognosis is often quite guarded. Jones (1984), Sgroi (1982), and Sloan and Meier (1983, c) have presented typologies of assaultive parents and conclude that some are so severely disturbed that they are virtually untreatable, especially within the short time-frame of their children's pressing developmental needs. A pragmatic and eclectic approach to treatment is usually indicated, accessing whatever resources can be marshaled to help in the healing process, including various combinations of other disciplines or modalities mentioned within this chapter.

## Psychology

Psychology has concerned itself with the modification of inappropriate behavior on the part of assaultive parents and assaulted children by offering insights into the origins of the behavior plus a variety of techniques for alleviating or eliminating it. Just as in other disciplines, there are many levels of training and areas of specialization in psychology; likewise, there are many levels of expertise. Generally speaking, a clinical psychologist, who has a Doctor of Philosophy degree (PhD) in Psychology and is licensed by the state psychology examining board, is best equipped to address the many complicated treatment needs of severely assaulted children. However, there are persons with lesser training and experience who can successfully apply behavior modification, individual and group counseling, rudimentary psychotherapy, play therapy, and other techniques, such as biofeedback training and progressive relaxation therapy, all of which should be supervised and monitored by a licensed clinician well versed in their application.

Just as is true of other previously mentioned disciplines, the psychologist should be a member of the diagnostic and treatment planning team, bringing up-to-date psychological expertise to each interdisciplinary conference and being able to represent an eclectic and pragmatic approach to the resolution of each client's psychological problems. In most of the disciplines mentioned in this chapter, as practitioners gain more experience, maturity, and sophistication in their particular disciplines, they tend to become more eclectic and pragmatic in their diagnostic and therapeutic application and interpretation. Thus, it is recommended that professionals practicing their disciplinary skills on an interdisciplinary team not only become well versed in the rationale and techniques of various schools of thought within their own disciplines but also obtain an appreciation and understanding of the approaches to therapy provided by other disciplines. Eclectic psychotherapy (Thorne, 1973) is derived from the most efficacious parts of a variety of psychotherapies, including existential, gestalt, reality, client-centered, psychoanalytic, learning theories, Adlerian, behavioral, rational-emotive, experiential, transactional, human potential, and others (Corsini, 1973).

As individuals demonstrate sufficiently encouraging progress and insight regarding their own behavior, it is often desirable and more efficacious to weave them into an existing appropriate group or to form a new group, which is composed of persons most likely to benefit from such a therapeutic modality. For optimum functioning and results, the therapeutic group should have an experienced leader (see section on Self-Help Groups later in this chapter). Sometimes a peer group can be used in a diagnostic fashion during intake, since some children and some adults interact more fully and openly with peers than with professionals, whom they perceive to be more foreboding.

Another traditional aspect of psychology has been its interest in observing, quantifying, and classifying behavior. Numerous standardized and experimental tests and procedures exist for assessing the entire gamut of human abilities and disabilities. The science of psychology can contribute multiple and varied estimates of a person's intellectual, emotional, and sociomoral status based on several widely accepted measures. A psychometrist, who is trained to measure numerous psychological functions, can obtain scores on tests of aptitudes, achievement, attitudes, interests, and personality to augment the understanding of clients and monitoring of their progress and change. These results are also extremely useful in research (Chapter 8).

## Radiology

This medical specialty is given brief mention because of its pivotal role in the dramatic rise in awareness of child assault (Silverman, 1980). The recent technological advances in radiology enable these medical specialists to determine whether or not a patient has suffered multiple bone fractures and stresses that are in different stages of healing due to repeated and presumably nonaccidental injuries. The now classic article entitled "The Battered Child Syndrome" (Kempe, Silverman, Steele, Droegemueller, and Silver, 1962) was coauthored by a radiologist (Droegemueller), who supplied ample compelling x-ray illustrations to prove their case. It is now routine for radiologists to do whole-body x-ray scans of children suspected of being victims of child assault; the increased availability of more sophisticated high-resolution computed tomography (CT) scans and other noninvasive imaging techniques employing electromagnetics promises to reveal much more precise descriptions of quite subtle physical damage and attendant neurophysiological dysfunction (Hanley, 1984).

## Recreation Therapy

Recreational activities encourage clients to use their leisure time in satisfying and pleasant pursuits, such as quiet reading or vigorous athletics. Clients should be encouraged to enjoy watching or participating in various sports, playing table games, doing handicrafts, preparing and eating their favorite foods, participating in activities such as backpacking, swimming, horseback riding, chess, checkers, 4H, and girl or boy scouts. Through this modality, which plays an integral part in the quality of any milieu therapy, clients are enabled to learn pro-social attitudes and behaviors toward their peers, including teammates, and toward various authority figures, including umpires, 4H leaders, and so forth. There is obviously some overlap with other modalities (especially art, dance, music, and play therapies), all of which are working toward producing a more fully functioning and happy human being. Specifically trained recreational therapists are credentialed

(RTR), but everyone who is in a helping relationship can share recreational ideas and join in such activities with the clients.

## Self-Help Groups

In the United States, self-help groups have recently gained and enjoyed considerable popularity. The participating clients readily establish rapport with one another and contribute to everyone's therapeutic movement. If a problem condition is a socially acceptable one, such as having diabetes or cancer, or being a survivor of a catastrophe, the victims often are brought together to share experiences to shore up one another during their suffering, bereavement, or other physical and psychological pain. When the condition has social sanctions against it or is too delicate to be made public (such as alcoholism, drug addiction, homosexuality, or unwed pregnancy, to name a few), the group may insist on the anonymity of its members, which is part of the rationale underlying such self-help groups as Parents Anonymous, Parents United, Daughters United, and other special groups of victims (e.g., Victims of Incest Can Emerge—VOICE) and perpetrators of various forms of child assault. In many cases the nearly overwhelming anger and underwhelming paranoia of newly referred parents and other perpetrators (or victims) can be significantly attenuated by having them participate in an intake group composed of experienced group members who have "been there" and whose empathy can be very effective in reducing the free-floating anger and suspicion of the new members toward participating in any treatment, whether voluntarily or in compliance with court orders. Such self-help groups should precede and may even accompany individual treatment sessions, which otherwise would be consumed in dealing with these initial and shared feelings and issues for some time before more individually prescribed and professionally managed therapy can be beneficially undertaken. It is generally agreed that a trained professional should be present to maintain the therapeutic tone and to protect the rights of each participant. Recent reports (Gray 1983, Leiber and Baker, 1977) of the success of thousands of self-help groups throughout the United States have led to the beginnings of self-help groups for assaulted children, led by qualified professionals, to help these young victims learn to cope more effectively with their feelings and consequently to function more acceptably and happily in their everyday lives. Just as with other promising intervention–prevention procedures, self-help groups are not a panacea for everyone; some clients simply do not wish to participate or are unable to function in such verbally loaded and assertive settings; others object to the lack of privacy, compromises with personal values, and the agonizing group pressure to deal with very delicate feelings and issues (Yassen and Glass, 1984).

## Social Work

As a single discipline, social work is perhaps best characterized as being primarily concerned with the direct provision and coordination of services to various client groups. Besides the somewhat standard MSW (Masters in Social Work) degree, clinical practitioners may also have an LCSW (Licensed Clinical Social Worker) degree, which authorizes the practitioner to provide individual therapy to adults and children. Social workers have specialized training and expertise in identifying and accessing community resources and frequently are responsible for intake and discharge of clients in many human services agencies and organizations. Most case workers and other professionals in departments of welfare or social services have some or most of their training in social work. They are especially helpful in obtaining meaningful social histories of clients and in giving assistance in determining who is or is not eligible for available programs and then helping to place those clients in appropriate settings for their optimal care.

This placement work runs the gamut from determining which hospital a pregnant teenager should enter for delivery or which abortion clinic would be best for her, to assisting geriatric patients in finding the most appropriate nursing home facilities and care. In the realm of the child assault, social workers are deeply involved in the entire process of removal of a child from parental custody. This includes tracking the child and family during various kinds of therapy and follow-up, participating in the planning for more permanent placement, whether it be reunifying the child with the biological parent or blood relative or placing the client in a temporary foster home awaiting adoption, arranging for formal adoption, or placing the child in a residential treatment program that is selected as suitable for dealing with the child's particular mental or emotional disturbance and physical disabilities. A comprehensive treatise of the social worker's many roles in child assault cases has been produced by Ebeling and Hill (1983).

In addition to being concerned with the nitty-gritty of helping people get their daily lives in order, social work has provided much leadership in family and marital therapy, as described in Chapter 6 and elaborated by Hartman and Laird (1983).

## Speech Therapy

A speech therapist is a trained professional usually possessing a master's degree in a field of communication disorders, speech pathology, or the like. The licensed clinician is able to assess and treat a wide variety of language disorders in children and adults.

A child's ability to communicate verbally is strongly influenced by the quality and quantity of the language available in the environment, especially during the preschool years. It is important to determine the cause of any given speech disorder, since it may be due to a lack of an appropriate adult model, a physical defect in the child's speech mechanism, a cultural difference in language articulation, a psychological barrier to risking verbal expression (such as in elective mutism often found in assaulted children), or numerous other causes. Since verbal communication is one of the first and most important abstract and symbolic human skills to develop, the results of many tests of children's mental, emotional, and social development depend on their ability to understand spoken directions and to express themselves verbally. Thus, a defect or delay in a child's ability to communicate may severely impair performance on assessments of other developmental abilities as the child grows older and abstract communication becomes increasingly more important.

Since speech and behavior are the output of an elaborate cybernetic process depicted by various information processing models (Meier, 1976a; Meier and Malone, 1979), it is also important to determine whether or not the central processor—namely, the brain or central nervous system—is getting accurate and adequate input. Computer technology continually reminds us of the GIGO principle—garbage in, garbage out. Thus, if speech is perceived (heard) as garbled by the child, the child's brain only has garbled information to process and will most probably produce garbled output. A physical defect(s) may be in one or more parts of the child's information processing system and require the skills of other specialists, such as an audiologist to check out the child's hearing, a neurologist to check the central nervous system, or a speech pathologist to evaluate the speech apparatus. The brain–computer analogy was stated in the following rhetorical question, "Where else can you find a computer that has over ten billion flip-flop circuits, occupies less than a cubic foot of space, will operate on the energy of a peanut for up to four hours, is totally mobile, and is produced with unskilled labor?" This rhetorical quip earned the writer an honorary Knighthood in The Order of Mark Twain (a scholarly society for the study of humor) plus numerous humorous and serious responses and challenges from the readers of *The New York Times,* in which it appeared in 1971.

Regardless of the cause of a given child's speech defects, it is up to the speech therapist to develop an effective approach toward helping the client cope with the defects and learn to communicate more clearly. This frequently requires enlisting the assistance of many other disciplines and resources.

## Spiritual–Holistic Therapies

Spiritual–holistic approaches to healing the whole person are advocated by many persons from a variety of disciplines. Examples of areas in which spiritual–holistic practices are found range from natural childbirth (Gold and Gold, 1977) to therapeutic touching (Downing, 1972; Halo, 1978), to improved nutrition (Kutsky, 1973), to psychotherapy (Smuts, 1961), to faith healing through meditation (Carrington, 1978; Das and Satsang, 1976), to humanistic medicine (Miles, 1978), to coping with death (Kübler-Ross, 1975). It seems fitting to close this review of therapeutic disciplines and modalities with a comprehensive view of the whole client and the entire life span from the cradle to the grave, the womb to the tomb—indeed, from the erection to the resurrection. Providing assaulted children and assaultive parents with therapeutic and growth opportunities to become complete, fully functioning human beings is an incredibly complex and commendable task to which the spiritual–holistic school of thought is dedicated (Bauman, Brint, Piper, and Wright, 1978). Spiritual therapy is defined as the application of spiritual knowledge in the treatment of all mental and physical disorders. It is based on the assumption that humans are spiritual beings, living in a spiritual universe, and that in proportion to their acceptance of this idea and to their success in demonstrating it, they may control the body and the material elements in harmony with their perception of a divine plan (Thomas, 1980). Such an extraterrestrial orientation embraces many controversial theories and unorthodox practices, some of which have had to be defended in court (Worthington, 1978). Nevertheless, it reminds the professional, paraprofessional, and layperson to regard a client as more than an underfed body, a broken arm, a phobic runaway, or a criminal monster. Effective and lasting therapies heal the body, mind, and spirit or soul of the same clients who may also be starved for affection, broken in spirit, running from themselves, or so demoralized (Frank, 1961) as to be scarcely human or culpable for their behavior. Chapters 7 and 8 elaborate upon some of the religious and sociomoral ramifications of spiritual–holistic therapy, which, if provided, requires a highly sophisticated professional clergyman on the interdisciplinary therapeutic team.

## Other Intervention–Prevention Considerations

There are numerous tidbits of accumulated wisdom about providing or applying the many aforementioned intervention–prevention approaches. Each discipline has developed its own guidelines and standards of accepted practice, which it enforces among its membership. Unfortunately each discipline also usually has its own language and set of mystical folklore, which makes interdisciplinary communication more difficult and closer case coordination and cross-discipline training mandatory (Davis, 1984). It is beyond the scope of this book to even attempt to capture and clarify the innumerable nuances and esoteric subtleties found within the many disciplines mentioned. This book represents a deliberate effort to address many of the most crucial areas in child assault by persons schooled and experienced in the respective disciplines and modalities most often called on to address them. In another work, this writer addresses the implicit and explicit rules of the interdisciplinary ball game to ensure smooth teamwork and to eliminate buck-passing and scapegoating (Meier, 1976a). Suffice it to say that any intervention–prevention effort should take into consideration the multiple perpetrator–victim–ecology factors described in Chapter 1, seeking to identify, prioritize, and alleviate or eliminate each contributing factor to ensure that another episode of child assault does not occur. A persuasive case exists for looking at the big picture of a child's total ecology in treating or preventing something as intimate as sexual assault (Conte, 1984) or as public as child neglect (Lally, 1984).

At the risk of throwing some cold water on many of the aforementioned ideas, it is imperative that many bright-eyed and bushy-tailed neophytes, and even some of the chronically Pollyanna-like oldtimers, imbued with unrelenting rescue fantasies, not be led to believe that the cure or preventive panacea has been discovered or developed. Nothing tempers clinical idealism as quickly as treatment failures and recidivism. Yet, as Gabinet (1983a), Jones (1984), Kempe and Kempe (1978), Meier (Chapter 1), and Steele (1976), to name a few, have repeatedly pointed out, child assault cases are extraordinarily complex and demanding, some parents are virtually untreatable, some professional teams are unworkable, and some intervention–prevention efforts seem actually to exacerbate the presenting problems in an iatrogenic fashion. One of the salutary features of an effective interdisciplinary team is the shared responsibility for the occasional and sadly inevitable failures plus the collective resources to make lemonade out of lemons when everything seems to be going sour.

The following three chapters focus on the three major categories of factors operative in most cases of assault against children—namely, parental–family factors (Chapter 6), ecological factors (Chapter 7), and child factors (Chapter 8).

Figures 5–1 through 5–8 are drawings by assaulted children in therapy at The Village of CHILDHELP, U.S.A.; the interpretive captions and related insights about art therapy earlier in this chapter were provided by Jean Bone, senior art therapist at The Village.

**Figure 5–1.** This self-portrait by an emotionally disturbed ten year old boy visually expresses his inner turmoil. The omission of hands and feet indicates his feelings of helplessness and lack of security. The face is covered with a grid, which signifies withdrawal and dejection. The colors of the original painting are the colors of a bruise— black, blue, and purple—signifying his deep emotional hurt. The figure is precariously perched on the edge of his chair and bent over in a dejected, withdrawn manner, unconsciously expressing his feelings of depression and hopelessness.

**Figure 5-2.** A self-portrait by a severely impaired and disturbed boy expresses his low self-esteem and feelings of helplessness and inadequacy. The form of the body is floating and ghost-like. The boundary lines of the head and body are not joined, suggesting a noteworthy lack of individuation. The omission of hands and feet emphasizes his helpless and hopeless feelings. Figures such as this are often drawn by clients with suicidal tendencies.

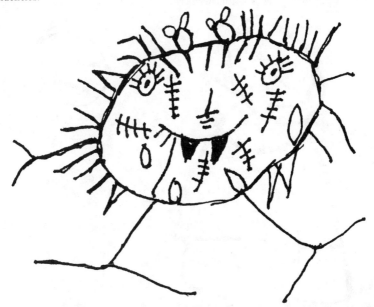

**Figure 5-3.** Spontaneous drawings are often indicators of physical abuse. This drawing by a five year old boy graphically describes his physical abuse. As he drew he verbally confirmed his visual description. "This is a hurt boy. He has cuts, bumps, scratches, and is covered with maggots. He is in the hospital." The carefully drawn eyelashes indicate confusion over sex roles.

**Figure 5-4.** This self-portrait and drawing of the client's mother indicates preoccupation with sex and possible sexual abuse. The overemphasis of hair and earrings generally has sexual connotations. The hearts also add to the sexual involvement of the client. The emphasis on belts and the shaded lower extremities show a psychic denial of the genital area of the body, an indicator of sexual assault. The omission of hands is a significant indicator of feelings of inadequacy and helplessness.

**Figure 5-5.** The repetition of symbolic forms and the omission of essential body parts can indicate arrested or disturbed emotional development. Repeated circular forms often indicate dependency and possible suicidal tendencies. The drawing on the right has denied the body altogether, which indicates difficulty experiencing the body psychically and could represent physical or sexual assault, or both.

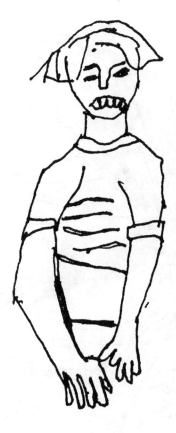

**Figure 5-6.** This drawing is typical of a child who has been sexually and physically assaulted. The body is omitted from the waist down, which expresses denial of the genital part of the body. The hands have been exaggerated which is indicative of physical assault. The emphasis on oversized teeth represents anger and aggression.

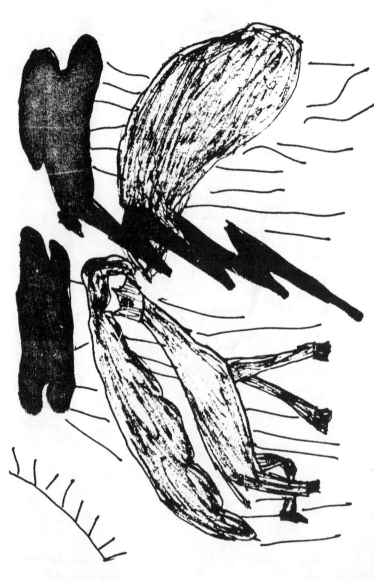

**Figure 5–7.** Assaulted children often represent their environment as threatening. Storms, which include clouds, rain, and lightning, are frequently repeated as symbols of these fears. In this drawing the horse is probably a fantasized self-portrait. The artist feels trapped by ominous, engulfing clouds. Rain is falling and progress is impeded by a bolt of lightning. The sun, a parent symbol, is in the upper left corner, separated from the horse (child) by storm clouds and rain.

**Figure 5–8.** Volcanoes in drawings of emotionally disturbed children frequently are symbolic of repressed anger and hostility. This environmental drawing by a six year old boy is a typical expression of anger, hostility, and frustration. The lower left and center is "Mt. St. Helens." The drooping tree at the center top, supported by meager roots, is a symbolic self-portrait. A violent sea with "huge waves" is depicted in the lower right corner. The sun, a parent symbol, is in the upper left corner. The volcano is violently erupting; boulders are flying and dropping into the sea. The parent sun is covered by smoke, helpless and unseeing. The tree self-portrait is "dying." This visual representation of unconscious feelings was accompanied by verbal confirmation of its significance to the child drawing it.

*Chapter 6*

# A Family Systems Approach to Child Assault

## Marshall Jung
## and Perry Cook

Child assault has been recognized as a major social problem by hospitals, schools, mental health centers, child welfare organizations, and family service and law enforcement agencies since the early 1960s when the "battered child syndrome" was identified and publicized by Kempe and his associates (1962). One of the early official definitions of child assault described it as "the physical or mental injury, sexual abuse, negligent treatment, or maltreatment of a child under the age of eighteen by a person who is responsible for the child's welfare under circumstances which indicate that the child's health or welfare is harmed or threatened thereby" (Public Law 91-247, U.S. Dept. H.E.W., 1974). Child assault has been found throughout the literature to be multifactorial (see Chapter 1). The many factors implicated in contributing to abuse of children include influence of American cultural tolerance for violence (Gelles, 1975); social stressors, such as unemployment, poverty, isolation of the family, and a feeling of powerlessness (Gelles, 1975; Justice and Justice, 1976; Kent, 1976; Straus, 1979, Wodarski, 1981); dysfunction of individual parents, including lack of parenting skills, overly high expectations for children, or psychopathology stemming from parents' own experience of being assaulted as children (Ackley, 1977; Kent, 1976; Oates, 1979; Spinetta and Rigler, 1972; Steele and Pollock, 1968; Straus, 1979;) and the vulnerability of a particular child to assault as a result of prematurity, physical defect, activity level, sex, or other factor (Belsky, 1980; Conger, Burgess, and Barrett, 1979; Justice and Justice, 1976; Ostbloom and Crase, 1980; Wodarski, 1981). Although there have been many descriptions of interventions aimed at mediating one or more of these dysfunctions, what is needed is an eclectic approach to treatment that also takes into account differential diagnosis on every level so that treatment can be tailored specifically for an individual family.

The purpose of this chapter is to describe a family treatment approach to child assault under the auspices of a community-based family service agency. The writers begin by discussing the influence the agency's orientation has on program development and the special characteristics family service agencies bring to the research, prevention, and treatment of child assault. They proceed to articulate their theoretical and philosophical bases in relationship to what has been written in literature. Essentially, the writers describe an eclectic, but integrated, multidimensional, multilevel, problem-oriented family systems approach to working with families in which child assault has occurred. The writers describe special issues associated with these families when they seek assistance. Methods and strategies to manage these issues effectively, particularly as they relate to interagency coordination, are addressed. The role of the practitioner in working with families in which child assault occurs also is examined. Finally, general practice principles are outlined to describe how the practitioner, with the family, can develop an appropriate treatment plan.

## AGENCY ORIENTATION

The overall mission of an organization will have a major influence on the programs and services it provides, including those involving child assault. Early child assault programs had their beginnings in hospital settings and, as Antler (1978) points out, "Child abuse was identified as primarily a medical problem requiring the leadership of physicians for its resolution." Organizations other than hospitals tend to emphasize what their organizational names imply. Child protective services may tend to place major emphasis on the protection of the child; mental health clinics on the psychological needs of the child and family; and child welfare agencies on the welfare of the child.

The Family Service Association of Riverside (FSAR), Inc., a private, nonprofit, nonsectarian, United Way Agency, has served the Western Riverside County community of approximately 230,000 people for nearly 30 years. The mission of the agency, under whose auspices the family therapy approach was designed and developed, is to promote the strengthening of family life through detecting, correcting, and preventing those conditions that tend to have an adverse effect on family functioning. As part of its family life education goal, the association was instrumental in helping to organize "Concern Group for Parents," an interorganizational group whose purpose, in part, is to encourage, facilitate, and organize family life education programs in the community. Many of these family life education programs address themselves to the issue of child assault.

# THEORETICAL FRAMEWORK

The numerous research studies aimed at developing typologies of the dynamics or causal factors that lead to child assault have all failed to explain why some parents assault their child(ren) and some do not. Typologies have been based on sociological and psychological factors, family or parent-child dynamics, or a combination of these influences. Some studies simply list and describe factors that are believed to contribute to assault (Meier and Sloan, 1983; Strauss, 1979). However, it must be recognized that typologies are just that—typologies. The combination of factors that can lead parents to assault their children is unique to each family. The treatment approach described in these pages takes into consideration that there is no one method of therapy that can meet the needs of all assaultive families, even families that may appear to have the same dynamics or presenting problems.

The FSAR model is in congruence with the predominant belief reflected in the literature on child abuse that there are normally multiple causal factors that lead to child assault (Antler, 1978; Belsky, 1980; Conger et al., 1979; Meier, 1983c; Ostbloom and Crase, 1980; see also Chapter 1). The model is built on a conceptual framework that recognizes that many variables influence the way in which individuals and families develop and behave. The individual, the family, and the environment are constantly interacting, each system influencing the other. Within a systems framework, both child assault and its treatment are viewed as resulting from interactions between two or more components in an embedded hierarchy of systems. The individual has his or her unique characteristics–traits with which he or she was born, such as intellectual capacity, physical characteristics, the self concept he or she has developed, and the behavior the person has learned to exhibit. His or her family has its unique characteristics also, which include the ways in which the members of the family communicate, the structure that has been established, and the coping mechanisms exhibited. The environmental systems (social, cultural, political, educational, and economic), like the individual and family systems, are continually changing and adapting to internal and external forces (Fig. 6-1).

The individual's family and environment are influenced not only by what is occurring in the present, but also by what has occurred in the past (Fig. 6-2). The interactions between the past and the present compound the already exceedingly complex problems of examining and attempting to determine how individuals and families develop, adapt, and change. Given the multitude of variables that influence individual and family behavior, the writers have accepted the belief that no one theory is adequate to describe that behavior.

It is a common practice among mental health practitioners to ask clients to conform to a given treatment model rather than selecting a model that can be most useful to the clients. It is incorrectly assumed by many practitioners that a sound theoretical framework will lead to a correct set of practice principles, which will then lead to correct techniques of intervention that can be applied to all clients. The FSAR family therapy model frees the therapist to select a theoretical framework from one theorist, practice principles from another, and use techniques from a third to meet the unique needs of his or her particular clients. It integrates theoretical concepts, practice principles, and techniques of intervention from a variety of conceptual frameworks into a holistic approach. The FSAR model incorporates the theoretical conceptualizations of Bowen (1978), Boszormenyi-Nagy and Spark (1973), and Framo (1979) who emphasize family or origin issues; Ackerman (1958), who reflects a psychodynamic theoretical orientation; Satir (1967), Haley (1976), and Jackson (1960), who emphasize communications theory; and Minuchin (1974), who developed the Structural Family Therapy Approach. The model also integrates knowledge of human physical, cognitive, and psychological development.

The FSAR model views the family, not the individual, as being the client. If a child is removed from a home in which child assault has occurred, for example, the removal is seen as protecting the family, since it is the family that is dysfunctional and in pain. It is generally assumed that presenting problems are not the real problems but instead represent dysfunctional family patterns. Hence, the focus of therapy is assisting the family in making changes so that the needs of individual members can be met. The model emphasizes the concept of rational ethics or the belief that each member of the family is entitled to happiness, a complex concept described in detail by Boszormenyi-Nagy and Spark (1973). In the achievement of that happiness the model recognizes the authority of parents to make decisions regarding child

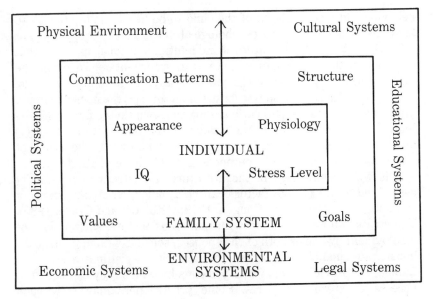

**Figure 6-1.** Interaction of individual, family, and environmental systems.

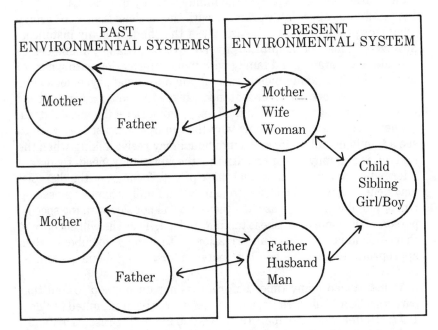

**Figure 6-2.** Interaction of past and present individual, family, and environmental systems.

behavior, but also the right of the child to be heard, understood, and have his or her social and psychological needs met appropriately.

The FSAR model is a multilevel and multidimensional approach that emphasizes the concept of simultaneous intervention. In using the model, the family therapist can work on any of the following levels: (1) the family in relationship to external factors; (2) the nuclear family; (3) the extended family; (4) various subgroups within the family; (5) the individual in relationship to the family; (6) the family of origin; or (7) any combination of the previous six. The level on which the therapist elects to work depends on the needs and tolerance of the family.

It is well documented in the literature that stress to the family associated with external factors can be a major variable influencing child abuse (Antler, 1978; Conger, 1979; Ostbloom and Crase, 1980). The stress can be associated with numerous factors, such as loss of employment by one or both of the spouses, social isolation, inadequate housing, or financial insecurity. The family therapist may assist such families by providing them with a means by which they can seek the necessary external supports. Some practitioners may view such assistance as "environmental manipulative services" (Ostbloom and Crase, 1980) or some other form of adjunct service, but the FSAR model views the assistance as part of the family therapy process. Quite often the family therapist will work only with the nuclear family to resolve whatever problems led to the assault of the child. In many instances, however, it may be helpful to involve extended family members to provide the therapist and family with more information with which to work or so that family members can gain additional psychological or emotional support. In other instances, it may be more advantageous to work with subgroups within the family, particularly the marital dyad.

There are also many reasons why the family therapist may wish to see a family member alone. An individual may resist talking when the rest of the family are present; the therapist may need to obtain information or have an individual share private feelings; or the therapist may believe it would be easier to join with a family member by seeing him or her alone. In any case, the therapist will not side with the specific person with whom he or she is talking. Indeed, he or she will encourage that individual to share information with family members when appropriate so that the conflicts between or among members can be resolved.

As mentioned many times before, it is not uncommon to find that parents who assault their child have themselves been assaulted (Ackley, 1977; Helfer and Kempe, 1976; Ostbloom and Crase, 1980). To understand this dynamic, the family therapist needs to turn to a variety of theoretical formulations, including social learning, object relations, and psychodynamic theories, as well as to theories associated with family loyalty. In such cases, the therapist normally finds unresolved family-of-origin issues, which often have direct bearing on the current family situation. In these cases, the therapist has the option of using a multigenerational approach to working with the family. The therapist can encourage the assaulter to work directly with his or her family of origin, either by inviting all members involved to the therapy sessions or, if this is not possible, by using such means as telephone calls and letter writing. If family members are deceased, the therapist can use symbolic means by which to resolve the issues. The abusing parent works directly with his or her parent(s) so that conflicts between them can be resolved in a mature manner and past dynamics need no longer negatively influence current family functioning.

The FSAR model is also multidimensional in that it takes into consideration cognitive, affective, behavioral, and systems dynamics. The family therapist has the option of shifting the emphasis among the cognitive, affective, and systems approaches. He or she can shift the emphasis in a session, over a period of time, or a combination of both. Most family therapists are multidimensional, but often they are not cognizant of this fact, and therefore fail to maximize their options in shifting the emphasis among the cognitive, behavioral, and systems approaches.

The FSAR model recognizes that numerous thoughts and feelings within the individual family members and transactions among these family members are occurring simultaneously. The more astute the therapist becomes, the more simultaneous interventions he or she can orchestrate. For example, the therapist, by a simple shift in body position and by touching the father gently on the arm, while encouraging an adolescent to talk with his father in such a way that the father is seen as the nurturing authority figure, can model patience, create a subgroup (father-son dyad), indicate to the son that his father loves him, block other family members from entering the subgroup, create hierarchy between son and father, join with both son and father, defuse resistance, break down old patterns of interactions, and resolve complex problems.

The FSAR model assumes that people do the best they can and that dysfunctional families are not significantly different from "normal" ones. It recognizes that individuals and families generally attempt to resolve their own problems and do not seek clinical services unless there is a crisis they cannot handle. The model allows the family to define what is dysfunctional within its unique family system. The exception to this process is when the family or one of its members comes to the attention of a social institution.

This therapeutic process emphasizes the strengths of a family. Families who need or seek assistance are feeling powerless to make changes that will resolve their conflicts. By emphasizing and building on strengths, the family therapist can quickly help restore the sense of control family members need.

The FSAR model assumes that families have the inherent ability to negotiate and make changes that will resolve their conflicts. The family therapist emphasizes the change process among family members and encourages and assists family members to interact with one another in a positive way to find solutions to their differences. If possible, conflicts are displayed rather than just discussed. For example, if a child exhibits temper tantrums, the therapist will encourage the child to have tantrums in the session. If a couple argues at home, they will be encouraged to do their arguing during the session. This is of particular value in court-referred cases, in which resistance renders self-report unreliable. The family can easily be led to enact their dysfunctional patterns in a treatment session. Finally, the model attempts to help families maintain natural support systems and social networks or, if necessary, to establish such connections within the families' own belief, cultural, or environmental systems. In summary, the FSAR model emphasizes simultaneous, multilevel, and multidimensional interventions to address multidimensional family problems such as child abuse.

## SPECIAL ISSUES GENERALLY RELATING TO FAMILIES IN WHICH CHILD ABUSE OCCURS

When particular families seek assistance for abuse, they bring with them complex constellations of problems, some of which are generic to most such cases. Often these families have been in contact with and influenced by representatives from other organizations. The integrity of the family boundary has been shattered. Typically, family members feel angry and defensive about the breaching of this boundary. Parents may have been arrested or imprisoned. Children may have been removed from the home. The family may have been ordered to seek counseling. The family that comes to the agency after experiencing these things is different from a self-referred family. Its members are undergoing a secondary crisis (in addition to that which caused the assault) around the broken boundary between themselves and institutions. The parents have abdicated their authority to legal powers. They are forced to participate in therapy. Their feelings of powerlessness only exacerbate the original perceived sense of powerlessness to control their own lives, which may have contributed to the abuse in the first place (Belsky, 1980; Kent, 1976; Steele and Pollock, 1968). These feelings constituted a major resistance to therapy, and must be dealt with (Nelson, 1975; Stanton and Todd, 1981).

A second generic issue is the need for coordination of services when several agencies are involved in working with a family (Elkind, Berson, and Edwin, 1977; Fauri, 1978; Stanton and Todd, 1981). This can cause further confusion in dealing with an already complex problem. A team approach, usually based on a hospital inpatient model, has frequently been used (Antler, 1978; Kristal and Tucker, 1975; Roth, 1978, Shamroy, 1980). The team, however, may be composed of members who bring different orientations, either because of personal training or agency mandate, to the treatment approach (Elkind 1977; Fauri, 1978). For example, the primary goal of the child protective services worker is to protect the child, whereas the teacher of a parenting skills class emphasizes individual dynamics. Often the result of such an approach is to break down a multidetermined problem into its separate components and to ignore the interactions among them. It is also not uncommon to have conflicts among the professionals involved, which, from a purely pragmatic point of view, impedes client progress and becomes quite unjustifiably expensive. The family members will become even more confused or establish a therapeutic alliance with the person they view as being in control of the case. They may be given conflicting messages, or may play off one part of the team against another in their attempt to deny responsibility for working on the problem. For these reasons, the FSAR model advocates a coordinated rather than a team approach, with one agency responsible for all interventions involving a family.

A third issue with assaultive families is the limitation of the usual client confidentiality. No matter what has contributed to the assault, one common factor in most cases is lack of impulse control. This means the family therapist must be alert to the continuing possibility of violence in the family and his or her responsibility for reporting it to the proper authorities. The therapist could also be required to submit reports to the court or child protective services. These limitations alter the usual client-therapist relationship and must be dealt with if the necessary trusting therapeutic relationship is to be established and maintained.

Finally, family service agencies have the difficult task of being asked to provide family therapy to child assault cases, while being denied the authority to do what they believe is in the best interest of the family. That authority is kept within the various child protective services departments and the judicial system. This can create problems if the professionals involved have divergent views on appropriate interventions. In some instances, the views can be so divergent that family service therapists have to become mediators or advocates for families.

## THE ROLE OF THE FAMILY THERAPIST

The practice of therapy is an art and as an art requires imagination, creativity, and skill. The FSAR model assumes that three separate skills are associated with being an effective family therapist: the ability to conceptualize theoretically, the ability to develop appropriate treatment plans, and the ability to operationalize the treatment plan. A skillful family therapist will be aware of what he or she is doing at any point in the session, recognize during the session the variety of means by which family members communicate (tone of voice, facial expression, body position, eye contact, touching, and so forth), and be able, in a variety of ways, to assist the family in gaining insights and making changes. Video taping and live supervision are training tools used by FSAR to maximize therapist skills. During the therapeutic process the therapist becomes a member of the family system and is influenced by them. The therapist must accept the role of expert in understanding individual and family dynamics. The therapist can only offer assistance; the family must accept that offer if change is to occur. The family therapist sometimes has the role of educator, providing information on parenting and communication. The therapist is a resource person who assists in obtaining community services. He or she is also called on as a consultant to other professionals in the case. The therapist might be asked to be an expert witness at a trial or hearing, or may perhaps coordinate the services of all the professionals involved.

The family therapist is in the unusual position of having the power to harm families, without changing the family system. He or she harms the family by giving them a negative therapeutic experience through being judgmental, providing incorrect information, or facilitating inappropriate treatment interventions. Consequently, family members with children who have been removed from the home can remain separated for an unnecessarily long period of time, even permanently. The therapist working with an assaultive family undertakes a heavy load. He or she must often see various subgroups in the family, necessitating more than one session per week. In addition, time will be spent in phone calls and meetings to coordinate agencies involved. Besides this extra work, stress is great on the therapist who is working sometimes angry clients, dealing with countertransference issues aroused by assault of a child, and having to make recommendations in potentially life-threatening situations. To minimize staff burnout related to all of these stressors, agencies should consider assigning their staff members varied caseloads. Although it is tempting to make one therapist the "child abuse expert" in the agency by assigning all such cases to him or her, the therapist in such a situation could easily become overloaded. Carrying a caseload of only assaultive families could blind a therapist to the distinctions among such families, resulting in his or her applying a "standard treatment," which would fit all the cases somewhat, but no particular case really well.

In summary, the family therapist ideally is a professional person who is educated and trained to assist dysfunctional families in an objective manner in making changes which will bring the family peace and harmony.

## APPLICATION OF THE MODEL

The initial phase of therapy is critical in determining the goals of treatment and the framework in which the family and therapist will work. The family therapist requests that all significant members of the family, even those who may have been removed from the home, attend the first session. During the first session, the therapist must accomplish many things, including the following: (1) join with each member of the family; (2) assess the strengths and weaknesses of the family members and the family as a unit; (3) evaluate whether or not the family is amenable to treatment; (4) assess and integrate the goals of each member of the family into the treatment plan; (5) determine which, if any, other professionals are involved in the case; (6) assess whether or not additional programs or services may be helpful to the family; (7) clarify the role of the therapist and the family in the therapeutic process; (8) minimize client resistance or reluctance to change; (9) help to create some immediate change; and (10) recommend to the family a framework in which the therapist believes family members will be able to obtain their stated goals. Although these items are addressed in the first session, they are refined, modified, and changed as therapy proceeds.

The joining with family members begins with introductory remarks and continues throughout the therapeutic process. Joining is not siding with a family member, for that only creates alienation somewhere in the system. It is the active effort on the part of the therapist to show the family members that he or she cares for them as individuals and as a family, understands and empathizes with each member, and is in many ways like them. Joining techniques go as far as the therapist's imagination; they include reinforcing positive behavior, speaking to the head of the household first, playing with children, self-disclosing, and speaking in a gentle, accepting manner. Throughout the therapy, the family therapist is assessing the strengths and weaknesses of the family. The therapist keeps in mind the principle of differential diagnosis, and that each family, although it may have similarities with others, must be assessed by its own set of characteristics. The assessment is based on numerous factors, including the family structure, communication system, social network, past history, cultural values, strength of the marriage, parenting skills, and psychodynamics of each member. The therapist attempts to maximize the strengths of the family by continually calling on each member of the family to utilize his or her resources. The family therapist recognizes that therapy cannot always be successful in reuniting or keeping together families who seek treatment. In many instances parents or children cannot or will not make changes necessary for keeping the family together. In rare instances, this to due to sociopathy in one or both parents (Oates, 1979; Steele and Pollock, 1968). The assessment of sociopathy must be made with care because it is rare and because the family's initial resistance may result in masking of affect (including shame), which can resemble sociopathy. In cases in which a parent is evaluated as being sociopathic, the family needs to be told that, because of the lack of motivation for change, family therapy will not be helpful to them and that (in cases of court ordered counseling) the therapist will send a report to the court to that effect.

When reunification of the family is not a viable goal, the therapist can help the family work on separation issues, conjointly if possible, or with separate subgroups if some members are not able to attend conjoint sessions. The goal here will be for the family to accept that they cannot live together, to grieve, and to let go. If this work is not done, the child and parents may be left with unresolved guilt, grief, and anger, which may be projected onto future relationships. Even if the parent is unable to respond appropriately to the child, the advantage of such separation work is that it allows the child to become aware of and express his or her feelings and to see the family as it really is, rather than to harbor distorted fantasies about it.

In making a differential diagnosis, the family therapist determines first whether the problem is a transitional or a chronic one. Transitional problems are those involving a normally well functioning family temporarily unbalanced by an identifiable stressor. Such problems are relatively easy to resolve and the prognosis tends to be good. An example is Oates' Type One Primary Abuse (1979). The assaultive act is an isolated incident, often perpetrated by an overstressed mother on an infant who may be premature or difficult to handle. The infant and other children in the family are well nourished and cared for, and parents manifest only minor personality problems. The assaultive parent may have been experiencing excessive fatigue or anxiety at the time of the assault, and he or she expresses considerable remorse afterward. It should be noted in this regard that the severity of assault does not always correlate with the severity of family dysfunction or aid in making a differential diagnosis. Oates notes that in cases of this type, the infant may suffer permanent neurological damage due to vulnerability to subdural hematoma from only one incident of hard shaking; yet the prognosis for the family, given that the assault is a transitional problem, is good.

In a differential diagnosis of either a transitional or a chronic case, the family therapist will weigh the balance of family strengths versus stressors with which they must deal. This is conceptualized by Ostbloom and Crase (1980) as a seesaw that must be balanced for successful family functioning. In the case of a transitional problem, the therapist will work to increase the family's ability to mobilize its considerable strengths to mitigate the effect of the immediate stressor. Family members can be helped to identify stressful situations and work out ways to support one another during these times. The family can also be helped to use outside support systems (extended family, child care services, friends, and so forth) to gain additional resources to balance stress. Chronic cases fall into several categories, but all are characterized by long-term dysfunction in one or more subsystems that cannot be attributed only to an identifiable stressor. In working with such families, the family therapist recognizes that numerous interventions, probably over a long period of time, will be necessary to complete therapy successfully. Figure 6–3 illustrates probable outcome of therapy based on differential diagnosis.

The family therapist recognizes that the goals of family members may conflict. Members of the family must be asked why they are attending the session and what they hope to accomplish. The therapist pays attention to verbal as well as nonverbal messages to assess goals members cannot or will not articulate. Finally, the therapist must somehow convince each family member that his or her concern(s) will be addressed.

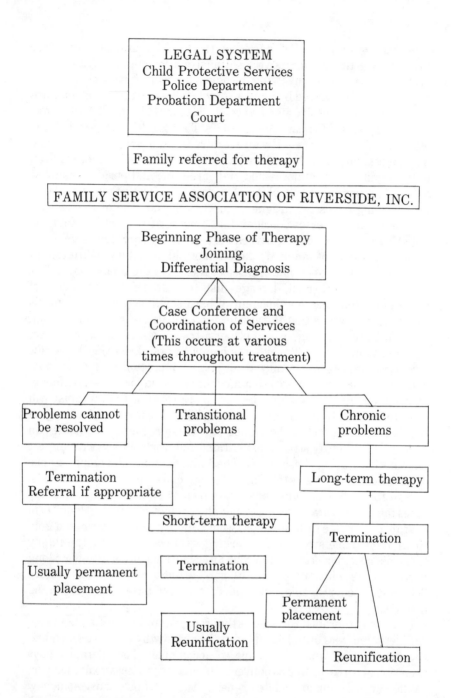

**Figure 6-3.** Flow chart.

As soon as possible, the therapist arranges for a case conference with the family and those significantly involved in the case, including foster parents. The purpose of the conference is to coordinate services, clarify the roles of all participants, and assist the family in understanding their support system.

The family therapist offers to assist the family in obtaining additional services or programs. In so doing, the therapist encourages family members to look for resources within their own environment, thus maximizing the opportunity for family members to develop friendships within their neighborhoods. Too often families are asked to participate in artificial groupings involving people who have little in common other than their problems. This can result in family members' continuing to identify themselves in terms of their dysfunction. The FSAR is involved in agency networking and has many supportive resources available to offer to its clients. The therapist keeps in mind that it is the responsibility of family members to follow through on obtaining resources. The therapist offers assistance to the family but does not encourage dependency. Families are often confused about the role of the family therapist because of the family's involvement with many other professionals prior to coming to the agency. The therapist clarifies his or her role in assisting the family by indicating what the therapist can and cannot do, and by honestly discussing the limits of the family's right of confidentiality and the possibility that the therapist might be called on as an expert witness in court. The therapist needs to share with the family members that they have a right to know what he or she is thinking about them, and they are entitled to review his or her case records. The family members are also entitled to disagree in writing to noted diagnoses and impressions in their case records. Finally, the therapist must help the family to recognize that he or she is not sitting in judgment of them, but is rather a facilitator for change.

There are many reasons why family members resist participation in therapy. The family therapist must assess what family members are resistant to and why. Among the questions the therapist asks himself or herself are the following: Is the family resistant to me, other members of the family, or other professionals or organizations involved in the case? Is the resistance due to anger, fear, mistrust, inability to change, or the need to retain some sense of control? Is it a combination of some of these things? The therapist keeps in mind that while resistance can be dysfunctional, it can also be a normal and healthy defense mechanism. The practice principles and techniques to minimize dysfunctional resistance are many and include working at a pace at which family members are comfortable, being supportive and sensitive to the family's pain, and having all family members participate equally in the therapy.

If, as is often the case in assaultive families, resistance arises from parents' past unhappy experiences with authority figures, the therapist has to walk a fine line between maintaining control of the therapy and minimizing his or her stimulus value as an authority figure.

The family therapist recognizes that often families come to the agency feeling powerless, overwhelmed, and fragmented. To begin the process of helping the family feel it has power to take control and resolve its problems, the therapist will work toward assisting the family in making changes—in the first session if possible. Families assume that the family therapist will recommend a framework in which therapy will be conducted. The therapist's recommendation will be based on what the family articulates as its need or on the therapist's own diagnostic impressions. The therapist will be flexible in his or her presentation and will support recommendations made by family members even though he or she may be in disagreement with them. For example, he or she may feel that a child does not need to be seen in individual sessions, but will do so at the request of the parents. What is most important to the therapist is that the overall treatment plan lead to a satisfactory resolution of the family's problems.

Because the family will display its characteristic dysfunctional interaction pattern around whatever issue is presented, the therapist can reduce resistance in the family by accepting its agenda and using it to effect systemic change. During the initial phase of therapy, the family therapist is assessing the cause of dysfunction by having the family enact problems in session and observing individual members' physical and mental status and style of relating. Communication patterns in the family, fixed sequences of behavior, boundaries and alliances within the family, triangling, and roles will become apparent. The therapist will also elicit important demographic information and data related to the family's support system and family of origin. At the same time, the therapist works at joining the family and becoming trusted and accepted by them so he or she can manage the system from within.

In child assault cases, this initial phase of therapy will include the case conference. The direction of therapy will move from being more structured in initial phases to less structured by the time of termination. Initially, the therapist is more controlling and directive as he or she lends ego strength to the family in crisis. As therapy progresses, the therapist will gradually encourage the family to assume control as members gain the power to do so. The more dysfunctional the family, the slower this process will be.

In the middle phase of therapy, the family therapist is less central and family members are working more directly with each other. The therapist is less active with the family members and is more in charge of obtaining information, utilizing resources, and clarifying issues that need to be addressed. Time is spent redefining issues, gaining greater understanding of how the family adapts, and making significant changes to improve family functioning.

During the ending phase of therapy, the therapist and family members feel that the family has come to understand and accept the causal factors for the family's dysfunction. In addition, the family has made changes that have resolved or diminished the problems that brought them to therapy initially. Finally, the therapist and the family members believe the family is in control and has the internal strength and coping skills to resolve future problems.

## SUMMARY

As child assault has been found to be a problem with multiple causations that can involve dysfunctions at one or more levels within an embedded hierarchy of systems, a multilevel, multidimensional family systems approach to differential diagnosis and treatment of families is advanced. The FSAR model aims at coordinating all treatment services through a single therapist to avoid confusion among the many agencies usually involved in such cases and to plan interventions aimed at alleviating all the interrelated causes of assault in a particular family. The approach is considered appropriate in dealing with all types of assaultive families seen at a community based family service agency.

## Case Study: The J. Family

The following case is a simple illustration of how therapy can be ineffective if a therapist facilitates resistance by allowing himself or herself to be primarily an evaluator of truth. It also speaks against a belief by many family therapists that an assaulter must always verbally accept responsibility for his or her behavior if therapy is to be successful. Finally, the case illustrates that there is often no such thing as a perfect solution, and that there are many unfair things in life that people must learn to accept. To grow and mature, individuals must learn both to resolve conflicts and to accept those that are unresolvable.

The J. Family was referred to the FSAR agency by Child Protective Services because Mr. J. had sexually molested his 15 year old daughter, Mary, for several months. The J.'s are a white, middle income family with both parents employed. Mr. J. is the natural father and his wife the stepmother. The Court had found Mr. J. guilty of the sexual assault and consequently Mary was removed from the home and placed in foster care. Still living with the couple was Mr. J.'s 13 year old daughter, Jan. Mr. and Mrs. J. and Mary were involved in family group oriented therapy elsewhere. It was part of the court's reunification plan that Mr. and Mrs. J. participate in marital therapy and that when conflicts between the two were resolved, family therapy would begin.

Marital therapy was brief, as the couple had a fairly stable relationship. During the initial phase of family therapy, in which the entire family participated, Mr. J. kept insisting that he did not molest his daughter. Mary just as adamantly insisted that he did. Mrs. J. believed her husband while Jan sided with her sister. When reminded that he had stated in court that he had abused his daughter, Mr. J. responded by stating that he felt he was going to be convicted in any case and that he might make it easier on himself if he stated he was guilty. The therapist felt nothing could be accomplished unless Mr. J. accepted responsibility for the abuse and requested a consultation because there was no movement in therapy.

The therapist was asked by the consultant if he wanted to prove that Mr. J. was guilty of the molestation or if he wished to help the family resolve its various problems so that it could be reunited and the dysfunctional patterns that led to the molestation be stopped. In agreeing to the latter, the therapist shifted the focus from judging the father to exploring what needed to be done to improve the relationship between family members and thereby return Mary to a home in which she could feel safe and have her social and psychological needs met. By maintaining focus on improving family relationships, the family worked together to resolve its problems to the point where Mary returned home.

Mr. J. never admitted to the abuse. Prior to being reunited with her parents, Mary was seen in individual sessions to resolve her conflicts associated with the abuse. She naturally believed it was unfair that her father did not accept responsibility for his behavior. The therapist agreed. The therapist was, however, able to assist in helping Mary not to assume responsibility for what had happened and to forgive her father even though he was too threatened to admit to his problem. The therapist also helped Mary recognize that it was often an unfair world and that recognizing and accepting that unfairness was a sign of maturity. Mary returned to the family feeling in charge of her life and comfortable in the home because of the changes that had been made in the family dynamics. She had confidence in herself and in the conviction that, because her parents now exhibited an appropriate spousal relationship with one another and parental relationship with the children, abuse would not recur.

# Case Study: The G. Family

The following case illustrates how multilevel interventions can simultaneously address several interacting causes of abuse and how change in one part of the system can reverberate throughout the other parts.

The G.'s are a low income Hispanic family consisting of a mother and father in their midthirties and their three biological children. The father had been disabled three years before and had been unemployed since that time. His role in the family had changed drastically from provider to full-time parent and homemaker, and he was feeling overburdened and depressed. The mother was angry at having to become the sole wage earner in the family and was fed up with her husband's withdrawal. The children reacted to the lack of control and open hostility at home in various ways. Fourteen year old Missy began failing in school and running away. Ten year old Tommy began wetting and soiling himself, lighting fires, and stealing. Six year old Colette tried to keep everyone happy but did not seem to hear when her parents wanted her to do something. Both mother and father, on several occasions, had lost control and hit the children until finally the Child Protective Services agency was called by the oldest daughter's school.

The therapist approached an early session with these things in mind: restoring the father's status in the family, relieving his depression, reducing mother's anger at having to do everything alone, bringing the marital pair closer together, emphasizing the hierarchy in the family, and solving one of the children's problems. She first met with the parents alone to get them to identify what was the worst child problem for them and to work out an approach to manage that specific problem. She then brought all three children into the room and had the father alone (on the grounds that he was home more hours with the children) explain to his son what the parents expected of him with regard to doing his own laundry when he soiled himself and what the consequences would be if he failed to comply. He also listened and responded to Tommy's feelings about the problem. This simple intervention was typical of a long string of such strategies used in the middle phase of therapy, in that it effected a change in a single session and worked on multiple levels. The parents had to agree on a goal and work together. The father was elevated and momentarily brought out of his depression to take charge. The mother was temporarily relieved of stress. The children saw their parents as supporting one another and in control. In addition, a step was taken toward eliminating one child's symptom.

Marital problems spilling over onto the children are often uncovered later in therapy, as they were with the G. family. After the session just described and others like it, mother began to express anger and dissatisfaction in the way her husband was managing the children. In spite of her earlier avowals of wanting him to do more, as he became more assertive she became angrier and angrier and was unable to let him talk to any of the children without interrupting. The therapist was then able to spend several sessions alone with the couple working on their marital problem. Just the act of calling such sessions was an intervention on the theme of boundary-setting, as the family received a clear message that spousal and parental roles are different and that marital problems should not concern the children. It also gave the couple the opportunity to resolve previously unexpressed grief and anger over the father's disability and resultant sexual dysfunction.

Obvious extrafamilial stressors for this family were the father's lack of employment and the oldest daughter's school problems. The first was addressed by helping the father gather information from his physician on types of work he would be able to do from vocational training programs and from the local adult education department on coursework needed to obtain his high school diploma. The father was helped in an individual therapy session to coordinate this information and plan career goals. This intervention simultaneously addressed removing a serious stressor from the family and relieving the father's depression by giving him a sense of power over his life and hope for the future. The second outside stressor, the daughter's academic problem, was worked on by having the parents contact the school to find out specifically what she needed to do to raise her grades. The parents then worked in a family therapy session to get their daughter to tell them how she felt about school and to agree to a contract regarding makeup work she would do with her father's help as needed. This intervention simultaneously addressed a family problem, increased both father's and daughter's self-esteem, and brought these two, who had expressed dissatisfaction with their alienation from one another, closer together in an appropriate parent-child interaction. These interventions are but a few examples of how the therapist in this case was able to work simultaneously on several levels to help the G. family eventually resolve dysfunctional patterns which had created an abusive situation.

## Case Study: The M. Family

The following case illustrates a successful resolution to a family's problems can occur when previous therapies have been unsuccessful, there are multiple problems within the family, similar problems are exhibited across generations, and a number of professionals have been and currently are involved with the case. The treatment plan included case conferences, working with various levels of the family simultaneously and over a period of time, and encouraging family members to work directly with the person or persons with whom they were in conflict.

The M. family was referred to the agency by a child-oriented agency. The presenting problem was that Sue, age 15, had been sexually molested regularly by her father between the ages of 4 and 11. The referring therapist, who had seen Sue in individual psychotherapy for one year, believed that Sue had many unresolved intrapsychic conflicts resulting from the molestation. The referring therapist believed that therapy had been unsuccessful and that possibly family therapy could help Sue and her mother, who was having problems with the other children.

The M.'s are a white, low income, single parent family. Mr. and Mrs. M. had been divorced for two years, and Mrs. M. had custody of their four children, Sue, Becky (age 12), George (age 9), and Brian (age 5). Mr. M. moved to another state immediately following the divorce. Mrs. M. was completing study for a master's degree. Living in the home were Mrs. M., Sue, and Brian. During the first session, which included all the children, it was learned that Mrs. M. was having difficulty with (1) Becky, who was in a children's psychiatric group home because of uncontrollable anger and suicide attempts and ideation; (2) George, who had been arrested for burglary, convicted, and placed in a foster home; and (3) Sue, who continued to show signs of anger and depression, and who refused to accept her mother's parental authority. Mrs. M. was feeling overwhelmed, helpless, angry, and not fully supported by those who were attempting to help her children. Sue felt angry during the first part of the session because she felt another professional person was "interfering" in her life. Becky was quiet and withdrawn during the session and would express little. George was restless and often behaved in a very immature manner. The mother had difficulty controlling his behavior. Brian acted appropriately for his age. In spite of the family's problems, it showed many signs of strength. Mrs. M. was a caring, genuine, nurturing, insightful, goal oriented, and highly intelligent woman, who had an intact social network. The children were warm, loving, genuine, friendly, intelligent, respectful, and active in their respective schools. All the family members agreed they wanted to live in peace together as a family, but did not know how this could be accomplished. In obtaining information about the family, the therapist learned that Mr. M. had favored Sue and throughout her childhood treated her as a "love object." He was harsh with the other children and on occasion would abuse them physically. Mrs. M. was aware of the abuse of all the children and would, on occasion, physically abuse them herself. It was also learned that Mrs. M. and her three siblings had been sexually abused for years by her father. It was not until toward the end of her marriage that Mrs. M. went to the authorities with her problems. At that point, Mr. M. was ordered to leave the home. As part of the reunification plan, the couple was ordered into individual, marital, and family group oriented therapy. For two years, Mr. M. refused to participate in any form of therapy and finally proceeded to divorce his wife. Mrs. M. participated in individual and group therapy, which she found helpful. Sue was asked to participate in group and individual therapy, but withdrew because she did not find it helpful. She wanted to live with her father, but could not do so because of his refusal to participate in any form of therapy. Following the divorce, Mrs. M. had to move into an overcrowded living situation, which only exacerbated the family's problems.

During the first session, the therapist found an opportunity to join with Sue. As Sue talked about her father, she became very tearful. At that point, the family members were asked to leave so that Sue and the therapist could talk alone. The therapist was able to get Sue to talk about the pain associated with the loss of her father. Unlike previous therapists and her mother, who insisted that she must have angry and resentful feelings towards her father, the current therapist made Sue feel supported and understood. The therapist was able to get Sue to agree to be seen alone and to explore her feelings about herself, her parents, and the rest of the members of the family.

The court ordered that Becky and George could not return home until Mrs. M. found larger accommodations. Consequently, the therapist suggested, and Mrs. M. agreed, that family therapy with those two children could wait until they returned home. In the meantime, Mrs. M. would also be seen individually. In addition, a meeting of all the professionals involved in the case was called so that a coordinated effort to help the family could be arranged.

Initially, treatment focused upon helping Sue to understand her feelings about herself and her family, particularly her mother and father. It also focused upon helping Mrs. M. resolve her problems with both her parents and stop projecting on to Sue many of the unresolved feelings she had towards her family of origin and her former husband. After a few sessions, Mrs. M. was requested to meet with her parents regularly to resolve the issues between them. Their relationship improved significantly. When Sue was able to identify the feelings she had towards her mother, conjoint sessions were held with the two. They were successful in resolving their differences. Shortly thereafter, Mrs. M. found a job and was able to rent a home. Becky and George returned home, at which time family therapy sessions began. Mrs. M. was feeling in control and very good about herself, which contributed significantly toward quickly resolving the various family conflicts.

Upon the successful completion of reuniting the family, Mrs. M. and Sue were asked to visit Mr. M. to resolve their problems with him. Under the supervision of a family therapist in the state in which Mr. M. lived, Sue and her mother were able to reach a satisfactory understanding with Mr. M. Therapy was terminated.

*Chapter 7*

# Interdisciplinary and Community-Based Approaches to Treating and Preventing Child Assault

*Morris J. Paulson*

Successful child abuse intervention requires multiple health disciplines and multiple agency networking (Helfer, 1976; Helfer, Schneider, Hoffmeister, and Tardi, 1977; Paulson et al., 1974b). Cohen (1977) in examining the interface between multidisciplinary teams and the community, describes the genesis and the development of the Child Protection Team in terms of a need for prompt interagency communication among professionals working the area of child assault. Each professional and each discipline brings to the team a special expertise and understanding. Each must be willing to interface and network with collaborating peers and agencies, recognizing that such a collaborative effort is necessary for effective intervention.

A coalition of such professionals and agencies in areas both urban and rural constitutes the local child abuse council. In a number of states state-wide consortiums of child abuse councils have developed, whose membership comprises representation from all local councils within the state. Such councils have the following functions: (1) to develop a state-wide communication network among local councils; (2) to consult with and provide technical assistance within councils to foster greater multidisciplinary involvement; and (3) to study and make recommendations as needed to public and private services agencies involved in child abuse intervention (Directions, 1980).

Councils and consortiums should include members from social services, law enforcement, education, and juvenile courts, as well as representatives from day care centers, alcohol and drug treatment centers, probation, public health, mental health, nursing, medicine, dentistry, religion, and all local child abuse treatment providers. Across the nation, there are a number of national child abuse treatment and prevention centers, plus the federally funded National Center on Child Abuse and Neglect; these centers provide a consultation and dissemination of information service to local and state child abuse centers. The effectiveness of such interagency collaboration, be it local, state or federal, lies in the degree to which individual members can share ideas and resources, and can provide personal and professional support for each other's activities and programs (Paulson, 1982, 1983).

# IMPLEMENTING A COMMUNITY-BASED TREATMENT PROGRAM FOR CHILD ABUSING FAMILIES

## The Diagnostic and Treatment Center

In developing goals and objectives for a diagnostic and treatment center, the professional team must first undertake a needs assessment study for the catchment area being served. Who are the families in need? What are the socioeconomic and ethnic or cultural characteristics of the community that may impact on or influence the identified objectives of the center? What are the needs of the referring agencies and can these needs be met within the specific goals of a diagnostic and treatment center? How also can meaningful networking be developed among all community agencies that will then expedite maximum treatment effectiveness with minimal personnel-agency conflict (Paulson, 1978b)?

The purpose of a child abuse treatment program is to maximize patient care and to reduce the real or potential risks of further assault to a child. It is therefore imperative that the implementation of goals and treatment does not in itself result in institutional abuse, or iatrogenic abuse of the child or the parents—for example, failure to recognize that traditional Anglo norms used for evaluation and diagnosis of a child abuse case may not be valid or reliable in assessing parenting behaviors, practices, and attitudes of families from various cultural-ethnic backgrounds, either self-referred or agency-referred (Daniel, Hampton, and Newberger, 1983). Every treating facility must take a leadership role in identifying and understanding such ethnic differences, to avoid community criticism that middle-class, Anglo values, expectations, and norms are being applied inappropriately in assessing non-middle-class, non-Anglo educationally or occupationally disadvantaged families (Helfer and Kempe, 1969; Paulson and Blake, 1969; Paulson, Schwemer, Afifi, and Bendel, 1977; Paulson, Schwemer, and Bendel, 1976).

In the same way that rigid professional stereotyping must be avoided in developing, implementing, and executing diagnostic and treatment programs, agencies must also avoid use of overly orthodox, conservative, and inflexible professional staffs. There must be awareness that traditional, insight-oriented, long-term psychoanalytic type treatment programs may often be inappropriate, ineffectual, and cost ineffective. Self-examination, introspection, and free association may not be the treatment of need for those many families whose living reality is one of bare survival, unemployment, or marginal or absent support systems. For many, the needs for direction, structure, support, advice, and limit setting are much more essential than years-long exploration of repressed and suppressed memories and experiences dating back to early life. The ultraconservative clinician, psychiatrist, or physician, steeped in doctrines of psychoanalytic psychotherapy, may well experience personal and professional conflict and early "burn out" when confronted with intervention needs foreign to orthodox orientations and traditional styles of mental health practice.

Will a diagnostic and treatment center provide opportunities for staff home visits, for which the primary purpose is to provide in-home psychotherapy as well as in-home assessment and evaluation? How willing is the therapist to sit with a family, surrounded by crying infants or children, and engage in a therapeutic encounter that is not structured by a 50 minute hour, nor scheduled on an hour-by-hour basis? Sitting in a disheveled home, amid the odor of an unscrubbed bathroom, seeking to establish a relationship of trust and openness (while at the same time surrounded by suspicion, distress, and hostility from an unmotivated patient or spouse), is an experience that will age and mature clinician-caregivers; yet these often are the essential ingredients of successful intervention.

Sharing and support are lifelines for any group membership. How does a group and how does the therapist respond to situations of poignant pain and sadness? A sobbing, grieving mother tells the group how, after her two year old child was brutally beaten and killed by her husband, she went to the funeral home alone, picked out a small white casket for her child, and then returned home to finish sewing a dainty pink dress for her daughter's funeral. The bereavement expressed by this mother was a moving and positive therapeutic experience for the mother. Sadness experienced by the group was a uniting dynamic for all group members as they shared the sadness of this mother's sorrow. Equally traumatic but even more stressful to the therapist is attending a coroner's autopsy of a young child who was tortured, burned, and beaten to death by a psychotic mother. Violent assault and death of a child are the stark realities of life which professionals must face when they choose to work in the area of domestic violence and child assault. Not every help giver, no matter what his or her specialty and training may be, is suited to working with such family conflict. It is therefore essential that agency selection of lay and professional staffs be based on sound, comprehensive personal interviews, as well as on honest appraisal and evaluations submitted by supervisors from previous educational or treatment facilities.

What is the responsibility of those human services agencies involved in decisions regarding permanent placement, relinquishment, and adoption of children whose parents are declared unfit or unable to provide necessary parental care, control, and custody? Too many children are subjected to years of multiple foster home placements, only to find that when parents are ultimately judged incompetent to reparent the child, the child, because of age or misbehavior, is now considered difficult or impossible to place. The tragic impact of parental assault is compounded by multiple separations and too frequent neglect and assault by licensed and unlicensed foster parents. For these children, repeated foster placements have been failure experiences, reinforcing already existing feelings of abandonment, separation, and loss, with its later manifestations of anger, rage, rebellion, and antisocial behavior.

## Out-of-Home Placement

For many children, the emotional trauma of one-time or ongoing physical or sexual assault is compounded by their being taken into protective custody, often in the middle of the night. If multiple sibs are at risk, they also are taken into protective custody, and because of limited shelter-home resources for siblings, they are frequently separated for periods of time ranging from weeks to months. This terror of separation from both parents and sibs is augmented by the anticipated fear that all other adults will be violent and assaultive. Even so, the judicial system and the protective services departments do exercise wisdom—a wisdom based (it is hoped) on sound, thorough, and complete interviews, evaluations, and workups. Too often, however, necessary information is missing. Professional consultation is frequently minimal, with dependency court decisions based on expediency rather than on the best interest of the child or full understanding of the dynamics and psychopathology of the family. Faced with the aforementioned realities of community networking, it is therefore essential that treatment centers, both public and private, develop acute crisis evaluation procedures and continued treatment resources for those children separated from their parents. Peer support through group therapy has proved highly effective for those abused and molested children separated from their parents (Paulson, Strouse, and Chaleff, 1982).

Sharing the common trauma of assault and separation, latency age and adolescent boys and girls quickly related to each other's needs, anxieties, and experiences. Ventilation, catharsis, and peer socialization help to reestablish personal esteem and reduce feelings of responsibility and guilt, which an assaulted child often develops when reliving his or her experience of violent parental assault, molestation, or incest. For the child facing the possibility of permanent out-of-home placement, or for the child being placed for adoption, it is essential that continued support and therapy be provided to permit understanding and acceptance of what may be perceived as ultimate rejection by his or her parents—that is, adoption. Following permanent placement or adoption, there is continuing need for ongoing therapy—for the assaulted child as well as for the newly identified parents or parent surrogates. This transitional period may well result in separation anxiety, emotional withdrawal, regressive behaviors, or antisocial acts on the part of the placed child. It is hoped that continued group and family therapy will reduce the traumatic impact of permanent parental separation. Similarly, long-term planning for children whose parents are incarcerated for an extended period of time must be undertaken. Return of such a parent does not necessarily mean that that parent is ready, willing, and able to assume immediately those parenting roles that are necessary to assure positive attachment, emotional linkage, and adequate parenting.

Owing to fiscal constraints and limited placement resources, group homes for children of all ages are, of necessity, developing. Although reality needs were, in part, a stimulus for such programs, it was also recognized by child-care workers and health professionals that the same principles found in successful group therapy with adults (Feldman and Wodarski, 1975; Kaplan and Sadock, 1971; Rosenbaum and Berger, 1975; Yalom, 1975) were also applicable to children living in well-run, well-organized group homes. Here, the hard-to-place child is many times able to identify with positive characteristics of peers through social learning and emulation. For multiple sibs separated from parents, the group home provides security, support, and maintenance of nuclear family bonds. Group-home parents, wisely selected and soundly trained in the psychology of child assault intervention, become ideal parent models. Parents and peer group members become a recapitulation of the nuclear family unit. Sibling rivalries and child-parent conflicts can be identified and, it is hoped, resolved, either through wise parenting alone, or in conjunction with formal group therapy programs. These can be provided by an outside professional staff, within the confines of the group home itself.

An extension of the concept of group homes can also be applied to sibling homes, where again, under the aegis of skilled and psychologically astute parent surrogates, the sibling relationship can be kept intact, the bonds of reassurance and support can be preserved, and the terror of separation from siblings and parents will be ameliorated. In urban areas having major colleges and universities, there are multiple opportunities to use mature graduate and undergraduate students as group-home parents. With a grounding in such behavioral and social sciences as education, psychology, sociology, and social work, students can bring a theoretical understanding to the practical, daily living challenges of house parents. Already existing at the University of California, Los Angeles (UCLA), is such a group of almost 100 students. Named Project MAC, volunteer students go three times per week to MacLaren Hall, a county receiving facility for children. Here assaulted, neglected, molested, and abandoned children, unable to be placed immediately in a suitable foster home or a temporary crisis shelter, are cared for until longer term jurisdiction is determined by the juvenile dependency court. Both male and female members of Project MAC are given many opportunities to engage on a personal and group level with children of all ages, from newborn to age 18. Through group activity, through sports and recreational programs, through dramatic productions, and through educational and tutorial programs, these young men and women provide excellent role models for those children in temporary custody. As parent surrogates and lay therapists, they have excellent skills, resources, and emotional maturity, all qualities that are ideal for group-home parents or for rehabilitation programs dedicated to the diagnosis and treatment of abused children and their parents.

## Family Crisis Centers

The startling increase in documented domestic violence reflects an increasingly violent society. Homicide directed against government leaders is passed off as mere political assassination. Defense attorneys use "homicide while under the influence of drugs" as a legal maneuver for avoiding responsibility for acts of violence. Homicide of children, a major consequence of domestic violence, is now the fifth leading cause of death of children. With such documented increase in domestic violence, the family crisis center has become a refuge for mothers and children who are subjected to threats or acts of violence from assaultive and often times alcoholic husbands and fathers. Some shelters provide 24 hour care for mothers and children for up to several weeks. At this writing, however, there is too frequently not yet available a shelter home for the battered wife and her children.

The Children's Bureau of Los Angeles (1982) is a nonprofit, nonsectarian, United Way Agency, accredited by the Child Welfare League of America, serving children and families in crisis throughout Los Angeles County since 1904. Having as its primary goal the reunifying and preservation of families, Children's Bureau provides counseling and psychotherapy for all family members. In addition, it operates a number of therapeutic group homes for children, ages 4 through 13, many of whom were assaulted, and whose emotional problems require intensive therapeutic intervention and professional treatment. In addition, the Bureau provides adoptive services, parent education classes, and foster family care whereby 24 hour placement in certified homes is offered those children who need to live away from their families because the crisis is of such magnitude that the family cannot safely function as a unit.

One of the most effective intervention programs of Children's Bureau is the 24 hour Family Crisis Center, which offers up to 72 hours of shelter in homelike surroundings to infants, children, and parents in danger of assault. In addition, the center provides emergency overnight shelter for children with or without parents, 24 hour telephone open-line contact for immediate access to temporary emergency shelter and crisis intervention counseling at no fee, as well as referrals to appropriate community services. Staffed by clinical social workers, parent educators, house parents, volunteers and Spanish speaking translators, the Family Crisis Center provides a much needed and highly respected program of primary and secondary prevention and treatment for families traumatized by child assault in all of its serious manifestations.

The Los Angeles county Inter-Agency Council on Child Abuse and Neglect (ICAN-1984) has sponsored six neighborhood family stress centers, based primarily on the success of a pioneer model program, Cedar House, in Long Beach, California. Supported in great part by local industry, such programs provide a model for community response throughout the nation. A full spectrum of interdisciplinary services are provided. These services are as follows:

1. Twenty-four hour crisis response to family stress, including emergency homemakers, emergency funds, and group care.

2. Preventive services for high-risk families, including parenting classes, prenatal classes, respite day care. Preventive programs are

offered to schools, preschool agencies, well baby clinics, and hospital personnel.

3. Protective services consultation with the local Department of Public Service and local law enforcement agencies, in which the assigned police liaison and children's services worker review all reports of suspected child assault coming into the center, with the policy of cooperative coordination to assure fulfillment of the requirements of the Child Abuse Reporting Law.

4. Treatment services, in which the primary goal is protection of the child, and in which the treatment program focuses on replacing the assaultive parenting practices with more appropriate childrearing practices. Such services would include family and child counseling, mental health services, psychiatric consultation, public health collaboration, homemaker and emergency caretaker services, respite day care, parenting classes, job and house finding, transportation to and from therapy, out-of-home care, referral to self-help groups like Parents Anonymous, Parents United, and Alcoholics Anonymous, and referral, outreach, and follow-up for program evaluation.

Each satellite community center is administered locally. Although an advisory board oversees the project, a multidisciplinary team networks closely with the community, maintaining close professional affiliations with local child trauma councils and statewide child abuse consortiums. Using local funds primarily, such model intervention programs can be developed within each community catchment area, with the locale determined by areas of highest need.

The California Department of Social Services has published a document (Oliver, 1980) that describes not only the development and implementation of six statewide community-based service programs for the prevention and treatment of child assault, but it also examines three areas of concern: (a) innovative approaches to funding, (b) issues in treatment, and (c) barriers to service delivery.

Four specific issues in the treatment of physical assault were identified: (1) parent resistance to treatment; (2) environmental impoverishment and its relationship to physical neglect; (3) treatment of choice for the total family; and (4) parental difficulties in distinguishing assault from discipline. Those treatment issues specific to incest and sexual assault were the following: lack of standard criteria for determining the need for out-of-home placement; therapist conflict and ambivalence regarding mandatory reporting; negative effects of court involvement on the victims of assault; absence of a valid and reliable working definition of sexual assault; lack of needed and appropriate treatment facilities; lack of interdisciplinary cooperation in treatment of sexual assault; and worker burnout.

In examining barriers to service delivery, the following concerns were identified by Oliver (1980): (1) criminalization versus decriminalization; (2) effectiveness of coercive or mandatory treatment; (3) determination of when diversion is more effective than incarceration; (4) the questionable value of psychotherapy when the immediate problems are in great part related to social and economic oppression, and absence of support services; (5) need for alternative and expanded child care resources; (6) improved foster care resources and parenting failures of foster parents; (7) resources for placing and treating the hard-to-place child; and (8) resistance of foster parents to involving natural parents in visitation.

Analysis of the six statewide child abuse treatment programs provides vital information that can be useful in the development of a community sponsored, community-based treatment resource program for physically, sexually, and emotionally abused children and their families.

Discovery House in Calgary, Alberta, Canada (1984), is also a shelter for battered spouses and their children, offering long-term refuge from a violent home life. This refuge is available to those who need additional time away from an acute crisis situation to explore alternative possibilities, to evaluate immediate and present family situations, and to make relevant changes if necessary. Discovery House also offers 24 hour security to the family, with each supplied a fully furnished apartment, complete with dishes and bedding. It provides one and two bedroom apartments and a common room for workshops and interfamily discussion. Residents may stay up to three months, with each paying a reasonable rent. The lay and professional staffs are equipped to answer questions on financial assistance, legal guidance, employment, educational opportunities, day care, housing, and professional counseling. Discovery House provides a broad range of workshops and weekly discussion groups, using appropriate audiovisual tapes and films for enhancing discussion, and providing greater insight and understanding into family dynamics of domestic violence and spouse assault. Children living within the shelter are provided with recreational programs, including swimming, crafts, and field trips, as well as opportunities for peer counseling led by staff members. Recognizing that adjustment to violence extends beyond this period of temporary security and support. Discovery House has also an outreach program called New Start. Immediately upon entrance into Discovery House each family is matched with a trained volunteer, who in many ways serves as a parent aide. During the time in residence at Discovery House, and up to a maximum of six months, the family and a New Start volunteer work together, planning and implementing steps necessary for the rehabilitation of the family. Subsequent to leaving Discovery

House, the volunteer fulfills many of the functions of a compassionate and caring parent surrogate, a family advocate, and a trusted listener and friend. With such an extension into the community and with the volunteer facilitating a network with other community resources and agencies, the victims of domestic violence are thus provided additional resources for maximizing their rehabilitation.*

# ETHNIC VALUES: A THERAPEUTIC CHALLENGE

Population statistics show a marked increase of minorities in highly urbanized cities, especially among the sunbelt states of the Southern United States. There have been increasing influxes of non-English speaking, undocumented aliens and Asian immigrants, many having minimal English speaking skills. Counties and states nationwide are now faced with major social service crises. With decreasing fiscal resources for maintaining health and social welfare needs, and lacking bilingual and multilingual professionals and staffs, human resources agencies are, throughout the country, unable to respond to the overwhelming needs for their services. Immigrants bring with them their own childrearing practices and values, some of which are antithetical to those prescribed by community, state, and United States health and welfare codes. Yet society is unable to intervene in helping these families adapt to a new code of parenting practices. Even in many relatively long-established minority communities, there are minimal opportunities for child health care and minimal opportunities for parents to learn the fundamentals of childrearing and effective parenting (Newberger and Cook, 1983).

The long-established black community, most of which is English speaking, by that fact has one less conflict area than does the non-English speaking minority family. Integrated throughout the community, the

---

*Editor's Note: A project similar to Discovery House was established in 1972 in Amsterdam. Called "De Triangel" (1979), this sociotherapeutic institute occupies a large apartment building in Amsterdam where over 15 troubled families live together for approximately six months while they receive a variety of diagnostic and therapeutic services.

Although the similarity in name to the technical family therapy called "triangling" (Bowen, 1978; Minuchin, 1974) seems coincidental, the Triangel Institute certainly employs all types of modern therapeutic techniques. A visit to the institute and a review of published literature reveals that De Triangel helped restore and maintain the integrity of more than 350 families in the past decade. The paralyzing and negative binding effects of pathological family dynamics are analyzed and modified in this intensive therapeutic microcommunity, which may serve as a useful model in intervention–prevention of child assault (see Chapter 5).

minority family becomes part of the locale. Living, at times, within a predominantly ghetto area, many minority families are frequently isolated from opportunities and advantages available to the more affluent. Lacking such opportunities and support systems, the economically and educationally disadvantaged minorities often become the families at risk for physical neglect and abuse of children (Daniel et al., 1983).

In many first generation families, multiple adjustment conflicts are specific to childrearing and family life. Many immigrant families emphasize the patriarchal role of the father, with traditional expectations for conformity and obedience on the part of the wife as well as the children. Especially in those families in which English is not spoken and families live within their own ethnic sphere, there is a sociological reinforcement of traditional values and a slow process of acculturation. The school-age child acculturates much more quickly than do the parents, by experiencing other socioeducational stimulation and by being exposed to a variety of Anglo-type parenting attitudes and practices that may be more liberal and permissive than those within their own home.

When the teacher identifies signs of assault and refers to protective services agencies, it is here there is greatest need for an understanding of crosscultural differences in childrearing. The social services and legal systems must intervene primarily to protect the health and welfare of the child. However, all plans for rehabilitation must recognize these cultural-linguistic differences when referring the families for psychotherapy (Gabinet, 1983b).

For many, rehabilitation should be primarily reeducational, with a cognitive approach to a better understanding of more appropriate childrearing practices and role expectations (Newberger and Cook, 1983). Here, clinical and emotional insight may be quite secondary. Such families in group therapy frequently avoid discussion of personal-family-marital problems; indeed, exploration of sexual feelings and practices is met with marked denial and inhibition. Family stress may express itself much more through somatic and psychosomatic distress. A group process provides reassurance and greater ease in sharing and discussing emotional issues, whereas, in contrast, individual therapy is often more inhibiting and less dynamic. Using male-female cotherapists, whether in conjoint, family, or group therapy, gives each of the parents a symbolic role model with whom to identify and relate. A macho male is often more willing to accept interpretation and confrontation from a male therapist, whereas many times a female client identifies more with and feels supported by the reassurance and insightful statements of the female cotherapist. Invariably in therapy, the focus of child assault intervention is on the marital relationship, rather than on in-depth exploration of intrapsychic conflicts. Many families marked with interpersonal isolation and aloneness, have an inability to publicly reveal empathic tenderness or intimacy to the spouse or to the children. Such parents will often demand from the therapist answers, directions, and guidance. Reflection and nondirective techniques are many times less effective than a straightforward statement or discussion from the therapist. When, for example, the undocumented alien is referred for therapy, one of his or her primary concerns is deportation and survival. Motivation for insight therapy is minimal. Altering of childrearing attitudes and practices thus has minimal priority compared to the concern about the legal system, the absence of a support family, and the lack of medical care or housing.

## The Asian Community: Our Newest Families

The influx of vast numbers of Asians to the United States in the 1970s brought with it many medical-social-psychological responsibilities for human resources agencies (Sue and McKinney, 1975). The traditional Asian family is raised in a patriarchal, close knit home, where a philosophy of self-sufficiency and self-sustenance often prohibits reaching out for emotional support from others. The roles of mother and children appear to reflect a subservient and acquiescing lifestyle, with minimal challenge to the power role of the father. Preservation of their Oriental culture and family values is the expectation and demand of newly arrived Asian parents raising their children in an Occidental culture.

What happens when such immigrant families, stressed by changing cultural values and economic anxieties, find themselves reported to or identified by social services or law enforcement agencies for suspected assault or neglect of a child? Unable to understand why their traditional parenting practices may have brought them into conflict with health services agencies, they are often resistant to mental health intervention. The absence of bicultural and bilingual mental health workers further complicates the process of identification, assessment, referral, and treatment. When, for example, identified assaultive parents are referred for family therapy or group therapy, many of the processes postulated by Yalom (1975) fail to develop. For a child to show anger and confront the authority of the parents is an almost impossible task for the traditional Asian child. Many Asian parents view outspoken retorts by their increasingly Americanized children as disloyalty, disrespect, and disregard for family traditions.

It is important to also realize that the term "Oriental" or "Asian" is a generic term identifying many different ethnic subgroups, each having its own characteristic dialect, culture, tradition, lifestyle, and childrearing practices. As the immigrant family changes into second, third, or fourth generation "Westerners," there is an admixture of cultural norms, which poses even more conflict for the traditional family members who, still living in the philosophy of the nuclear family, continue to exercise pressures, values, and grandparent expectations upon the younger family members.

Chien and Yamamoto (1982), in exploring the effectiveness of various psychotherapeutic modalities for Asian Americans, note the importance of Confucianism in teaching family traditions. They list several fundamental ethics that obviously and directly influence the process of Occidental mental health intervention. For example, intimacy between father and son, propriety between husband and wife, order between elder and junior, and trust among friends are all values which, in a dynamic, reactive, process-oriented family therapy, may inhibit the expression of deep-lying, primary process feelings, drives, and recollections. Chien and Yamamoto further caution that "Respect of the parents and seniors, obedience, and close family ties . . . are values desirable in the Confucian dominated culture, yet are often interpreted as 'passive aggressive,' 'non-assertive,' or 'over-dependent on authority' in the eyes of those Anglos not familiar with Confucianism. Such culturally sensitive understanding is important because it is relevant to the conduct of family therapy, to the interpretation of psychotherapeutic content and process, and to understanding Asian family life" (Chien and Yamamoto, 1982).

What then is the role of the psychotherapist who either by cultural heritage or by deep understanding of such philosophical ethics sees the psychotherapeutic need to explore and analyze existing family conflicts, which are so complexly intermixed with Asian family values, obedience, conformity, and respect? Sexual growth and development, masturbation, and adult sexuality are areas of intimacy rarely shared by Oriental family members with health delivery personnel. Psychological intervention and psychiatry are, for the Asian, primarily associated with psychotics and acutely mentally ill patients; they are not viewed as interventions for families experiencing parent-child stress, marital conflict, sexual dysfunction, or severe depression. Whereas an act of suicide on the part of the Japanese military is seen as a noble act in defense of the motherland, non-military suicide by a family member is regarded as shameful, a degradation of the family name, and a tragedy rarely shared outside the family, not even with a mental health worker.

Therefore, any agency developing a diagnostic and treatment program in a catchment area with an Asian or Asian-American population, must use careful and considered attention to a needs assessment evaluation that recognizes especially the cultural heritage of the Orientals as it pertains to social service and mental health intervention (Sue, 1977). For these people, there is nothing more sacred than traditional family life. When child assault intervention requires a careful and intimate study, examination, and exploration of family history, parent-child relationships, sexual intimacy, and assaultive parenting practices, the first response of the family may be silence, noncooperation, or even withdrawal from further professional contacts. Intensive, long-term therapeutic intervention is seen as threatening, whereas exploration of the personal life of the family in greater depth regarding those stress areas that are considered sacred and not to be shared with outsiders is even more frightening. For this reason, short-term therapy, focusing on symptom removal, is often the treatment of choice. Concomitant physiological and psychosomatic symptoms that mask underlying depression or other personal-social conflict are more acceptable for primary medical intervention. When these biophysical stresses are relieved, often through medication, the Asian patient or family may elect to terminate therapy. Such a "flight into health" must be carefully weighed by the therapist as he or she presents to such families the need for more intensive, depth-oriented intervention.

In the same way that Asian parents may culturally resist confrontation, catharsis, and probing psychodynamic exploration of their inner lives, so may the Asian children similarly resist therapeutic intervention. Fear of confronting authority of the parents, feelings of disloyalty and disobedience for criticizing the parents, and apprehension over sharing highly personal inner feelings are all part of the mixed emotions felt by many Asian children when first undergoing a program of psychotherapy. Separated from their assaultive family, required to testify against their physically and sexually assaultive parents in a dependency hearing, placed in a foster home, and undergoing a program of psychotherapy, these children may be seen as recalcitrant, noncommunicative, and nonresponsive to traditional Western psychotherapy. The therapist must be patient, tolerant, wise to family and cultural values, and, above all, nonjudgmental. Nonverbal techniques such as play therapy, art therapy, puppetry, and finger painting are techniques by which the assaulted, neglected or molested child may initially be reached in therapy (see Chapter 5). Group therapy with age-appropriate peers also becomes an additional vehicle for supportive exploration of intrapsychic, interpersonal, and family related conflicts within the Asian and the Asian-American child and its parents.

# The Culturally Mixed Community

Psychotherapists must recognize the important influence of ethnicity and culture on the diagnosis and treatment of family violence. Examining cultural definitions of normality and pathology, McGoldrick, Pearce, and Giordano (1982) address issues in family therapy that are specific to such ethnic groups as Native American, black, Mexican, Puerto Rican, Cuban, Asian, and numerous European and mid-East cultures. Clinical judgments in psychological and psychiatric assessment are (it is hoped) based on a foundation of well-grounded education, training, and professional experience. It is, however, recognized that countertransference feelings may influence attitudes and decision-making processes in the therapist. McGoldrick, Pearce, and Giordano (1982) raise a provocative question about the practitioner's cultural background and how it affects perceptions of families' responses to psychotherapy. Whether mental health intervention is primarily diagnostic and referral, or whether it encompasses such techniques as individual, group, brief treatment, or Gestalt therapy, the ethnic variability within the therapist-client relationship is an essential aspect of rehabilitation and emotional growth within the patient (Maurer and Williams, 1983).

Because child assaulting families are many times seen as socially isolated, uncommunicative, spontaneously violent, and resistant to therapeutic intervention, it is essential that family dynamics and interpersonal relationships be altered or modified. Whether it is through a social learning approach, implosion therapy, Gestalt confrontation, or any number of other dynamic process therapies, intervention in the field of domestic violence must consist of a variety of practical intervention strategies that are effective in working with the wide range of socioeconomic statuses in society and applicable to the increasing cultural and ethnic mix that now characterizes the most recent census description of the United States of America (see Chapter 5).

Much of the literature on group therapy intervention has focused on Caucasian populations, or a mixed ethnic population in which Caucasians appear to be the major ethnic group. The great majority of published findings describe clinical samples derived from populations of patients in community health centers, hospital-based inpatient treatment programs, and medical center outpatient psychiatric clinics; most of these patients can be described as of middle to lower socioeconomic status, with mixed ethnicity and with English as the primary language (Paulson and Chaleff, 1973; Paulson et al., 1974b; Paulson et al., 1975a).

For some groups, the major goal is to work primarily in specific conflict areas, such as divorce, alcoholism, suicide ideation, delinquency, drug addiction, or loss and bereavement. Slavson (1956), an exponent of a specific problem as the basis for selecting group therapy members, writes,

> I have consistently recommended grouping of patients in analytic group psychotherapy with adults—unlike that in activity groups for children—on the basis of similarity of pathology or syndrome. Such similarity enhances identification among the members of the group, evokes empathy as well as more insightful interpretation and better understanding of each other's problems and that of one's own . . . . Similarity of the nuclear problem accelerates the therapeutic process, not only for the group but for the individual patients as well, since a communication by one applies to others and therefore evokes responses and memories in all . . . . The group becomes in effect one patient, which makes possible treatment through the group as differentiated from the treatment of patients in a group. (pp. 53–54)

For other groups, there is less of a focus on specific reasons for referral, and greater focus on interpersonal relationships, peer isolation, or marital discord as a reason for referral. Success and failure in group therapy have been widely studied (Feldman and Wodarski, 1975; Kaplan and Sadock, 1971; Rosenbaum and Berger, 1975) with Yalom (1975) documenting a number of concepts and processes found in more successful groups. Paulson and colleagues (1974b) describe a long-term, open-ended group therapy program with self-referred and court-referred assaultive parents, emphasizing in their paper the dynamic interplay among group members as an essential ingredient for therapeutic growth. The simulation of real-life family relationships, the conscious and unconscious identification of the male and female cotherapists as parent surrogates, and the understanding of the love-hate relationship between group members are processes in group therapy which, when understood and abreacted to, lead to significant insight and conflict resolution. When people recognized that many behavioral and interpersonal conflicts are a result of earlier learned experiences, disturbed family relationships, and acute socioeconomic stress, the application of family therapy, group marital therapy, encounter groups, and traditional male-female mixed dynamic groups can prove therapeutic and highly rehabilitative (Paulson, 1982).

Compared to the plethora of articles on English-speaking groups, relatively little has been written on group psychotherapy with adults whose speaking and reading language is Spanish-English or entirely Spanish. However, since the mid-1970s, a number of articles and textbooks have explored the effectiveness of group psychotherapy with Hispanics who speak only Spanish. Most recently, Acosta (1982) described a number of psychodynamic and group processes inherent in providing group psychotherapy to Spanish-speaking clients. He strongly endorsed the use of group therapy as an effective treatment modality for Spanish-speaking Hispanic patients and focused on such treatment issues as acculturation stress, family breakdown, discrimination, and somatization of psychological problems.

Becerra, Karno, and Escobar (1982) explored the mental health of Hispanic Americans, examining such clinical perspectives as social and cultural issues, religious and cultural influences, social networking, diagnosing of schizophrenia, substance abuse, gang membership, treatment of the Hispanic child, group therapy, the Anglo consulting psychiatrist, and clinical services for Hispanics.

Mental health workers have explored other therapeutic issues central to the treatment of the Hispanic patient. These issues include the use of behaviorally oriented group therapy in treating low-income, Spanish-speaking clients (Herrera and Sanchez, 1976); the role of brief group therapy to facilitate use of mental health services by Spanish-speaking patients (Normand, Iglesias, and Payne, 1974); and the psychodynamic meaning of transference and culture in Latino therapy groups (Werbin and Hynes, 1975).

Zavala (personal communication) summarizes a number of very relevant findings and generalizations specific to the treatment of the Hispanic family as follows:

1. Group therapy is useful and effective in working with Latino patients.

2. The mixing of Anglos and Latinos frequently results in a high drop-out rate for those with little mastery of the English language. It is most important, especially for the therapist, to have a good understanding of the Latino culture and the nuances of the Spanish language within each of the several Latino subcultures.

3. The application of group therapy techniques and treatment methods for Latinos is essentially similar to those used with Anglo or black patients. Although these concepts are as applicable to one culture as to another, there may be specific cultural attitudes and values that must be especially understood in the application of group treatment modalities. For example, exploring of sexual feelings and behavior in a mixed-sex Latino group may be much more inhibited and suppressed than in a comparable group of Anglos. Yet, confrontation, abreaction, transference, catharsis, and the many recognized mechanisms of defense are as important and as relevant in working with Latinos as they are in working with Anglos.

4. Many Latinos, especially females, exhibit multiple psychosomatic complaints, which mask underlying conflicts related to anger, depression, sexual dysfunction, and marital discord. It is as if the psychophysiological distress is more personally, socially, and culturally accepted than is the public acknowledgment of emotional and psychological pain and conflict. As a point of caution, it is important

that the therapist recognize this defense of somatization. For many patients, the early amelioration of physical distress and therapy can be described as a flight into health. Feeling this temporary relief from physical pain, many may wish to terminate therapy without achieving emotional insight and understanding of the conflict and discord that led to the earlier symptom development. This writer's experience in supervising Latino students treating a group of Latino women speaking and understanding only Spanish permitted an excellent comparison of the effectiveness of group therapy with Latinos and with Anglos. The solidarity and cohesion in the groups, as described by Yalom, were beautifully demonstrated in this Latino group of females, who at the beginning of therapy referred to themselves as "Las Afligidas" (the "anguished ones"), and who later in therapy renamed their group "Las Compañeras," denoting the recuperative strength of shared companionship.

5. Disclosure and openness in expressing guilt-laden behavior is often slow to develop in Latino groups. Behavioral and cognitive approaches are many times seen as less ego threatening and less anxiety provoking than more psychodynamic and transactional kinds of therapeutic interventions. Behavioral approaches focusing on such areas as modifying and developing specific social skills and assertiveness were seen as less threatening than were such approaches as Gestalt therapy, confrontation, and implosion therapy.

In summary, it is evident that the process of group psychotherapy with Latinos can be as effective as it is with Anglos and blacks. It provides multiple feedback opportunities, it has a reintegrating and restorative function for the lonely, depressed, anguished, and angry individual. For those with limited interpersonal skills, and for those having restricted emotional understanding of the relationship between somatic stress and emotional and marital conflicts, group psychotherapy techniques and principles are highly remedial.

Although the above-mentioned findings describe a number of clinical studies, there is a dearth of methodologically sound, empirical studies assessing outcome indices of group psychotherapy intervention with Latinos. Moreover, there is a scarcity of articles examining the application of group techniques to the teaching of parenting skills to the Latino assaultive family. Although principles of child growth and development are well known, the group application of such principles to minority families has, at times, been only minimally effective in altering and modifying supposedly maladaptive parenting practices— primarily because of conflicts centering on differentiation between discipline, punishment, and assault. Reared in a family milieu where, for generations, a traditional lifestyle has been modeled, emulated, and passed on, many parents will respond within their own family in a way that is deemed culturally, socially, and personally appropriate. Parent laxity, absence of limit setting, or an ultraliberal lifestyle may, for some families, make for emotional and physical neglect of a child. Rigidity, high conformity demands, and ultraconservative parental behaviors, attitudes, and values can make for child-parent conflict and rebellion, actions which may provoke the parents to severe corporal punishment, and, in the extreme, parental violence and physical assault. Even more, the transient movement of many minority families seeking greater economic and employment opportunities results in a separation from traditional family lifestyles, with their nuclear and extended family supports, to a new and unknown community with mixed sociocultural lifestyles and minimal personal-social supports. It is here that the family may experience increased child-parent stress, with minimal means of coping. It is for such families, however, that programs of group psychotherapy intervention, based on a comprehensive understanding and experience with minority culture values and childrearing practices, can be most effective, both in primary prevention of assault as well as in secondary intervention with already identified, traumatized children.

What can be done for the highly urban, economically and educationally deprived, multicultural community, where many or most families have had minimal or no prenatal care? For the Latino, black, or Oriental family, there may be minimal educational opportunities for parenting classes or for prenatal or postnatal training. It is here that health educators and institutions must provide resources for maximizing health care opportunities (Daniel et al., 1983). Group programs of prenatal education can provide the minority mother (and, it is hoped, the father) with an understanding of such concepts as bonding, attachment, and "en face" interaction, as well as an understanding of the importance of knowing developmental milestones from birth through late childhood. Shared experiences regarding parental expectations allow for understanding and support among group members. Identity formation, arousal and aggression, role expectation of parents, separation anxiety, individual differences, and mother-infant interaction can be taught and discussed both in group parenting classes and in programs of group psychotherapy for minorities. Although the individual minority parent may be uninformed and fearful of revealing such lack of understanding, there is a communal sense of support and sharing that helps in the understanding of catharsis, discipline, abuse, social class differences, positive and negative reinforcement, language development, sexual growth, self-esteem, and sibling conflict.

In the one-to-one therapy relationship, such concepts are at times difficult to share, and at times they are hard for parents to comprehend. The individual therapist is many times reluctant to cast himself or herself in the role of active educator or teacher. This is a traditional inhibition, which frequently prevents many therapists from taking a role of advice-giver or behavioral director. It is most important that therapists working in the area of child assault prevention and treatment be flexible in both orientation and response. The reality needs of many assaultive families respond best to direct intervention, short-term, group types of therapeutic rehabilitation, multiple agency networking, and a level of maturity in the therapist that shows understanding, compassion, firmness, and decisiveness, and, at all times, a capacity for flexibility, adaptability, and egalitarianism in the patient-therapist relationship. The "nature-nurture" controversy has, for example, many sociocultural aspects that can rarely be discussed in detail in a one-to-one therapeutic relationship; however, in a group interaction program, such attributes provide discussion, debate, and sharing of personal, family, and ethnic cultural values. Behavior modification and operant conditioning are core concepts in prenatal, postnatal, and parent-toddler training, and they are also suitable for small group education. As a part of a comprehensive intervention program for assaultive parents, the integration of more structured and formal education with dynamic, process-oriented, group psychotherapy becomes a means of preventing the initial act of parental assault of a child, and also a means for rehabilitating the already identified assaultive family.

# EXPANDED INTERVENTION SERVICES

## Community Planning

Magrab (1982), in examining the increasing need for services to chronically ill and handicapped children, especially in light of decreasing federal supports, states, "The real hope for coordinated cost-effective services is in communities. Communities are where the important arrangements can be made—among professionals, agencies, and families; state and national authorities should support this. Planning for services at the community level is going to be the key in the next decade" (p. 105). Although recognizing the contributions of the interdisciplinary process, Magrab emphasizes a need to also turn to an untapped resource—parents and other family members. Realizing that the great majority of child assault occurs as a result of parenting failures related to discipline and childrearing, it is important that the professionals and the community combine to provide massive new opportunities for parenting improvement classes, classes for the young adult, classes for pregnant parents, and classes for caregivers of neonatal and postnatal infants. "We need new models, models that spiral—trainers who train trainers, who train trainers; the psychologist who trains day care workers, who train the parents—prevention strategies must become the watchword of developing impact programs with families and children early on to reduce the need for some special services throughout a lifetime" (Magrab, 1982, p. 105).

Yet, we must be aware that success of any parenting class is a function of interest and motivation of participating parents. Child management training and programs on child growth and development are frequently offered to economically and educationally disadvantaged minority families by middle-class, Anglo professionals. Follow-up analyses of such programs reveal resistance or outright rejection of the program because the minorities at times feel that such trainers cannot really understand, identify with, or appreciate the realities of the disadvantaged minority-class members. Firestone and Witt (1982) reviewed two studies (Eyberg and Johnson, 1974; Patterson, 1974), each reporting attrition rates ranging from virtually no defectors to attrition as high as 50 per cent, depending on the nature of the identified client population. Self-referred families having a strong, positive motivation and belief in the use of psychological and educational approaches to change impaired child, parent, and family patterns of conflict had a much higher degree of success, both in the process of psychotherapy and in the parent-training component of family rehabilitation. For agency-referred families, who often feel unfairly accused of child assault, the effectiveness of these types of therapeutic approaches too often have been less than successful. "Inasmuch as treatment, rejection, and premature termination appear to be a persistent problem in all forms of therapy, including parent training, these disengagements require exploration for several reasons. It is expected that those disengaging from therapy receive minimal if any benefits, while they are costly in terms of therapeutic resources. In addition, some families who may be more likely to benefit from intervention, are placed on long waiting lists or denied treatment altogether" (Firestone and Witt, 1982, p. 209).

Intervention inadequacies for both Anglos and minorities must therefore be viewed in terms of institutional, agency, and professional failures. It is the critical intermeshing of the client, the agency, and the professional health providers that assures maximum rehabilitation of the abusing, neglecting, and sexually molesting family (Paulson, 1978).

# Home Visits and Intervention

Child assault researchers and clinicians are more and more recognizing the importance of home visits and observations of the child-parent interaction as an important component in intervention and rehabilitation of families. Using home observation scales, much data can be derived studying maternal-infant interaction and its relationship to neglect, failure to thrive, bonding and attachment, and the long-term growth and development of the mental and physical health of the infant. The pioneer work of Spitz (1945) in his study of "hospitalism" and marasmus in young children, has provided important clinical data from a macroanalytical approach. Pollitt, Eichler, and Chan (1975), in their comparative study of mothers of failure to thrive infants with a matched control group, found that mother-infant interaction was the most differentiating element. "In interaction with their children, the control group was more verbal, showed more physical contact, and contact was more often positively reinforcing and warm. In addition, mothers in the control group showed twice as many instances of positive affect" (p. 525).

If maltreatment of children and nonorganically based failure to thrive are indices of parenting failures, what can be done to identify their early precursors? Alfasi (1982), in a brief review of the literature, states that the microanalysis of mother-infant intervention is becoming an increasingly respected tool in clinical research. Alfasi, in describing this microanalysis study of mother-infant interaction states,

> Microanalysis of mother-infant interactions may be used to eliminate behavioral deviations in clinical syndromes. A three month old failure to thrive infant was videotaped while playing with his mother and with a female stranger. Videotapes were analyzed for a variety of maternal and infant behaviors on a second by second basis. Scores for this dyad were then compared with scores for a group of 19 other babies who did not show the failure to thrive syndrome. The results show that the mother of this baby used extremely high levels of stimulation in a variety of sensory modalities but showed little positive affect. By contrast, in playing with this baby, the stranger tended to use lower levels of stimulation in the areas of positive (stimulation) vis-à-vis the baby and touch. It is suggested that the mother's intrusive over-stimulation, perhaps coupled with deficits on the part of the infant, resulted in serious interactional asynchrony. The infant's failure to develop normally might thus reflect the absence of a happy, reciprocal exchange between mother and infant.
>
> (Alfasi, 1982, p. 111)

It is thus evident that multiple disciplines, multiple theoretical approaches, and multiple identification and treatment programs can be used in working successfully with assaulted children and their parents. Both macro- and micro-analysis investigations of mother-infant interactions can provide a sensitive and measurable index of unusual or disordered interaction.

> Whether because of innate difficulties or because of early experience, the infant who develops failure-to-thrive is one who may show a serious deficit in his ability to titrate incoming stimulation, thus leaving him or her extremely vulnerable to over-stimulation. The mother of such an infant may also show deficits in her interactive abilities. Unable to read her infant's cues accurately, and therefore unaware of the infant's vulnerability, she may respond in an inappropriate and over-stimulating way . . . . Deprived of a positive, reciprocal exchange with the mother, the infant may show a breakdown in normal developmental processes, leading to the symptom of Failure-to-Thrive.
>
> (Alfasi, 1982, p. 111)

The ultimate success in reducing and, it is hoped, eliminating such aspects of domestic violence as child assault will depend not only on community and federal support of intervention programs but also on the integration of professional skills and understanding coupled with specialized service procedures and techniques of social science assessment. The application of well-proved, traditional mental health procedures, and the creative interaction of new measures of intervention such as microanalysis of parent-infant interaction, will maximize the prevention and treatment of child abuse (Paulson, 1983).

## THE MENTAL HEALTH WORKER AS HOME VISITOR

Social workers have traditionally filled the role of home visitor in assessing or monitoring medical, social, and health care needs of home-bound families (Halpern, 1984). Working closely with public health nursing, numerous families have thus been supported, sustained, and enabled to live more adequately outside of hospitals, institutions, and convalescent homes. Why, though, are physicians increasingly reluctant or unwilling to make home visits or house calls? Why are psychiatrists and psychologists similarly reluctant to make either occasional or regularly scheduled house calls? Gurian (1978) discusses a number of practical and emotional issues that cause both patient and psychiatrist sufficient discomfort to limit such a model of therapeutic intervention. Kempe (1976) describes the important networking role of home visitors, who provide support, encouragement, social stimulation, and an extension of the therapeutic process into the homes of assaultive families. Most home visitors are lay therapists, trained as specialists in the area of child assault prevention, identification, and therapeutic intervention. For the home-bound child and parent, this special visitor becomes an extension of the nuclear family, the idealized parent who is supportive, understanding, giving, and nonjudgmental. For the therapist-visitor, such a home visit provides unique opportunities to see, to understand, and to feel the experiential life of the assaultive family. It is noteworthy that one of the principal findings from an evaluation study of 11 national demonstration programs for treating child assault was that lay therapist–counselors, parent aides, or Parents Anonymous groups acting as home visitors were the single most cost-effective provision to prevent future abuse (Cohn, 1979).

Gurian (1978) describes this phenomenon of entering into the private world of the patient, stating,

> The family that asks any professional—a physician, for example—to enter their home, decides to open their borders, relax their guard, expose their specialness, listen to judgments, receive directives, and assume a relatively passive and perhaps dependent role. This is the "paranoid" side of the territorial imperative. The "trusting" side is a wish to share one's privacy and to open one's home as one's heart in welcoming the outsider. (p. 592)

For the family willing to allow such entrance into the privacy of their home, there may well be much openness and receptivity. But for many assaultive families, the request for a home visit magnifies already existing suspicion, distrust, and paranoid thoughts that the family has toward both professionals and agencies. In many phases of psychotherapy, the social stresses within the home or the cross-generational tensions within the extended family lead to crisis moments, which may constitute threats of violence or even death to one or more family members. A traditional 50 minute office visit will many times not provide an accurate appraisal of a potentially life-threatening situation. It is in such situations that a mature, emotionally secure mental health worker can make an immediate home assessment. If the crisis is potentially violent, or if the family does not allow such a home evaluation, the cooperation and support of law enforcement professionals must be sought. Police not only provide security for the home visitor or clinician but also provide access into a home, even without a court order. In any well-organized and well-staffed community agency or mental health organization, the specific services of psychiatrists, psychologists, social workers, and other members of the mental health team should be routinely available for house calls or home visits. "Even when most of an evaluation must be carried out elsewhere, it is important that a direct evaluation of the person's home situation be made. In addition to telling much that is useful about people's lives, such evaluation makes it possible to bring services to those . . . persons who cannot or will not leave their homes to come to a clinic, hospital, or agency" (Butler and Lewis, 1973, p. 23).

Generalizing from the role of gereopsychiatrist to the home visiting role of all mental health workers, Gurian (1978) concludes, "In order to be useful within these boundaries, the psychiatric house call may have to be stylistically flexible and still provide responsible case management. We must work toward models that provide community focused comprehensive mental health services as part of an integrated human services delivery system."

# RELIGIOUS FAITH: A DYNAMIC ELEMENT IN PSYCHOTHERAPY

Mental health workers in general and psychodynamic psychotherapists in particular have traditionally isolated the patient's religious belief system from the healing processes of psychotherapy. For many professionals, religion is seen as a dependency crutch, as a way of placing accountability and responsibility in the hands of others rather than in the hands of the individual struggling to find solutions to personal conflict. Menninger (1938), speculating on the dynamics of reassurance—whether it comes from a trained professional or from the ear of an attentive listener—writes,

> For an individual overwhelmed by his own hostility and other emotional conflicts, even the tacit assurance that somebody loves him enough to listen to him, and prescribe for him, or advise him, is, of itself, a tremendous reassurance. It is no wonder, therefore, that people get well as a result of the conscious or unconscious psychotherapeutic influence of all kinds of quacks, faith healers, and fakers, as well as reputable physicians, psychoanalysts and others. These transference cures, however, are well known to be illusory since insecure individuals are very apt to develop these feelings again and seek for renewed assurance of affection and love. (p. 149)

In examining the role of religious faith in the daily process of living, it is important to differentiate the bizarre, delusional religious beliefs of a psychotic person from the deep and abiding religious faith of a more healthy individual, whether the religion be Christianity, Judaism, or another form. Even while accepting, as Menninger states, "insecure individuals are apt to . . . seek for renewed assurances of affection and love," it is also important to recognize that *secure* individuals, such as psychiatrists, psychoanalysts, psychologists, religious leaders, and all of humanity, also need "assurance of affection and love." For some, meaningful interpersonal relationships are sufficient to provide such assurance of affection and love. For others, interpersonal relationships combined with a deep personal religious faith provide an increased sense of security, and an increased depth in living, loving, and relating. Menninger summarizes the ambiguous role of religion in the curative process of mental health intervention, stating,

> It is doubtless true that religion has been the world's psychiatrist throughout the centuries. That religion may have caused much suffering, as well as cured much, is also not to be gainsaid . . . . Unfortunately, too, many people cannot accept either the gratification or the restrictions of religions because their intelligence or emotional conflicts forbid it. For these, it is of little help; but for the millions of others, it is and will continue to be an indispensable mode of salvation, i.e., reconstruction. (p. 156)

Two decades after Menninger wrote the foregoing sentences, Feifel (1957) wrote, "One should be cautious in considering the religious person as invariant. Some may adopt religion as a kind of defense against the 'slings and arrows of outrageous misfortune.' Then there are those individuals who incorporate their religious beliefs into every day living activities" (p. 43). More recently, McLemore (1982) explored the role of Christian faith in the healing process of psychotherapy. Some Christian believers view psychotherapy as almost blasphemous, as a reflection of a lack of faith and a lack of belief in the power of prayer. For others, a combination of counseling, faith, hope, and a belief in a power beyond oneself provides the strengths that bring people through the abyss of depression and the despair of hopelessness.

Does religious faith have any place in the treatment and rehabilitation of families involved in domestic violence? What should psychotherapists do, and how should they respond, when assaultive mothers and fathers, both self-referred and agency-referred, profess in therapy the importance of religion in their daily living? It is important to affirm that child assault is no stranger to race, religion, color, creed, or socioeconomic status. Religious beliefs per se do not prevent assault of a child. In fact, in many fundamentalist religions, the power role of the parents, the Old Testament beliefs in punishment for sin, and the fear of a constantly tempting world are dynamics that make many parents tragically overreact in the discipline and punishment of their children. The need to "drive out the devil" is many times the justification given by a religious, neurotic, overly punishing, assaultive parent, as well as the explanation of a psychotic, delusional assaultive caregiver.

Therapists must be aware of the manifold dynamics of their patients (Paulson and Blake, 1969). In those situations in which religion or a belief in God is used as a rationalization, as a defense, or as a displacement of responsibility and guilt, such faulty thinking must be part of the confronting processes of insight psychotherapy. On the other hand, a belief in the omnipotent presence and power of a supreme being can be a reinforcing, reassuring affirmation that one is not alone, even in the midst of despair. Like the outstretched hand that touches, like the hug that reassures, like the cradling arms of a mother holding a feverish young child, like the presence of the kindly bedside practitioner in a moment of anguished waiting, many believers experience an inner strength and a sustenance that allows them to hope, to believe, and to face the immediate moments of doubt, despair, dread, death, or even the fear and pain of living.

It is the experience of many health professionals working in the area of child assault that religion, like any other aspect of family life, can be a meaningful part of the therapeutic process. The therapist may be atheist or agnostic, fundamentalist or ultra-liberal, yet, in terms of both traditional psychoanalytic thinking and behavioral doctrine, there has been much resistance to recognizing the positive role of religion in the curative process of psychotherapy. An abiding faith in the powerful reassurance of the rabbi, priest, or minister is attested to by many. Pastoral counseling is a recognized part of modern-day psychological intervention. The sustaining strength of a chaplain in times of peace and war, and his or her supportive role in the hospital in counseling the bereaved and giving solace to those facing life-threatening uncertainties, attest further to the power of faith in coping with immediate and acute crises of living and dying. Whether religion per se provides long-term insight and conflict resolution is a function of the client's many related, intrapsychic, interpersonal, and familial-cultural values, as well as the therapist's expressed or unexpressed values and beliefs regarding religion. For the family sustained in part by faith, it is important that the therapist does not deny or impugn the power of religion. When therapists and clients have belief systems that are consonant with each other there can be a significant contribution to personal growth. It is a courageous mental health worker who, believing in the power of faith and prayer can likewise share his or her own experiences of personal faith with clients when it is therapeutically indicated.

The Village of CHILDHELP, U.S.A., a project of CHILDHELP, U.S.A./INTERNATIONAL, a nonsectarian, nonprofit, residential treatment center for assaulted children and their families, added a small nondenominational chapel to its treatment facilities. This chapel provides an appropriate setting for a variety of spiritual experiences for the assaulted children in residence. The founders have always stressed the importance of religion and access to a chapel in developing a holistic, comprehensive program for treating assaulted children and their troubled families (see Chapter 8). Too often traditional roles of mental health intervention–prevention have centered primarily on health delivery disciplines. It is only recently that the additional contributions of law, law enforcement, lay therapy, and volunteer modalities on the interdisciplinary team have been expanded to include the important contributions of theology and religion in the rehabilitative processes with assaultive families (see Chapter 5).

McLemore's book (1982) is a stimulating introduction to philosophical, moral, and religious aspects of contemporary psychology. It provides a careful, critical insight into Christian psychology and calls for believers to hold theology and psychology in balance, without compromise. Unfortunately, references to "Christian" practices or beliefs throughout the book may imply that such principles and guidelines apply only to that specific faith group. McLemore examines Christianity in terms of behavior therapy, Rogerian therapy, biofeedback, hypnosis, transactional analysis, marriage and family therapy, existential therapy, interpersonal therapy, group therapy, cognitive behavior modification, Gestalt therapy, body oriented therapy, and psychoanalysis. In one of his final chapters, McLemore discusses the place of Christ in the healing process of psychotherapy. Although this chapter may appear to be of use only to members of the Christian faith for therapeutic intervention, the term "God" or "Supreme Being" could be substituted for the word "Christ"; the same tenets could be applied in coming to terms with God and self.

In the same way that mental health professionals cannot afford to disregard the important role of "the church" (in its broad sense), neither can the church disregard the resources of mental health.

These resources must be worked in to the warp and woof of caring within the church universal. While at times 'the church' has regarded psychology as its enemy, the psychologist is no more the necessary enemy of Christ [God] than the biologist. It is only the religious beliefs, or unbeliefs, of individual scientists or practitioners that are problematic . . . . It is the therapists who have most addressed the need for self-disclosure, for emotional dialogue, for intelligent compassion. They have done what the church is charged to do—care effectively for people.

(McLemore, 1982, p. 236)

# LATENCY AGE SUICIDAL BEHAVIOR AND CHILD ASSAULT

Adolescent and adult suicidal behavior have been well documented and studied. Faced with seemingly hopeless conflict, lacking emotional or family supports, unable to face the guilt within and the judgment of society, there is for many only one means of escape—suicide. Child psychiatrists have examined the concept of childhood suicide, but in most cases the age range of children studied has been from early adolescence to young adulthood. It is only in the last few years that medical and behavioral scientists have studied carefully suicidal behavior of latency age, preadolescent children.

Many outcome studies on the sequelae of assault and severe neglect identify developmental disabilities, school failures, social withdrawal, peer conflict, and delinquency as only a few of the consequences of abuse (Martin, 1976). The violence of acute and chronic assault leaves physical as well as emotional scars. It might be expected that assaulted children, faced with continual physical assault and sensing a life of immediate hopelessness and despair, might see intended death and suicide as one escape from intolerable family pressures and emotional pain. Relatively few studies, however, have examined suicidal behavior as a chosen act of escape from life's terrors by children who have been abused (Green, 1978).

Paulson and Stone (1974, 1978, 1983) studied 34 suicidal children ranging in age from four to 12 years. The dynamics of subintended and intended death were found to be associated with family violence, alcoholism, divorce, previous suicide or suicidal attempts of family members, intense sibling rivalry, and overly severe parental discipline. But, in examining the medical and case histories of these 34 children, not a single case was at that time identified in the terms of "child abuse." Yet it is evident that in almost all of these 34 cases, extreme emotional rejection, abandonment, marital separation, and domestic violence were the precursors to the suicidal act or suicidal thought.

The taboo against accepting the fact of latency age suicidal behavior is almost as great as is the taboo against recognizing family incest. It is vital that parents, teachers, day care workers, social service workers, health professionals, and even coroners be aware that young children can be so unhappy and so depressed that they purposely try to kill themselves. The emotional and physical pain of living is often more feared than death itself. Coroner's offices nationwide rarely document the cause of death of children under 12 years old as suicide. For many of these suicidal children, somatic symptoms, school failures, and peer conflicts mask the underlying acute depression and sadness. In studies of acute adult depression and suicidal behavior, the "depressive equivalent" has been considered the unconscious and unidentified manifestation of possible suicide. In a similar manner, the depressive equivalent in childhood psychopathology must be recognized for what it really is. The continuing experience of somatic symptoms and school failures occurring in a setting of domestic violence must alert health care workers and educators to the possible presence of child assault, molestation, incest, and its too frequent consequence, self-destructive and suicidal behavior.

The concept of permanency or nonreversibility of death does not develop until approximately seven to eight years of age. Prior to this age, unhappy and acutely depressed children, often identified as "accident prone," may engage in behaviors that are self-destructive (Daniel et al., 1983), yet feel on some level that even though he or she dies today, he or she returns tomorrow (Paulson and Stone, 1974, 1978). For many children over six, the child's death is attributed to accidental poisoning and accidental injury. This may well be a serious error in medical-professional judgment. It is true that many children see pills and regard them as candy to be eaten. In the same way, many children engaged in street play may chase a ball into the road and accidentally be hit by a car. Yet, too often, the "accidental poisoning" or "accidental injury" of a child over seven, when carefully studied, reveals an act of intended or subintended death. Purposeful running in front of a car by an unhappy, depressed child is a too frequent attempt to escape from intolerable emotional pain—pain that too many times was inflicted by an assaultive parent.

It is therefore essential that every case of "accidental injury" or "accidental death" of a child over seven years old be examined not only in terms of suicidal intent, but also for evidence of a potentially violent home life steeped in child assault, neglect, and spouse assault. Professionals must be alert to indices of family stress and violence. They must learn how to identify and properly refer these cases. They must learn how to manage the "at-risk" child, the parents, and the family. Whether it be through the process of psychodynamic intervention, or whether it be in terms of behavioral intervention, environmental manipulation, and community networking, it is necessary that caregivers and social scientists provide better health for our children. The sociological nature of the child's environment must be studied. The familial-cultural roots of the family must be carefully documented. The idiosyncratic characteristics of the marriage, the parents, and the child must be understood. The absence or presence of a basic understanding of child growth and development and of appropriate child rearing practices must be identified. With such a comprehesive understanding of the family and its roots, professionals are in a much better position to provide primary prevention programs or, if necessary, secondary intervention resources for both parents and their assaulted children.

# SILENCE: A DYNAMIC PROCESS IN THERAPEUTIC INTERVENTION

Because the great majority of child assaulting families are either court-referred or agency-referred, the diagnostic and treatment center is one of the first agencies to experience the wrath and anger of parents who have been reported by the schools, interrogated by law enforcement, and, following extended protective services and expensive court proceedings, referred for treatment (Paulson, 1982; Paulson and Blake, 1969). Denying the act of assault and feeling self-righteous about their parental rights to discipline and punish their children, many assaultive parents become unmotivated, guarded, fearful of exposing their own anxieties and fears, and distrustful of professionals. The family interaction is often characterized by overcontrolled hostility, followed by sudden and unpredicted eruptions of verbal and physical assault. At other times, the family life is one of uncontrolled, constant violence, with the most vulnerable family member often being the young child or infant. In these situations, the therapist must facilitate understanding and insight, hopeful that through the therapeutic process more adequate and socially acceptable means to express anger will be found. The experiencing of anger and aggression in therapy, although scary and painful for the patient (and sometimes for the therapist), is part of the growth in understanding, in emotional control, and in family and interpersonal communication.

For many, silence is a means of exercising control over emotions and feelings. For others, raised within a violent family, silence is a means of survival. Whatever the dynamics of silence may be, it must be seen as an avoidance of intimacy. It may be a conscious and purposeful way of isolating oneself from interpersonal relationships that pose too many risks and dangers. Yet, silence in the right setting can also be therapeutic. It can be the time for thoughtful introspection and reappraisal of oneself and one's behavior in relationship to others. There are times in the therapeutic encounter when an individual may not share a specific opinion or thought because of the "nonreadiness" of others to accept and understand what, if spoken, might be too traumatic, too confronting, or too ego shattering. There is a time and place for everything, even silence. The therapeutic process, however, will provide practical techniques for healthy restructuring of those maladaptive behavior patterns, for those emotionally blocked periods of silence, and for those mechanisms of defense that are countertherapeutic and destructive to all family members.

# OUTLOOK FOR THE FUTURE

The last two decades since the pathfinder textbook of Helfer and Kempe (1968) have brought to the attention of both lay and professional health delivery agencies the fact that domestic violence and child assault have been the tragic lot of children for centuries. Diagnosis and treatment have been greatly refined in quality and quantity. The community in general is now aware of the need for early identification and reporting. Still necessary are the manpower resources and the financial supports for expanded primary prevention and secondary treatment.

It is well recognized that early and positive bonding and attachment between mother and newborn are the essential foundations for later personal-social maturity. It is equally evident that the pregnant, unwed mother is becoming one of the high-risk elements for the future assault of the unborn child. Although heroic measures have been designed to treat the assaulted child, such secondary care will never be sufficient to effectively resolve conflicts existing today in the violent home. There is hope, however, that treatment agencies will, as part of their intervention, direct special attention, time and professional resources to the high-risk family.

The Village of CHILDHELP, U.S.A. (see Chapter 8), is a dramatic example of what the private sector can do when people who really care are not afraid to "move mountains." Supported by private and public donations, The Village brings a multidisciplinary home environment to an exciting new venture into the area of residential care for the severely assaulted child. Networking with the community agencies and collaborating with specialist professionals, The Village combines an outreach prevention program with a nationally recognized treatment, education, and research program. It is a model, parts of which can be successfully emulated nationwide, if the community citizens and professionals are willing to link arms in a common cause, forego concerns over "turfdom," and combine their applied clinical understanding and research findings to further the cause of child assault prevention.

The local child trauma councils and the statewide consortiums of child abuse councils networking together with the lay and professional community can provide a high level of consultation and liaison. It is hoped that such consulatation will be directed toward a broadside approach to prevention programs, focusing or family life and family communication, as well as focusing on specific programs of education. Such education must include the pregnant woman, the postnatal family, and the cooperation of parents in infant-parenting classes. Working with schools, neighborhood institutions of higher learning, public health departments, social service agencies, law enforcement, and the judiciary, such organizations as community based councils and consortiums can bring maximum intervention opportunities to the high-risk families, and to the already identified assaulted children and their parents.

*Chapter 8*

# CHILDHELP, U.S.A./ INTERNATIONAL:
# A Comprehensive Approach to the Identification, Evaluation, Management, and Prevention of Assault Against Children

*John H. Meier*

This chapter is designed to recount the dramatic conception and dynamic growth and development of the CHILDHELP organization in the undaunted pursuit of a challenging human services mission motivated by a firm philosophy. A brief recapitulation of its origins is followed by a description of the present activities and achievements. If the past 25 years are prologue, the exciting early stages of what is now the CHILDHELP organization augur well for an even more challenging future currently in the planning stages. Since planning becomes increasingly crucial for the orderly evolution of a complex organization, it is important to review past trends to ensure consistent and coherent next stages in the organization's developmental process. Planning has been pragmatically defined as "an improvisation on a general sense of direction" (Cleveland, 1972). It is the purpose of this chapter to point out that general sense of direction derived from the written, spoken, and implied philosophy as well as the actual behavior of the CHILDHELP organization. It is hoped that by retracing the major milestones of this all-encompassing mission, philosophers (dreamers) and practitioners (change agents) throughout the world can benefit from these novel CHILDHELP approaches to identifying, evaluating, managing, and preventing assault against children.

As stated in the Preface and in Chapter 1, with continued immersion in the work of compensating for the deliberate and often violent destruction of children, it becomes increasingly clear to this writer and many colleagues that these innocent and powerless children are victims of what would be considered and prosecuted as assault and battery if inflicted by one adult on another adult. Therefore, the somewhat softer terminology of "child abuse and neglect" has been replaced by the stronger terms "assault against children" and "child assault" to remind the reader of the seriousness of the damage done to those whom medical pioneers in the field had called "battered children" (Helfer and Kempe, 1980; Kempe et al., 1962). This is not intended to strengthen the indictment against the perpetrators of these assaults; they, too, need help and understanding, since in most cases only one short generation earlier they too were victims of similar violent assaults.

## CHILDHELP PHILOSOPHY AND PURPOSE

To appreciate how an organization has evolved it is essential to know how and why it was conceived. The underlying philosophy is frequently reflected in such things as articles of incorporation and by-laws when the organization is in fact legally formalized. Although there is additional interesting history preceding such formal arrangements, some of which will be briefly mentioned in subsequent sections, it is important to consider first what the incorporating Board of Directors originally stated to be their purpose for incorporating: namely, for "the charitable purpose of encouraging material and spiritual assistance in support of homeless and needy children, including those who are neglected, abused or abandoned" (IOI, 1959). This purpose briefly states and further implies an underlying holistic philosophy which embodies a commitment to the whole child, that is, the child's physical, social, emotional, intellectual and spiritual well-being.

CHILDHELP, therefore, exists for several purposes: (1) to help meet the needs of a limited number of assaulted children and their dysfunctional families in a unique residential living environment augmented by a variety of enriched learning and therapeutic experiences; (2) to provide a comprehensive continuum of exemplary services that can also serve as a training and research opportunity for preparing more professional and paraprofessional people to work in the common cause of eliminating assaults against children; (3) to sponsor a variety of demonstration pilot projects, appropriate parts of which can be refined and replicated in other parts of the United States and throughout the world; (4) to provide a research laboratory and resource information center addressing all aspects of child assault and sharing information and findings with other persons and agencies working in related areas; and last, but not least, based upon the foregoing four endeavors, (5) to lead the way toward the primary prevention of assault against children by advancing the state of the art and science regarding child and family development theory and practice (e.g., the continuum includes public awareness campaigns, parenting education, national research programs, a national hot line, and community-based primary and secondary evaluation, treatment, and prevention programs).

Such a comprehensive and altruistic philosophy regarding the total welfare of others springs from a genuine faith in, hope for and charity towards mankind.

# EVOLUTION OF A PRIVATE-SECTOR RESPONSE TO A PUBLIC-SECTOR PLEA

CHILDHELP has a long and intriguing history. In 1959, Sara Buckner O'Meara and Yvonne Lime Fedderson, to whom this book is dedicated, were selected from 500 actress applicants to represent America on a good will tour of the Far East. While in Tokyo, Mrs. O'Meara and Mrs. Fedderson "adopted" 11 half-American, half-Japanese homeless orphans whom they found wandering the streets following a devastating typhoon. They found a home for the children with Mrs. Kim Horiuchi, who lived in a ramshackle, unheated, one-room hut where she was already caring for a group of Japanese–American orphans. The two American women promised that money and clothing would be sent toward support of all of the children. Before returning home Mrs. O'Meara and Mrs. Fedderson had about 100 mixed-blood children in their philanthropic fold.

Back in the United States, these two women devoted all the time they could to raising funds for their "adopted orphans." The effort grew by word of mouth; a nucleus of volunteers formed and International Orphans, Inc. (IOI) was born and officially incorporated as a nonprofit organization with the aforementioned mission. Resources from the efforts of IOI chapters built and maintained four orphanages for thousands of children in Japan.

In 1966, the two founders were invited to Washington, DC and were requested to work with the Third Marine Amphibious force to help orphans who were victims of the Vietnam war. Five orphanages, a hospital, and a school were built and maintained in Vietnam over the next four years. When the American troops left Vietnam, IOI organized a baby-lift that transported hundreds of homeless children to the United States for adoption.

As the United States involvement in Vietnam subsided in the middle 1970s, the very serious domestic problem of assault against children was brought to the attention of Mmes. O'Meara and Fedderson. The U.S. Senate Subcommittee on Children and Youth (chaired by the then Senator Walter Mondale) revealed that child abuse in the United States had assumed epidemic proportions; the American Medical Association indicated that it was one of the leading causes of death in young children. California's then Governor Ronald Reagan, his concerned wife Nancy, and his top staff in that state's Department of Public Social Services echoed the national alarm. This caused Mmes. O'Meara and Fedderson and the IOI board to decide to redirect the IOI organization's energies and talents toward meeting the needs of assaulted children, initially those in their own back yard of Southern California. The decision represented an exemplary private-sector response to an ominous and exploding public-sector need.

CHILDHELP, Inc. (the new legal name replacing IOI in 1982) is a nonprofit, charitable, and humanitarian organization supported primarily by the private contributions of individuals, corporations, foundations, and CHILDHELP's own chapters and auxiliaries. Generous gifts and grants have enabled CHILDHELP to grow and develop; of course, it would be impossible and inappropriate in this textbook to enumerate all of the persons who have donated their time, talents, and material wealth to CHILDHELP.

No one person is responsible for all that has been achieved in just a few years, during which the present CHILDHELP concept has evolved from a glint in the eye. It has gone from an exciting conception and pregnancy, through a somewhat strenuous birth and early infancy, and is now a robust toddler known as CHILDHELP, U.S.A./ INTERNATIONAL. To mix the metaphor, just as all winning teams collectively do great things that no single person could accomplish alone, they do require a quarterback and a coach and cooperative, competent teammates in order to succeed.

Indeed, there would be no CHILDHELP or reason for this chapter without the caring and charismatic combination of the two founding women, National President Mrs. Don (Yvonne) Fedderson and Chairman of the Board Mrs. Robert (Sara) O'Meara. The history of philosophy teaches us that ideas do have consequences. In the musical "South Pacific" one of the songs says that one must have a dream in order to have a dream come true. These two ladies, supported by legions of loyal followers, dared to dream impossible dreams and to have the courage and conviction to endure the occasional nightmares required to make such dreams come true.

Of course, these two talented yet modest women are the first to acknowledge the scores of CHILDHELP Chapter volunteer "midwives," now numbering over 1000, and the numerous attending "obstetricians" and consulting "developmental specialists" who have assisted in CHILDHELP's birth and well-baby care.

The incredible and horrifying facts about assaulted and abandoned children in the United States (see Chapter 1) and in California alone—with numbers leaping from 55,000 in 1975 to over 100,000 in 1979 (the International Year of the Child) and doubling again by 1984—prompted CHILDHELP to create and operate a lighthouse program rather than curse the darkness of these human tragedies. The master plan called for an exemplary continuum of interdisciplinary services and related projects for assaulted children and their dysfunctional families. The first component was to be an excellent residential treatment and research center for the most severely assaulted children to live in and to be healed while their assaultive parents received appropriate help. Plans for other components in the continuum were less detailed, since designing, building, and opening The Village was practically all-consuming. Although conceived in love and properly planned prenatally, what had been anticipated as a leisurely gestation period for creating the entire Village from nothing was suddenly accelerated.

## THE VILLAGE OF CHILDHELP: A MAJOR MISSION MILESTONE

Suddenly, the ready-made physical setting for The Village became available unexpectedly in the form of 10 magnificent buildings on 120 acres of beautiful rural land at a price the CHILDHELP (then IOI) organization could not refuse. Thus, in phoenix-like fashion, arising from the smoldering remains of a residential ranch for emotionally disturbed teenage boys, The Village arose to serve younger children (2 years through 12 years of age), whose histories of various types of assault place them at high risk of subsequently becoming juvenile delinquents and adult criminals if they did not get the kind of caring available at The Village. A principal concern was remediation of the effects of past maltreatment of children and prevention of any further episodes by offering the victims and their families the best intervention programs and procedures presently known in order to make a better future for them—and in turn for society at large.

Although CHILDHELP is now providing service, training, and research in a variety of ways on behalf of assaulted children throughout the world (see later sections of this chapter), a major milestone was reached when The Village (originally named Children's Village, U.S.A.) opened its residential doors in April, 1978. Over the entrance of the administration building for The Village is emblazoned the motto: "All Who Enter Here Will Find Love." Assaulted children who reside at The Village experience concentrated loving care by being totally immersed in a milieu of competent caregivers (not caretakers) who are trained to give care wherever and whenever it is needed. Lay and professional visitors are immediately impressed by The Village's homelike cottages, the dining and kitchen facilities, the recreational, educational, and administration buildings, the meadows, orchards, barn, and the children's chapel, each of which has been underwritten by a single benefactor or an identifiable group. These visible features give concrete testimony to the immense faith, hope, and charity that enable the entire CHILDHELP organization to flourish. Knowledgeable visitors also realize that expenditures for staff salaries, children's needs, consumable supplies, and maintenance are not visible, but that they are equally enduring (and endearing) characteristics of The Village's therapeutic milieu.

For the past decade or so, there has been much rhetoric and considerable effort to remove children from large group settings and to place them in allegedly more homelike smaller group homes and foster families, typically located in ordinary urban community surroundings. Some parents, lay citizens, and professionals climbed on the national bandwagon for deinstitutionalization, vociferously advocating the closing down of all large group homes and institutions for severely handicapped children and adults as inherently inadequate and dehumanizing for the children and families involved (Wolfensberger, 1971). Establishing a new residential program like The Village was deemed unwise by these critics and described as a step backwards—(Blatt and Kaplan, 1974; Bush, 1980; and numerous others). Yet, just seven years later, it is clear that opening The Village's doors was a giant step—but in the right direction—judging from the hard empirical data and the soft humane evidence now available. Through its innovative and comprehensive interdisciplinary residential treatment program at The Village, CHILDHELP has already had an enormous and well-documented impact both on the more than 200 assaulted children who have lived at The

Village and on many of their assaultive, dysfunctional families (Meier, 1980b, 1980c, 1981, 1983a, 1983c, 1984a; Shaw and Meier, 1982b; Scholz and Meier, 1983; Sloan and Meier, 1983a). In retrospect, others have discovered that the indiscriminate and precipitous deinstitutionalization efforts not only backfired but may have been ethically irresponsible (Feldman, 1983; see also Chapter 4); a similar backlash has been experienced in the community mental health movement, which implemented deinstitutionalization policy only to displace patients into even less satisfactory general hospitals, nursing homes, prisons, and skid rows (Shadis, 1984).

# THE VILLAGE: NUCLEUS OF CHILDHELP ACTIVITY

It is a rare opportunity to step outside of the frenetic daily activity and to pause and reflect about where the CHILDHELP organization came from, is now, and intends to go, especially when the writer is being consumed by the day-to-day breathtaking pace and unrelenting demands of meeting today's, tomorrow's, and sometimes yesterday's deadlines. There is little time or energy left after tending to the needs of over 70 assaulted children in residence at The Village, counseling with their dysfunctional families, serving an additional 60 or more normal children and families from the local community who use the Village programs every day, and hosting visitors, salespersons, trainees, and multitudes of other persons.

The Village, which is now only one of several major CHILDHELP projects, has grown at an unanticipated and unprecedented rate. To chronicle such a burgeoning growth and development is difficult, to say the least. To fully document the many thrills and disappointments, ebbs and flows of feelings, and the other human elements composing the unique CHILDHELP organization is probably not possible and has not been attempted in this chapter. Furthermore, and perhaps most important in the long run, the pilot experimental Village effort is discovering many important things about what are and are not effective intervention–prevention practices—which knowledge and skills can ripple out from the unique Village laboratory to help smooth the troubled waters wherever in the world there is a need for compassionate and competent caring for assaulted children and their dysfunctional families.

# THE VILLAGE ENVIRONMENT, FACILITIES, AND PROGRAM

Indeed, all who enter the doors of The Village do find love—and much more, since "Love is Not Enough" (Bettelheim, 1950). They find as well the healing presence of many dedicated and trained professional and para-professional persons and volunteers, well-groomed grounds and attractive buildings, pleasant homelike cottage living units, delicious and nourishing meals, exciting and satisfying indoor and outdoor activities, and many educational and therapeutic opportunities. Love is indeed a many splendored thing and The Village is one of its most splendid manifestations. Just as the hospitals that deal with the most complicated physical illnesses are equipped with the finest and most expensive facilities and apparatus so, too, The Village is an intensive care unit and is outfitted with the best materials and personnel available for coping with the most complex cases of child assault—at least the children who survive.

The location of The Village outside a large urban center is a deliberate and well-advised choice. It is close enough to several thriving small communities to permit participation in their services, such as small public schools, various children's activity clubs (such as 4-H, Youth Soccer, Little League, and Scouts), and multiple church activities, especially those now provided in liason with the Village's nondenominational and charming children's chapel situated on the campus. Located in a magnificent, open, hilly area surrounded by beautiful mountains (Beaumont), there is relatively little pollution and unlimited natural resources to strengthen the therapeutic impact of the entire milieu on each child (see Chapter 5). The Village program and environment enables assaulted children to heal their physical, emotional, and spiritual wounds while learning how to become more effective persons; that is, becoming individuals who elicit more caring and nurturing responses from other people—instead of the previous hostile, violent reactions.

It has been estimated that the reported and known cases of child assault constitute only a tip of an iceberg in relationship to the real prevalence (see Chapter 1). Likewise, the state of the art and science for best dealing with the varieties and complexities of child assault and for successfully coping with their multi-problem families is woefully inadequate (see Chapter 5). CHILDHELP is breaking through new frontiers in this vast challenge of modeling more humane and pleasant environments and experiences for all of the children and families of the world. It is doing so by exemplifying one of the best comprehensive programs in the world for assaulted children and their dysfunctional families.

## SOME FEATURES OF THE VILLAGE DAILY LIVING

Family-style living in comfortable and pleasant cottage units provides a stabilizing home experience with all of the normal joys and challenges of multi-age siblings, family togetherness, and sharing.

Traditional ethical and moral values are stressed throughout The Village and supported by a nondenominational religious program; the addition of a full-time chaplain and the completion of the on-grounds children's chapel have dramatically augmented and upgraded this aspect of meeting the spiritual needs of assaulted children living at The Village. The experience of cruel treatment at the hands of other humans creates a greater need for a child to learn about and to believe in a kind and loving supreme being or "force" and to incorporate a transcendental purpose to life.

Simply living in the caring cottage environment and participating in the many play and recreational experiences provides a wide variety of therapeutic opportunities daily. The popular ranch program, including caring for the many donated horses, ponies, and myriad small animals, has enabled several children to come out of their shells as they communicate their feelings, perhaps for the first time, to a living creature that does not talk back and listens as long as necessary. Various group activities, such as team games and sports, give children enjoyable experiences in teamwork and responsibility. Frequent field trips (including mountain and desert backpacking) throughout Southern California provide entertainment, information, and challenging experiences for children (and adults) of all ages.

Trained child caregivers attend to each child's individual needs, as would competent and conscientious parents. To ensure each child's optimal growth and development, the number of children in each cottage unit is limited to ten, with an adult staff of two or more "round the clock." Each cottage has a trained social worker as supervisor and each caregiver has primary responsibility for two children in the unit group. The in-service education program for caregivers utilizes formal academic sessions (with undergraduate or graduate credit), individual supervision, educational conferences, and continued on-the-job training. The therapeutic milieu (see Chapter 5) of each cottage unit is the focal point around which other services revolve. An application of behavior modification principles, with a generous sprinkling of humanistic values (Woolfolk and Richardson, 1984), underlies the Progressive Behavior System, which is premised on unconditional positive regard for each child and is designed to reinforce desirable behaviors ("Catch 'em being good") and to extinguish undesirable behaviors that have previously caused trouble for the child (Rondeau, 1983).

Specific treatment prescriptions are geared to each individual child's needs, which are carefully and completely delineated in the intake evaluation and resultant individual treatment plan and monitored and documented in The Village's problem-oriented chart system. Physicians, nurses, psychologists, social workers, special educators; speech, occupational, recreational, and art therapists; clergy; lawyers; parent-aide volunteers; and other professionals (including a consultant child psychiatrist and occasionally other specialists) use a variety of treatment methods to augment the therapeutic effect of the child caregivers (see Chapter 5 for a more detailed account of various interdisciplinary intervention–prevention approaches for assaulted children and their dysfunctional families). Careful orchestration of these clinical services ensures a harmonious therapeutic and healing experience for each client.

Individual or group psychotherapy is provided for each child on a regular basis, usually at least one hour per week in one or more sessions as needed. An extensive art therapy program is only one of the many special treatment modalities regularly used at The Village; assaulted children frequently give clues through drawings to their attitudes, behavior, and experiences which they are either unwilling or unable to talk about. Whatever form of expression the child selects, the results are frequently illuminating and revealing to the trained therapist or caregiver.

An individually prescribed educational program meets the children's unique academic needs and challenges their particular abilities and interests. School-age children at The Village are mainstreamed into nearby Beaumont public schools whenever possible. For school-age children who are not ready or able to benefit from regular public school education, appropriately tailored learning experiences are provided in The Village's special classrooms and programs to prepare them to enter the regular public school program as soon as possible. A Satellite Day Care program, sponsored and administered by the Riverside County Public Schools, and a federally funded Head Start program are also located on The Village campus. Children under school age enjoy and benefit from these learning and socialization opportunities in which they interact with children from the neighboring communities of Beaumont and Banning.

## PROGRAM FOR PARENTS: AN ESSENTIAL INGREDIENT

Parents of resident children come to The Village to participate in a variety of structured and unstructured supervised activities, which are conducted primarily on the weekends but are also individually arranged if necessary to accommodate parent schedules at other times during the week. Designed to assess a family's potential for reunification, and to encourage and facilitate the process whenever possible, these sessions include a variety of rehabilitative activities for parents.

The parents receive help in coping with their personal and parenting problems and training to become more effective parents. An extensive outreach program of lay and professional counselors works within The Village and as part of a growing outreach network (Meier, 1984c) to cover the geographical catchment areas to which the children and families return. As the child and family progress through this therapeutic intervention–prevention sequence, The Village gradually reunites them under its protective supervision, until it is clear that the assaultive behavior is unlikely to recur and that a more acceptable home situation has been established.

When it is judged that the natural family situation has a very low probability of ever being an adequate place in terms of the child's best interests, The Village continues to provide an excellent home for the child for as long as it is therapeutically indicated (Whittaker, 1979). The Village also cooperates with various official adoption agencies to help find placements for eligible children (Weitzel, 1984) and works closely with the prospective surrogate parents and families to ensure an appropriate situation for both the child and the new family (for a more detailed description of The Village's Parent Program, see Sloan and Meier, 1983a).

## A LOS ANGELES CHILDHELP CENTER

An innovative outreach center in East Los Angeles represented the next major facility and program to be undertaken by CHILDHELP. This project is housed in a complex purchased by the City of Los Angeles and granted to CHILDHELP for housing another link in the chain of primary and secondary intervention–prevention endeavors sponsored by CHILDHELP. The CHILDHELP Los Angeles Center is headquarters for (1) an experimental emergency foster care network for placing brothers and sisters together instead of separating them when they are removed from endangering homes (Mayeda, Jensen, and Meier, 1983; Ward, 1984); (2) an interdisciplinary family evaluation and treatment planning service primarily for the Los Angeles Juvenile Court but available to other qualified referral sources; (3) a satellite outreach program for "graduates" from The Village program to ensure some continuity of care and follow-up (Meier, 1984c); (4) a national 24 hour toll-free hotline (1-800-4A-CHILD) providing professional counseling for clients and current information and referral services for professionals and agencies working with assaulted children in collaboration with the CHILDHELP-sponsored Kempe Center family evaluation project; (5) a family education and crisis center for primary and secondary intervention–prevention of child assault, likely to occur in identified dysfunctional families; and (6) other components to be determined on the basis of new needs that arise. A panel of representative interdisciplinary professional experts advises CHILDHELP on this Los Angeles effort to ensure that it addresses the most pressing needs of assaulted children and their dysfunctional families in a sprawling megalopolis that has the highest number of child assault cases in the United States (see Chapter 1).

## NATIONAL PUBLIC EDUCATION AND CRISIS INTERVENTION–PREVENTION

CHILDHELP sponsors a National Campaign for the Prevention of Child Abuse, a multimedia primary prevention effort. A one hour television special regarding CHILDHELP's efforts to eliminate assault against children has been shown repeatedly in major cities throughout the United States during the past several years and raised the consciousness of millions of citizens. The hotline received over 30,000 calls during 1984 alone, some reporting suspected abuse and family crises, others seeking counseling, information literature, and related help; this hotline is staffed by trained counselors and is active 24 hours a day, 7 days a week. Furthermore, CHILDHELP offers a variety of public educational programs and materials, including a series of free pamphlets, millions of which are distributed to junior high school students throughout the United States, to help them understand and even to report assaults against themselves or their friends; CHILDHELP tent cards for public and professional offices, advertisements in national magazines, and special stamps have been produced and distributed throughout the United States to arouse the public awareness and to encourage prompt reporting of any suspected child assault. This national effort also promotes individual involvement of the general citizenry in worthy local community child assault intervention–prevention projects. CHILDHELP staff and Board Members have participated in a wide variety of planning and presentation panels at local, national, and international professional conventions addressing numerous issues regarding child assault.

## VOLUNTEER PROGRAM AND VISITORS

Volunteers, a vital part of the entire CHILDHELP organization from its very beginnings, perform a variety of duties, from serving on the National Board to painting corral fences. After a careful orientation program, they are assigned to appropriate projects that interest them the most and where they are needed. At The Village, volunteer opportunities include helping in the church-related programs, the foster grandparent program, ranch program, day care center, weekend reception and tourguiding, tutoring, thrift shop operation, recreation programs, research projects, music and art instruction, children's birthday parties, and various other special projects. One such demonstration pilot project enlists a group of retired elderly foster grandparents to serve as parent aides for low income and high risk families to prevent child assault, to strengthen the families, and to serve as a model for expanding Head Start and similar preschool and day care programs (Meier, 1984b).

Other organizational activities also benefit greatly from the donated time and talents of Hollywood celebrities, Olympic and professional athletes, and other professionals who assist with the promotion of CHILDHELP projects. Nearby military base personnel and service organization members continue to give generously of their time and talents in refurbishing and maintaining CHILDHELP facilities.

Visitors are always welcome at any of the CHILDHELP projects, since this is a very effective way of sharing ideas and practices; tours are conducted by appointment, with special arrangements made for large groups.

## RESEARCH TO ENSURE EXCELLENCE AND REPLICABILITY

CHILDHELP is the only known laboratory program of its kind with an active research component for the study and application of existing methods and the development and testing of new methods to treat and eliminate assault against children. Evaluating which aspects of the various CHILDHELP programs work well and which do not is the continuing responsibility of the Research Division. Such feedback from constant self-analysis ensures program quality control, improvement, and integrity. The extensive and intensive Research Division activities and findings have already begun to distinguish many of CHILDHELP's pilot efforts as useful models, parts of which are now being implemented or considered for replication at various sites throughout the world.

There are, at this writing, over 40 research projects, scientific reports, master's theses, doctoral dissertations, monographs, and books in various stages of completion that focus on child assault (Meier, 1984a). As affiliations with collaborating universities and colleges continue to grow and develop, it is expected that the Research Division will make substantial contributions toward advancing the state of the art and science regarding the complex dynamics of assault against children and effective strategies for its intervention–prevention.

## NATIONAL NETWORK OF CHILDHELP SPONSORED RESEARCH

To enlarge its scope, data base, national image, and academic sophistication, CHILDHELP has established several sponsored research efforts throughout the United States and at five major universities— namely, Columbia University, Harvard University (Children's Hospital Medical Center), and the Universities of California (at Los Angeles and Riverside), Chicago, and Florida (at Gainesville [Medical Center]). Individual applied research projects are under the direction of a senior faculty member at each institution. Reports of these research projects are available from the CHILDHELP Research Division.

# MORAL DEVELOPMENT: A MISSING INGREDIENT IN ASSAULTIVE PARENTS?

In addition to the specific research projects at the universities, there is an umbrella CHILDHELP project in which the universities have all agreed to participate. This universal project is an exploratory investigation into the moral development of parents who have assaulted their children compared with parents who have not. It was inspired by testing and observations of assaultive parents and assaulted children in the Village population, a conviction on the part of the CHILDHELP National Board and staff that spiritual development is essential for becoming a whole person, and such statements as the following:

> Some day, maybe, there will exist a well-informed, well-considered, and yet fervent public conviction that the most deadly of all possible sins is the mutilation of a child's spirit; for such mutilation undercuts the life principle of trust, without which every human act, may it feel ever so good and seem ever so right, is prone to perversion by destructive forms of conscientiousness.
>
> (Erikson in Kempe and Helfer, 1980, p. 2)

A review of the literature and informed scholarly opinion have led to the discovery that there is an apparent and conspicuous absence of what has been defined as "morality" in those parents who have assaulted and mutilated the spirits of their children (Meier, 1983b). Unfortunately, the term "morality" is nearly as global and confusing as the term "love" and therefore requires additional definition before it can be systematically and scientifically studied. A child's lack of moral development probably reflects the influence of an amoral or demoralized parent (Frank, 1961; see also Chapter 1). Thus, if the components of moral development could be teased out, identified, observed, quantified, analyzed, and ultimately reconstituted, it might be possible to identify critical elements in parent education to help prevent child assault from occurring. It therefore becomes necessary to learn about the components of moral development and measures thereof in parents who have assaulted or not assaulted their children to determine what is missing and might be supplied to those parents who have assaulted or are at significant risk of assaulting their children.

Through the Research Division of CHILDHELP (plus a review of the relevant literature and correspondence with other scholars), and with the cooperation of the five aforementioned universities, several promising procedures for assessing various aspects of moral development in adults and particularly in parents have been identified (Jensen and Meier, 1983). Phase I of the research has administered these procedures to a national sample of assaultive and nonassaultive parents to determine which of the procedures or parts of the procedures are most sensitive and useful in identifying which aspects of moral development, if any, differentiate assaultive from nonassaultive parents. Phase II of this research program builds upon the findings of Phase I by creating training materials and procedures for parenting education and child caregiver training for residential programs such as The Village of CHILDHELP. Phase III of this effort translates the parent training materials into teacher-usable curriculum materials for introducing moral development concepts to children in elementary and secondary school since these children all too soon will become the next generation of parents and must be prevented from assaulting their children, thus perpetuating the vicious cycle.

## SELECTED HIGHLIGHTS OF RESEARCH FINDINGS

Since efforts to scientifically evaluate client progress and program effectiveness in residential treatment have been plagued by inadequate client and program descriptions (Curtis et al., 1984; Durkin and Durkin, 1975; Wurtele, Wilson, and Prentice-Dunn, 1983), such descriptive information has been collected at The Village from its inception. Although several technical reports and graphic profiles are available regarding the first seven years of The Village operation (Meier, 1980b, c; 1981; 1983b, c; and 1984a), it is revealing to consider some selected highlights from relevant demographic, clinical, and psychometric characteristics of the children and their families.

Several of the preceding sections have described The Village's therapeutic milieu and program designed to counteract the previous deleterious effects of ecological factors contributing to assault against children; some examples of in-house studies indicate that a rewarding environment in Village cottages is far more efficacious than a punishing one (Rondeau, 1983), that the children perceive the living circumstances at The Village very positively (Shaw and Meier, 1982a; corroborated by top-notch ratings on the Caldwell HOME ratings, 1979), and that various behavior modification efforts by child caregivers can be improved and become quite efficacious (Shaw and Meier, 1982b).

A majority (68 per cent) of the 200 children at The Village had histories of being both abused and neglected, whereas only about 16 per cent of the approximately 200,000 children surveyed by the American Humane Association's national studies (AHA, 1979, 1981, 1983) experienced such severe assault (Fig. 8–1). Since the assault was generally more severe for Village children, more of them were reported by law enforcement (25 per cent) and social service agencies (22 per cent) and fewer by friends, neighbors, or relatives than in the AHA sample. The Village children both individually and collectively suffered a wider variety of assaults and more severe assaults than the average child in the AHA sample; these included physical and emotional neglect (60 per cent), cuts and bruises (55 per cent), sexual assavlt (40 per cent), brain and internal injuries (35 per cent), and educational neglect (25 per cent) and demoralization (Frank, 1981) as a precursor to their own mental illness and becoming themselves child assaulters (Fig. 8–2).

The Village children are from a variety of ethnic backgrounds: Caucasian (63 per cent), Spanish surname (15 per cent), black (9 per cent), mixed (8 per cent), Asian (4 per cent) and Native American (1 per cent). Although more than one half (61 per cent) come from Los Angeles County, others were residing in other Southern California counties—Orange (14 per cent), Riverside (12 per cent), San Bernardino (9 per cent), San Diego (3 per cent), and Imperial and Ventura (1 per cent). The Village children range in age from two to twelve years at intake, with the average age being around six years of age; there have been about 20 per cent more boys than girls placed at The Village.

The majority (over 100) of the school-age children at The Village have attended local public schools in nearby Beaumont. Although it is preferable to mainstream or normalize The Village educational program as much as possible, severely assaulted children often require considerable help before they can participate in regular public schools; thus, The Village has three classes for special-needs elementary school children who have such severe learning disabilities, emotional disorders, and other handicaps that they are prevented from benefiting from the regular public schools. Moreover, The Village has two Head Start classes (one third Village children and two thirds community children), plus a day care preschool program under the auspices of the host Riverside County Schools; these two preschool programs serve about 60 additional children from nearby communities whose low SES families benefit from this CHILDHELP/Riverside County collaborative effort.

Standardized tests of intelligence and achievement indicate that, on the average, Village children are somewhat below the national norms on such tests owing to their deprived lives (Diamond, 1984; Meier, 1970), elevated stress (Brown and Rosenbaum, 1983) and neuropsychiatric dysfunction (Hanley, 1984). With some exceptions they do better on performance items (WISC-R) than on verbally loaded items (Fig. 8–3) partly because of hearing and speech problems in addition to general deprivation of language in their homes.

The children typically enter The Village program with a very low sense of self-worth (Harter, 1979), which then rises to unrealistically high levels due to emphasis placed on developing self-esteem in the treatment program (Scholz and Meier, 1983).

Measures of problem behaviors (Achenbach and Edelbrock, 1982), after the two to five week honeymoon period of good behavior immediately after entry, show dramatically high ratings on practically all problem behaviors (both externalizing and internalizing), with a slight dip in somatic complaints, perhaps due to a higher pain threshold, a sort of psychosomatic anesthesia developed to cope with assaults (Fig. 8–4).

Duration of stay at The Village has ranged from one month to more than five years. The average length of residency at The Village over the past seven years is about 20 months; this average time is being reduced more recently due to pressures to reduce the number of children in out-of-home care. Those who are ultimately reunited (50 per cent) with their biological parent(s) stay about 20 months. Children whose parents clearly are not willing or able to take them back are placed in either preadoptive or foster homes (23 percent) after about 26 months of preparation focused on both the children and the prospective adoptive parents. Those few who have to be placed in more structured and secure institutions (10 per cent) stay at The Village an average of 10 months. Approximately 90 per cent of the more than 100 children who have graduated from The Village have gone to what are regarded as more permanent placements. This is especially noteworthy in view of their previous placement histories, which often begin before two years of age and may reach as many as 13 placements over three to ten years of time that has elapsed before they enter The Village. These multiple changes and separations constitute additional trauma and are a form of systemic or tertiary iatrogenic assault, which complicates and prolongs the time required for healing.

The nearly 200 assaultive families with children presently or previously at The Village have manifested more extensive and intensive problems than is typical of the more than 15,000 families in the AHA survey. Some of the prevalent factors are low socioeconomic status (over 75 per cent earn less than $9,000 per year [Fig. 8–7]); broken, single-parent family (65 per cent); family still intact but with marital discord (75 per cent), including spousal assault in at least one third of the couples; lack of understanding and tolerance for normal child development and behavior (40 per cent), often accompanied by mental illness akin to demoralization (Frank, 1981), as described in earlier chapters; and social isolation (45 per cent) (Fig. 8–8). Because the mother spends most of her time with the children, she is the prime perpetrator of child assault (75 per cent), especially against children under ten years of age; as children approach the age of puberty and as marriages dissolve into new relationships, more fathers, step-parents, friends, and relatives become involved in the assault, including a dramatic increase in sexual assault (Fig. 8–9).

It is clear that most of the children at The Village make statistical and really significant advances in intellectual (WISC-R, Weschler, 1974), social (Vineland SMS, Doll, 1965), self-esteem (Harter, 1979), emotional (Scholz and Meier, 1983), physical (Meier, 1983c), and behavioral (Achenbach, 1979a) realms. It is apparent, but not yet empirically demonstrated, that they are developing well in personality and spiritual and moral realms. It is apparent, and currently being empirically demonstrated, that the children are developing well in crucial personality, spiritual, and moral domains as well (Jensen and Meier, 1983). Other assessments done by art, occupational, recreational, and speech therapists also indicate remarkable development in most of The Village children during their residence. As Kempe points out in the Introduction, just relieving the suffering and making possible these spurts of growth and development in assaulted children, even for short durations of their stay at The Village, is quite gratifying. Moreover, observing and participating in the process in which numerous confused and desperate parents gradually get their personal and parental acts together (Sloan and Meier, 1983a) in preparation for reunification with their rehabilitated children is encouraging.

Having been forewarned about the possibility of assault occurring to a child in residential treatment (Blatt and Kaplan, 1974; Rindfleisch, 1984; Savelis, 1983), The Village has been extremely careful in staff recruiting and training (Nelson, 1975) as well as in monitoring all program activities (Cavara and Ogren, 1983). Although there have been a few questionable incidents, which were carefully investigated and rectified as necessary, the children in residence have fared extremely well (Shaw and Meier, 1982a), especially compared to their probable fate had they been left alone or placed in less caring or less therapeutically oriented settings (Bush, 1980).

Nevertheless, the proverbial proof of the pudding is how well reunifications or new permanent placements progress and endure.

Although it is too early to draw any firm conclusions from limited follow-up data, it is evident that most (over 80 per cent) of the families fully cooperating with follow-up procedures are faring well. However, in this case, no news is potentially bad news, since parents in trouble may not want to become involved again in the formidable care system if they can avoid it. Thus, in spite of repeated registered mailings of follow-up packets, with assurances of confidentiality and payments for their time and effort, coupled with phone calls and occasional home visits to assist in completing the periodic reports (three months after discharge, six months after discharge, then every year thereafter), fewer than 50 per cent of the responsible adults have regularly returned completed packets. Relatively good cooperation (63 per cent) has been obtained from reunified families, in which good rapport was developed with the parents, who received therapy and parenting education under Village auspices; on the other hand, poor cooperation from foster (19 per cent), adoptive (12 per cent), and institutional (6 per cent) placements is characteristic to date.

The recidivism rate of reportable assault or at least placement failure among the former group is less than 10 per cent, whereas it appears to be approaching 25 per cent in the latter three options. It is hoped that the aforementioned Los Angeles CHILDHELP Center, with an increased investment of time and talent in reaching out to families before (while children are at The Village) and after placement of children with them, will help to bridge this information and intervention–prevention gap (see Chapter 5 and Meier [1984b] for use of paraprofessionals in this capacity). It is an additional and compounded tragedy to invest thousands of dollars' worth of elaborate intervention–prevention efforts in out-of-home care only to see it eroded by a lack of aftercare devices that must be provided to ensure that a permanent placement remains satisfactory for all concerned (Meier [1984c]; see Chapters 4 and 7 for recommended sociolegal and community changes needed to help effect this aftercare feature).

Figures 8–1 through 8–9 are representative of many such data displays and profiles derived from several years of The Village's operation, during which nearly 200 (196) assaulted children and their families were studied. To put the data in some perspective, The Village population is compared with the much larger population studied by the American Humane Association (AHA, 1984) using the same variables whenever possible and appropriate. These figures give a graphic representation of and elaboration on the preceding text. More detailed and technical data and monographs about The Village and other CHILDHELP endeavors are available from CHILDHELP's Research Division (Meier, 1984a).

# THE CHILDHELP INTERNATIONAL INFLUENCE

The rapid growth of CHILDHELP's visibility and impact has enabled it to take its place among the other leading organizations that are shedding light on and providing communication about the worldwide cancer of assault against children and ways to stop it. CHILDHELP national Board Officers and senior executive staff have played various roles in international organizations, such as the International Union for Child Welfare, the International Society for the Prevention of Child Abuse and Neglect, and the International Society for the Scientific Study of Mental Retardation. Moreover, CHILDHELP cosponsored, with the North Atlantic Treaty Organization and California State University at Fresno, an advanced training seminar regarding research and innovations for the study, treatment, and prevention of child abuse (Leavitt, 1983). The CHILDHELP organization has enjoyed and learned from visits by many dignitaries and scholars from all over the world, representing programs and organizations dedicated to the exposure and elimination of assault against children in their respective countries.

All of this requires large amounts of human and material resources. When IOI directed its charitable efforts toward developing the multifaceted programs now incorporated in CHILDHELP, U.S.A./INTERNATIONAL, it represented an exemplary private-sector response to an ominous and exploding public-sector need. Indeed, CHILDHELP's continuum of services, training, and research is becoming an important part of the critical mass needed to eliminate from the face of the Earth all assault against children.

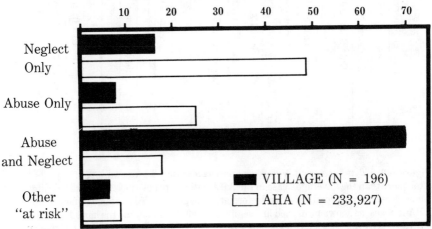

**Figure 8-1.** *Cases classified by abuse and neglect.* The children at The Village have suffered significantly more serious assault than the American Humane Association (AHA) national sample of abused and neglected children.

PERCENT

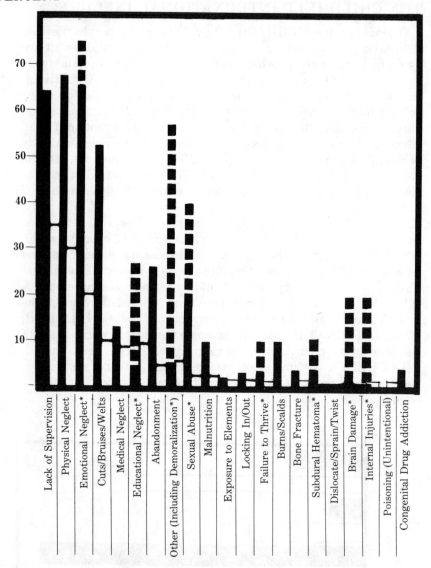

**Figure 8–2.** *Types of assault*. Village children have suffered a wide variety of assaults, often more than the "average" case in the AHA national population. Asterisks indicate factors for which anecdotal and clinical information suggest that Village families far exceed AHA families, as shown by dashed line segments that extend beyond the hard data base represented by solid-black bar segments. From a CHILDHELP national research study, preliminary findings (Jensen and Meier, 1983).

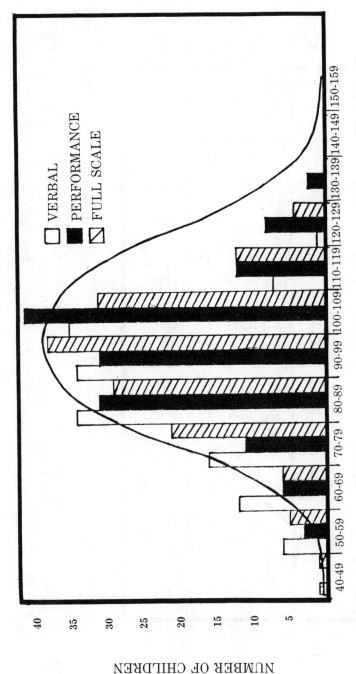

**Figure 8-3.** *Individual intelligence scores for Village children (N = 146).* The children at The Village perform in general somewhat below average, as shown by the shift to the left (negative skew) under the normal curve; this lower functioning is largely due to their deprived lives and occasionally due to brain damage or dysfunction. With some exceptions, Village children do better on performance related items than on verbally loaded items. Intake scores are taken from the Weschler Intelligence Scale for Children-Revised (Weschler, 1974). Some dramatic improvement is seen for some children after participating in The Village's enriched and therapeutic milieu.

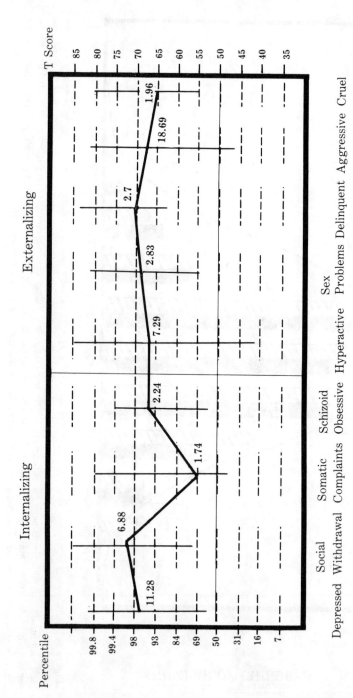

**Figure 8-4.** *Profile of behavior problems for Village girls, 6 to 11 years old (N = 29).* The averages all run at or above the 95th percentile, with the exception of the somatic complaints, suggesting a sort of psychic anesthesia or higher threshold of pain in these assaulted children. All averages are far above the range for normal children, who cluster around the 50th percentile. This scale (*The Child Behavior Profile*; Achenbach, 1980) is one of many scales, instruments, and procedures used to document client progress and to monitor program efficacy.

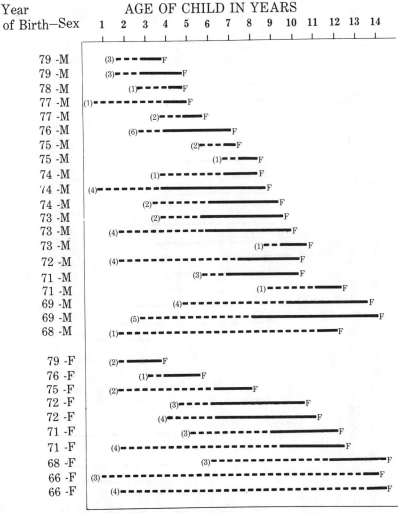

Year of Birth—Sex

AGE OF CHILD IN YEARS

**Figure 8–5.** *Placement histories of Village children who have been placed in foster care or Fost-Adopt (foster care with intention to adopt) settings (N = 30).* Almost all of the children at The Village have been in previous out-of-home placements; each of these changes and separations typically constitutes an additional trauma and is a form of systematic abuse, which prolongs the time required for healing. These data contributed to the formulation and passage of national legislation (PL 96-272—the Adoption Assistance and Child Welfare Act of 1980) to mandate improved permanency planning and implementation.

Key: Blank spaces at the left signify time when child was living at home prior to placement; number in parentheses indicates number of placements prior to The Village; dashed line indicates time in out-of-home placement(s) other than The Village; solid line indicates time in placement at The Village; F denotes placement in foster care or Fost-Adopt.

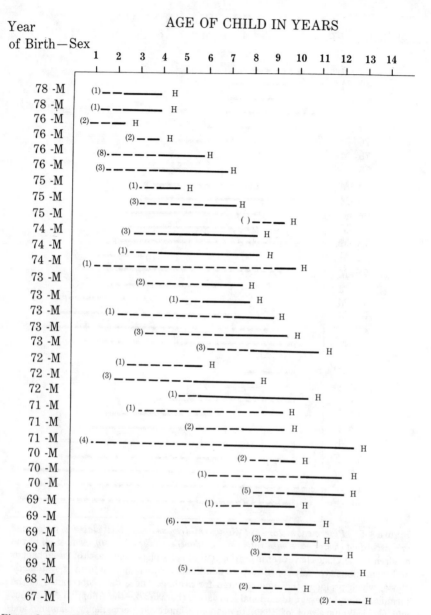

**Figure 8–6.** *Placement histories of male Village children who have been returned to their natural homes (N = 33).* Follow-up studies indicate that the majority are doing well; an aftercare program (Meier, 1984c) is needed to ensure that more will do well over an extended length of time. Symbols and abbreviations are the same as in Figure 8–5 except that H signifies the child was reunited in home of biological parent(s).

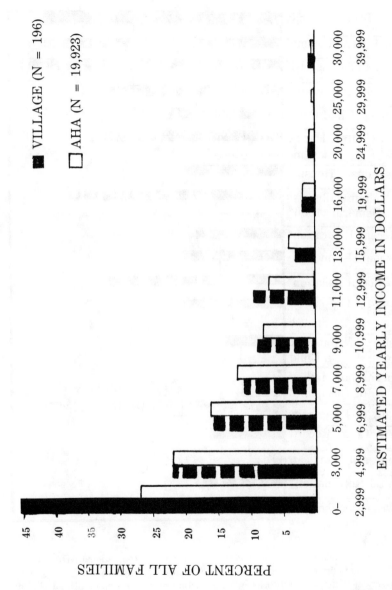

**Figure 8-7.** *Estimated family income.* The Village families correspond with the national AHA sample in that the majority are of low socioeconomic status. The dashed line segments represent estimates based upon anecdotal information, since verifiable family income data are not available on many Village families.

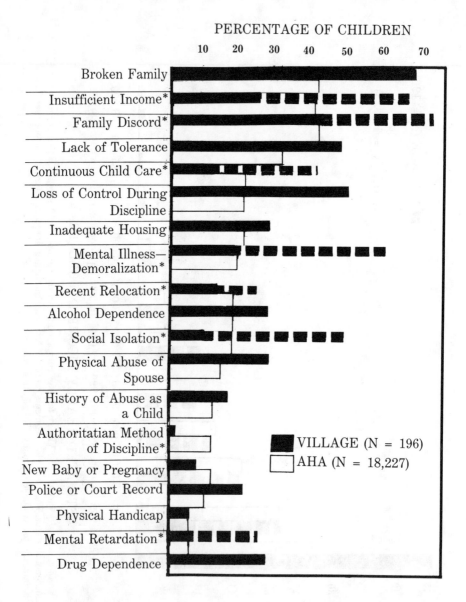

**PERCENTAGE OF CHILDREN**

**Figure 8-8.** *Factors present in families.* Compared with the national AHA sample, The Village families have more extensive and intensive problems which contribute to more serious assault(s). Asterisks indicate factors on which anecdotal and clinical information suggest that Village families far exceed AHA families, as shown by the dashed line segments that extend beyond the hard data line.

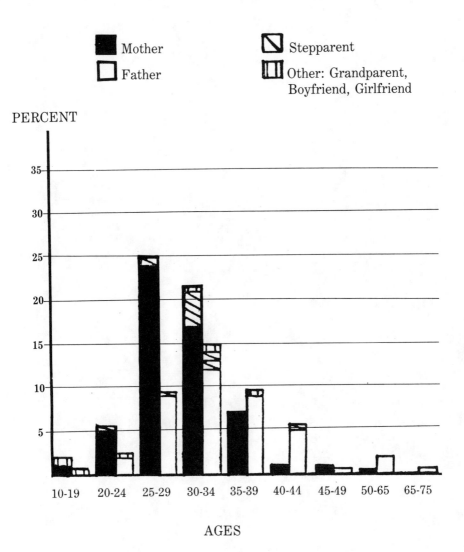

**Figure 8–9.**  *Age and sex of perpetrators of assault against Village children (N = 196).*
The female caregiver, during early childrearing years, is the most frequent perpetrator
of assault against children—largely because she is with the child(ren) most of the time.
However with the passage of time and concomitant changes in family composition, male
perpetrators become increasingly prominent. Percentages may total more than 100 per
cent since there were two or more perpetrators in some cases.

# REFERENCES

Aber, J. (1980). The involuntary placement decision: Solomon's dilemma revisited. In G. Gerber, C. Ross, and E. Zigler (Eds.), *Child abuse: An agenda for action*. New York: Oxford University Press.

Abrams, H., Naehring, E., and Zuckerman, M. (1984). *Preventing abuse and neglect: A staff training curriculum for facilities serving developmentally disabled persons*. Miami Shores, FL: Barry University Press.

Achenbach, T. M. (1978). *Research in developmental psychology: Concepts, strategies, methods*. New York: Free Press.

Achenbach, T. M. (1979a). The child behavior profile: An empirically based system for assessing children's behavioral problems and competencies. *International Journal of Mental Health, 7*, 24–42.

Achenbach, T. M. (1979b). The child behavior profile: I. Boys aged 6–11. *Journal of Consulting and Clinical Psychology, 46*, 478–488.

Achenbach, T. M., and Edelbrock, C. (1982). *Manual for the child behavior checklist and revised child behavior profile*. Burlington, VT: University Associates in Psychiatry.

Ackerman, N. W. (1958). *The psychodynamics of family life*. New York: Basic Books.

Ackerman, N. W. (1966). *Treating the troubled family*. New York: Basic Books.

Ackerman, N., Lieb, J., and Pearce, J. (Eds.). (1970). *Family therapy in transition*. Boston: Little, Brown.

Ackley, D. (1977). A brief overview of child abuse. *Social Casework, 58*(1), 21–24.

Acosta, F. (1982). Group psychotherapy with Spanish-speaking patients. In R. Becerra, M. Karno, and J. Escobar (Eds.), *Mental health and Hispanic Americans: Clinical perspectives*. New York: Grune and Stratton.

Adams, W. V. (1976). The physically abused child: A review. *Journal of Pediatric Psychology, 1*(2), 7–11.

Ainsworth, M. D. (1980). Attachment and child abuse. In G. Gerbner, C. Ross, and E. Zigler (Eds.) *Child abuse: An agenda for action*. New York: Oxford University Press.

Ainsworth, M. D., Blehar, M. C., Waters, E., and Well, S. (1978) *Patterns of attachment: A psychological study of the strange situation*. Princeton, NJ: Wiley.

Akins, F. R., Akins, D. L., and Mace, G. S. (1981). *Parent-child separation: Psychosocial effects on development*. New York: Plenum.

Alexander, H. (1980). Long-term treatment. In C. H. Kempe and R. Helfer (Eds.), *The battered child* (3rd ed). Chicago: University of Chicago Press.

Alfaro, J. D. (1978). *The relationship between child abuse and later socially deviant behavior*. Unpublished report to New York Select Committee on Child Abuse.

Alfasi, G. (1982). A failure-to-thrive infant at play: Applications of microanalysis. *Journal of Pediatric Psychology, 7*(2), 111.

Alvarez, J. (1956). *Helpful hints to puzzling diagnoses*. Rochester, MN: Mayo Clinics.

American Humane Association (1976–1981). *National analysis of official child neglect and abuse reporting: Annual report*. Denver: Author.

American Humane Association (1984). *Highlights of official child neglect and abuse reporting: 1982*. Denver: Author.

American Humane Association (1984, January 5). *Legislative alert* (Vol. 2, No. 1, pp. 1–21). Denver: Author.

American Psychiatric Association (1980). *Diagnostic and statistical manual* (3rd ed.). Washington, DC: Author.

Antler, S. (1978). Child abuse: An emerging social priority. *Social Work, 23*(1), 58–61.

Armstrong, L. (1978). *Kiss Daddy goodnight: A speakout on incest.* New York: Hawthorn Books.

Ayres, A. (1966). *Southern California Test Battery.* Los Angeles: Western Psychological Services.

Bachrach, L. L. (1980). Model programs for chronic mental patients. *American Journal of Psychiatry, 137*(9), 1023–1031.

Badinter, E. (1981). *Mother love, myth and reality (motherhood in modern history).* New York: Macmillan.

Baldwin, J. A. and Oliver, J. E. (1975). Epidemiology and family characteristics of severely abused children. *British Journal of Preventative and Social Medicine, 29*(4), 205–221.

Barbour, P. J. (1983). Adopt a family—dial a granny. *Child Abuse and Neglect, 7,* 477–478.

Baron, R. C., and Piasecki, J. R. (1981). The community versus community care. In R. D. Budson (Ed.), *Issues in community care.* San Francisco: Jossey-Bass.

Bauman, E., Brint, A. I., Piper, L., and Wright, P. A. (Eds.). (1978). *The holistic health handbook: A tool for attaining wholeness of body, mind, and spirit.* Berkeley, CA: And/Or Press.

Bavolek, S. J., Comstock, C. M., and McLaughlin, J. A. (1983). *The nurturing program: A validated approach for reducing dysfunctional family interactions.* Eau Claire, WI: University of Wisconsin Press.

Becerra, R., Karno, M., and Escobar, J. (1982). *Mental health and Hispanic Americans.* New York: Grune and Stratton.

Beery, K. (1967). *Developmental test of visual motor integration: Administration and scoring manual.* Chicago: Follett Educational Corporation.

Beit-Hallahmi, B., and Rabin, A. I. (1977, July). The kibbutz as a social experiment and as a child-rearing laboratory. *American Psychologist, 32*(6), pp. 532–541.

Belsky, J. (1980). Child maltreatment: An ecological integration *American Psychologist, 35*(4), 320–335.

Bender, L. (1956). Psychopathology of children with organic brain disorders. Springfield, IL: Charles C Thomas.

Benward, J., and Densen-Gerber, J. (1975). *Incest as a causative factor in antisocial behavior: An exploratory study.* New York: Odyssey Institute.

Bergler, E. (1946). *Unhappy marriage and divorce: A study of neurotic choice of marriage partners.* New York: International Universities Press.

Berliner, L., and Stevens, D. (1979). Special techniques for child witnesses. In L. G. Schultz (Ed.), *The sexual victimology of youth.* Springfield, IL: Charles C Thomas.

Berry, G. W. (1977). Therapeutic interventions with incestuous families. *Audio Digest, Psychiatry, 6,* 14.

Besharov, D. J. (1981). Toward better research on child abuse and neglect. *Child Abuse and Neglect, 5*(4), 383–390.

Besharov, D. J. (1983). Protecting abused and neglected children: Can law help social work? *Family Law Reporter, 9*(41), 4029–4037.

Bettelheim, B. (1950). *Love is not enough.* New York: Free Press.

Billingslea, R. (1979). Soft neurological signs in audiometric testing of abused children. Professional correspondence. Beaumont, CA: CHILDHELP Research Division.

Birrell, R. G., and Birrell, J. H. W. (1968). The maltreatment syndrome in children: A hospital survey. *Medical Journal of Australia, 2,* 1023.

Bishop, F. I. (1971). Children at risk. *Medical Journal of Australia, 1,* 623–628.

Blatt, B., and Kaplan, F. (1974). *Christmas in purgatory.* Syracuse, NY: Human Policy Press.

Bobath, B. (1963). Treatment principles and planning in cerebral palsy. *Physiotherapy, 49,* 122.

Boszormenyi-Nagy, I., and Spark, G. M. (1973). *Invisible loyalties: Reciprocity in intergenerational family therapy*. New York: Harper and Row.

Bowen, M. (1978). *Family therapy in clinical practice*. New York: Jason Aronson.

Bowlby, J. (1969). *Attachment and loss*. New York: Basic Books.

Boyd, L., Jr., and Remy L. (1978). Is foster-parent training worthwhile? *Social Service Review*, pp. 275–296.

Bross, D. C. (Ed.) (1984). *Multidisciplinary advocacy for mistreated children*. Denver: National Association of Counsel for Children.

Bross, D. C., and Munson, M. M. (1980). Alternative models of legal representation for children. *Oklahoma City University Law Review, V*, 561–618.

Brown, B., and Rosenbaum, L. (1983). Stress and competence. In J. M. Humphrey (Ed.), *Stress in childhood*. New York: AMS Press.

Bryce, M., and Lloyd, J. C. (Eds.) (1981). *Treating families in the home: An alternative to placement*. Springfield, IL: Charles C Thomas.

Budson, R. D. (1981). Challenging themes in community residential care systems. In R. D. Budson (Ed.), *Issues in Community Residential Care*. San Francisco: Jossey-Bass.

Burgdorf, K. (1980). *Recognition and reporting of child maltreatment*. Rockville, MD: Westat.

Burgess, A. W., and Holmstrom, L. L. (1975). Sexual trauma of children and adolescents: Pressure, sex and secrecy. *Nursing Clinics of North America, 10*, 551–563.

Burgess, A. W., Groth, A. N., Holmstron, L. L. and Sgroi, S. M. (1978). *Sexual assault of children and adolescents*. Lexington, MA: Lexington Books.

Bush, M. (1980). Institutions for dependent and neglected children: Therapeutic option of choice or last resort? *American Journal of Orthopsychiatry, 50*(2), 239–255.

Butler, S. (1979). *Conspiracy of silence: The trauma of incest*. New York: Bantam Books.

Butler, R., and Lewis, M. (1973). *Aging and mental health*. St. Louis: C. V. Mosby.

Bytner, C. V., Griffin, L. S., Jenkins, W. W., and Ray, E. O. (1979). A positive approach in evaluating potential adoptive families and children. In S. R. Churchill, B. Carlson, and L. Nybell (Eds.), *No child is unadoptable*. Beverly Hills, CA: Sage Publications.

Calderone, M. S., and Johnson, E. W. (1981). *The family book about sexuality*. New York: Harper and Row.

Caldwell, B. M. (1979). *HOME observation for measurement*. Little Rock: University of Arkansas.

California Commission on Peace Officer Standards and Training (1980). *Investigation of child abuse and neglect*. Sacramento, CA: Author.

Call, J. D. (1984). Child abuse and neglect in infancy: Sources of hostility within the parent infant dyad and disorders of attachment in infancy. *Child Abuse and Neglect, 8*, 185–202.

Campbell, M., Cohen, I. L., and Small, A. M. (1982). Drugs in aggressive behavior. *Journal of American Academy of Chid Psychiatry, 21*(2), 107–117.

Campos, J. J. (1984). A new perspective on emotions. *Child Abuse and Neglect, 8*, 147–156.

Cantwell, H. B. (1983). Vaginal inspection as it relates to child sexual abuse in girls under thirteen. *Child Abuse and Neglect, 7*, 171–176.

Carrington, D. (1978). Using modern forms of meditation psychotherapy. In S. Boorstein and K. Speeth (Eds.), *Explorations in transpersonal therapy*. New York: Aronson.

Carter, J. E., and McCormick, A. O. (1983). Whiplash shaking syndrome: Retinal hemorrhages and computerized axial tomography of the brain. *Child Abuse and Neglect, 7*, 279–286.

Cattell, R. B. (1965). *The scientific analysis of personality*. Baltimore: Penguin.

Cautley, P. W. (1980). *New foster parents: the first experience*. New York: Human Sciences Press.

Cavara, M., and Ogren, C. (1983). Protocol to investigate child abuse in foster care. *Child Abuse and Neglect, 7*, 287–295.

Chess, S. (1960). Diagnosis and treatment of the hyperactive child. *New York Journal of Medicine, 60,* 2379–2385.

Chess, S., and Thomas, A. (Eds.) (1980). *Annual progress in child psychiatry and child development.* New York: Brunner/Mazel.

Chien, C., and Yamamoto, J. (1982). *Effective psychiatry for Asian Americans and Pacific Islander patients.* New York: Plenum.

Children's Bureau of Los Angeles (1982). *Family Crisis Center.* Los Angeles: Author (pamphlet).

Christoffell, K., and Liu, K. (1983). Homicide death rates in childhood in 23 developed countries: U.S. rates atypically high. *Child Abuse and Neglect, 7,* 339–345.

Cleveland, H. (1972). *The future executive: A guide for tomorrow's managers.* New York: Harper and Row.

Cohen, A. (1977). Multidisciplinary teams or interagency coalitions: A comparative analysis. *Protective Services Resource Institute, 2,* 1.

Cohn, A. H. (1979). Effective treatment of child abuse and neglect. *Social Work, 24,* 513–519.

Cohn, A. H., Ridge, S. S., and Collignon, F. C. (1975). Evaluating innovative treatment programs in child abuse and neglect. *Children Today, 4*(3), 10–12.

Coleman, S. H. (1924). *Humane Society leaders in America.* Albany, NY: American Humane Association.

Colon, F. (1978). Family ties and child placement. *Family Process, 17,* 289–312.

Conger, R., Burgess, R. L., and Barrett, C. (1979). Child abuse related to life change and perceptions of illness: Some preliminary findings. *The Family Coordinator, 28*(1), 73–78.

Connors, K. (1980). *Food additives and hyperkinetic children.* New York: Plenum.

Conte, J. R. (1984, May-June). Progress in treating the sexual abuse of children. *Social Work,* pp. 258–263.

Corsini, R. (Ed.) (1973). *Current psychotherapies.* Itasca, IL: Peacock.

Cousins, M. (1979). *Anatomy of an illness as perceived by the patient: Reflections on healing and regeneration.* New York: Norton.

Curran, D. (1983, October 5). *Family dealings more in the open.* Redlands, CA: Daily Facts.

Curtis, P. A., Rosman, M. D., and Pappenfort, D. M. (1984). Developing an instrument for measuring psychosocial assessment in clinical child welfare. *Child Welfare, 63*(4), 309–318.

Cutler, J. P., and Bateman, R. W. (1980, Fall). Foster care case review: Can it make a difference? *Public Welfare,* pp. 45–61.

Daniel, J., Hampton, R., and Newberger, I. (1983). Child abuse and accidents in black families: A controlled comparative study. *American Journal of Orthopsychiatry, 53*(4), 645–653.

Daniels, M. (1980, August 2). So who's sick? That loving pet can be just what the doc ordered. *Chicago Tribune,* pp. 1, 9–10.

Das, B. H., and Satsang, D. S. (1976). *Between pleasure and pain: The way of conscious living.* Berkeley, CA: Dharma Sara Publications.

Davis, L. V. (1984, May-June). Beliefs of service providers about abused women and abusing men. *Social Work,* pp. 243-250.

DeFrancis, V. (1969). *Protecting the child victim of sex crimes committed by adults.* Denver: American Humane Association.

DeFrancis, V. (1975). *The court and protective services: Their respective roles.* Denver: American Humane Association.

Delaney, J. J. (1976). New concepts of the family court. In R. E. Helfer and C. H. Kempe (Eds.), *The family and the community.* Cambridge, MA: Ballinger.

De Triangel (1979). Socio-therapeutisch Instituut, Lauriergracht 55, 1016RG, Amsterdam.

Devereux, E. C., Shouval, R., Bronfenbrenner, U., Rodgers, R. R., Kavenski, S., Kiely, E., and Karson, E. (1974). Socialization practices of parents, teachers, and peers in Israel: The kibbutz versus the city. *Child Development, 45*, 269–281.

de Young, M. (1984). Counterphobic behavior in multiply molested children. *Child Welfare, 63*(4), 333–339.

Diamond, M. (1984). A love affair with the brain. *Psychology Today, 18*(9), 61–73.

Dinkmeyer, D., and McKay, G. (1982). *The parent's handbook: Systematic training for effective parenting.* Circle Pines, MN: Guidance Service.

Directions (1980). H.E.W. Region IX, Child Abuse and Neglect Resources Center, *15*(1).

Disborn, M. A., Doerr, H., and Caufield, C. (1977). Measuring the components of parents' potential for child abuse and neglect. *Child Abuse and Neglect, 1*, 279–296.

Dishon, C. (1970, January). Skeezer: The canine child therapist. *Today's Health,* pp. 16–18.

Discovery House (1984). *A shelter for battered wives and their children.* Calgary, Alberta, Canada: Author.

Doll, E. A. (1965). *Vineland social maturity scale.* Circle Pines, MN: American Guidance Service.

Donley, K. (1979). Single parents as placements of choice. In S. R. Churchill, B. Carlson, and L. Nybell (Eds.), *No child is unadoptable.* Beverly Hills, CA: Sage Publications.

D'Onofrio, A., Robinson, R., Isett, M., Roszkowski, M., and Spreat, S. (1980). Factors related to contact between mentally retarded persons and their parents during residential treatment. *Mental Retardation, 18*, 293–294.

Downing, G. (1972). *The massage book.* New York: Random House.

Dubanowski, R. A. (1983). Corporal punishment in schools: Myths, problems, and alternatives. *Child Abuse and Neglect, 7*, 271–278.

Dubin, W. R., and Ciavarelli, B. (1978). A positive look at boarding homes. *Hospital and Community Psychiatry, 29*(9), 593–595.

Duquette, D. (1981). Legal roles. In K. Faller (Ed.), *Social work with abused and neglected children.* New York: Free Press.

Durkin, R. P., and Durkin, A. B. (1975). Evaluating residential treatment programs for disturbed children. In M. Guttentage and E. L. Streaning (Eds.), *Handbook of evaluation research* (Vol. 2). Beverly Hills, CA: Sage Publications.

Ebeling, N. B., and Hill, D. A. (Eds.) (1983). *Child abuse and neglect: A guide with case studies for treating the child and family.* Littleton, MA: PSG.

Egeland, B., Breitenbucher, M., and Rosenburg, D. (1980). Prospective study of the significance of etiology of child abuse. *Journal of Consulting and Clinical Psychology, 48*(2), 195–205.

Egeland, B., Sroufe, L. A., and Erickson, M. (1983). The developmental consequence of different patterns of maltreatment. *Child Abuse and Neglect, 7*, 459–469.

Elias, M. (1982, April 7). Dependence court: Children in a web of bureaucracy. *Los Angeles Times,* pp. 9–12.

Elkind, J. S., Berson, A., and Edwin, D. (1977). Current realities haunting advocates of abused children. *Social Casework, 58*(19), 527–531.

Ellerstein, N. S. (Ed.) (1981). *Child abuse and neglect: A medical reference.* New York: John Wiley and Sons.

Ellman, G., Silverstein, C. I., Zingarelli, G., Shafer, E. W., and Silverstein, L. (1984). Vitamin-mineral supplement fails to improve IQ of mentally retarded young adults. *American Journal of Mental Deficiency, 88*(6), 688–691.

Elmer, E. (1967). *Children in jeopardy.* Pittsburgh, PA: University of Pittsburgh Press.

Elmer, E., and Gregg, G. S. (1967). Developmental characteristics of abused children. *Pediatrics, 40*, 596–602.

Emde, R., and Brown, C. (1978). Adaptation after the birth of a Down's syndrome infant: A study of six cases, illustrating differences in development and the counter-movement between grieving and maternal attachment. *Journal of the American Academy of Child Psychiatry, 17*(2), 299–323.

Erickson, J. (1976). *Activity, recovery, growth: The communal role of planned activities.* New York: Norton.

Erikson, E. H. (1950). *Childhood and society.* New York: Norton.

Eyberg, S., and Johnson, S. (1974). Multiple assessment of behavior modification with families. *Journal of Consulting and Clinical Psychology, 42,* 594.

Faber, A., and Mazlish, E. (1980). *How to talk so kids will listen and listen so kids will talk.* New York: Rawson Wade.

Fanshell, D., and Shinn, E. B. (1978). *Children in foster care: A longitudinal investigation.* New York: Columbia University Press.

Fauri, D. P. (1978). Protecting the child protective service worker. *Social Work, 23*(1), 62–64.

Feifel, H. (1957). Some aspects of the meaning of death. In E. Shneidman and N. Farberow (Eds.), *Clues to suicide.* New York: McGraw-Hill Book Company.

Feingold, B. (1975). *Why your child is hyperactive.* New York: Random House.

Feldman, R., and Wodarski, J. (1975). *Contemporary approaches to group treatment.* San Francisco: Jossey-Bass.

Feldman, S. (1983). Out of the hospital, onto the streets: The overselling of benevolence. *Hastings Center Report, 13*(2), 5–7.

Felker, E. H. (1974). *Foster parenting young children: Guidelines from a foster parent.* New York: Columbia University Press.

Ferenczi, S. (1933). Confusion of tongues between adults and the child. In S. Ferenczi (Ed.), *Final contributions to the problems and methods of psychoanalysis* (pp. 155–167). New York: Basic Books.

Feshbach, N. D., and Howes, C. (1983). *Project report.* Beaumont, CA: Research Division, CHILDHELP, U.S.A./INTERNATIONAL.

Finkelhor, D. (1979a). *Sexually victimized children.* New York: Free Press.

Finkelhor, D. (1979b). What's wrong with sex between adults and children? Ethics and the problem of sexual abuse. *American Journal of Orthopsychiatry, 49,* 692–697.

Finkelhor, D., and Hotaling, G. T. (1984). Sexual abuse in the national incidence study of child abuse and neglect: An appraisal. *Child Abuse and Neglect, 8,* 23–33.

Firestone, P., and Witt, J. (1982). Characteristics of families completing and prematurely discontinuing a behavioral parent training program. *Journal of Pediatric Psychology, 7*(2), 209.

Foley, V. (1974). *An introduction to family therapy.* New York: Grune and Stratton.

Framo, J. L. (1977). In-laws and out-laws: A marital case of kinship confusion. In P. Papp (Ed.), *Family therapy: Full length case studies* (pp. 167–181). New York: Gardner Press.

Framo, J. L. (1979). Personal reflections of a family therapist. In J. Howells (Ed.), *Advances in family psychiatry* (Vol. I). New York: International Universities Press.

Frank, J. D. (1961). *Persuasion and healing: A comparative study of psychotherapy.* Baltimore: Johns Hopkins University Press.

Frank, J. D. (1981). Therapeutic components shared by all psychotherapies. Audiotape lecture in the Master Lecture Series on Psychology: *Psychotherapy research and behavior change.* New York: Audio Transcripts, Ltd.

Freud, S. (1896). The aetiology of hysteria. In J. Strachey (Ed.), *The Complete Works of Sigmund Freud.* London: Hogarth Press (1955).

Freud, S. (1933). *The complete introductory lectures of psycho-analysis.* New York: Norton.

Freudenberger, H. J. (1974). Staff burn-out. *Journal of Social Issues, 30*(1), 159–165.

Friedman, R. M., Baron, A., Lardieri, S., and Quick, J. (1982, November). Length of time in foster care: A measure in need of analysis. *Social Work*, pp. 499-503.

Friedman, S. B. (1972). The need for intensive follow-up of abused children. In C. H. Kempe and R. E. Helfer (Eds.), *Helping the battered child and his family* (pp. 79-92). Philadelphia: J. B. Lippincott.

Frodi, A. (1981). Contributions of infant characteristics to child abuse. *American Journal of Mental Deficiency, 85*, 341-349.

Frost, R. (1923). *New Hampshire* (p. 87). New York: Henry Holt.

Furstenburg, F. (1976). *Unplanned parenthood: The social consequences of teenage childbearing.* New York: Free Press.

Gabinet, L. (1983a). Child abuse treatment failures reveal need for redefinition of the problem. *Child Abuse and Neglect, 7*, 395-402.

Gabinet, L. (1983b). Shared parenting: a new paradigm for the treatment of child abuse. *Child Abuse and Neglect, 7*, 403-411.

Gagnon, J. H. (1965). Female child victims of sex offenses. *Social Problems, 13*, 176-192.

Gaines, R., Sandgrund, A., Green, A. H., and Power, T. (1978). Etiologic factors in child maltreatment: A multivariate study of abusing, neglectful mothers. *Journal of Abnormal Psychology, 97*(5), 531-540.

Galdston, R. (1971). Violence begins at home. *Journal of American Academy of Child Psychiatry, 10*, 336-350.

Garbarino, J. (1977). The human ecology of child maltreatment: A conceptual model for research. *Journal of Marriage and the Family, 39*, 721-735.

Garbarino, J., and Crouter, A. (1977). *The problem of construct validity in assessing the correlates of CA/N.* Unpublished manuscript, Boys Town Center for the Study of Youth Development, Omaha, NE.

Garbarino, J., and Plantz, M. C. (1984). An ecological perspective on the outcomes of child maltreatment: What difference will the differences make? In D. Bross (Ed.), *Multidisciplinary advocacy for mistreated children.* Denver: National Association of Counsel for Children.

Geis, C., and Monohan, J. (1976). The social ecology of violence. In T. Lickona (Ed.), *Moral development and behavior* (pp. 342-356). New York: Hold, Rinehart, and Winston.

Gelles, R. (1972). *The violent home.* Beverly Hills, CA: Sage Publications.

Gelles, R. J. (1973). Child abuse as psychopathology: A sociological critique and reformulation. *American Journal of Orthopsychiatry, 45*, 363-371.

Gelles, R. J. (1975). The social construction of child abuse. *American Journal of Orthopsychiatry, 45*, 365.

Gelles, R. J. (1977). Violence toward children in the United States. In S. Nagi (Ed.), *Child maltreatment in the United States: A challenge to social institutions.* New York: Columbia University Press.

Gelles, R. J. (1979). *Family violence.* Beverly Hills, CA: Sage Publications.

Gelles, R. J. (1984). Child abuse in the context of violence in the family and society. In D. Bross (Ed.), *Multidisciplinary advocacy for mistreated children.* Denver: National Association of Counsel for Children.

George, C., and Main, M. (1979). Social interactions of young abused children: Approach, avoidance, and aggression. *Child Development, 50*, 306-318.

Giaretto, H. (1976). Humanistic treatment of father-daughter incest. In R. E. Helfer and C. H. Kempe (Eds.), *Child abuse and neglect: The family and the community* (pp. 143-158). Cambridge, MA: Ballinger.

Gifford, C. D., Kaplan, F. B., and Salus, M. K. (1979). *Parent aides in child abuse and neglect programs* (DHEW Publication No. OHDS 79-30200). Washington, DC: U.S. Government Printing Office.

Gil, D. G. (1968). Incidence of child abuse and demographic characteristics of person involved. In R. E. Helfer and C. H. Kempe (Eds.), *Child abuse and neglect: The family and the community* (pp. 143–158). Cambridge, MA: Ballinger.

Gil, D. G. (1970a). *Violence against children in the United States.* Cambridge, MA: Harvard University Press.

Gil, D. G. (1970b). Violence against children. *Journal of Marriage and the Family, 33,* 637–648.

Gil, E. (1982). Foster parents: Set up to fail. *Child Abuse and Neglect, 8,* 121–123.

Gill, M. (1979). Foster care/adoptive family: Adoption for children not legally free. In S. R. Churchill, B. Carlson, and L. Nybell (Eds.) *No child is unadoptable.* Beverly Hills, CA: Sage Publications.

Gill, M., and Amadio, C. M. (1983). Social work and law in a foster care/adoption program. *Child Welfare, 62*(5), 455–467.

Giovannoni, J., and Becerra, R. (1979). *Defining child abuse.* New York: Free Press.

Gold, C., and Gold, E. J. (1977). *Joyous childbirth: Manual for conscious natural childbirth.* Berkeley, CA: And/Or Press.

Goldberg, K., and Dooner, M. (1981). Rethinking residential treatment. *Child Welfare, 60*(5), 355–358.

Golding, W. (1978). *Lord of the flies.* New York: Coward (Putnam).

Goldstein, J., Freud, A., and Solnit, A. J. (1979). *Before the best interest of the child.* New York: Macmillan.

Goocher, B. E. (1975). Behavioral applications of an educateur model in child care. *Child Care Quarterly, 4*(2), 84–92.

Goodenough, F. (1926). *Measurement of intelligence by drawings.* New York: Harcourt, Brace and World.

Gordon, T. (1970). *Parent effectiveness training.* New York: Wyden.

Gray, E. (1983). *What have we learned about preventing child abuse?* Unpublished working paper 009. Chicago: National Committee for Prevention of Child Abuse.

Green, A. H. (1978). Child abuse. In B. Wolman, J. Egan, and A. Ross (Eds.), *Handbook of treatment of mental disorders in childhood and adolescence.* Englewood Cliffs, NJ: Prentice-Hall.

Green, A. H. (1980). *Child maltreatment: A handbook for mental health and child care professionals.* New York: Jason Aronson.

Green, A. H., Gaines, R. W., and Sandgrund, A. (1974). Child abuse: Pathological syndrome of family interaction. *American Journal of Psychiatry, 131*(8), 882–886.

Griswold, B. B., and Billingsley, A. (1969). *Personality and social characteristics of low income mothers who neglect or abuse their children.* Final Report: Grant #PR1100 R., Washington, DC: Children's Bureau, Welfare Administration, U.S. Department HEW.

Groth, A. N. (1978). Patterns of sexual assault against children and adolescents. In A. W. Burgess, A. N. Groth, L. L. Holmstrom, and S. M. Sgroi (Eds.), *Sexual assault of children and adolescents.* Lexington, MA: Lexington Books.

Guerin, P. (Ed.) (1976). *Family therapy.* New York: Gardner Press.

Gruber, A. R. (1978). *Children in foster care: Destitute, neglected, betrayed.* New York: Human Sciences Press.

Gurian, B. (1978). The psychiatric house call. *American Journal of Psychiatry, 135*(5), 592.

Haddock, M. D., and McQueen, W. M. (1983). Assessing employee potentials for abuse. *Journal of Clinical Psychology, 39*(6), 1021–1029.

Haley, J. (1971). *Changing families: A family therapy reader.* New York: Grune and Stratton.

Haley, J. (1976). *Problem-solving therapy: New strategies for effective family therapy.* New York: Jossey-Bass.

Hall, C. S., and Lindzey, G. (1957). *Theories of personality.* New York: Wiley and Sons.

Halo, K. (1978). Nursing in transition. In E. Bauman, A. T. Brint, L. Piper, and P. A. Wright (Eds.), *The holistic health handbook: A tool for attaining wholeness of body, mind, and spirit.* Berkeley, CA: And/Or Press.

Halpern, R. (1984). Lack of effects for home-based early intervention: Some possible explanations. *American Journal of Orthopsychiatry, 54*(1), 33–42.

Hanley, J. (1984). *New windows, new vistas, old views.* Unpublished paper presented at the Eleventh Symposium of Neuropsychiatric Issues in the Law, Medicine, and Education, Kamuela, HI. Southern California Neuropsychiatric Institute.

Harlow, H. F. (1958). The nature of love. *American Psychologist, 13,* 673–687.

Harmon, R. J., Morgan, G. A., and Glicken, A. D. (1984). Continuities and discontinuities in effective and cognitive motivational development. *Child Abuse and Neglect, 8,* 157–167.

Harris, D. (1963). *Children's drawings as measures of intellectual maturity.* New York: Harcourt, Brace and World.

Harter, S. (1979). *Perceived competence scale for children.* Denver: University of Denver.

Hartman, A., and Laird, J. (1983). *Family-centered social work practice.* New York: Free Press.

Hathaway, S. R., and McKinley, J. C. (1967). *Minnesota multiphasic personality inventory* (revised manual). New York: Psychological Corporation.

Haynes, C. F., Cutler, C., Gray, J., and Kempe, R. S. (1984). Hospitalized cases of nonorganic failure to thrive: The scope of the problem and short-term lay health visitor intervention. *Child Abuse and Neglect, 8,* 229–242.

Heinicke, C. M. (1984). The role of pre-birth characteristics in early family development. *Child Abuse and Neglect, 8,* 169–181.

Helfer, R. (1976). Child abuse and neglect: Early identification and prevention of unusual child-rearing practices. *Pediatric Annals, 5,* 91.

Helfer, R., and Kempe, C. H. (1968). *The battered child* (1st ed.). Chicago: University of Chicago Press.

Helfer, R., and Kempe, C. H. (Eds.) (1976). *Child abuse and neglect: The family and the community.* Cambridge, MA: Ballinger.

Helfer, R., and Kempe, C. H. (1980). *The battered child* (3rd ed.). Chicago: University of Chicago Press.

Helfer, R., Schneider, C., Hoffmeister, J., and Tardi, B. (1977). *Manual for the use of the Michigan screening profile of parenting.* East Lansing, MI: Department of Human Development, Michigan State University.

Herrera, A. E., and Sanchez, V. C. (1976). Behaviorally oriented group therapy: A successful application in the treatment of low income Spanish speaking clients. In M. R. Miranda (Ed.), *Psychotherapy with the Spanish speaking: Issues in Research and service delivery* (Monograph No. 3). Los Angeles: University of California, Spanish Speaking Mental Health Research Center, p. 73.

Hightower, K. (1982). Follow-up of parents of children discharged from the Village of Childhelp, U.S.A. Beaumont, CA: Research Division of CHILDHELP U.S.A./INTERNATIONAL.

Hoffman, M. L. (1970). Moral development. In P. Mussen (Ed.), *Carmichael's manual of child psychology* (Vol. II, pp. 261–359). New York: John Wiley and Sons.

Holden, C. (1984). Baby Doe compromise imminent. *Science, 225,* 294–295.

Hollingshead, A. B. (1957). *Two factor index of social position.* New Haven, CT: Yale University Press.

Holmes, T. H., and Rahe, R. H. (1967). The social readjustment rating scale. *Journal of Psychosomatic Research, 11*(2), 213–218.

Hunner, R. J., and Walker, Y. E. (1981). Exploring the relationship between child abuse and delinquency. Montclair, NJ: Allanheld, Osman, and Company.

Hyman, C. A., and Parr, R. (1978). A controlled video observational study of abused children. *Child Abuse and Neglect, 2*, 217–222.

Hyman, F. A., and Wise, J. H. (1979). *Corporal punishment in American education.* Philadelphia: Temple University Press.

Interagency Council on Child Abuse and Neglect (ICAN) (1978). *Neighborhood family stress centers.* Los Angeles: Author.

International Association of Chiefs of Police, Inc. (1977). *The police perspective in child abuse and neglect,* (p. 4). Gaithersburg, MD: Author.

International Orphans, Incorporated. (1959). *Articles of incorporation for International Orphans, Incorporated.* Woodland Hills, CA: Author.

Jackson, D. D. (1968). *Therapy, communication and change.* Palo Alto, CA: Science and Behavior Books.

Jackson, D. D. (1960). *The etiology of schizophrenia.* New York: Basic Books.

Jacobs, M. (1980). Foster parent training: An opportunity for skills enrichment and empowerment. *Child Welfare League of America, 59*(10). 615–624.

Jacobson, N. S., and Margolin, G. (1979). *Marital therapy: Strategies based on social learning and behavior exchange principles.* New York: Brunner/Mazel.

Jellinek, M. S., and Slovik, P. M. (1981). Divorce: Impact on children. *New England Journal of Medicine, 305*, 241–253.

Jenkins, R. L. (1970). Interrupting the family cycle of violence. *Journal of Iowa's Medical Society, 30*, 85–89.

Jensen, M., and Meier, J. H. (1983). *Moral development: Implications for research and intervention in child abuse.* Monograph #9, 8/83. Beaumont, CA: Research Division of CHILDHELP, U.S.A./INTERNATIONAL.

Johnson, B., and Morse, H. A. (1968). Injured children and their parents. *Children, 15*, 147–152.

Johnson, J., Floyd, B. J., and Isleib, R. (1983). *Parent, child, and social variables as predictors of child abuse: Implications for a temperament mismatch view of abusive behavior.* Beaumont, CA: CHILDHELP Research Division.

Jones, D. (1984). *Interviewing the sexually abused child. II: Principles and practice.* Denver: C. Henry Kempe Center for the Prevention and Treatment of Child Abuse and Neglect.

Jones, M. A. (1976). Reducing foster care through services to families. *Child Today, 5*, 7–10.

Jones, M. A., Magura, S., and Syne, A. W. (1980). Effective practice with families in protective services: What works? *Child Welfare, 59*(8), 60–67.

Jones, M. L. (1977). Aggressive adoption: A program's effect on a child welfare agency. *Child Welfare, 56*(6). 401–407.

Justice, B., and Duncan, : . F. (1976). Life crises as a precursor to child abuse. *Public Health Reports, 91*, 110–115.

Justice, B., and Justice, R. (1976). *The abusing family.* New York: Human Sciences Press.

Kahane, R. (1975). The committed: Preliminary reflections on the impact of the kibbutz socialization pattern on adolescents. *British Journal of Sociology, 26*(3), 343–353.

Kanner, A. D., Coyne, J. C., Schaefer, C., and Lazarus, R. S. (1981). Comparison of two modes of stress measurement: Daily hassles and uplifts versus major life events. *Psychosomatic Medicine, 43*(3), 97–118.

Kaplan, H., and Sadock, B. (1971). *Comprehensive group psychotherapy*. Baltimore: Williams & Wilkins.

Katz, S., McGrath, M., and Howe, R. A. (1976). *Child neglect laws in America*. Washington, DC: American Bar Association Section on Family Law.

Kean, R. B. (1984). The battered child and the exclusionary role: A practical outline of search and seizure law for the law enforcement officer investigating child abuse and neglect. In D. Bross (Ed.), *Multidisciplinary advocacy for mistreated children*. Denver: National Association of Counsel for Children.

Keith-Lucas, A., and Sanford, C. W. (1977). *Group child care as a family service*. Chapel Hill, NC: University of North Carolina Press.

Kellogg, R. (1967). *The psychology of children's art*. New York: Random House.

Kelly, J. B., and Wallerstein, J. S. (1976). The effects of parental divorce: Experiences of the child in early latency. *American Journal of Orthopsychiatry, 46*(1), 20–32.

Kempe, C. H. (1976). Approaches to preventing child abuse: The health visitor concept. *American Journal of the Disabled Child, 130*, 941.

Kempe, C. H. (1979). Recent developments in the field of child abuse. *Child Abuse and Neglect*, 3, ix–xv.

Kempe, C. H., and Helfer, R. (1973). *Helping the battered child and his family*. Philadelphia: J. B. Lippincott.

Kempe, C. H., and Kempe, R. S. (1982). *Sexually abused children and adolescents*. Cambridge, MA: Harvard University Press.

Kempe, C. H., Silverman, F. N., Steele, B. F., Droegemueller, W., and Silver, H. K. (1962). The battered child syndrome. *Journal of American Medical Association, 181*, 105–112.

Kempe, R. S., and Kempe C. H. (1978). *Child abuse*. Cambridge, MA: Harvard University Press.

Kent, J. T. (1976). A follow-up study of abused children. *Journal of Pediatric Psychology, 1*, 25–31.

Klaus, M., and Kennell, J. (1976). *Maternal-infant bonding: The impact of early separation or loss on family development*. St. Louis: C. V. Mosby.

Klein, J. W. (1973, Spring). A new professional program development for the child-care field—the child development associate. *Child Care Quarterly, 2*, 56–60.

Kohlberg, L. (1976). Moral stages and moralization: The cognitive developmental approach. In T. Lickona (Ed.), *Moral development and behavior: Theory, research and social issues*. New York: Holt, Rinehart and Winston.

Korbin, J. E. (1980). The cultural context of child abuse and neglect. *Child Abuse and Neglect, 4*, 3–13.

Kristal, H. F., and Tucker, F. (1975). Managing child abuse cases. *Social Work, 20*(5), 392–395.

Krugman, R. D. (1983). *Point counterpoint*. National Center on Child Abuse and Neglect, 6th National Convention, Baltimore.

Krugman, R. D. (1984). The relationship between unemployment and physical abuse in children. In D. Bross (Ed.), *Multidisciplinary advocacy for mistreated children*. Denver: National Association of Counsel for Children.

Krugman, R. D., and Krugman, M. K. (1984). Emotional abuse in the classroom: The pediatrician's role in diagnosis and treatment. *American Journal of Diseases of Children, 138*, 284–286.

Kübler-Ross, E. (1975). *Death: The final stage of growth*. Englewood Cliffs, NJ: Prentice-Hall.

Kutsky, R. (1973). *Handbook of vitamins and hormones*. New York: Van Nostrand Reinhold.

Kwiatkowski, H. (1978). *Family therapy and evaluation through art*. Springfield, IL: Charles C Thomas.

Lachar, D., and Gdowski, O. L. (1979). *Actuarial assessment of child and adolescent personality: An interpretive guide for the personality inventory for children profile.* Los Angeles: Western Psychological Services.

Lally, J. R. (1984). Three views of child neglect: Expanding visions of preventive intervention. *Child Abuse and Neglect, 8,* 243–254.

Lamb, R. H. (1981). Maximizing the potential of board and care homes. In R. D. Budson (Ed.), *Issues in community residential care.* San Francisco: Jossey-Bass.

Landis, J. (1956). Experiences of 500 children with adult sexual deviants. *Psychiatric Quarterly, 30,* 91–109.

Lawder, E. A., Lower, K. D., Andrews, R. G., Sherman, E. A., and Hill, J. G. (1969). *A follow-up study of adoptions: Post placement functioning of adoption families.* New York: Child Welfare League of America.

Leak, G. K., and Christopher, S. B. (1982). Freudian psychoanalysis and sociology: A synthesis. *American Psychologist, 37,* 313–322.

Leavitt, J. (Ed.) (1983). *Child abuse and neglect: Research and innovation.* The Hague, Netherlands: Martinus Nijhoff.

Lee, R. E., and Hull, R. K. (1983). Legal casework and ethical issues in "risk adoption." *Child Welfare, 62*(5), 451–454.

Lefkowitz, M., Eron, L., Walter, L., and Hensmann, L. (1977). *Growing up to be violent.* New York: Pergamon.

Leiber, L. L., and Baker, J. M. (1977). Parents anonymous—self-help treatment for child abusing parents: A review and an evaluation. *Child Abuse and Neglect, 1,* 133–148.

Lenoski, E. F. (1973). *Translating injury data into preventive and health care services— physical child abuse.* Unpublished manuscript. Los Angeles: University of Southern California School of Medicine.

Levinson, B. M. (1969). *Pet-oriented child psychotherapy.* Springfield, IL: Charles C Thomas.

Levinson, B. M. (1972). *Pets and human development.* Springfield, IL: Charles C Thomas.

Levinson, D. J. (1978). *The seasons of a man's life.* New York: Alfred A. Knopf.

Lickona, T. (1976). *Moral development and behavior: Theory, research and social issues.* New York: Holt, Rinehart and Winston.

Lieberman, F. (1979). *Social work with children.* New York: Human Sciences Press.

Light, R. (1973). Abused and neglected children in America: A study of alternative policies. *Harvard Education Review, 43,* 556–599.

Lindsey, D. (1982, November). Achievements for children in foster care. *Social Work,* pp. 491–496.

Linn, M. W. (1981). Can foster care survive? In R. D. Budson (Ed.), *Issues in community residential care.* San Francisco: Jossey-Bass.

Linn, M. W., Caffey, E. M., Klett, J., and Hogarty, G. (1977). Hospital versus community (foster) care for psychiatric patients. *Archives of General Psychiatry, 34,* 78–83.

Linton, T. E. (1971). The educateur model: A theoretical monograph. *Journal of Special Education, 5,* 155–190.

Lipton, M. A., and Mayo, J. P. (1983). Diet and hyperkinesis—an update. *Journal of the American Dietetic Association, 83*(2), 132–134.

Los Angeles County Sheriff's Department (1981). *Manual of Policy and Procedure.* Unpublished manual. Los Angeles: Author.

Lowenfeld, V. (1954). *Your child and his art.* New York: Macmillan.

McClelland, D. (1973). Testing for competence rather than intelligence. *American Psychologist, 28,* 1–14.

McCord, J. (1979). Some child rearing antecedents to criminal behavior in adult men. *Journal of Personality and Psychology, 37*, 1477–1486.

McGoldrick, M., Pearce, J., and Giordano, J. (1982). *Ethnicity and family therapy.* New York: Guilford Press.

McLemore, C. (1982). *The scandal of psychotherapy: A guide to resolving the tensions between faith and counseling.* Wheaton, IL: Tyndale House Publishing.

Madden, J., O'Hara, J., and Levenstein, P. (1984). Home again: Effects of the Mother-Child Home Program on mother and child. *Child Development, 55*, 636–647.

Magrab, P. (1982). Services for children: Challenge for the 1980's. *Journal of Pediatric Psychology, 7*(2), 105.

Main, M., and Goldwyn, R. (1984). Predicting rejection of her infant from mother's representation of her own experience: Implications for the abused-abusing intergenerational cycle. *Child Abuse and Neglect, 8*, 203–217.

Martin, H. P. (1976). *The abused child: A multidisciplinary approach to development issues and treatment.* Cambridge, MA: Ballinger.

Martin, H. P. (1979). Child abuse and development. *Child Abuse and Neglect, 3*, 415–421.

Martin, H. P. (1984). Intervention with infants at risk for abuse or neglect. *Child Abuse and Neglect, 8*, 255–260.

Martin, H. P., and Rodeheffer M. (1976). Learning and intelligence. In H. Martin (Ed.), *The abused child: A multidisciplinary approach to developmental issues and treatment.* Cambridge, MA: Ballinger.

Maurer, A. (1976). *Aftermath of physical punishment ages 1 to 10.* Direction: Child abuse and neglect project H.E.W. Region IX. June, Number 2.2. Unpublished paper presented at the Western Psychological Association Convention, San Francisco.

Maurer, A., and Williams, G. (1983). Violence against children reconsidered. *Journal of Clinical Child Psychology, 12*(3), 231–368.

Mayeda, T., Jensen, M., and Meier, J. H. (1983). *Brothers and sisters emergency care program to alleviate separation trauma in child assault cases: Description, research design, and some initial impressions.* Monograph #18, 9/83. Beaumont, CA: Research Division, CHILDHELP, U.S.A./INTERNATIONAL.

Mayeda, T., and Meier, J. H. (1983). *University collaborative research networking: Rationale, operation, and initial observations from CHILDHELP, U.S.A. National Network.* Monograph #13, 9/83. Beaumont, CA: Research Division. CHILDHELP, U.S.A./INTERNATIONAL.

Mayer, M. F. (1958). *A guide for child-care workers.* New York: Child Welfare League of America.

Mednick, S. A. (1977). A bio-social theory of the learning of law-abiding behavior. In S. A. Mednick and K. D. Christiansen (Eds.), *Bio-social bases of criminal behavior.* New York: Gardner.

Meier, J. H. (1970). Autotelic training for deprived children. *Psychiatric Therapy Quarterly, 10*, 30-45.

Meier, J. H. (1973). *Screening and assessment of young children at developmental risk.* Washington, DC: U.S. Government Printing Office.

Meier, J. H. (1975a). Early intervention and prevention of mental retardation. In A. Milunsky (Ed.), *The prevention of mental retardation and genetic disease* (pp. 385–407). Philadelphia: W. B. Saunders Co.

Meier, J. H. (1975b). Screening, assessment and evaluation procedures for infants at developmental risk. In N. Hobbs (Ed.), *Classification of exceptional children* (pp. 497–543). San Francisco: Jossey-Bass.

Meier, J. H. (1976a). *Developmental and learning disabilities: An interdisciplinary approach to their evaluation, management, and prevention in children.* Austin, TX: Pro-Ed Publications.

Meier, J. H. (1976b). Foreword. In R. E. Melfer and C. H. Kempe (Eds.), *Child abuse and neglect: The family and the community.* (pp. xv–xvi). Cambridge, MA: Ballinger.

Meier, J. H. (1977a). Found: Long-term gains from early intervention studies. In B. Brown (Ed.), *Found: Long-term gains from early intervention.* American Association for the Advancement of Science, Symposia Series (pp. 1-10). Boulder, CO: Westview Press.

Meier, J. H. (1977b). Head Start program: Identification and reporting of child abuse and neglect—policy instruction. *Federal Register, 42*(17), 4970–4971.

Meier, J. H. (1978). Current status and future prospects for the nation's children and their families. In *Family Factbook* (pp. 229–242). Chicago: Marquis Academic Media.

Meier, J. H. (1979a). *Brief statement regarding the relationship between alcohol abuse and child abuse/neglect.* Beaumont, CA: Research Division, CHILDHELP, U.S.A./INTERNATIONAL.

Meier, J. H. (1979b). [Relationship between child abuse and juvenile delinquency/crime.] Testimony at Public Hearing for California Department of Youth Authority. Beaumont, CA: Research Division, CHILDHELP, U.S.A./INTERNATIONAL.

Meier, J. H. (1979c). *Violence family style.* Presented at a State-of-the-Art Conference Regarding Family Therapy, Theory and Practice. Beaumont, CA: Research Division, CHILDHELP, U.S.A./INTERNATIONAL.

Meier, J. H. (1980a). Assessment of developmental levels. Presented at American Medical Association Academy of Child Psychiatry Meeting, Chicago. In series: *The physician and the mental health of the child.* Monroe, WI: American Medical Association.

Meier, J. H. (1980b). *Children's Village, U.S.A.* Statement and backup material for Congressional Field Hearings on Child abuse prevention and treatment programs. Committee on Ways and Means. Washington, DC: U. S. Government Printing Office, Serial #96-108.

Meier, J. H. (1980c). *I.O.I.'s Children's Village, U.S.A.: Annual Report.* Beaumont, CA: Research Division, CHILDHELP, U.S.A./INTERNATIONAL.

Meier, J. H. (1981). Children's Village, U.S.A.: A caring community. In E. Hodges and R. Rouch (Eds.), *Caring.* Chicago: National Committee for Prevention of Child Abuse.

Meier, J. H. (1982). Corporal punishment in the schools. *Childhood Education, 58*(4), 236–237.

Meier, J. H. (1983a). [CHILDHELP, U.S.A./INTERNATIONAL.] Testimony before U.S. House Select Committee on Children, Youth and Families. Monograph #19, 12/83. Beaumont, CA: Research Division, CHILDHELP, U.S.A./INTERNATIONAL.

Meier, J. H. (1983b). *Corporal punishment and child abuse: Some observations and relationships.* (Edited and updated paper originally presented at the Forum on Corporal Punishment in the Schools by J. H. Meier at the American Psychological Association 84th Annual National Convention, Washington, DC) Monograph #1, 3/83. Beaumont, CA: Research Division, CHILDHELP, U.S.A./INTERNATIONAL.

Meier, J. H. (1983c). *Research division progress report (1981–1982).* Beaumont, CA: Research Division, CHILDHELP, U.S.A./INTERNATIONAL.

Meier, J. H. (1984a). *Current child abuse facts and figures.* Monograph #21, 5/84. Beaumont, CA: Research Division, CHILDHELP, U.S.A./INTERNATIONAL.

Meier, J. H. (1984b). *Primary prevention of child assault: Grandparent aides strengthen low-income high-risk families and expand Head Start.* Monograph #24, 11/84. Beaumont, CA: Research Division, CHILDHELP, U.S.A./INTERNATIONAL.

Meier, J. H. (1984c). Secondary prevention of child assault: Provision of specialized foster-adoptive placements and reunification after-care to prevent drift and recidivism. Monograph #25, 12/84. Beaumont, CA: Research Division. CHILDHELP, U.S.A./INTERNATIONAL.

Meier, J. H. (1984d). The responsibility for violent behavior: Acts of God vs. rites of families. Unpublished paper presented at the Eleventh Symposium on Neuropsychiatric Issues in the Law, Education, and Medicine, Kamuela, HI. Southern California Neuropsychiatric Institute.

Meier, J. H., and Malone, P. J. (1979). *Facilitating children's development. Volume I: Infant and toddler learning episodes. Volume II: Learning episodes for older preschoolers.* Austin, TX: Pro-Ed. Publications.

Meier, J. H., and Martin, H. P. (1970, 1972, 1974). Developmental retardation. In C. H. Kempe, H. K. Silver, and D. O'Brien (Eds.), *Current pediatric diagnosis and treatment* (pp. 459–464, 538–563, 459–565, respectively). Los Altos, CA: Lange Medical Publications. (English, Spanish, Italian, Serbo-Croatian, Polish, and Turkish versions.)

Meier, J. H., Nimicht, G. P., and McAfee, O. (1968). An autotelic responsive environment nursery for deprived children. In J. Hellmuth (Ed.), *Disadvantaged child* (Volume II, pp. 299–399). Seattle, WA: Special Child Publications.

Meier, J. H., and Sloan, M. P. (1983). *Acts of God and/or rites of families: Accidental versus inflicted child disabilities.* Monograph #12: 3/84 Beaumont, CA: Research Division, CHILDHELP, U.S.A./INTERNATIONAL.

Meier, J. H., and Sloan, M. P. (1984). The severely handicapped and child abuse. In J. Blacher (Ed.), *Severely handicapped young children and their families: Research in review.* New York: Academic Press.

Meier, R. (1984). Preliminary study to compare normal versus abused children's drawings. Unpublished paper and narrated slide presentation. Riverside, CA: University of California.

Mele, S. (1984). Frequently litigated issues in criminal cases involving family violence. In D. Bross (Ed.), *Multidisciplinary advocacy for mistreated children.* Denver: National Association of Counsel for Children.

Menninger, K. (1938). *Man against himself.* New York: Harcourt, Brace and World, Inc.

Miles, R. B. (1978). Humanistic medicine and holistic health care. In Bauman, E., Brint, A. I., Piper, L., and Wright, P. A. (Eds.), *The holistic health handbook: A tool for attaining wholeness of body, mind, and spirit.* Berkeley, CA: And/Or Press.

Miller, S. H. (1983). *Children as parents: Final report on a study of childbearing and childrearing among 12 to 16 year olds.* New York: Child Welfare League of America.

Minuchin, S. (1974). *Families and family therapy.* Cambridge, MA: Harvard University Press.

Mora, G. (1974). Recent psychiatric developments (since 1939). In S. Arieti (Ed.), *American Handbook of Psychiatry* (Vol. 1). New York: Basic Books.

Morris, M. G. (Ed.). (1977). *Education for parenthood.* Cambridge, MA: Educational Development Associates.

Morris, M. G., and Gould, R. W. (1963). Role reversal: A necessary concept in dealing with the "battered child syndrome." *American Journal of Orthopsychiatry, 33,* 298–299.

Morse, C. W., Sahler, O. J., and Friedman, S. B. (1970). A three-year follow-up study of abused and neglected children. *American Journal of Diseases of Children, 120,* 439–446.

Motorola Teleprograms (Producer). (1977). *Double jeopardy* [Film]. Shiller Park, IL: Producer.

Myers, B. L. (1981). Incest: If you think the word is ugly, take a look at its effects. In K. MacFarlane, B. Jones, and L. Jenstrom (Eds.), *Sexual abuse of children: Selected readings* (pp. 98–101). Washington, DC: National Center on Child Abuse and Neglect, Department of Health and Human Services, U.S. Government Printing Office.

Nagi, S. (1977). *Child maltreatment in the United States: A challenge to social institutions.* New York: Columbia University Press.

National Committee for the Prevention of Child Abuse (1978). In H. Donovan and R. J. Beran (Eds.), *Dealing with sexual child abuse* (Vol. 2). Chicago: Author.

National Committee for the Prevention of Child Abuse (1981). *Child Abuse campaign magazine* (ad no. CA-3120-79). Chicago: Author.

National Legal Resource Center for Child Advocacy and Protection (1979, May). *The child abuse legal representation: Suggestions for effective implementation.* Washington, DC: Author.

Naumburg, M. (1966). *Dynamically oriented art therapy: Its principles and practice.* New York: Grune and Stratton.

Nelson, J. C. (1975). Dealing with resistance in social work practice. *Social Work, 56*(10), 587–592.

Newberger, C. M., and Cook, C. J. (1983). *Parent awareness and child abuse and neglect: A cognitive developmental analysis.* Cambridge, MA: Harvard University Press.

Newberger, E. H. (Ed.) (1982). *Child abuse.* Boston, MA: Little, Brown.

Newberger, E. H., Newberger, C. M., and Hampton, R. L. (1983). Child abuse: The current theory base and future research needs. *Journal of American Child Psychiatry, 22*(3), 262–268.

Nimnicht, G. P., McAfee, O., and Meier, J. H. (1969). *The new nursery school.* New York: Silver Burdett.

Normand, W., Iglesias, J., and Payne, S. (1974). Brief group therapy to facilitate utilization of mental heath services by Spanish speaking patients. *American Journal of Orthopsychiatry, 44*(1), 37.

Northern California Criminal Justice Training and Educational System (1978). *Countering Child Abuse.* Unpublished training book. Sacramento, CA: Author.

Norton, D. G., and Huttenlocker, J. (1983). *Pattern of interaction in families at risk for abuse.* Beaumont, CA: CHILDHELP Research Division.

Oates, M. (1979). A classification of child abuse and its relation to treatment and prognosis. *Child Abuse and Neglect, 3,* 907–915.

Oates, R. K., and Hufton, I. W. (1977). The spectrum of failure to thrive and child abuse: A follow-up study. *Child Abuse and Neglect, 1,* 119–124.

Oliver, D. (1980, April). *Bridging the gap: Issues, problems, and program designs of six community based child abuse treatment programs.* Department of Social Service, Health and Welfare Agency, State of California.

Oliver, J. E., and Taylor, A. (1971). Five generations of ill treated children in one family pedigree. *British Journal of Psychiatry, 119*(552), 473–480.

O'Keefe, R. A. (1974). *A guide for planning and operating home-based child development programs.* Washington, DC: Administration for Children Youth and Families, HEADSTART.

Ooms, T. (Ed.). (1979). *Teenage pregnancy and family impact: New perspectives on policy.* Washington, DC: George Washington University.

Orwell, G. (1949). *1984.* New York: Signet Classics.

Ostbloom, N., and Crase, S. A. (1980). A model for conceptualizing child abuse causation and intervention. *Social Casework, 61*(3), 164–172.

Ounsted, C., Oppenheimer, R., and Lindsay, J. (1974). Aspects of bonding failure: The psychopathology and psychotherapeutic treatment of families of battered children. *Developmental Medicine and Child Neurology, 16*(4), 447–456.

Palmer, S. (1972). *The violent society.* New Haven, CT: College and University Press.

Papp, P. (Ed.) (1977). *Family therapy: full length case studies.* New York: Gardner Press.

Parke, R. D., and Collmer, C. W. (1975). Child abuse: An interdisciplinary analysis. In

M. E. Hetherington (Ed.), *Child development research* (Vol. 5). Chicago: University of Chicago Press.

Parmalee, A. H. (1984). Infant mental health and biological risk. *Child Abuse and Neglect, 8*, 219–226.

Patterson, G. R. (1974). Retraining of aggressive boys by their parents. Review of recent literature and follow-up. *Canadian Psychiatric Association Journal, 19*, 142.

Paulson, M. J. (1975). Child trauma intervention: A community response to family violence. *Journal of Clinical Child Psychology, 1*, 29.

Paulson, M. (1976). Multiple intervention programs for the abused and neglected child. *Journal of Pediatric Psychology, 1*, 83.

Paulson, M. (1978a). Early intervention and treatment of child abuse. *Psychiatric Opinion, 15*, 34.

Paulson, M. (1978b). Incest and sexual molestation: Clinical and legal issues. *Journal of Clinical Child Psychology, 7*, 177.

Paulson, M. (1982). Identifying and helping the child abusing family. In Robert O. Pasnau (Ed.). *Psychosocial aspects of medical practice* (Vol. 1, pp. 61–75). Menlo Park, CA: Addison-Wesley Publishing Company.

Paulson, M. (1983). Physical and emotional abuse of children: Prevention and intervention strategies. In C. E. Hollingsworth, *Providing for the emotional health of the pediatric patient* (pp. 169–206). Jamaica, NY: Spectrum Publications.

Paulson, M., Afifi, A., Chaleff, A., Liu, V., and Thomason, M. (1975a). A discriminant function procedure for identifying abusive parents. *Suicide* (formerly *Life Threatening Behavior, 5*, 194.

Paulson, M., Afifi, A., Chaleff, A., and Thomason, M. (1975b). The MMPI scale for identifying "at risk" abusive parents. *Journal of Clinical Child Psychology, 4*, 22.

Paulson, M., Afifi, A., Thomason, M., and Chaleff, A. (1974a). The MMPI: a descriptive measure of psychopathology in abusive parents. *Journal of Clinical Psychology, 30*, 387.

Paulson, M., and Blake P. (1969). The physically abused child, a focus on prevention. *Child Welfare, 68*(2), 86.

Paulson, M., and Chaleff, A. (1973). Parent surrogate roles: A dynamic concept in understanding and treating abusive parents. *Journal of Clinical Child Psychology, 11*, 38.

Paulson, M., Savino, A., Chaleff, A., Sanders, W., Frisch, F., and Dunn, R. (1974b). Parents of the battered child: A multidisciplinary group therapy approach to life threatening behavior. *Life Threatening Behavior, 4*, 18.

Paulson, M., Schwemer, G., Afifi, A., and Bendel, R. (1977). Parent Attitude Research Instrument (PARI): Clinical vs. statistical inferences in understanding abusive mothers. *Journal of Clinical Psychology, 33*, 848.

Paulson, M., Schwemer, G., and Bendel, R. (1976). Clinical application of the Pd, Ma and (OH) experimental MMPI scales to further understanding of abusive parents.

Paulson, M., and Stone, D. (1974). Suicidal behavior of latency age children. *Journal of Clinical Child Psychology, 3*, 50.

Paulson, M., and Stone, D. (1978). Suicide potential and behavior in children. *Journal of Clinical Child Psychology, 7* 50.

Paulson, M., and Stone, D. (1983). Theoretical and clinical issues in severe depression and latency age suicidal behavior of children. In C. E. Hollingsworth (Ed.), *Pediatric consultation liason psychiatry*. Jamaica, NY: Spectrum Publications.

Paulson, M., Strouse, L., and Chaleff, A. (1982). Intra-familial incest and sexual molestation of children. In J. Henning (Ed.), *Children and the law: Children's rights and children's attitudes*. Springfield, IL: Charles C Thomas.

Pawl, J. H. (1984). Strategies of intervention. *Child Abuse and Neglect, 8*, 261–270.

Paykel, E. S., Prusoff, B. A., and Uhlenhuth, E. H. (1971). Scaling of life events. *Archives of General Psychiatry, 25*, 340–347.

Pelton, L. H. (1978). Child abuse and neglect: The myth of classlessness. *American Journal of Orthopsychiatry, 48*(4), 608–617.

Pelton, L. H. (Ed.) (1981). *The social context of child abuse and neglect.* New York: Human Services Press.

People vs. Brown, 12 Cal.App.3d 600, 605.

People vs. Roman, 256 Cal.App.2d 265, 260.

People vs. Smith, In re: Dawn O., 58 Cal.App.3d 160, 162–63.

Peters, J. J. (1973). Child rape: Defusing a psychological time bomb. *Hospital Physician, 9*, 46.

Peters, J. J. (1976). Children who are victims of sexual assault and the psychology of offenders. *American Journal of Psychology, 30*, 398–412.

Phillips, M. J., Shyne, A. W., Sherman, E. A., and Haring, B. L. (1971). *Factors associated with placement decisions in child welfare.* New York: Child Welfare League of America.

Pickney, A. (1972). *The American way of violence.* New York: Random House.

Plumez, J. H. (1982). *Successful adoption: A guide to financing a child and raising a family.* New York: Harmony Books.

Pollitt, E., Eichler, A., and Chan, C. (1975). Psychosocial development and behavior of mothers of failure to thrive children. *American Journal of Orthopsychiatry, 45*, 525.

Queen's Bench Foundation (1976). *Sexual abuse of children.* San Francisco: Project on child victims of sexual assault.

Radbill, G. (1974). A History of child abuse and infanticide. In R. Helfer and C. H. Kempe (Eds.), *The battered child* (pp. 3-25). Chicago: University of Chicago Press.

Reagan, N. (1982). *To love a child.* New York: Bobbs Merrill.

Reid, J. B., and Taplin, P. S. (1977). *A social interactional approach to the treatment of abused children.* Unpublished manuscript.

Reid, J. B., Taplin, P. S., and Loeber, R. (1982). A social interactional approach to the treatment of abusive families. In R. Stuart (Ed.), *Violent behavior: A social learning approach to prediction, management, and treatment.* New York: Brunner/Mazel.

Rindfleisch, N. (1984). How much of a problem is resident mistreatment in child welfare institutions? *Child Abuse and Neglect, 8*, 33–40.

Rondeau, C. (1983). *The efficacy of reward versus punishment: A comparison of two cottage units.* Monograph #2, 3/83. Beaumont, CA: Research Division, CHILDHELP, U.S.A./INTERNATIONAL.

Rosenbaum, M., and Berger, M. (1975). *Group psychotherapy and group function.* New York: Basic Books.

Rosenzweig, S. (1944). An outline of frustration theory. In J. McV. Hunt (Ed.), *Personality and behavior disorders.* New York: Ronald Press.

Roth, R. A. (1978). *Multidisciplinary teams in child abuse and neglect programs.* Washington, D. C.: National Center on Child Abuse and Neglect, Special Report.

Rush, F. (1977). The Freudian cover up. *Chrysalis, 1*, 31–45.

Russell, D. E. (1984). The prevalence and seriousness of incestuous abuse: Stepfathers vs. biological fathers. *Child Abuse and Neglect, 8*, 15–22.

Satir, V. (1967). *Conjoint family therapy.* Palo Alto, CA: Science and Behavior Books.

Savelis, J. (1983). Child abuse in residential institutions and community programs for intervention and prevention. *Child Abuse and Neglect, 7*, 473–475.

Schaefer, C. (1978). *How to influence children.* New York: Van Nostrand Reinhold.

Schmitt, B. D., and Beezley, P. (1976, March). The long term management of the child and the family in child abuse and neglect. *Child Abuse and Neglect Pediatric Annals*, pp. 60–78.

Schmitt, B. D. (1978). *The child protection team handbook.* New York: Garland.

Scholz, J. P., and Meier, J. H. (1983). Competency of abused children in a residential treatment program. In J. Leavitt, (Ed.), *Child abuse and neglect: Research and innovation.* The Hague, Netherlands: Martinus Nijhoff.

Schoenthaler, S. J. (1983). Diet and crime: An empirical examination of the value of nutrition in the control and treatment of incarcerated juvenile offenders. *International Journal of Biosocial Research, 4*(1), 25–39.

Segal, S. P., and Baumohl, J. (1981). Toward harmonious community care placement. In R. D. Budson (Ed.), *Issues in community residential care.* San Francisco: Jossey-Bass.

Selye, H. (1956). *The stress of life.* New York: McGraw-Hill.

Selye, H. (1975). *Stress without distress.* New York: Signet.

Senate of Canada (1977–79). *Childhood experiences as causes of criminal behavior.* Hull, Quebec, Canada: Canadian Government Publishing Centre.

Senate Report 93-308 (1973, July 10). *Child abuse prevention and treatment act.* Committee on Labor and Public Welfare.

Sgroi, S. M. (1975). Sexual molestation of children: The last frontier in child abuse. *Children Today, 4*, 18-21.

Sgroi, S. M. (1978). Introduction: A national needs assessment for protecting child victims of sexual assault. In A. W. Burgess, A. N. Groth, L. L. Holmstrom, and S. M. Sgroi (Eds.), *Sexual assault of children and adolescents* (pp. xv–xxii). Lexington, MA: Lexington Books.

Sgroi, S. M. (1982). *Handbook of clinical intervention in child sexual abuse.* Lexington, MA: Lexington Books.

Shadish, W. R. (1984). Policy research: Lessons from the implementation of deinstitutionalization. *American Psychologist, 39*(7), 725–738.

Shamroy, J. A. (1980). A perspective on childhood sexual abuse. *Social Work, 25*(2), 128–132.

Shaw, V. L., and Meier, J. H. (1982a). Child consumer survey: An analysis of children's attitudes toward their residential care. In J. Leavitt (Ed.), *Child abuse and neglect: Research and innovation.* The Hague, Netherlands: Martinus Nijhoff.

Shaw, V. L., and Meier, J. H. (1982b). *The role of the child in abuse: Direct observation, intervention and implications for preventing institutional abuse.* Woodland Hills, CA: CHILDHELP, Inc., Annual Report, FY 80-81, pp. 17–21.

Shengold, L. L. (1979). Child abuse and deprivation: Soul murder. *Journal of the American Psychoanalytic Association, 27*, 533–599.

Shinn, E. (1968). *Is placement necessary? An experimental study of agreement among caseworkers in making foster care decisions.* Unpublished dissertation. New York: Columbia University School of Social Work.

Silverman, F. N. (1980). Radiologic and special diagnostic procedures In C. H. Kempe and R. E. Helfer (Eds.), *The battered child* (3rd ed.). Chicago: University of Chicago Press.

Simon, S. (1976). *Caring, feeling, touching.* Niles, IL: Argus Communications.

Slader, D. (1978). The legal and social limitations upon state involvement in a parent-child relationship. In M. Lauderdale, R. Anderson, and S. Cramer (Eds.), *Child abuse and neglect: Issues on innovation and implementation.* Proceedings of the Second Annual National Conference on Child Abuse and Neglect, Volume 1, DHEW Publication #0HDS 78-30147, Washington, DC

Slavson, S. (1956). *The fields of group psychotherapy.* New York: Science Editions.

Sloan, M. P., and Meier, J. H. (1983a). Reuniting abused children and their parents: Procedures and preliminary results. In J. Leavitt (Ed.), *Child abuse and neglect: Research and innovation.* The Hague, Netherlands: Martinus Nijhoff.

Sloan, M. P., and Meier, J. H. (1983b). Sociobiological aspects of child abuse. In J. Leavitt (Ed.), *Child abuse and neglect: Research and innovation.* The Hague, Netherlands: Martinus Nijhoff.

Sloan, M. P., and Meier, J. H. (1983c). Typology for parents of abused children. *Child Abuse and Neglect, 6*(4), 443–450.

Smith, P., and Bohnstedt, M. (1981). *Child victimization study.* Sacramento, CA: Social Research Center of the American Justice Institute.

Smuts, J. C. (1961). *Holism and evolution.* New York: Viking.

Solnit, A. J. (1984). Theoretical and practical aspects of risks and vulnerabilities in infancy. *Child Abuse and Neglect, 8,* 133–144.

Solomon, T. (1973). History and demography of child abuse. *Pediatrics, 51*(2), 773–776.

Spinetta, J., and Rigler, D. (1972). The child abusing parent: a psychological review. *Psychological Bulletin, 77,* 296–304.

Spitz, R. (1945). Hospitalism: An inquiry into the genesis of a psychiatric condition in early childhood. *Psychoanalytic Study of the Child, 1,* 53.

Spitz, R. (1946). Anaclitic depression. *Psychoanalytic Study of the Child, 2,* 313–324.

Spitzer, R. L. (1980). *Diagnostic and statistical manual of mental disorders: DSM III.* Washington, DC: American Psychiatric Association.

Stanton, M. D., and Todd, T. C. (1981). Engaging "resistant" families in treatment. *Family Process, 20*(3), 261–294.

Starr, R. H., Jr., and Dietrich, K. N. (1984, September). *Preventive implications of a research-based model of the ecology of child abuse.* Unpublished paper presented at the Fifth International Congress on Child Abuse and Neglect, Montreal, Canada.

Steele, B. (1970). Parents: abuse of infants and small children. In E. Anthony and T. Benedek (Eds.), *Parenthood: Its psychology and psychopathology.* Boston, MA: Little, Brown.

Steele, B. (1975). *Working with abusive parents from a psychiatric point of view.* Washington, DC: U.S. Department HEW, Office of Child Development, OH75-70.

Steele, B. (1976). Experience with an interdisciplinary concept. In R. Helfer and C. H. Kempe (Eds.), *Child abuse and neglect: The family and the community.* Cambridge, MA: Ballinger.

Steele, B. F., and Pollock, C. (1968). A psychiatric study of parents who abuse infants and small children. In R. E. Helfer and C. H. Kempe (Eds.), *The battered child* (pp. 89–134). Chicago: University of Chicago Press.

Stewart, R. W. (1984). Owner-grandmother indicted in preschool sex molestation case. *Los Angeles Times,* March 24, Part II, pp. 1, 5.

Stoller, R. J. (1974). Hostility and mystery in perversion. *International Journal of Psychoanalysis, 55,* 425–434.

Stone, L. E., Tyler, P. T., and Mead, J. J. (1984). Law enforcement officers as investigators and therapists in child sexual abuse: A training model. *Child Abuse and Neglect, 8,* 75–82.

Straus, M. A. (1979). Family patterns and child abuse in a nationally representative American sample. *Child Abuse and Neglect, 3,* 213–215.

Straus, M. A., Gelles, R. J., and Steinmetz, S. K. (1980). *Behind closed doors: Violence in the American family.* Garden City, NY: Anchor/Doubleday.

Sue, S. (1977). Community mental health services to minority groups: Some optimism, some pessimism. *American Psychologist, 32,* 616.

Sue, S., and McKinney, H. (1975). Asian Americans in the community mental health system. *American Journal of Orthopsychiatry, 45,* 111.

Summit, R. (1978). Sexual child abuse, the psychotherapist, and the team concept. In H. Donovan and R. J. Beran (Eds.), *Dealing with sexual abuse* (Vol. 1, pp. 19–33). Chicago: National Committee for the Prevention of Child Abuse.

Summit, R. C., and Kryso, J. G. (1978). Sexual abuse of children: A clinical spectrum. *American Journal of Orthopsychiatry, 48,* 237–250.

Swanson, J. M., and Kinsbourne, M. (1980). Food dyes impair performance of hyperactive children on a laboratory learning test. *Science, 207,* 1485–1487.

Swenerton, H., and Jarvis, W. T. (1983). Diet and criminal behavior. Unpublished position paper of the California Council Against Health Fraud, Loma Linda, CA. *Teenage pregnancy: The problem that hasn't gone away* (1981). New York: The Alan Guttmacher Institute.

Thomas, C. L. (Ed.) (1980). *Taber's cyclopedic medical dictionary* (13th ed.). Philadelphia: F. A. Davis.

Thorne, F. (1973). Eclectic psychotherapy. In R. Corsini (Ed.), *Current psychotherapies.* Itasca, IL: Peacock.

Tjossem, T. D. (Ed.) (1976). *Intervention strategies for high-risk infants and young children.* Baltimore: University Park Press.

Toffler, A. (1981). *The third wave.* New York: Bantam Books.

Tower, C. C. (1984). *Child abuse and neglect: A teacher's handbook for detection, reporting and classroom management.* West Haven, CT: NEA Professional Library.

Tracey, J. J., and Clark, H. H. (1974). Treatment for child abusers. *Social Work, 19,* 339–342.

Tracy, J. J., Ballard, C. M., and Clark, E. H. (1975). Child abuse project: a follow-up. *Social Work, 20*(5), 298–299.

Tyler, A. H., and Brassard, M. R. (1984). Abuse in the investigation and treatment of intrafamilial child sexual abuse. *Child Abuse and Neglect, 8,* 47–53.

University of Southern California, Delinquency Control Institute (1980). Child abuse: Intervention, referral, investigation. Unpublished training manual. Los Angeles: Author.

U.S. Department HEW, Office of Human Development (1974). *Child Abuse Prevention and Treatment Act.* Public Law 98-457. Washington, DC: U.S. Government Printing Office.

U.S. Department HEW, Office of Human Development, Office of Child Development, Children's Bureau, National Center on Child Abuse and Neglect (1975). *Child abuse and neglect: The problem and its management* (Vol. 1: An overview of the problem). Washington, DC: U.S. Government Printing Office.

U.S. Department HEW, Office of Human Development (1977). *Basic course for residential child care workers.* DHEW Publication No. (OHDS) 79-30213.

Van de Kamp, J. K. (1983). *Child abuse prevention handbook* (rev. ed.). Sacramento, CA: California Department of Justice.

Van den Berghe, P. L. (1979). The human family: A sociobiological look. In J. S. Lockard (Ed.), *The evolution of human social behavior.* New York: Elsevier.

Van Hagen, J. (1983). One residential center's model for working with families. *Child Welfare, 62*(3), 233–241.

Vasaly, S. M. (1976). *Foster care in five states: A synthesis and analysis of studies from Arizona, California, Iowa, Massachusetts, and Vermont.* Washington, DC: U.S. Department of HEW, Office of Human Development.

Wald, M. (1975). State intervention on behalf of neglected children: A search for realistic standards. *Stanford Law Review, 27,* 985–1019.

Walsh, K. W. (1978). *Neuropsychology: A clinical approach.* London: Churchill Livingston.

Walsh, W. J. (1983). Body chemistry, violent actions shown linked. *Chicago Tribune,* Sept. 1, p. A-27.

Ward, M. (1984). Sibling ties in foster care and adoption planning. *Child Welfare, 63,* 321–332.

Weiss, B. (1982). Food additives and environmental chemicals as sources of childhood behavior disorders. *Journal of the American Academy of Child Psychiatry, 21*(2), 144–152.

Weiss, J., Rogers, E., Darwin, M. R., and Dutton, C. F. (1955). A study of girl sex victims. *Psychiatric Quarterly, 29,* 1–27.

Weitzel, W. J. (1984). From residential treatment to adoption: A permanency planning service. *Child Welfare, 63,* 361–365.

Werbin, J., and Hynes, K. (1975). Transference and culture in a Latino therapy group. *International Journal of Group Psychotherapists, 25*(4), 396.

Weschler, D. (1974). *Weschler intelligence scale for children—revised.* New York: Psychological Corporation.

West's Annotated California Codes (1981). Volume 7, Sections 193–1091. St. Paul, MN: West.

Whittaker, J. (1979). *Caring for troubled children.* San Francisco: Jossey-Bass.

Whittaker, J. K., and Garbarino, J. (Eds.) (1983). *Social support networks: Informal helping in the human services.* New York: Aldine.

Wineman, D. (1969). *The other 23 hours.* New York: Aldine.

Wirt, R., Lachar, D., Klinedinst, J., and Seat, P. (1977). *Multidimensional description of child personality: A manual for the personality inventory for children.* Los Angeles: Western Psychological Services.

Wodarski, J. (1981). Treatment of parents who abuse their children: A literature review and implications for professionals. *Child Abuse and Neglect, 5,* 351–360.

Wolfensberger, W. (1971). Will there always be an institution? II. The impact of new service models. *Mental Retardation, 2*(6), 31–38.

Woolfolk, R. L., and Richardson, F. C. (1984). Behavior therapy and the ideology of modernity. *American Psychologist, 39*(7), 777–786.

Worthington, L. (1978). Unorthodox healing and the law. In Bauman, E., Brint, A. I., Piper, L., and Wright, P. A. (Eds.), *The holistic health handbook: A tool for attaining wholeness of body, mind, and spirit.* Berkeley, CA: And/Or Press.

Wurtele, S. K., Wilson, D. R., and Prentice-Dunn, S. (1983). Characteristics of children in residential treatment programs: Findings and clinical implications. *Journal of Clinical Child Psychology, 12*(2), 13–144.

Yalom, I. (1975). *The theory and practice of group psychotherapy.* New York: Basic Books.

Yassen, J., and Glass, L. (1984, May-June). Sexual assault survivors groups: A feminist practice perspective. *Social Work,* pp. 252–257.

Young, L. (1964). *A study of child neglect and abuse.* New York: McGraw-Hill.

Zigler, E. (1979). Controlling child abuse in America: An effort doomed to failure. In E. Newberger and R. Bourne (Eds.), *Critical perspectives on child abuse.* Lexington, MA: D. C. Heath.

# Author Index

# S

# T

# U

# Subject Index

47,380

| DATE | | |
| --- | --- | --- |
| JAN 3 1 1987 | APR 1 2 1989 | NOV 2 6 1992 |
| FEB 1 8 1987 | APR 2 3 1989 | MAR 2 9 1993 |
| Mau 23 | NOV 2 8 1989 | APR 1 3 1993 |
| APR 0 6 1987 | MAR 1 3 1990 | FEB 1 5 1994 |
| APR 0 8 1987 | MAR 3 0 1990 | FEB 1 5 1994 |
| OCT 8 1987 | | MAR 2 9 1994 |
| NOV 1 8 1987 | APR 1 0 1990 | APR 1 3 1995 |
| | | MAR 3 0 1995 |
| DEC 8 1987 | APR 1 0 1991 | |
| NOV 0 8 1988 | OCT 2 9 1991 | |
| FEB 1 1 1989 | MAR 2 6 1992 | |
| | AUG 3 1992 | |

© THE BAKER & TAYLOR CO.